FASCIST DIRECTIVE
Ezra Pound and Italian Cultural Nationalism

The Ezra Pound Center for Literature
at the University of New Orleans

The Ezra Pound Center for Literature Book Series is a project dedicated to publishing a variety of scholarly and literary works relevant to Ezra Pound and Modernism, including new critical monographs on Pound and/or other Modernists, scholarly studies related to Pound and his legacy, edited collections of essays, volumes of original poetry, reissued books of importance to Pound scholarship, translations, and other works.

Series Editor: John Gery, University of New Orleans

Editorial Advisory Board

Barry Ahearn, Tulane University
Massimo Bacigalupo, University of Genoa
A. David Moody (Emeritus), University of York
Ira B. Nadel, University of British Columbia
Marjorie Perloff, University of Southern California
Tim Redman, University of Texas at Dallas
Richard Sieburth, New York University
Demetres P. Tryphonopoulos, Brandon University
Emily Mitchell Wallace, Bryn Mawr College

Also Available in the Ezra Pound Center for Literature Book Series

William Pratt, Editor, *The Imagist Poem: Modern Poetry in Miniature*
Patrizia de Rachewiltz, *Trespassing*
Caterina Ricciardi, John Gery, and Massimo Bacigalupo, Editors, *I poeti della Sala Capizucchi/The Poets Of The Sala Capizucchi*
Zhaoming Qian, Editor, *Modernism and the Orient*
John Gery, Daniel Kempton, and H. R. Stoneback, Editors, *Imagism: Essays on Its Initiation, Impact and Influence*

FASCIST DIRECTIVE
Ezra Pound and Italian Cultural Nationalism

Catherine E. Paul

© 2018 by Clemson University
All rights reserved

First published 2016

ISBN: 978-1-942954-72-9 (paperback)

Published by Clemson University Press
at the Center for Electronic and Digital Publishing,
Clemson University,
Clemson, South Carolina.

Cover photo used by permission of Instituto Luce/Alinari
Archives Management, Florence.

For information about Clemson University Press,
please visit our website at www.clemson.edu/cedp/press.

Typeset in Adobe Garamond Pro by Carnegie Book Production.

Contents

List of Abbreviations	vii
List of Figures	ix
Acknowledgments	xv
Introduction	1
1. Italian Cultural Nationalism	19
2. Renaissance Revisited: Pound's Foray into Italian Cultural Nationalism	47
3. The Bundle and the Pickax: Fascist Cultural Projects	83
4. Ezra Pound and/or the Fascist *Gerarchia*	141
5. The Fascist Cultural Nationalism of the Vivaldi Revival	159
6. Italian Fascist Exhibitions and Pound's Fascist Directive	199
7. Propaganda Art: Can a Poet be a Traitor?	237
Appendix: Vivaldi scores in Pound's hand	269
Select Bibliography	277
Notes	281
Index	339

Abbreviations for Works by Ezra Pound

ABCR *ABC of Reading* [1934] (New York: New Directions, 1987)
C   *The Cantos*, 13th ed. (New York: New Directions, 1995)
CI   *Carte italiane 1930–1944: Letteratura e arte*, ed. Luca Cesari (Milano: Archinto, 2005)
EPEC *Ezra Pound's Economic Correspondence, 1933–1940*, ed. Roxana Preda (Gainesville: University Press of Florida, 2007)
EPM   *Ezra Pound and Music: The Complete Criticism*, ed. with commentary R. Murray Schafer (New York: New Directions, 1977)
EPS   *"Ezra Pound Speaking": Radio Speeches of World War II*, ed. Leonard W. Doob (Westport: Greenwood Press, 1978)
EPVA *Ezra Pound and the Visual Arts*, ed. Harriet Zinnes (New York: New Directions, 1980)
GB   *Gaudier-Brzeska: A Memoir* (New York: New Directions, 1970)
GCR   *Guido Cavalcanti Rime* (Genova: Edizioni Marsano S. A., [1932])
GK   *Guide to Kulchur* [1938] (New York: New Directions, 1970)
J/M   *Jefferson and/or Mussolini* (New York: Liveright, 1936)
LE   *Literary Essays*, ed. T. S. Eliot [1954] (New York: New Directions, 1968)
P&P   *Poetry and Prose: Contributions to Periodicals*, ed. Lea Baechler, A. Walton Litz, James Longenbach, 11 vols (New York: Garland Press, 1991) [cited by volume number and page number]
SL   *Selected Letters, 1907–1941*, ed. D. D. Paige (New York: New Directions, 1971)
SP   *Selected Prose, 1909–1965*, ed. William Cookson (New York: New Directions, 1973)

List of Figures

Chapter 2

1. Ezra Pound, title page of *Guido Cavalcanti Rime* (Genova: Edizioni Marsano S. A., [1932]). (Beinecke Rare Book and Manuscript Library) Copyright © 1935 by Ezra Pound. Reprinted by permission of New Directions Publishing Corp.

2. Ezra Pound, *Guido Cavalcanti Rime* (Genova: Edizioni Marsano S. A., [1932]), Plate 4, "Donna mi prega," Ms. Ld. Laurenziano. (Beinecke Rare Book and Manuscript Library) Copyright © 1935 by Ezra Pound. Reprinted by permission of New Directions Publishing Corp.

Chapter 3

3. Antonio Floridi posing with a *fascio littorio* made from ears of wheat. Farm owned by Camillo Frizzoni, in Morengo in the province of Bergamo; on the *fascio*, a photograph of the Duce, 1926. (Alinari Archive, Florence)

4. Palazzo delle Esposizioni, Rome. (Photograph by the author)

5. Façade of the Palazzo delle Esposizioni, covered for the Mostra della Rivoluzione Fascista, according to a design by Adalberto Libera and Mario de Renzi, Rome (c. 29 October 1931–21 April 1932). (Alinari Archive, Florence)

6. Giuseppe Terragni, *The Year 1922 leading up to October* (Sala O), Mostra della Rivoluzione Fascista, Rome. (Alinari Archive, Florence)

7. Guido Mauri and Esodo Pratelli, *The Year 1921* (Sala N), Mostra della Rivoluzione Fascista, Rome. (Alinari Archive, Florence)

8. Mario Sironi, Salone d'Onore (Sala R), Mostra della Rivoluzione Fascista, Rome. (Alinari Archive, Florence. Sironi: © 2016 Artists Rights Society (ARS), New York / SIAE, Rome)

9. Reconstruction of Mussolini's office at the headquarters of *Il Popolo d'Italia* on the via Lovanio, Sala del Duce (Sala T), Mostra della Rivoluzione Fascista, Rome. (Alinari Archive, Florence)

10. Lamppost featuring Romanizing imagery, via dei Fori Imperiali, Rome. (Photograph by the author)

11. Demolition in St. Peter's Square for the construction of the via della Conciliazione, 1936. (Leoni Archive / Alinari Archives, Florence)

12. Men at work demolishing and leveling the Velian Hill, between the Colosseum and Piazza Venezia, for the construction of the via dell' Impero, Rome, 17 February 1932. (Istituto Luce / Alinari Archives Management, Florence)

13. Marble maps celebrating the extent of the Roman Empire, Basilica of Maxentius and Constantine, via dei Fori Imperiali, Rome. (Photograph by the author)

14. Benito Mussolini, on the roof of a house on vicolo Soderni near Ripetta, inaugurates the demolition in the piazza Augusto Imperatore, for the bimillennium of Augustus, 22 October 1934. (Istituto Luce/Alinari Archives Management, Florence)

15. Ezra Pound, *Jefferson and/or Mussolini* (London: Stanley Knott, 1935; New York: Liveright, 1936), p. 113. Copyright © 1935, 1936 by Ezra Pound; renewed 1963 by Ezra Pound. Reprinted by permission of Liveright Publishing Company.

16. Shops around the courtyard of House of the Lararium, Ostia Antica, c. 1920–30. (Alinari Archive, Florence)

17. Detail of the mosaic pavement of the frigidarium in the Baths of the Cisiarii, Ostia Antica, c. 1920–30. (Alinari Archive, Florence)

18. Black-and-white mosaics from the Foro Mussolini, now Foro Italico, Rome. (Photograph by the author)

19. Postcard of Foro Mussolini, Fountain and Monolith, Rome, mailed by Ezra Pound to Olga Rudge 18 June 1937. (Olga Rudge Papers, Yale Collection of American Literature, Beinecke Rare Book and Manuscript Library) Copyright © 2016 by Mary de Rachewiltz and the Estate of Omar S. Pound. Reprinted by permission of New Directions Publishing Corp.

Chapter 5

20. Cover of program, "Concerto dalla Collezione Chilesotti," November 1933. (Olga Rudge Papers, Yale Collection of American Literature, Beinecke Rare Book and Manuscript Library, by permission of New Directions Publishing Corporation)

21. Ezra Pound, "Studi Tigulliani," *Il Mare* (14 March 1936). (Olga Rudge Papers, Yale Collection of American Literature, Beinecke Rare Book and Manuscript Library) Copyright © 2016 by Mary de Rachewiltz and the Estate of Omar S. Pound. Reprinted by permission of New Directions Publishing Corp.

xii   *Fascist Directive*

22. Olga Rudge, *Thematic catalogue of the instrumental works of Antonio Vivaldi in the Giordano and Foà Collections, National Library, Turin* (1936), microphotograph of first page. (Olga Rudge Papers, Yale Collection of American Literature, Beinecke Rare Book and Manuscript Library) Copyright © 2016 by Mary Rudge de Rachewiltz.

23. Example of one of Ezra Pound's microphotographs from Sächsische Landesbibliothek, Dresden. Actual photograph measures 4.5 inches wide by 3.5 inches tall. (Now in Olga Rudge Papers, Yale Collection of American Literature, Beinecke Rare Book and Manuscript Library) Copyright © 2016 by Mary de Rachewiltz and the Estate of Omar S. Pound. Reprinted by permission of New Directions Publishing Corp.

24. Ezra Pound, transcription of "Concerto in La" (Vivaldi's Concerto in A for violin, 3 violins "per eco," strings and harpsichord, RV 552), draft copy. Pound's work is in ink and Rudge's corrections are in pencil. (Olga Rudge Papers, Yale Collection of American Literature, Beinecke Rare Book and Manuscript Library) Copyright © 2016 by Mary de Rachewiltz and the Estate of Omar S. Pound. Reprinted by permission of New Directions Publishing Corp.

25. Ezra Pound, transcription of "Concerto in La," violin part. (Olga Rudge Papers, Yale Collection of American Literature, Beinecke Rare Book and Manuscript Library) Copyright © 2016 by Mary de Rachewiltz and the Estate of Omar S. Pound. Reprinted by permission of New Directions Publishing Corp.

Chapter 6

26. Tempio Malatestiano, Rimini. (Photograph by the author)

List of Figures   xiii

27. Façade of the Palazzo delle Esposizioni, modified for the Mostra Augustea della Romanità, under the direction of G. Q. Giglioli, Rome, photographed on the occasion of the official visit of Adolph Hitler, 3–9 May 1938. (Leoni Archive / Alinari Archives, Florence (AVQ-A-003696-0112))

28. Exhibited reliefs and casts, Mostra Augustea della Romanità, Rome, 23 September 1937. (Archivio Storico Istituto Luce)

29. Reconstruction of the temple of Augustus and Ancyra, made for and exhibited at the Mostra Augustea della Romanità, Palazzo delle Esposizioni in Rome, 1937–38. (Alinari Archive, Florence)

30. Stele of Axum, Rome, 2003. (Photograph by the author)

31. Ezra Pound, "EVROPE—MCMXXXVI," *The Globe* 1:2 (May 1937): 106. Copyright © 2016 by Mary de Rachewiltz and the Estate of Omar S. Pound. Reprinted by permission of New Directions Publishing Corp.

32. Envelope mailed by Ezra Pound to Olga Rudge 19 October 1937, featuring a stamp celebrating the bimillennium of Augustus, 1937. (Olga Rudge Papers, Yale Collection of American Literature, Beinecke Rare Book and Manuscript Library) Copyright © 2016 by Mary de Rachewiltz and the Estate of Omar S. Pound. Reprinted by permission of New Directions Publishing Corp.

33. Envelope mailed by Ezra Pound to Olga Rudge 22 October 1937, featuring stamps celebrating the bimillennium of Augustus, 1937. (Olga Rudge Papers, Yale Collection of American Literature, Beinecke Rare Book and Manuscript Library) Copyright © 2016 by Mary de Rachewiltz and the Estate of Omar S. Pound. Reprinted by permission of New Directions Publishing Corp.

34. Front of dust jacket, Ezra Pound, *Guide to Kulchur* (London: Faber and Faber, 1938). Copyright © 1938 by Ezra Pound. Reprinted by permission of the New Directions Publishing Corp.

35. Base of a pillar, 1481–89, Tullio and Pietro Lombardo, Santa Maria dei Miracoli, Venice. (Alinari Archive, Florence)

36. Model of the Roman Empire during the time of Emperor Constantine, exhibited in the Mostra Augustea della Romanità, 1937–38, Rome. (Alinari Archive, Florence)

Chapter 7

37. Ezra Pound, extract from Canto 79, *Cantos* (New York: New Directions, 1993), p. 506. Copyright © 1934, 1937, 1940, 1948, 1956, 1959, 1963, 1966 and 1968 by Ezra Pound. Reprinted by permission of the New Directions Publishing Corp.

38. Frescoes celebrating the imperial wars in Addis Abeba and Somalia with cleaning supplies, courtyard of Casa Madre dei Mutilati di Guerra, Rome, 2004. (Photograph by the author)

39. Graffiti on marble markers in the Foro Mussolini, now Foro Italico, Rome, 2004. (Photograph by the author)

Acknowledgments

I am beyond grateful to Wayne K. Chapman and John Morgenstern of Clemson University Press for their interest in this project and their tireless work in helping this book come to be.

Any errors are my own, but I am grateful to the many scholars who read, assisted with, and responded to parts or all of this manuscript at various points: Anderson Araujo, Susanna Ashton, Massimo Bacigalupo, David Barnes, George Bornstein, Ronald Bush, David Cappella, Stefano Maria Casella, Reed Way Dasenbrock, Mary de Rachewiltz, Mary DeShazer, Margaret Fisher, John R. O. Gery, Michaela Giesenkirchen, Martin Jacobi, Justin Kishbaugh, Peter Liebregts, Elizabeth Loizeaux, Alec Marsh, Brian McGrath, A. David Moody, Ira Nadel, Sean O'Sullivan, Jay Paul, Roxana Preda, Robin Schulze, Michael Silvestri, Ellen Keck Stauder, Demetres Tryphonopoulos, James Winn, and Barbara Zaczek.

This book could not have been completed without generous fellowship support. A National Endowment for the Humanities and Consiglio Nazionale delle Ricerche Fellowship for Research on Italian Cultural Heritage enabled me to complete the manuscript. I am grateful to the directors and participants of two separate National Endowment for the Humanities Summer Seminars held in 2001 and 2004 at the American Academy in Rome, where I first conceived of this project and conducted crucial research among Italian publications: Elizabeth Bartman and Jane

Fejfer, "Topographies of Collecting" (2001) and Stephen Dyson, "Archaeology and Ideology in Rome" (2004). A Donald C. Gallup Fellowship in American Literature, from Yale University's Beinecke Library enabled the research in the Ezra Pound and Olga Rudge Papers that underpins this whole study. Finally, many years of support from Clemson University's Department of English, College of Architecture Arts and Humanities, and the University Research Grant Committee enabled vital archival study, writing time, and site visits.

For kind and extensive assistance, I thank the staffs of Yale University's Beinecke Rare Book and Manuscript Library, the Library of the American Academy in Rome, the Biblioteca Nazionale di Torino, and the Clemson University Library. Valued assistance with images came from the Alinari Archives, Archivio Centrale dello Stato, Archivio Storico Istituto Luce—Cinecittà, the Artists Rights Society (ARS) in New York, the SIAE in Rome, and the Beinecke Rare Book and Manuscript Library.

Previously unpublished writings of Ezra Pound and Olga Rudge. © 2016 by Mary de Rachewiltz and Estate of Omar S. Pound; reprinted by permission of New Directions Publishing Corp.

A version of part of Chapter 3 appeared as "Ezra Pound in Mussolini's Rome" in William Pratt and Caterina Ricciardi (eds), *Roma/Amor: Ezra Pound, Love and Rome* (New York: AMS Press, 2013), 51–63.

A version of part of Chapter 5 appeared as "Ezra Pound, Alfredo Casella, and the Fascist Cultural Nationalism of the Vivaldi Revival" in Massimo Bacigalupo and William Pratt (ed.), *Ezra Pound, Language and Persona* (Genoa: University of Genoa, 2008), 91–112.

A version of part of Chapter 6 appeared as "Italian Fascist Exhibitions and Ezra Pound's Turn to the Imperial" in *Twentieth-Century Literature* 51:1 (Spring 2005): 64–97.

For support beyond what I can express, I thank Sean Scuras.

Introduction

In 1938, American poet Ezra Pound published *Guide to Kulchur*, a book so radically different from his earlier writing that readers may not have believed that it was written by the same firebrand aesthetician who had advocated in 1913 that poets go in fear of abstractions. But *Guide to Kulchur* was only the latest example of a new kind of prose that Pound had been writing—fiercely invested in politics and the mobilization of cultural heritage to its service. *Fascist Directive* studies Pound's prose of the 1930s to reinterpret his devotion to Italian Fascism, which continues to anger, fascinate, and confuse readers. Insufficiently considered in scholarly treatments of Pound, however, are the important aspects of the Fascist regime's use of culture to foment Italian national identity, which have been uncovered by scholars of literature, history, art history, urban design, and music. These studies reveal the cultural, mythical, rhetorical, and intellectual aspects of that regime—more than enough new knowledge to require a reappraisal of perhaps the most famous, certainly the most notorious, American in Italy in that era, and perhaps the entire twentieth century.

Unlike previous discussions of Pound's adoption of Italian Fascism, which focus mostly on his political and economic interests, *Fascist Directive* reveals the importance of the cultural projects of Mussolini's Fascist regime to Pound's evolving modernism, and to his changing prose style. In the period following the Risorgimento,

Italy was (more or less) politically unified, but culturally divided. Linguistic, historical, economic, and artistic differences kept industrialized northern Italians from feeling that they were compatriots with Italians of the agricultural south.[1] These divisions contributed to the weakness of the new Italy. During the Fascist period, Mussolini's government sponsored exhibitions, design competitions, archaeological restorations, concerts, educational reforms, birthday celebrations of ancient writers, and vast architectural projects to highlight Italy's unifying cultural heritage and to invigorate new design—all with the intent of producing a rich sense of Italianness. For a writer like Pound, who lived in Italy during this period and himself had long argued for the importance of the arts, Mussolini's projects were immensely appealing—so appealing, in fact, that he was willing almost to disown aesthetic positions that had been crucial to him not long before. Yet, scholars have not addressed the role of these Fascist cultural projects in Pound's transformation. In a sense, Spiro Kostof's expression of dismay from 1973—that while we have paid attention to the so-called International Style of modernism, "That other international style of Nationalism … has yet to receive a serious historical assessment"[2]—remains painfully appropriate in our discussions of Pound's versions of literary modernism. The sad result is that Pound's investment in Fascism seems perplexing: when we read Pound's Fascism as motivated only by economics (a subject in which he grew very interested during the 1920s and 1930s), or by his love of Mussolini, we wonder what happened to the poet. By bringing Italian primary sources and new approaches to the cultural project of Mussolini's regime to bear on Pound's work (including unpublished material from the Pound Papers and untranslated contributions to Italian periodicals), *Fascist Directive* shows how Pound's writing came to embody the contradictions derived from involvement in Italian politics and culture.

In Pound's writings of the late 1930s and after, his ideas about art and literature differ dramatically from those that characterize his early period in London, the period during which he made himself into a modernist. In his essay "Ubicumque Lingua Romana" (1938), he states that if he were asked to devise a syndicate for writers, "Among other things I should treat literature as communications service, not as the quantitative production of merchandise."³ In a letter to C. H. Douglas from the same year, Pound wrote, "The masterworks or the best of its time is like orders from the STAFF, from the high command."⁴ These assertions that poets, like other propaganda artists, work in the service of a regime, passing on a leader's ideas to the masses, shock readers of Pound's early poetry and essays, who may remember his claims in "The Serious Artist" (1913) that "art never asks anybody to do anything, or to think anything, or to be anything" and that "It exists as the trees exist."⁵ Similarly, his vision for obtaining culture in *Guide to Kulchur* (1938) departs abruptly from that of his earlier writings. Prior to this text, Pound offers his readers the tools for understanding a poem: those tools might include primary texts, cultural background, or even photostatic reproductions of manuscript sources. In *Guide to Kulchur*, however, he provides a synthesis that requires a new kind of reading to make sense. In examining Pound's writings from the Fascist period together with the cultural Nationalist projects of Mussolini's regime, I demonstrate that Pound's aesthetic and intellectual shifts grew out of his investment not only in the ideas of Mussolini's Italy, but also in the wider aims of Italian cultural Nationalism, and in the regime's rhetorical and iconographic devices. While Pound began by using the regime's rhetoric and iconography to bring recognition to scholarly and poetic projects he would have pursued anyway, he became more and more invested in that rhetoric, finally overhauling his approach to pedagogy and critique to follow that of Mussolini's Italy.

Moreover, Pound's adoption of the more troubling aspects of Fascism, including its racism and anti-Semitism, makes him the perfect case for examining the relationships between art and propaganda. Mussolini's regime commissioned a great deal of "propaganda art," much of it aesthetically as well as politically interesting. Similarly, a great deal of Pound's poetry and prose from the 1930s and 1940s has a clear political mission, even as it continues to innovate. I argue for an understanding of such art that brings its aesthetic and political aspects together.

Pound's case requires that we ponder the question, raised by fellow poet H. D. in her memoir *End to Torment*: Can a poet be a traitor? Based on Pound's arrest resulting from his broadcasts on Radio Rome, we know that the United States government thought so. But how does such a verdict understand the relationships between art and propaganda? And how might a renewed exploration of these relationships alter such a verdict?

There are persistent questions that face any Pound scholar, that I have been asked again and again: Why write about a Fascist? Isn't that an endorsement? And/or: Doesn't Pound's political affiliation render his aesthetic work troubling enough that it should not be celebrated? Some say yes, so they ignore him—and chide those who would devote scholarly attention to his work. Others try to force a wedge between his poetry and politics—preferring to focus on the early poetry, or arguing that his famous *Pisan Cantos* represent a turning away from Mussolini and Fascism, and even a self-critique for those investments. But more and more, scholars of Pound are recognizing the need to bring the complicated parts of his work together, and it is to this project that my book contributes. Where his so-called "Fascist Cantos" were once repressed—left out of the New Directions *Cantos* volume—they are now included, and so discussed, but then most commonly denigrated as inferior poetry. More of Pound's writings from his time in Italy—writings that speak to his investment in Mussolini's regime—are being republished in their original languages and translated into others, making them available to scholars grappling with Pound's significance to twentieth-century literature. In *Fascist Directive*, I similarly bring to the fore previously undiscussed aspects of Pound's career, in hopes that they may help us to make sense of his work and its significance.

It has never been more important to understand the appeal of extreme movements, and the complicated relationships between individuals and nations. Recent decades have again seen the rise of ardent Nationalism and far-right political movements—both of which have been hugely influential. Contrary to postwar hopes, we continue to see anti-Semitism, racism, sectarian violence, genocide, xenophobia resulting in part from increased immigration, Nationalist rallies, movements to establish states based on the enforcing of group identity and ideology, and spectacular demonstrations of power. These movements and spectacles make starkly clear the ways that narrow insistence on national and group identity—and the display thereof—can both polarize and enforce compliance. It is desirable and often too easy to believe these extreme positions the exclusive property of demagogues and their lemming-like followers, but Ezra Pound's case necessarily reminds us that such is not always the case.

The great danger of dismissing or ignoring writers, artists, and thinkers with ugly views is that we miss the chance to learn from them. If a philosopher argues for what it means to be in the world, *and* adheres to National Socialism, we need to consider why. If a filmmaker makes great films *and* abuses young women, we need to consider why. And if a poet breaks the pentameter, helping to change the course of poetry writing in English, *and* spouts hateful propaganda, we need to consider why. None of these cases present easy answers—which is why we have to keep thinking, talking, and writing about them. In Pound's case, this means that it is our historical, political, aesthetic, and human responsibility to try to understand the reasons for his investment in Mussolini's Fascist regime and for his anti-Semitic thinking. We need to understand the connections between Pound's early work and his Fascist period, how his thinking about art joined with his political aspirations, and what role he imagined for an individual artist or thinker in a larger state project. *Fascist Directive* contributes to this endeavor, and while it presents no easy answers, it does provide new material for our continued consideration.

I do not intend for anything I write here to be taken as an apology for Pound or his politics. I admire much of Pound's poetry and prose—but I do not share his views, nor do I want to justify or excuse them. To understand his views, however, we must discern their appeal—and that means not slipping too quickly into condemnation, but rather allowing ourselves to dwell, if only briefly, in the uncomfortable space of espousal. It is easy, for instance, to mock the grandiosity of Mussolini's self-presentation. It is easy to point to connections between the *passo romano* of Fascist processions and the Nazi death camps—not that we should ever forget these connections. And it is easy, with hindsight, to read the early years of the Fascist era, when many artists and intellectuals found value in Fascism, through the later years and horrific acts that make it impossible to find an appeal. But what is less easy and no less important is to explore the reasons that many intelligent and creative people found Fascism attractive, and devoted tremendous energy to its growth and sustenance.

It is not by chance that *Fascist Directive* focuses its critical attention on Pound's prose writings. The period of his engagement with Fascism is the peak of Ezra Pound's prose publication, both in the form of innumerable periodical contributions (in English and Italian) and in his major pamphlet and monographic works, including *How to Read* (1931), *ABC of Economics* (1933), *ABC of Reading* (1934), *Social Credit* (1935), *Jefferson and/or Mussolini* (1935), *Guide to Kulchur* (1938), *What Is Money For* (1939), *Carta da Visita* (1942), *L'America, Roosevelt e le cause della Guerra presente* (1944), *Oro e lavoro* (1944), *Introduzione alla natura economica degli S.U.A.* (1944), and *Orientamenti* (1944). Although Pound had published plenty of prose criticism before, it was during the Fascist period that prose tracts became a major form for him. There is a powerful drive in him during this period to declare, explain, and try to convince. These texts are more "directive" than is his poetry or some of his earlier prose, in that they incorporate an almost legalistic or authoritarian tendency to direct, guide, or rule.

During the Fascist period, Pound develops and cements a sort of "directive prosaics," or method for laying out his ideas in prose. The word "prosaic" typically implies a sense of dullness or a lack of the poetic, and Pound himself had played on this implication in his opening of "I Gather the Limbs of Osiris" (1911), in which he introduced his method of Luminous Detail, which he quippingly called "A Rather Dull Introduction." There he argues that "The aim of right education is to lead a man out into more varied, more intimate contact with his fellows" (*SP*, 21). The institutions of education in the humanities—of which he was no fan—tend rather to produce barriers "of books and mutual misunderstanding" (*SP*, 21). Works of literature are produced and edited with the scholar, rather than the general public in mind, and Pound therefore prefers facts that "give us intelligence of a period" over those that "tell us nothing we did not know" (*SP*, 22). What begins in the 1910s as a discussion of the production and consumption of literature and art would transform during the 1930s to a profound concern with the relationships between the arts and the political success and influence of a nation.

From the 1910s into the early 1930s, Pound's prose works display a real anxiety about the act of explaining. Towards the end of "I Gather the Limbs of Osiris", Pound claims that he will be "strictly pedagogical," but even in so doing, what he offers is not a "special introduction" or "annotation" to the works of troubadour poets, but rather the direction to read Arnaut, because having done so, "any other Provencal canzon is clearer to one" (*SP*, 43). And *How to Read* and *ABC of Reading* both proceed—as do many of his letters concerning poetry—by providing a reading list, which, presumably, if studied cannot but educate. In *How to Read* (1931) he charges that "the best history of painting in London was the National Gallery, and that the best history of literature, more particularly of poetry, would be a twelve-volume anthology in which each poem was chosen ... because it contained an invention, a definite contribution to the art of verbal expression" (*LE*, 17). He gives over pages at a time of *The Spirit of Romance* (1910) to quotations from Dante and Lope de Vega. As Pound's prose evolves during the 1930s, however, he becomes less anxious about the act of explanation, such that *Guide to Kulchur* has abandoned this earlier method altogether in favor of faith in his ability to explain, in his authority to produce a truly directive text.

In addition to denoting a guide or set of directions, "directive" can refer to a legal or religious mandate or a set of military orders. It is therefore particularly appropriate to our thinking about Pound's prose and its engagement in politics and propaganda. Whereas his poetry during this time moves in directions that may open up possibilities of interpretation, and which might therefore more easily be championed by critics and poets alike, his prose seems rather to shut down reader engagement in favor of his declaiming voice, leaving many critics lamenting its changes. But as John Whittier-Ferguson has identified, these prose works (and even some of the 1930s cantos) "constitute an immense body of writing and represent a sustained endeavor that addresses ... the complex disjunctions between artist and audience" that trouble many modernist writers.[6] Whether through the titles of these works, which convey a sense of a primer or guide, or through frequent direct address to readers, Pound insists that in conveying his knowledge to his prospective reader, he can enrich that reader's ability to be an informed and invested citizen. In this way, his prose treatises of this period, informed as they are by Fascist approaches to employing culture in the service of politics, come to show tremendous confidence in their own authority, and indeed trade on that authority as a means of shaping culture.

Because Pound's prose provides such a rich and inadequately explored field of study, my focus is there instead of on his cantos of the period. One issue in the generic distinction between poem and essay is the question of belief and argument. We are content to let a poem exist, to grapple with its meanings and making without necessarily assuming that its author—who, of course, may or may not be its speaker—is "trying to say something." We might even believe that the aesthetic aspects of a poem could negate or at least balance out troubling subject matter. Indeed, those elements of craft might even give us a way to skirt disagreeable content. Not so with a prose essay. A book like *Jefferson and/or Mussolini* troubles Pound's fans and long ago fell out of print likely because it argues for Mussolini's virtues and for the rightness of Fascism, and uses one of the American founding fathers to do so. For this reason, I find it crucial to attend directly to Pound's more direct and sometimes less crafted statements—statements we find in magazine articles, books, and letters, and which we are asked to take more at face value than we might a poem.

Pound's prose always asks us to acknowledge it as a literary creation, however, which may complicate typical assumptions about the directness of the prose essay. Pound's frequent use of abbreviations, colloquialisms, profanity, slang, non-standard spelling, and the like create an impression of informality, that his statements are made off the cuff. It seems that this writing must be what he truly believes, because it appears to be so "uncrafted." At the same time, however, this kind of prose writing relies on a chosen style, and we should be cautious of taking it at face value any more than we would lines of poetry.

In a sense, Pound's proliferation of prose tracts during this period represents an escape from the poetic, whether that be the persona-heavy shorter poems that he all but stopped writing by this time, or the pentameter-heaving ideogrammic longer poems that characterize the *Cantos*. For Pound, prose writing represents a space of education, political contemplation, exploration of ideology, striving for social change, and cultural advocacy, and we must continue to think of these elements as a part of his *literary* agenda.

By reading Pound's prose treatises of the 1930s in the context of his profound investment in Italian Fascist cultural Nationalism, we can begin to see why this form becomes so important to him and to his larger artistic mission, and even why his prose production dropped off so dramatically after the war. Indeed, it is time that we come to consider his prose as a part of Pound's artistic production and mission, rather than assigning it an ancillary role.

Fascist Directive enters into a larger conversation about Pound's Fascism, and scholars are constantly bringing new material to bear on the aspects of Pound that can be the most troubling and complex. Most recently, A. David Moody's multi-volume biography of Pound has positioned Pound's writings in the larger narrative of his life, his second volume treating events in Italy as an important background and motivator to Pound's writings.[7] Matthew Feldman's *Ezra Pound's Fascist Propaganda, 1935–45* offers an archivally rich Geertzian "thick description" of Pound's case, the framework of his propagandistic thinking, how it relates to the sacralization of the Italian Fascist regime, paying significant attention to Pound's correspondence, radio broadcasts, and the various forms that Pound's propaganda takes.[8] David Barnes's work to understand the importance of the cultural aspects of Fascism in Pound's thinking about the regime and in the *Cantos* is also vital to this endeavor.[9] These scholars all acknowledge in their discussions of Pound that our understanding of him in this period must consider the numerous components contributing to his views and writing, a project to which *Fascist Directive* contributes.

Fascist Directive likewise depends heavily on previous scholarly work about Ezra Pound, and it complements others in the field by offering new understanding of Pound's modernism and his Fascism. Tim Redman's *Ezra Pound and Italian Fascism* remains the most important scholarly treatment of Pound's engagement with Fascism, and I have relied heavily on its insights in my own research.[10] Luca Gallesi has linked Pound's investment in Mussolini to the intellectual context of London before and after the Great War, demonstrating connections among Italian Fascism, the Arts and Crafts movement, Guild Socialism, and A. R. Orage's *The New*

Age.¹¹ Without the work of Redman, Leon Surette, Luca Gallesi, Peter Nicholls, Alec Marsh, and Paul Morrison on the relationships between Pound's profound investment in economics and his interest in Italian Fascism, we would not understand what may have been the strongest reason for Pound's investment in Mussolini.¹² Pound's anti-Semitism remains a real problem for readers of his poetry and prose and for thinkers about modernism, and I have thought a great deal about the interpretations of this issue put forth by Surette, Robert Casillo, and Wendy Flory as I have tried to grapple with its connection to my own project.¹³ I do not aim to discount these scholars' conclusions about the centrality of economics to Pound's championing of Mussolini. *Fascist Directive* builds on this scholarship to broaden our understanding of Pound's Fascism by revealing its cultural bent.

Fascist Directive is hardly the first study of Pound to consider his engagement with culture and the arts. In *Inventing the Italians* Reed Way Dasenbrock has provided a wide examination of Pound's investment in Italy's cultural past, but acknowledges that the work on Pound's engagement with contemporary Italy remains to be done.¹⁴ Similarly, Lawrence Rainey's rich work *Ezra Pound and the Monument of Culture* demonstrates the importance of Italian culture to Pound, both in the writing and producing of texts but, like Peter Robinson's exploration of Pound's relationship to the visual arts, privileges the culture of the past.¹⁵ Rainey's brilliant book gestures to the connections between Pound's interest in past Italian culture and in Fascism, but does not really examine the Fascist cultural projects on which Pound built. In Italian, Niccolò Zapponi has addressed many of Pound's interactions with Italy and Italians, but there is much to say about interactions not addressed in his study.¹⁶ My book brings recent scholarly discussions of Fascism to bear on Pound's thinking, allowing new insights into his engagement with the arts.

Fascist Directive does take up cultural subjects that have been discussed by Pound scholars in the past, but with different focus and conclusions. Anne Conover's *Olga Rudge and Ezra Pound* illuminates that relationship and its importance to Pound's work, but as a primarily biographic study, it does not explore Italian Fascist material.[17] Stefano Maria Casella's nuanced work on Pound's *Cavalcanti*, for instance, historicizes Pound's exploration of Italian culture, but its focus is not on the arts patronage and cultural development of the Fascist period.[18] *Fascist Directive* draws substantially on this important scholarship, and adds additional material to our understanding of the cultural bent of Pound's Fascist interests and the Fascist inflection of his cultural endeavors.

Over the years, much of Pound's unpublished writing and significant documents concerning his life have been edited, translated, and published, and I have depended on work by Omar Pound and Robert Spoo, R. Murray Schafer, Massimo Bacigalupo, Leonard W. Doob, Lawrence Rainey, and C. David Heymann in researching this project.[19] As Pound's *Pisan Cantos* and his Italian Cantos have figured prominently in my thinking about his engagement with Fascism, writings about these works by Bacigalupo, Ronald Bush, and Patricia Cockram have been crucial to my understanding.[20] As the notes to this volume demonstrate, I position my new insights about Pound within an ongoing conversation initiated and maintained by these scholars.

Fascist Directive relies heavily on new insights into the cultural practices of Mussolini's regime provided by recent scholarship about Italian Fascism. Of particular importance have been treatments of the Fascist regime's mobilization of culture in the "communications service" of the regime, to use Pound's language. Joshua Arthurs's *Excavating Modernity*, Ruth Ben-Ghiat's *Fascist Modernities*, Giorgio Ciucci's "Italian Architecture during the Fascist Period," Simonetta Falasca-Zamponi's *Fascist Spectacle*, D. Medina Lasansky's *The Renaissance Perfected*, Harvey Sachs's *Music in Fascist Italy*, Jeffrey T. Schnapp's *Staging Fascism*, and Marla Susan Stone's *The Patron State* all address different aspects of this pervasive project, and have both pointed me to projects that were important to

Pound and revealed tropes that undergirded the cultural mission of Mussolini's regime.[21] Other works—such as Emily Braun's *Mario Sironi and Italian Modernism* and Philip V. Cannistaro and Brian R. Sullivan's *Il Duce's Other Woman*—focus on particular artists and cultural administrators who helped shape this project.[22] Increasingly, the primary texts from this period are being republished and translated, though many more remain hidden in archives or housed in decaying journals.[23] Numerous collections of essays, such as those edited by Matthew Affron and Mark Antliff, Richard J. Golsan, Claudia Lazzaro and Roger J. Crum, and Henry A. Millon and Linda Nochlin, have provided specialized treatment of specific examples of the kinds of project undertaken by Mussolini's regime.[24] As my notes show, and as is the case in my reliance on scholarship on Pound, these references are far from comprehensive, though they do point to some of the work most important to my study. In many ways, *Fascist Directive* uses Ezra Pound as a way for scholars of Anglo-American modernism to see the rich appeals and accomplishments of Italian modernism during the Fascist period.

The chapters that follow trace Ezra Pound's engagement with Fascist Italian cultural Nationalism in order to demonstrate how that engagement changed Pound's prose modernism. Chapter 1 offers a framework of the cultural Nationalism that had been growing in Italy since the Risorgimento, but which had taken on great importance during the first decades of the twentieth century. Well before Mussolini came to power, Italian intellectuals were trying to reconcile bombastic Nationalism with regional identity and a wider European avant-garde. It is in this period that Pound begins to form a sense of Italy, but it is a sense shaped largely by the writings of Anglo-American travelers. The Pound we see in this chapter has not yet encountered the more radical Nationalist thinking of Italians, and has not been converted to Fascism. Despite the interval between Pound's first visit to Italy and his taking up residence there later, this chapter lays out the conflicts facing intellectuals after the Risorgimento and sorts the threads of cultural

Nationalism in Italy before the March on Rome in 1922. It also considers the ways in which "culture" was understood—both in Italy and by Pound—and what it meant to employ the country's cultural heritage as the basis for a political movement, a nation, or a corpus of poetic work. In short, this chapter sets the stage.

Chapter 2 contextualizes and explores Pound's first participation in the cultural Nationalist project of Fascist Italy: his edition of *Guido Cavalcanti Rime*, published in Italy in 1932. Like many Italian artists and intellectuals at this time, Pound saw in the art of the Italian *quattrocento* (or early Renaissance) material for enriching modern Italian culture. At this same time, Pound was realizing that Mussolini, too, looked to the Italian cultural heritage as a means of building a strong nation. Pound's elaborate edition showcased the work of a late medieval Italian poet, an immediate predecessor of Dante, who had already become a central figure of Italian Nationalism. I argue that Pound wanted to make Cavalcanti a worthy Nationalist compatriot of Dante. I examine the writings of Bernard Berenson, F. T. Marinetti and Cipriano Efisio Oppo, Carlo Carrà, Margherita Sarfatti, as well as Mussolini himself, together with artwork generated by the Novecento and *Valori Plastici* groups, whose work emulated the formal characteristics of early Italian Renaissance painting. Through my reading of *Guido Cavalcanti Rime*, I show how the project of cultural Nationalism claimed Pound, such that he wedded his work to Fascist Italy's.

Chapter 3 reveals how aware Pound was of the many and various cultural projects undertaken by Mussolini's regime. Although Pound's economic writings of the 1930s have contributed to the misconception that Pound abandoned art for economics, his many periodical writings of the period demonstrate how closely he followed cultural matters in Italy. He wrote about the drive toward cultural unification, the cult of Mussolini, the importance of modernism to the Fascist project, the cult of *Romanità*, and the archaeological transformation of the city of Rome. This chapter reads those writings, together with his highly political and propagandistic *Jefferson and/or Mussolini* (1935), to demonstrate the importance of Italy's politically driven cultural projects to Pound's changing aesthetic sense.

Between the writing of *Jefferson and/or Mussolini* and its publication—a period of about two volatile years—Pound corresponded extensively with most of the intellectual and cultural leaders in Mussolini's regime, including Margherita Sarfatti, Camillo Pellizzi, Galeazzo Ciano, Giuseppe Bottai, Roberto Farinacci, and of course Mussolini himself, searching for ways in which his writings could be used in service of the regime's cultural missions. In this correspondence, Pound continues to experiment with means of formulating and communicating his ideas. The brief fourth chapter draws these letters together, clarifying the reasons for Pound's desire to participate in Mussolini's regime. It shows why—despite his passion—Pound's vision of cultural Nationalism was not politically viable.

Since Pound could not participate in these national projects, he devised a cultural Nationalist project of his own. Chapter 5 shows Pound acting the cultural administrator, albeit on a very local, self-driven project: the revival of the music of Antonio Vivaldi. Pound saw this work as both enriching the culture of his adopted home, Rapallo, and offering a musical model for the mining of Italy's rich cultural heritage in service of modern Nationalist culture. Where his earlier work with cultural artifacts had remained in the realm of the aesthetic, here he adopts an explicitly political objective. His collaborative work with Olga Rudge (and sometimes with Italian composer Alfredo Casella) toward bringing the largely forgotten music of Vivaldi to modern listeners was usually framed in a distinctly Fascist cultural rhetoric. This chapter uses new archival evidence—including scores, clippings, letters, and pamphlets—to demonstrate both Pound's use of Fascist rhetoric in this endeavor and his involvement in the actual music of the revival (something previous scholars have denied). An appendix at the back of the book catalogues the manuscripts of Vivaldi, largely but not exclusively transcribed by Pound, used in the Tigullian concerts and housed in the Pound and Rudge papers in Yale's Beinecke Library.

Chapter 6 examines the shift in Pound's treatment of culture toward the more imperial model that followed Mussolini's declaration of empire in 1936. After that declaration, Pound's prose shifts significantly, drawing on imperial discourse to argue for his conceptions of culture and adopting a directive mode that completes the transformation that began with his turn to Mussolini. Nevertheless, Pound's growing conception of culture is hardly the Nationalist structure that Mussolini built; rather, it tears down national boundaries to imagine a truly transnational culture. The chapter reads Pound's *Guide to Kulchur* (1938) together with the Mostra Augustea della Romanità (1938), an exhibition celebrating the bimillenium of Augustus's birth. Unlike earlier Fascist exhibitions, which used a participatory model to draw visitors into their message, the Augustan exhibition presented its ideas didactically, discouraging visitor interaction or critique. Likewise, Pound's *Guide to Kulchur* assumes an authoritative posture to teach readers what culture is and how to engage with it. Reading the *Guide* in this context not only reveals Pound's interest in empire, but also helps to make sense of this highly confusing work. More generally, this chapter speaks to the ways in which a writer's sense of aesthetic mission can change direction when it is co-opted to a particular political position.

Chapter 7 brings together the findings of the previous chapters to resolve how Ezra Pound's modernism changed as a result of his engagement with Mussolini's regime, and to gesture to the relationships between his prose innovations and his poetic composition. Here, we come quickly to the question raised by Pound's investment in Fascism: Can a poet be a traitor? I use H. D.'s *End to Torment* to analyze the relationships between Pound's politics and poetry at the end of the Second World War. Her response to his arrest and incarceration, and to his anti-Semitic wartime broadcasts, can stand in for that of many other readers, at that time and since. I connect claims made in those broadcasts to the workings of the *Pisan Cantos*, written during his captivity at the Disciplinary Training Center in Pisa. These poems are widely considered some of the most aesthetically rich of his *Cantos*, and by showing their powerful links to his broadcasts—some of his ugliest anti-Semitism and most dramatic espousals of Mussolini's Italy—I gesture to how his literary work was transformed by his engagement with the cultural projects of Mussolini's regime. Because of these relationships and transformations, Pound's poetry offers an important locus for considering the relationships between the art and politics of the twentieth century.

Rather than focus on political ideology itself, *Fascist Directive* attends to the ways that states deploy cultural projects in the service of Nationalism. Still, it is important to clarify what is meant here by "Fascism." When I use this term, I refer only to the situation in Mussolini's Italy and Pound's sense of it—not to that in any other state, like Hitler's Germany or Franco's Spain, where the term might accurately or loosely be applied. As many of the scholars already noted here have demonstrated, Pound's interest in Italian Fascism was partly economic, partly political, partly based on a mythic conception of the Duce, and partly rooted in Pound's own historical and fantastical sense of how leaders and states might thrive. At times, his sense of Italian Fascism derives from close attention to current events; at others, it seems to grow rather out of more imaginative practices of analogy, idealization, and hope. My book focuses primarily on how Italian cultural Nationalist projects contribute to Pound's imagining of Fascism—a project as creative as it is ideological.

Scholars disagree about whether to capitalize "Fascism." Some capitalize it to acknowledge it as a very specific ideology of a very specific historical period. Some do not, using it to refer to a cluster of similar movements, or wishing not to seem to valorize a term, which, together with many others, was capitalized in Italian Fascist propaganda although it is not in common Italian usage. In this book, I capitalize terms like Fascism, Fascist, *Romanità*, *Italianità*, *Toscanità,* and *Gerarchia* to acknowledge their very specific historical meanings; I likewise capitalize the terms designating such artistic and political groups and movements as the Futurists, Nationalists, Socialists, Rationalists, *Vociani*, and proponents of *Strapaese* and *Stracittà*. In so doing, I also acknowledge that for Pound they took on the ontological status of proper nouns even though he often followed the Italian practice of not capitalizing them.

Pound's devotion to Mussolini and his endeavors leads to confusion, dismay, and immediately to the questions of what Pound knew when, what he believed, and where he stood. Rather than aim to settle these questions once and for all, which as responsible historians we cannot do, I prefer to acknowledge them and let them stand. As we compile archival facts, examine literary creations, consider statements and claims, we must recognize this combination in Pound's Fascism of fact and fantasy, reality and myth, description and creation.

To be clear: in saying that Pound's Fascism is at least in part his own creation, I am not letting him off the hook, saying he was not really a Fascist, or that he did not really believe in Mussolini, or that he did not mean the many horrible things he said in defense of Fascism. Rather, I believe we must look thoughtfully at what he made of Fascism in his writing and why Fascism was such a productive ideology for him. *Fascist Directive* takes this inquiry as its focus.

CHAPTER 1

Italian Cultural Nationalism

Ezra Pound's initial experiences in Italy offer no indication of how that nation would change him during the Fascist period. His early visits are largely about missed opportunities and limited vision. When he moved to Europe in 1908, for instance, he was looking for ways to reinvigorate his writing, but he would conclude that Venice had nothing to offer him, that he had to move on to London. And indeed, the English capital enabled him to construct a kind of modernism that the *Serenissima* withheld. But already at that same time, though unbeknownst to Pound, Italians were in the midst of reimagining their own modernity and their relationship to their cultural heritage. And while Pound did not discover their innovative ideas then, these same ideas would later enable him to build on but also rethink the very modernism he made in London and Paris. This chapter first examines Pound's encounter with Venice in 1908, and the reasons for his inability to engage then with burgeoning Italian Nationalism and modernism. Then, I turn to the ways in which Italians were beginning to employ their cultural heritage to strengthen their nation, even before the Fascist era, and lay out some of the strategies the Fascists borrowed from these early movements. Finally, I will look briefly at Pound's return to Italy after the March on Rome, and set the stage for his adoption of Italian methods of making modernism through a deployment of the cultural heritage of the past.

"But how you onnerstan' Venice!!"

When Ezra Pound went to Europe in 1908, he wanted to transform English and American poetry. Disillusioned with American academic life, he found himself in Venice and invested in the living arts. Pound believed he could see the vacuousness of the American art world, and his own youthful arrogance let him believe that he had the answers. He was confident that time in Europe, where he could be free from American provincialism, would let him develop an art that would dismantle accepted notions of the aesthetic. Sadly, Venice was probably not the right place for a young American to start such a revolution. For one thing, the city was hardly a blank slate. Pound had read too much Henry James, Robert Browning, and John Ruskin to approach the city with anything other than the highest expectations. James had written in 1882 that Venice was "of all the cities in the world ... the easiest to visit without going there" since "Everyone has been there, and everyone has brought back a collection of photographs."[1] And even the monumental John Ruskin had written of the now much-photographed Ponte de' Sospiri (or "Bridge of Sighs"), "a work of no merit, and of a late period ... owing the interest it possesses chiefly to its pretty name, and to the ignorant sentimentalism of Byron."[2] If Ruskin, who by Pound's day had become one of the best-known English-language commentators on the merits and shortcomings of the Most Serene Republic, found himself overburdened by English writing about Venice (in this case, the fourth canto of *Childe Harold's Pilgrimage*), then how could Pound find a fresh perspective?

Still, in the time he spent there, Pound wrote poems that would be the basis of his early modernist style. And by the end of his stay, he was sure that he fully comprehended this romantic city. In one of his last letters to his mother from that stay, he noted that one of his poems had appeared, "translated by the 'Dirretore' himself" in *La Bauta*, a publication Pound described as "The Venetian Colliers." When Pound gave the director, Marco Londonio, more poems to read, he says that Londonio responded, "But how you onnerstan' Venice!! You onnerstan' it all," leading him to conclude, "If I can make Venetian verse to suit the Venetians, I suppose it ought to satisfy me."[3] But despite this reported flattery, these poems were not "Venetian verse" so much as an engagement with English pre-Raphaelitism.

In fact, Pound's understanding of Venice at this time was very much that of highly aestheticizing Anglo-American travelers. This is hardly surprising, given Pound's wider tendency to rely on late Romantic assessments of culture and given that the travelers' discourse of Venice was well established by William Dean Howells, Horatio F. Brown, Augustus Hare, Henry James, and the ubiquitous Baedeker guides, as well as by fictionalized versions of James, Edgar Allan Poe, and Mark Twain.[4] The look and feel of Venice were so clearly articulated that it was impossible to so much as arrive without having one's actions, route, or even responses prescribed. Eminent travel writer Augustus Hare seems almost to anticipate Pound's notion of the periplum when he emphasizes that Venice is really two cities in one: one is visible from the land and one from water, and any traveler who misses one or the other sees only half of the city.[5] These writings collectively shape a traveler's visit to Venice, starting with the approach to the city—should one arrive by the modern train or the more romantic boat?—emphasizing the importance of gondolas, detailing the important monuments to see and how to see them, even mentioning the *Caffè Florian* on the Piazza San Marco.[6] As Pound wrote in the first of his "Three Cantos" (1917), "True, it was Venice, / And at Florian's and under the north arcade / I have seen other faces, and had my rolls for breakfast, for that matter; / So, for what it's worth, I have the background."[7] This background is a litany of the key stops in Venice—as defined by this travel discourse—and thus a demonstration of his credentials for what could become his new masterwork. And Pound's sense that a traveler's view of a city is all one needs to be an expert would drive his early modernism.

For many Anglo-American visitors—especially those writers and artists looking for a richer experience than that expected by a standard traveler on the Grand Tour—the popularity of Venice was a problem. In "Venice" (1882), Henry James's imagined "sentimental tourist" bemoans the fact that this city, which he so wants to be the first to discover, is already so thoroughly walked, gondoled, explored, and described:

> The Venice of to-day is a vast museum where the little wicket that admits you is perpetually turning and creaking, and you march through the institution with a herd of fellow-gazers. There is nothing left to discover or describe and originality of attitude is completely impossible. This is often very annoying; you can only turn your back on your impertinent playfellow and curse his want of delicacy. But this is not the fault of Venice; it is the fault of the rest of the world.[8]

James's attention to the ways in which the city suffers from overvisitation was extensive. He insinuates that the authentic pleasures of Venice have been replaced by shoddy showmanship or commercialization: "The barbarians are in full possession and you tremble for what they may do," he wrote. "You are reminded from the moment of your arrival that Venice scarcely exists any more as a city at all; she exists only as a battered peep-show and bazaar." Tourists "infest" the city, and peddlers sully such prominent sites as St. Mark's: "There is a great deal of dishonour about St. Mark's altogether, and if Venice, as I say, has become a great bazaar, this exquisite edifice is now the biggest booth."[9] For the city to be selling aesthetic experience cheapens both the art and the experience.

Pound similarly comments parenthetically, early in the first of "Three Cantos," "(I stand before the booth, the speech; but the truth / Is inside this discourse—this booth is full of the marrow of wisdom.)"[10] This metaphor persists throughout the "Three Cantos," an acknowledgement both of the showmanship of art and an expression of anxiety about art's flimsiness. Still, Pound wants Venice to remain the historical and traditional beauty that he had come to expect from the writings of other poets, in part because that sense of beauty was central to his modernism.

Like most other anglophone writers whose visions were shaped by John Ruskin, Pound emphasizes the "stones of Venice," the monuments around him. For Pound, these monuments create the setting for the beginning of his experience as an expatriate writer. "Accademia & Franchesi Palace also within sight of the trees I use to loaf under," he notes in his first letter to his father from Venice.[11] He sent postcards to his parents, featuring pictures of the Canal Grande and the Chiesa della Salute, as well as the Chiesa S. Giorgio dal Molo. The current Canto 3 shows Pound sitting "on the Dogana's steps / For the gondolas cost too much that year …" (*C*, 3:11). His view of the Grand Canal, of the edge of the Piazza San Marco, is one any tourist could appreciate, and Pound's sojourn in Venice at this time was perhaps too brief for him to lose the aestheticizing eye of the highly cultured Anglo-American visitor.

But perhaps we can forgive the young Pound. As Margaretta Lovell has noted, very few Venetians appear in the work of most Anglo-American visitors.[12] Their discussions center on other visitors like themselves, and because of limitations of language and because Venetian society tended to ignore outsiders, they rarely offer insight into the goings-on of actual Venetians. The exceptions to this absence, of course, are the gondoliers and beggars, or the occasional market woman viewed from afar. "Having visited the group of buildings around S. Mark's," writes Augustus Hare, "the traveler cannot do better than engage a gondolier at the Piazzetta and bid him row leisurely up and down the Grand Canal, which the Venetians call *Canalazzo*." Advising visitors where to find gondolas and how to engage them, Hare also notes:

> Here a peculiar class of beggars are always stationed, pretending to pull your gondola to shore, and really doing

you no service whatever, called by the Venetians *gransieri*, or crab-catchers. Here we may see that the type of the lagunes, especially the masculine type, is now that which Gozzi describes as "bianco, biondo, e grassotto," rather than the dark, bronzed, and grave figures of Giorgione.[13]

Perhaps Hare is building on James's "Venice" essay, where James notes that seeing a painting of Venice in London's National Gallery sends him back immediately to Venice:

> You may sit before it for an hour and dream you are floating to the water-gate of the Ducal Palace, where a certain old beggar who has one of the handsomest heads in the world—he has sat to a hundred painters for Doges and for personages more sacred—has a prescriptive right to pretend to pull your gondola to the steps and to hold out a greasy immemorial cap.[14]

This conversation among texts creates expectations for readers anticipating their own visits, and to discover a different city probably would require more time than the few weeks Pound spent in Venice in 1908.

Pound's descriptions of the city follow the patterns established for him by his Anglo-American predecessors. His first letter to his father—which noted confidently, "There is only one Venice"—described his connections to a wider community of Anglo-American visitors: "The Robertsons (Scotch Church Pastor) delightful. Some pleasant folks at Hotel Milan who feed and gondole me now & then."[15] In a later letter, he identifies these people as "a certain Miss Wells, well along in the afternoon of life & a 'plain Massachusetts person' Norton by name whose papa happens to be Charles Elliot Norton, our ~~first so~~ foremost American Dante Scholar, & whose unkle has a gentle little job as President of Harvard," and "Lauder, who I presume synonymous with 'art in Scotland' was also at the

'Milan' during their stay." The other Venetians Pound mentions in this correspondence are composer Pietro Mascagni, whom he met at the Lido, and the A. Antonini who would publish his *A Lume Spento*. Still, he comments, "you know Venice is nothing but a rather small wet village where you can see most anybody if you hang around long enough."[16] He follows other anglophone tourists in his definition of "anybody." Pound left the city with a book of poems in hand, having realized that he could not make the cultural changes he needed there, but had to move on to London. Perhaps he was right: the overdetermined nature of a holiday in Venice stood in the way of his seeing a truly *Italian* Venice.

Had Pound been less obsessed with James's hours, Browning's troubadour, or Ruskin's stones, he might have seen around him Italians trying to find something to call Italy. What we think of as the Italian nation was fairly new in 1908: the unification process of the Risorgimento had begun in 1815, and although Rome was declared the capital of the Italian state in 1861, it was not annexed to the kingdom of Italy until 1870, and the territories of Venezia Giulia and Trentino would not be annexed until the First World War. Numerous groups of artists in different regions of Italy were trying to determine what a particularly Italian modernism might look like. At this time in Florence (another required stop on the Grand Tour), the writers around the avant-garde journal *La Voce* were negotiating a relationship between the experiments of the European avant-garde and a more Nationalistic modernism rooted in the local tradition. In 1904 Florentine Giuseppe Prezzolini distinguished between two Italies—"the one decadent, oratorical, ineffectual, the other forward-looking, active, creative." He urged the new generation of avant-garde writers, artists, and politicians to destroy the first to make way for the second.[17] The first decade of the twentieth century saw the initiation of a wide array of literary and Nationalist publications, seeking alternatives to the Giolitti regime and D'Annunzian decadence.[18] Pound traveled through Milan about a year before Marinetti published his

Futurist Manifesto. In many Italian cities, including Venice, there were groups of young thinkers (contemporaries of Pound) who were eager to see Italy modernize and compete in an international arena: the weekly Venetian paper *Mare Nostro* was one of many manifestations of this relaunching of the Nationalist movement.[19] Pound does not seem to have been aware of any of this, and given his own pre-Raphaelite aesthetic at the time and his rejection of Marinetti and Futurism in London, he probably would not have thought much of these proto-Futurist experiments.[20]

Modernist and Nationalist Italian writers of Pound's generation were well aware that the tourist view of their country was confining them to an eternal past. Whatever beauty major monuments and long-standing traditions held, they obstructed a vibrant and economically viable future. All over Italy, artists and patrons sought escapes from the holds of tradition. In Venice, for instance, a new art gallery had just been founded to feature the work of young, innovative artists—artists typically excluded from the more academic world of the Venice Biennale. The Gallery of Modern Art in Ca' Pesaro opened in 1902, and held its first exhibition in 1908, showing works by artists who later would join with the Milanese Futurists to challenge Italy's reputation as a land of dead monuments. In his inaugural speech on 26 July 1908, Count Nani Mocenigo, President of Opera Bevilacqua La Masa, emphasized Ca' Pesaro's mission to launch young artists:

> We are telling, particularly our young artists: hurry to this gym where your talent inspired and cultivated by Truth and Beauty, will shine in your work, and in this noble and fair competition you will win the prize which resides in the triumph of those who dedicate themselves to hard work and to high ideals.[21]

In early 1910, a group of Futurist painters wrote: "In the eyes of other countries, Italy is still a land of the dead, a vast Pompeii, white with sepulchers." They called for a "cultural resurgence" to follow the "political resurgence": using the Italian word *risorgimento* in both phrases, they linked this need for cultural regeneration to the recent unification of the Italian nation.[22] And as Emilio Gentile has shown, their desire to revive Italian culture coexisted with similar desires on the political front. In 1909, Benito Mussolini, not yet a Fascist, wrote in a rather Futurist way that Italy was

> gradually losing the characteristics of a cemetery. Where lovers once dreamed and nightingales once sang, the factory whistles are now screaming. Italy is pulling ahead in the great stadium where the Nations are running the great Marathon of World supremacy. The heroes are giving way to producers. Having once fought, we now work. The plow is making the earth fecund and the pneumatic drill is gutting the city. Italy is preparing itself to fulfill a major role in a new epoch of human history.[23]

This view of the Italian nation specifically rejects the view expressed by Anglo-American tourist discourse and espoused by Pound during his first visits. Where such travel discourse lamented Italian modernization as ruining Venice, Mussolini saw promise. And where Pound looked around Venice for poetic inspiration, Mussolini noted the need to move on, to shift from romanticism to modernism.

There are a number of reasons why Pound was unlikely to have found this side of Italy when he was in Venice for several months in 1908. Although a number of the journals espousing Nationalist ideology had national circulation, and Pound's Italian was good enough that he could have read such writings, 1908 was a particularly quiet year in terms of Nationalist publication, thanks to an economic downturn, the Bosnian crisis, and wide concern about problems of emigration.[24] More importantly, however, such was not the Italy Pound sought in 1908, wanting Browning's inspiration and a start for his own poetic career. Indeed, based on his publication in *La Bauta*, and verbal response from that magazine's director, he thought he had tapped into modern Italian, or at least Venetian, literary life. It would not be until the 1930s that Pound would gain enough understanding of and interest in Italian modernism and Nationalism to wed his literary mission to the cultural objectives of the Italian nation.

Certainly Pound envisioned himself at this time as a modern artist, and of course the poetry he published in Venice and went on to produce in London helped to define Anglo-American modernism, but his approach to modernism at the time differed greatly from that of the Italian Futurists and other Italian modernists. The Italy in which it is rooted, therefore, is not modern, avant-garde Italy, but the old Italy of a glorious past, defined not by its role on the world (or even European) stage, but by the exceptional products of its history. In 1908–20, his early years in London, Pound laid out in his poetry and prose an aesthetic that has come to dominate at least a part of our sense of Anglo-American modernism.

He considered his own role with respect to the vast literary tradition by delving into the literary past, finding glistening gems meriting returns, and putting them on display for readers in his poetry and prose. Imagining himself as the mythical Isis, breathing life into the scattered limbs of tradition, he celebrated in "I Gather the Limbs of Osiris" (1911–12) a method of "luminous detail," by which crucial individual details are allowed to stand alone, separated from the detritus surrounding them, to "give us intelligence of a period."[25] Many of his early poems followed this method, reviving lost limbs of the past, giving readers medieval Provence and Tuscany, classical China, and the elegiac world of Anglo-Saxon seamen. In other words, his London modernism was about finding a new way of seeing the beautiful but lost remnants of the past. His role, as an appreciator of culture, was to present to his readers the tools with which to come to appreciate art and poetry. His criticism—think, for instance, of *The Spirit of Romance* (1910) and "I

Gather the Limbs of Osiris" (1911–12)—overflowed with lengthy quotations, whereby readers could learn how to come to their own conclusions. Criticism should "startle a dull reader into alertness," he wrote in "A Retrospect" (1913): rather than explaining literature to readers, it should bring them into a state in which they might better engage with the literature themselves (*LE*, 4). In the same essay, he wrote, "I think we need a convenient anthology rather than descriptive criticism" (*LE*, 13): most important to people's understanding of literature is that they have access to that literature, and the act of reading will accomplish what no mere description from a critic—however deft—could. Pound's assertions in this period about poetry's place follow the *ars gratia artis* school of thought. In "The Serious Artist" (1913), he famously asserted that "art never asks anybody to do anything, or to think anything, or to be anything." Instead, "It exists as the trees exist" (*LE*, 46). That art is a part of the natural world, a part of life that offers no argument, but simply a creation of the artist's hands and mind, allows it to be considered separately from other human products—from tracts, advertisements, and so on.

Pound's idea that the culture of the past might fortify a nation politically had its roots in his London modernism, and his sense that modern ways of making art differed from those of the past. By the end of his London years, he could see that any decent modern nation needs good art. But in Italy, his resuscitation of the culture of the past took on a decidedly political quality. He would never let go of his celebration of those artists like Wyndham Lewis, Henri Gaudier-Brzeska, and Jacob Epstein, but when he moved to Italy in 1924, he was searching for new ideas. Like the Venice that he had loved and left in 1908, he was stuck in the past, too focused on medieval models and antiquated verbiage to be as modern as he wanted to be. In the Fascist cultural Nationalist projects of Mussolini's regime, he would find new models for his writing, and a new means of engaging the cultural heritage of the past to make a vibrant present and future.

Using culture to unify a new nation

As a strategy for resolving Italy's many divisions, "cultural Nationalism" preceded the Fascist revolution. By "cultural Nationalism," I refer to a particular approach to understanding the structure of the Italian nation and strengthening the coherence of its national identity. Specifically, this approach begins with the assumption that all the citizens of a nation share a common culture, comprising history, religion, language, arts, and folkways. National identity can therefore be strengthened by encouraging citizens to share in cultural practices and in a sense of a collective past that can infuse the nation's present and future. In the case of Fascist Italy, elements of "high culture"—painting, classical music, classical archaeology, poetry, sculpture—dominated, but there was still an important place for such mass cultural elements as after-work leisure activities, mass exhibitions, foodways, and religious practices. Indeed, historian Claudio Fogu has argued that Fascist modernism complicates Andreas Huyssen's notion of the "Great Divide" between "high" modernism and "low" mass culture, and, within modernism, separating modernist and avant-garde projects.[26] There is some room for dissent in such a structure, and for small variations in experience and cultural elements which may not be shared, but if the disparate elements come to overwhelm those that are shared, then the nation loses—or, in the case of post-Risorgimento Italy, never gains—coherence. Fascist thinkers saw in the Italian cultural heritage a remedy to this problem. This approach would appeal to Pound, who had long argued for the wider cultural importance of good painting, poetry, architecture, and music.

Although the Risorgimento brought political union to Italy, the new nation remained culturally fragmented. When the nation of Italy was unified during the 1860s, and Rome finally captured in 1870, the leaders of the Risorgimento understood that they were bringing together regions with strong traditions, long histories, and important economic, religious, and linguistic differences.

As Christopher Duggan has noted, northern Italians tended to see Southerners as a politically backward population, led into unrest by common criminals. It was widely believed that "Africa began somewhere just beyond Rome," and "by depicting the south as a land of backwardness and corruption the Piedmontese created a moral climate in which the imposition of their own constitution, laws, and administrative system (not to mention personnel) on the rest of the country appeared wholly justified." Not surprisingly, southern Italians resisted the northerners' imposition of uniformity, centralization, mandatory military service, parliamentary government, and the sense that all power (including, especially, the king himself) would derive from and be located in the north.[27] Much to the chagrin of thinkers early in the twentieth century, however, Italians did not attend adequately to these cultural differences, focusing instead on political unification.[28] Although there had been much optimism immediately following unification, much of that faded as intellectuals and artists realized that although Italy now had a federal government residing in Rome, not enough had been done to give the fledgling nation a coherent identity.

The factors dividing Italy in the years before the Risorgimento were powerful. Municipal rivalries and divisions between cities and the countryside had been part of Italian history for centuries.[29] The lack of a unifying infrastructure in the form of connecting roads and railways combined with mutually indecipherable dialects and incompatible systems of measurement to make the regions of Italy seem too distinct to unify. Indeed, as John Auchard has noted, "time in Italy was considered a local phenomenon, varying approximately four minutes for every degree of longitude." "Without the 'Table of Italian Hours' [featured in most guidebooks to Italy]" Auchard notes, "the punctual foreigner might be stunned by a train's apparently early departure from a Roman or Neapolitan railroad station."[30] The lack of a strong national capital city contributed to the lack of moral collectivity.[31] Other fragmenting factors included the continued conflict between the papacy and the Italian state, disputes between local and national initiatives, and the divisive appeal of prominent Nationalist figures. For all these reasons, historian Christopher Duggan has concluded that

> The Risorgimento as a political and cultural movement had been the work of a small minority of the population inspired by a vision of the nation that owed much to literary and artistic fantasy and to a willing suspension of disbelief in the face of the fractured reality of much of the peninsula.[32]

What remained after the political unification was to attempt to make this fantasy into a reality.

In the year preceding unification and that immediately following, the vision of a unified Italy relied as much on poets and mythologizers as politicians and soldiers. Early in the nineteenth century, poet Ugo Foscolo had hoped that attention to Italy's glories—especially literary glories—might help modern Italians resist the domination of foreign powers. Literature's purpose, he argued in one lecture, is to "preserve the value system and traditions of a community" and help combat forces that might diminish these values and traditions.[33] Milanese poet Alessandro Manzoni, writing in 1821 in the context of revolutions in southern Italy and attempts to liberate Lombardy and the Piedmont from Austrian control, composed an ode describing Italy's people as "one in arms, language and faith, memories, blood and heart" and therefore willing to rally around the Italian flag.[34] Nationalist Giuseppe Mazzini imagined Italy as a spiritual nation willed by God, and he emphasized a mythic vision of Rome—past and future—as a means of giving cohesion and identity to a prospective nation.[35] For Giovanni Gentile, one of the most important architects of Fascist thought, Mazzini's notion of nations as spiritual entities in which individuals immersed themselves proved important to a conceptualization of the Fascist state.[36] Mussolini stated in April

1927 that "The nation is … a moral, political and economic unit that finds expression integrally in the Fascist state."[37] His emphasis on the nation as a moral unit derives in large part from Mazzini, via Gentile. Beginning in the mid-1920s, Mussolini used the machinery of the Fascist state—including its cultural machinery—to galvanize every aspect of Italy's moral, cultural, and economic life, to unify the population.[38] All these thinkers, and the Fascist regime that grew out of their thought, were invested in the project of "making Italians" as a crucial part of "making Italy."[39]

As writers, thinkers, and painters looked to Italy's past for models, they came up against the question of which past to glorify. All agreed that the recent past was no high point in Italy's cultural history.[40] The pre-Risorgimento legacy of foreign domination and more recent obstacles to economic modernization left Italy weak. The vibrant optimism that came with Italian unification had given way to a stagnant traditionalism, leaving the Italian arts scene overrun with repetitively Baroque painting and such overly ornamented architectural eyesores as the Vittorio Emanuele monument in Rome.[41] The more distant past offered more fruitful territory. In the early nineteenth century, writer Vincenzo Cuoco had argued that a new Italy should model itself on the ancient Etruscans, claiming Etruria as a source not just of Roman civilization but of all world civilization.[42] Painter Pelagio Palagi found power and prestige in Italy's medieval history, though a medieval model was dangerous because it tended to emphasize divisions within Italy.[43] Writing in 1870, Nationalist poet Giosuè Carducci imagined modern Italy as a new Byzantium.[44] By the early twentieth century, ancient Rome and Renaissance city-states were preferred models. Images of Italy's glorious past—be it ancient, medieval, or Renaissance—modeled its future, offering a counterbalance to its rockier recent past.[45]

Central to the cultural Nationalism of the Fascist era was a belief in the necessity of cultural rebirth. In his influential writings about the consolidation of the Italian nation, Giuseppe Mazzini emphasized this idea, looking for a "Third Italy"—after the Roman Empire and the Renaissance—that would lead humanity toward "a new era of the Spirit." Historian Emilio Gentile identifies the key components of Mazzini's regenerative myth: "The ethical concept of life as service to the fatherland; the messianic vision of politics as a new lay religion; the belief that only a collective palingenetic experience, through struggle, sacrifice, and martyrdom, would foster the birth of a new Italian people."[46] And Walter L. Adamson has noted how prominent the language of regeneration was in the writings of the Florentine avant-garde during the 1900s and 1910s: "No word was more important to the message of *Leonardo*, or recurred more often in its pages, than 'renewal' and its various equivalents: 'rebirth,' 'reawakening,' 'renaissance,' 'regeneration,' 'resurgence,' 'resurrection.' Nor was any attitude more deprecated there than the one that simply contemplated the world rather than remaking it."[47] Fogu notes that this emphasis on spiritual regeneration was shared by cultural modernists, Catholic *modernisti*, and political Nationalists alike.[48]

As Tim Redman and others have amply demonstrated, Pound's concept of "cultural heritage" derives originally from the theories of Social Credit economist C. H. Douglas.[49] Among other ideas from Douglas quoted repeatedly by Pound is the notion of cultural heritage as the source of all values:

> The source of value is the cultural heritage; that is, the whole aggregate of mechanical inventions, their correlations and possible correlations, the improvement of seed and farming methods, and the customs and habits of civilization (subject to some selection and horse-sense, but, at any rate, treated as a potential and as a level of demand and perception.)[50]

In a letter to American Fascist Robert Summerville from the same month, July 1934, Pound wrote, "VALUE arises mainly from the cultural heritage, namely the aggregate of all mechanical inventions, mechanical correlations improved seed and agricultural methods, habits of civilized cooperation etc.," adding "THIS val[u]e belongs to no one man, and to no one clique or group" (*EPEC*, 114). Pound's sense of the cultural heritage, therefore, is not simply an Arnoldian vision of "the best which has been thought and said," but also a sense of life as lived, in terms of habits, technological innovations, and modes of social organization.

Pound realized that Benito Mussolini too relied on the strategies of cultural Nationalism. Pound wrote to the economist Odon Por in April 1934 that "the new real BASIS of value" is "cultural heritage," and goes on to note that this "fits with M[ussolini]'s objection to everything 'anti=storico.'"[51] In the *New York Herald* in the same year, Pound wrote, "Mussolini has taken his rank as the First European by a solid refusal to sabotage the cultural heritage, by a solid refusal to think that social justice can be attained only by abandoning every criterion that distinguishes the more civilized from the less civilized races."[52] Mussolini himself frequently argued for cultural heritage as an important tool for social change. "We must not remain solely contemplatives," Mussolini said in a speech to the students of the Academy of Fine Arts in Perugia that was later published in *L'Assalto* (Perugia) in early October 1926. "We must not simply exploit our cultural heritage [*patrimonio*]. We must create a new heritage to place alongside that of antiquity. We must create a new art, an art of our times: a Fascist art."[53] This notion that cultural heritage is active and changing motivated many of Mussolini's cultural projects. Jeffrey Schnapp and Barbara Spackman have noted that for the Fascist revolution to become permanent, it "would have to leave an indelible imprint on the Italian national psyche; it would have to penetrate the Italian subconscious and mold a new being: a genuinely 'fascist' political subject."[54] Using the culture of the past to make the art of the present and thereby change the future agreed with Pound's own aesthetics and would remain an important part of his Fascist-infused modernism.

As Emilio Gentile has noted, the project of national rejuvenation needed either new culture or new politics—or both, as the two are rarely easy to separate from one another.[55] Gentile identifies as important to this moment the concept of "modernist Nationalism"—a state of mind that emphasizes the myth of the nation but maintains an open attitude towards modernity as bringing massive social transformation and offering rich possibilities for new forms of collective life. Gentile calls this kind of Nationalism modernist because it wants "to reconcile intellectual culture, or *spiritualismo* ... with mass industrial society." And this form of Nationalism underlies Fascism, as well as many of the important avant-garde artistic movements of prewar Italy.[56] The result was that the culture that Fascism sponsored in its first decade—and that would suggest to Pound a new model for his own modernism—took elements from various existing movements, including political Nationalism, Milanese Futurism, and the Florentine avant-garde, and combined them to form its own social modernism.

The political Nationalist movement contributed much to the Fascist approach to cultural unification. The movement had been important to the campaigns of the Risorgimento, and the Italian Nationalist Party was a "secular, antiliberal, antisocialist political party of the right."[57] The Nationalists were realists, objecting to the inefficiency of Parliament, the corruption rampant in the capital, Socialism, provincialism, and the larger complacency in Italian life.[58] Nationalists' desire for an Italian unification which included regions that had been controlled by Austria meant that the port of Fiume—claimed by both Italy and Yugoslavia after the First World War, and briefly occupied by proto-Fascist forces led by poet and novelist Gabriele D'Annunzio—became a model for what the new Italy and its politically engaged artists could accomplish.[59] The Nationalists' emphasis on Italy's international stature remained crucial in the Fascist era, as intellectuals, artists, and government operatives continued to contemplate how modern

Italy could equal or surpass France and England.[60] Similarly, the Fascist regime shared with the Nationalists the desire to reclaim the Italian past from non-Italians, whether foreign occupiers, Grand Tour travelers, expatriates in Italy, or even foreign scholars.[61]

As Mussolini would, the Nationalists called for a remaking of Italians themselves.[62] And when such prominent Nationalists as Alfredo Rocco joined the Fascist Party, they brought with them Nationalist ideas and followers.[63] The Nationalists celebrated *Romanità*, or "Romanness," looking to ancient Rome for a model for modern Italian greatness, and advocated a colonial project that would restore Italy's former imperial glories.[64] In sum, the Nationalists' strategies and iconography shaped the Fascist approach to remaking regional citizens into national citizens, and many elements of the Nationalists' approach would make it into Pound's new Italian modernism.

So too the Milanese Futurists. Led by the poet F. T. Marinetti, they called for a complete break from tradition, the elimination of the baggage of the past, and the celebration of new technology, speed, and even war. Using their "manifesto of overwhelming and incendiary violence," they aimed to liberate Italy from the "fetid cancer of professors, archaeologists, tour guides, and antiquarians."[65] "Why should we look back over our shoulders, when we intend to breach the mysterious doors of the Impossible?" F. T. Marinetti asked in the famous "Founding and Manifesto of Futurism" (1909). "Time and space died yesterday. We already live in the absolute, for we have already created velocity which is eternal and omnipresent." Regular visits to museums and libraries—emblems of Italy's cultural past—were considered "as dangerous for artists as a prolonged guardianship under the thumb of one's family is for certain young talents intoxicated with their own genius and ambitious aims." Instead, artists should look to the future, to such modern mechanisms as airplanes and race cars, and to the power of crowds and violence for inspiration.[66] Marinetti called speed "a new form of beauty," describing a racecar, "with a hood that glistens with large pipes resembling a serpent with explosive breath" as more beautiful than the *Nike* of Samothrace. The Futurists wanted to eliminate those parts of Italian identity that had slowed the nation down.

No aspect of Italy's cultural past escaped their derision. Marinetti dismissed Dante's *Commedia* as "a filthy wormpit of commentators," a work whose battles have already been fought: rather than keeping their focus there, thinkers should look to modern works.[67] They reserved particular disdain for those places that foreigners loved best—Florence, Venice, Rome, "the three purulent sores of our peninsula." In admiring these historic cities, foreigners prevented their citizens from becoming participants in the culture of tomorrow.[68] Marinetti derided Venice and was determined to burn all gondolas and "fill the stinking little canals" of Venice "with the ruins of crumbling, leprous palaces."[69] That Pound had admired Venice when he visited in 1908 was not the only reason he commented, "when Mr. Marinetti and his friend shall have succeeded in destroying that ancient city, we [Americans] will rebuild Venice on the Jersey mud flats and use the same for a tea-shop" (*SP*, 107). Pound admired the bombast of the Futurist manifestos—and indeed emulated it in his contributions to *Blast* and elsewhere—but his vision of cultural renewal during the same period founded more upon a connection between past, present, and future. Although at the time he denied that the Futurists had anything of value to offer to the cultural world, by 1932 Pound had changed his mind, commenting in an interview with *La Stampa* (Turin) that "That movement that I, Eliot, Joyce and others initiated in London could not have been, without Futurism."[70] As a result of the Futurist influence, the cultural Nationalism that took root in the first decade of the Fascist era contained a deep skepticism about situating oneself in the past, and this new approach to the past affected Pound profoundly.

A third group, the Florentine *Vociani*, brought to Fascist cultural Nationalism an emphasis on regional identity and tradition.[71]

Coalescing in the years 1908–11 around Giuseppe Prezzolini and Giovanni Papini's Florentine journal *La Voce*—which Mussolini read from the beginning of its run—the *Vociani* were "united in their contempt for parliamentary democracy, bourgeois materialist values, and the compromises of reformist Socialism," all problems of the Giolittian era.[72] They differed dramatically from the Futurists and Nationalists by embracing a regionally determined sense of tradition as a means of molding a new future.

In Tuscany, some intellectuals feared that the culture of the Piedmont, the region with the greatest political and economic power, would smother that of the other regions. Others feared a bland homogeneity arising from the hybridizing of different regional identities.[73] For artists like Ardengo Soffici and such writers as Papini, both of whom were active in the Florentine avant-garde and later in wider Italian cultural movements of the 1920s and 1930s, *Toscanità*—or "Tuscanness"—meant a sense of home, a love of the Tuscan landscape, a celebration of the spirituality of the Tuscan people, and a sense that the power of the Tuscan past should infuse artistic and intellectual production in the present.[74] Later, Soffici joined with Carlo Carrà and Giorgio Morandi to form a movement known as *Strapaese* (or "supercountry") which opposed the *Stracittà* (or "supercity") representing the mechanistic tendencies of Futurism, the internationalizing aesthetics of the Novecento, and the urban focus of architectural Rationalism.[75] For the artists associated with *La Voce* and the *Strapaese*, celebrating regional identity could repel Nationalist homogenization, and Pound grew only more invested in these regions' history and culture.

When the Fascist government began envisioning a new Italy, it brought together many of these regional identities, political movements, and avant-garde groups. All these groups shared a desire for the aesthetic and intellectual work of the avant-garde and intelligentsia to "mediate the contrasts between the elite and the masses and create a cohesive national identity."[76] The modernist avant-garde of Italy—whether Futurist, *Vociano*, or Novecento—shared with the Nationalists the goal of national regeneration.[77] The blending of ideas from all these groups became ideological and aesthetic, "underpinning for the Fascist lay religion of the state."[78] Fascist rhetoric drew on these disparate extant strands, sharing their desire for cultural renewal and using some of their language and world view to accomplish its own ends.[79] The goal was to bring together *Toscanità* and *Romanità*, *Strapaese* and *Stracittà*, into one expansive and glorious vision of *Italianità*. As might be expected, this process took time, and the first decade of the Fascist era—from the March on Rome (October 1922) to the celebration of its ten-year anniversary with the Mostra della Rivoluzione Fascista—saw significant vying among groups each of which hoped that its vision of a new Italy would win out. As Roger Griffin has noted, "Fascism's multivalent, multifaceted nature as a utopian project of historical change" made it attractive to "any number of rival political visions ... as long as they were permutations of the core vision of Italian society's imminent rebirth from decadence."[80] In short, Fascism was a magnet for modernism, and these forms of Italian modernism would help to shape Pound's modernism of the 1930s.

The *Italianità* that developed during the 1920s and 1930s, in the context of Fascism's ascendancy, looks quite different from that imagined in earlier decades. Because so many of the intellectuals invested in the cultural projects of the Fascist regime had belonged to avant-garde movements before the First World War, and had therefore participated in some of these early attempts to solidify regional identities, there are traces of these regional identities in the Fascist conceptions of Italy. As Ruth Ben-Ghiat has argued, many Italian intellectuals saw the advent of a dictatorship as a chance to address the question of a unified Italian culture, feeling that the lack of such a coherent national cultural identity had left Italy vulnerable to cultural colonizing by other nations.[81] Such an appeal to intellectuals was a deliberate part of the Fascist strategy, which aimed to employ these thinkers, artists, and writers in the work of deploying Italy's cultural heritage in service of a new nation.

It is really no surprise, then, that this joining of the political and aesthetic would not just appeal to Pound, but become an important part of his own changing literary and cultural work.

Pound similarly recognizes the complexity of the Italian cultural context in *Jefferson and/or Mussolini*, that there existed in Italy a rich, but fragmented, culture: "In one sense they've all got some sort of culture, millenniar, forgotten, stuck anywhere from the time of Odysseus to the time of St. Dominic, to the time of Mazzini" (*J/M*, 25). The challenge, for a man who once identified himself as the gatherer of Osiris's limbs, is to make sense of these pieces as a whole. That all these movements were influencing and competing with one another for dominance meant that the *Italianità* that evolved during the late 1920s and early 1930s contained elements of the identity of different Italian regions and movements while at the same time looking beyond the strong identities of Italian regions to create a new, coherent nation.

Pound's return to Italy

Ezra Pound moved to Italy with his wife Dorothy in October 1924, and he was extremely receptive to the Italian strategies of cultural Nationalism. Having left London in 1920, and tired of Paris, where they had spent the intervening years, the Pounds settled in Rapallo, on the Ligurian Riviera. Pound quickly became enamored of Mussolini, whose Fascist "revolution" had started in northern Italy in the 1910s, coming to a visible climax with 1922's March on Rome. Pound's belief in the promise of Fascism came in part from Mussolini's economic solutions to Italy's unstable position in the interwar period, but Mussolini's cultural Nationalist projects also contributed significantly to his appeal. To ensure a glorious future for the new Italy, Mussolini employed artists to construct new works, and he imagined his building projects as an extension of those of ancient Roman emperors. He said in May 1922, shortly before coming to power, that "Fascism constructs its ideal and material edifices in the Roman way, stone by stone, and like the Roman ones, they will challenge time."[82] That these Romanizing edifices would be material *and ideal* demonstrates the extent to which individual artworks and monuments were to carry a strong ideological message and build a sense of national identity. Mussolini's desire to build a Fascist art—a desire he expressed in 1926 but which continued to motivate state patronage of the arts throughout the Fascist period—reflects his respect for the arts as a means of creating national identity. For Pound, Mussolini's approach was the perfect union of art and politics.

During the 1920s and 1930s, Pound's awareness of what was happening in Italy grew steadily, coming to shape his own aesthetic approaches. In *Indiscretions; or, Une Revue de Deux Mondes* (1923), we see—again in the context of Venice—an early glimpse of Pound's increasing awareness of the complexities of the Italian situation. Towards the beginning of the essay, Pound notes the name of his hotel in Venice, "which bears the hyphenated conjunction of a beer (Pilsen) and of the illustrious—but to the outer world somewhat indefinite saviour of his country, Manin ...." He then adds a footnote: "Fragility of local glory only too evident in the fact that the first reprobatory British proofreader effaced this Venetian name and substituted that of Mazzini."[83] This note mocks the ignorant proofreader who cannot distinguish Nationalist—and emphatically Venetian—Daniele Manin from the better-known Nationalist Giuseppe Mazzini. But it also offers a commentary on the complexity of the Italian case, reflecting on Nationalist campaigns and regional differences. One wants to read here a precursor to Pound's later claims, in *Jefferson and/or Mussolini*, to understand the Italian case better than any other foreigner. Most likely, what we are seeing here is an indication of curiosity about a different aspect of Venice than he was able to see in 1908. His mention later in that volume of Caporetto, an important First World War defeat for Italy, only emphasizes Pound's growing interest in modern—as opposed to historical—Italy.[84] Pound's investment in the workings of modern Italy, and in Italian cultural Nationalism, would only increase.

In 1924, Mussolini was consolidating his power, and trying to keep a positive public face on activities of which Italians would not always approve. He had dissolved Parliament in January and ordered new elections for April, and behind the political scenes he urged his followers to use violence to intimidate his opposition. The most prominent of these incidents involved the linking of Mussolini to the murder in June 1924 of Socialist deputy Giacomo Matteotti, a vocal opponent of Fascist violence.[85] Although Mussolini stayed in power, the incident was a blow to his authority; during 1924–25, he tried to distract the public from the Matteotti affair by focusing on cultural projects.[86] At this time, and as the years went on, Pound's own interest in Mussolini's cultural projects would cloud the American poet's view of the dictator's pattern of establishing power through violence against his opponents.

As Marla Stone has demonstrated, the Fascist state sought to build its legacy through support of living—and often avant-garde—artists. In the realm of architecture, the image of the artist as builder became quite literal, and the state commissioned numerous building projects in service of civic and national identity. Painters were imagined similarly as builders, although in a less literal sense, as they were more responsible for the ideal edifices. And although novels were not very successful as agents of social change, theater and cinema played important roles in reviving the masses' spiritual lives.[87] Similarly, poetry by pre-Fascist writers Giosuè Carducci, Giovanni Pascoli, and Gabrielle D'Annunzio was appropriate to the Fascist celebration of nation and modernity.[88] As Emily Braun has shown, "Reconstruction after the war called for a new sense of artistic competence: no longer one who undermines the foundations of bourgeois institutions, the artist became the master builder of the Fascist state, articulating the façade of a new classless society through edifying myths."[89] Where architects helped to define the new Italian nation by creating the space in which it would grow, painters and writers could articulate how individual Fascist subjects might relate to that state. Because art produced during this period is so frequently and intimately connected to the workings of state power, the aesthetics and politics of this period must be considered together, despite the desire of numerous modernists—like Pound—to separate them.

Whether subtle or glaring, state-sponsored cultural projects aimed to foment a sense of national, and Fascist, identity. For instance, Fascist exhibitions acted as communications services for the regime, celebrating wide-ranging aspects of Italian culture and arguing for their importance to making Italian—and Fascist—citizens.[90] Similarly, the journal *Capitolium*, initiated in 1924 and still in publication, worked during the Fascist period to connect present and past—modern building projects, say, with prominent archaeological discoveries in Rome—and to make the cultural past a consciously shared heritage that could be employed for present enrichment.[91] And in the realm of literature, this "exhibiting" included state-commissioned editions of writers like Dante, who were crucial to the consolidation of national identity.[92] State sponsorship of artists was a part of this same mission.

Not all artists made their evocation of Italy's past culture explicit. Many—and certainly the most sophisticated—employed subtler references, mixing historical sources with modern elements so that, as Jeffrey Schnapp has written, their work "gave rise to a complex, forward-looking interpretation of the regime's backward-looking ideals of Italianness and Romanness."[93] State patronage addressed not only the production but also the exhibition of works. As Marla Stone has shown, national cultural institutions—such as the state-supported Venice Biennale and Rome Quadriennale—took precedence over smaller local or regional institutions prevalent in Liberal Italy.[94] Jeffrey Schnapp has addressed the regime's use of spectacular entertainment to convey their ideas to people and create mass experience.[95] The more Pound learned of these state-sponsored projects, the more he saw them as a crucial part of the success of Mussolini's politics, and as a model for his own works.

Mussolini's politics and arts practices infused Pound's artistic projects and political sensibility. These various approaches appealed to Pound—sometimes working within his sense of how states ought to support artists, and sometimes offering new ways of imagining modernism. In Mussolini's regime, Pound newly imagined the relationship between the aesthetic and the political—realms he would never have brought together before. As we shall see, Pound's new thinking about the political and the aesthetic would transform his literary work. In the chapters that follow, I examine some important moments in the story of Fascist Italy's cultural Nationalist project to show how Pound's response to these endeavors shaped his modernism. We begin in 1932, when Pound's interest in Renaissance Italian poetry collided with a wider Italian rethinking of the Renaissance and its significance to the modern present.

CHAPTER 2

Renaissance Revisited: Pound's Foray into Italian Cultural Nationalism

> Originality and tradition are not contradictory terms. By returning to the purest traditions of Giottos, Masaccios, Paolo Uccellos, one does not renounce the originality of modern times, but only polishes off the rust and purifies our art of imitative alloys.
>
> —Margherita Sarfatti[1]

Towards the end of the first Fascist decade, Ezra Pound decided to become a part of the cultural Nationalist movement in Italy. Certainly his interest in modern Italy had been building at least since his move to Italy in 1924. But by 1932, he had found a way to take his own work and make of it a contribution to Italy's endeavors to find in its past a means of invigorating its future. As he would write in the unpublished essay "Italy: The Second Decennio" (1935 or 1936), "Fascism was a fight for cultural heritage."[2] Indeed, throughout his treatments of Mussolini, Pound emphasizes the role of Italy's cultural heritage in the Fascist move to make a modern, strong nation—thereby affiliating himself with the larger Italian cultural Nationalist movement.

This chapter examines the moment at which Pound insinuated himself into that movement. I explore the scene in which Pound found himself, identifying prominent strands in the conversation to which Pound was determined to make a contribution. I examine some of the prominent figures in the cultural work that began evolving in the first decade of the Fascist regime, 1922–32, others of which will be explored in more depth in Chapter 3. This decade represented the most optimistic period for Fascist and non-politically aligned intellectuals alike. The regime was in flux, still determining its own direction, and eager for the input of intelligent and creative minds. Experimental artists found themselves gaining entrance to prestigious exhibitions which previously had admitted only members of an academic elite. Editors of journals received attention from the state and were asked to contribute to state-sponsored projects of cultural renewal. Art critics with political leanings found ways to use their thinking about art to reform a degenerated society. All this happened in the context of a regime that was surprisingly open to an array of artistic and philosophical approaches—less interested in controlling thought than in benefiting from its ventures, however disparate or wild.

Of particular interest is the reappropriation of Renaissance culture by artists, theorists, politicians, and designers alike—all as part of the larger project, to use art critic and Fascist publicist Margherita Sarfatti's language, of finding previously ignored parts of tradition and "polishing off the rust," in order to make of them exciting, modern innovations. By building a sense of the cultural scene of Italy during the first decade of the Fascist regime, and then reading Pound's edition of *Guido Cavalcanti Rime* (1932) in the context of the Italy in which it was published, I demonstrate how Pound got involved in Italy's project of cultural rejuvenation, why he believed he could contribute, and how this investment claimed him.

Appropriating the Renaissance

Pound shared with his Italian contemporaries an admiration of the Renaissance. As Reed Way Dasenbrock has noted, Pound had looked to the Italian Renaissance as a model for the revitalization he wanted to see in the United States. "Whether from habit, or from profound intuition, or from sheer national conceit," Pound wrote in 1914, "one is always looking to America for signs of a 'renaissance.'"[3] Earlier in the same essay he notes that "the first step of a renaissance, or awakening, is the importation of models for painting, sculpture or writing," and he continues that "Flaminius and Amaltehus and the Latinists of the quattrocento and cinquecento began a movement for enrichment which culminated in the Elizabethan stage, and which produced the French Pléiade."[4] Like the members of the Italian avant-garde, then, Pound associated the cultural enrichment of that earlier period with his desire for strong contemporary patronage.

By this time, Pound was already concerning himself with the term "renaissance." He comments in *Patria Mia* (1913) that "renaissance" is not quite the word he wants, that "risvegliamento" would be the better Italian term: where *rinascimento* means "rebirth," *risvegliamento* has more of a sense of "awakening," "rekindling," or "revival"—or even "whetting," as of an appetite. He goes on to note the requirements for such an awakening:

> if one will study the *cinque cento* minutely, one will perhaps conclude that the earlier renaissance had two things requisite, the first, indiscriminate enthusiasm; the second, a propaganda. I mean that and just that. There was behind the awakening a body of men, determined, patient, bound together informally by kindred ambitions, from which they knew that they personally could reap but little.[5]

Given that Pound had been looking for such a cluster of men, with enthusiasm and a mechanism for getting their message out, he must have been star-struck by the role that intellectuals and artists were invited to play in Mussolini's Fascist regime.

That he calls the communication of the period's ideas "propaganda"—a term already accruing the negative implications we now associate with it—heightens the relationships he sees between "then" and "now." He would have appreciated Margherita Sarfatti's assertion in 1928 that "Revolutions in every domain of religion, society, philosophy, and art are made by altering the watchword." She noted that these new watchwords (or *parole d'ordine*) are launched "first within the governing elites and then by extending it to the mob: a watchword that stops them, surprises them, makes them reflect, and places them under the spell of action."[6] Not only did these Italian artists and thinkers have the enthusiasm already in place—as Pound had for America, they had been arguing for cultural revival in Italy since before the First World War. Now they had at their disposal the communications media of the Fascist regime: state-endorsed and state-sponsored art exhibitions, publicity in *Il Popolo d'Italia*, prizes and academies that would support them, and state patronage. "Great art does not depend upon comfort, it does not depend on the support of riches," Pound had written in 1914. "But a great age is brought about only with the aid of wealth, because a great age means the deliberate fostering of genius, the gathering-in and grouping and encouragement of artists."[7] What Pound saw in modern Italy was a nation on the verge of a great age, supported by a leader interested in the same kind of greatness to which artists and writers aspired.

Pound shared with many thinkers of his era a view of the Renaissance as a great age, an age defined by intellectual and artistic rejuvenation. In Italy, this period designated elsewhere as "the Renaissance" was often broken down further into centuries—the *trecento, quattrocento, cinquecento* (fourteenth, fifteenth, and sixteenth centuries).[8] In Italy, the period meant something else as well: a specifically *Italian* glorious past. To distinguish Pound's engagement with the Italian Renaissance during this period from that of his earlier writings, we need to look more closely at how Italian thinkers and painters were returning to the Renaissance as a source for modern experimentation. During the 1920s, addressing the question of what kind of art would best emblematize a new Fascist Italy, many artists and thinkers found the answer in a glorious traditionalism, with roots in the Renaissance. Many were quick to distinguish their resuscitation of the Italian Renaissance—and its cultural heritage—from that of foreigners who had made seemingly similar moves.[9] In his book on the early Renaissance Florentine painter Giotto, metaphysical painter Carlo Carrà pointed to the English Pre-Raphaelites as an example of a wrong way of approaching the art of the past. Such a group, he notes, "having their heads full of abstract ideology, sought in the artists of the fourteenth century, religiosity rather than artistic merit." He explains their error:

> They thus let it be seen that they were ignorant of the fact that religiosity has the same relation to art as any other vital activity, and should be considered only as a material for art, having the same value as any other material offered the artist by life and no more.[10]

Given Pound's own Pre-Raphaelite tendencies in his early poetry, such a comment marks a notable distinction. For the Italian artist of the twentieth century, Carrà asserts, Giotto provides an artistic model on formal grounds for his "forms are nearest to our own modes of understanding and sensing the construction of bodies in space."[11]

Margherita Sarfatti's championing of a "return to order" was extremely influential. During the 1910s, she was an art critic for the Socialist journal *Avanti!*, whose editorship Mussolini assumed in 1912. When Mussolini broke with the Socialist Party and started *Il Popolo d'Italia*, Sarfatti took her criticism there. The two began an affair by the fall of 1918, and Sarfatti became one of Mussolini's principal cultural advisors. With Mussolini she co-edited *Ardita* (1919–21), the literary review of *Il Popolo d'Italia*, and later *Gerarchia* (1922–43). During the early years of the Fascist regime, Sarfatti also actively educated Mussolini about the role that art could play in his vision of a politically revitalized Italy, encouraging him to study Machiavelli and the history of ancient Rome.[12] Consequently, Sarfatti's ideas about art shaped both the work of artists and the political appropriation of art; Pound corresponded with her and read many of her writings.

As we see from this chapter's epigraph, in 1921 Sarfatti wrote in *Il Popolo d'Italia* about a new direction for Italian art, and her statement about the confluence of originality and tradition became a sort of manifesto for artists:

> Italian art must return to method, order, and discipline. It must achieve a definite, full-bodied form, a precise sense of gravity, analogous to and convergent with that of the ancients; independent of foreign fashions and mercantile considerations.[13]

That she chooses Giotto, Masaccio, and Paolo Uccello is no coincidence for they were seen by this time as three of the greatest innovators in the early Florentine, and therefore Italian, Renaissance. In part, that reputation had grown out of Bernard Berenson's writings in *The Florentine Painters of the Renaissance* (1896). Thanks to the work of Emilio Cecchi, and despite Berenson being an American, the book had come to provide an important underlying theory in contemporary Italian aesthetic discussions.

Berenson's sense of Renaissance art rests largely on his theory of "tactile values" as a way of analyzing form. He lists Giotto and Masaccio as the most important innovators in this realm, arguing that the Florentine painters' treatment of form accounted for their great innovations, setting them apart from other painters of their day. "It was in fact upon form, and form alone, that the great Florentine masters concentrated their efforts, and we are consequently forced to the belief that, in their pictures at least, form is the principal source of our aesthetic enjoyment."[14] The representation and interpretation of form relies on the ability to "give tactile values to retinal sensations" and to make viewers more conscious of how they see. Simply seeing bodies, buildings, and other structures in day-to-day life, he notes, is rarely an opportunity for the heightened aesthetic experience that comes from conscious seeing. And yet, when that same experience occurs in art, and therefore in a setting of heightened awareness, the pleasure increases dramatically (*FP*, 10). Berenson valorized Giotto's revolutionary "power to stimulate the tactile imagination," and asserted that such stimulation of the tactile imagination makes the experience of viewing Giotto's pictures *more* powerful than viewing actual people because of their status as painted forms (*FP*, 6). For readers who believe in the power of tactile values, Giotto must therefore be a hero, as he was for Sarfatti and many artists of the time.

As Berenson had used the work of Giotto to define tactile values, he saw Masaccio as Giotto's most important successor. Berenson called Masaccio, "Giotto born again, starting where death had cut short his advance, instantly making his own all that had been gained during his absence, and profiting by the new conditions, the new demands" (*FP*, 27). He admired Masaccio's sense of the material and spiritual significance of his figures:

> Types, in themselves of the manliest, he presents with a sense for the materially significant which makes us realize to the utmost their power and dignity; and the spiritual significance thus gained he uses to give the highest import to the event he is portraying; this import, in turn, gives a higher value to the types, and thus, whether we devote our attention to his types or his action, Masaccio keeps us on a high plane of reality and significance. In later painting we

shall easily find greater science, greater craft, and greater perfection of detail, but greater reality, greater significance, I venture to say, never. (*FP*, 29)

For Masaccio's work, this combination of material and spiritual significance creates not only the sense that the figures portrayed could be touched (and therefore look real) but also the understanding of the importance of the scenes portrayed. By "significance," Berenson seems to mean a combination of "realism" and "the ability to convey information." A painting of a man that has material significance, for instance, registers as "a man" in the viewer's mind, and conveys through its form some information about what that man represents. When that same work has also spiritual significance, then the information conveyed goes beyond the physical to represent things unseen, whether they be the man's divine stature, his power, or his relationship to God.

For Italian painters of the early twentieth century, many of whom had been inspired by the formal innovations of Paul Cézanne and Giovanni Fattori, Masaccio's ability to convey meaning in his depiction of forms opened up possibilities for the painted representation of their modern condition. Berenson goes on to attribute power to the very figures in Masaccio's paintings. Because of their material significance, he imagines them as powerful in their own right, not merely as representations:

Then what strength to his young men, and what gravity and power to his old! How quickly a race like this would possess itself of the earth, and brook no rivals by the forces of nature! Whatever they do—simply because it is they—is impressive and important, and every movement, every gesture, is world-changing. (*FP*, 30)

When painters like Mario Sironi adopted the formal qualities that Berenson had described in Masaccio's figures, they wanted their massive painted figures, too, to be this impressive and important—to be powerful enough to seem capable of possessing the earth and changing the world.

Berenson does not share Sarfatti's and contemporary artists' admiration for Paolo Uccello. Sarfatti's comment above about the need for Italian art to "return to order" and look to Renaissance tradition is typical in linking these three masters as worthy of emulation, but Berenson determined that Uccello's interest in Nationalism and scientific problems overwhelmed the tactility of his figures. "His real passion was perspective," Berenson wrote, "and painting was to him a mere occasion for solving some problem in this science, and displaying his mastery over its difficulties." To Berenson, all the details in Uccello's paintings—Prostrate horses, dead or dying cavaliers, broken lances, ploughed fields, Noah's arks" (*FP*, 33)—are included in order to create as many mathematically converging lines as possible, noting that his "zeal" for precision and naturalism often compromised the realism of other elements of the picture. What Berenson saw as "dexterity for its own sake," solicited praise from Ardengo Soffici, who said of Uccello, "the mad person who did not know how to construct a horse according to anatomy, was one of the most fresh, the most sincere, the most courageous, and therefore the greatest painters of the *quattrocento* and of all time in Florence, in Italy, in the world."[15] Carlo Carrà specifically addressed critiques of Berenson and others, saying that from Uccello's emphasis on spirit over realism was born "the legend of his impotence in plastic, which today again is repeated by the great spirits. But impotence in art signifies genuineness, and therefore is a quality of delicacy, life that gets around in the perception."[16] After the qualities of Giotto's and Masaccio's art that had been so innovative became "drained of substance," it remained to Paolo Uccello to "sustain the weight and responsibilities of all the plastic inheritances."[17] And after more discussion of the artist's works, Carrà concludes: "Paolo Uccello was one of the best, most rare and wisest artists, among the many from whom we were born."[18] Arguing with

Berenson gave many Italian artists a way to valorize their cultural heritage without seeming to rely too heavily on foreign scholarship.

It may also have mattered to these Italian artists that the works discussed by Berenson are not usually museum pieces. Rather, he often tracks them down in churches still used for worship or in palaces, some of which had been transformed into working governmental buildings.[19] Berenson is *not* writing about the entombed, preserved past of the Italian Renaissance, but of a mass of images and monuments still part of the fabric of Italian life. For artists and thinkers who wanted to conceive of Italian tradition as something vibrant, such a setting was essential. Although museum culture could afford comparisons of the sort found in Berenson's treatment of Giotto, it now also carried the explicit condemnation of the Futurists, who likened museums to cemeteries. In "The Foundation and Manifesto of Futurism" (1908), F. T. Marinetti had blamed museums—together with libraries and suffragettes—for the artistic downfall he saw around him, declaring the Futurists' plan "to destroy museums, libraries, academies of every sort, and to fight against moralism, feminism, and every utilitarian or opportunistic cowardice."[20] For artists of the Italian avant-garde, art was not something to be admired merely for beauty, but something that could change points of view and even contribute to a wider project of cultural renewal, and Berenson's analysis made an important contribution to that project.

Most Italians encountered Berenson's conception of the workings of Renaissance art through the work of Emilio Cecchi. In 1920, Cecchi, who had been a literary contributor to *La Voce* and would go on to play a dominant role in the Cines film production complex in the 1930s, published in the Roman journal *Valori Plastici* a discussion of Berenson's writings. His essay mentions an impending translation of Berenson's writings, presumably by painter Roberto Longhi, to be published as a part of the "Libreria della Voce," a series of books associated with the Florentine journal *La Voce*, the same line that had in 1915 published the first biography of Benito Mussolini.[21] Berenson's contributions to the history of Italian art remained important for Cecchi for years to come. His *Trecentisti Senesi* (1928) draws on Berenson's attributions and assessments of Sienese paintings, even as it occasionally notes that Berenson's ideas could bear updating. In 1936, Cecchi published a translation of Berenson's *Italian Painters of the Renaissance*, as well as a separate volume translating the accompanying list of definitive attributions to each of the artists discussed; the two were printed as part of the "Collezione 'Valori Plastici,'" affiliated with the Roman art journal of the same name.[22]

Valori Plastici (1918–1922) was well into its second volume at the time it published Cecchi's review. The journal was published by painter Mario Broglio, and provided a forum for conversations about art, featuring columns by such important Italian artists as Carrà, Soffici, Giorgio de Chirico, and Alberto Savinio, and by other Europeans including Max Jacob, Jean Cocteau, and André Breton.[23] The journal regularly featured reproductions of artworks from prominent avant-garde art movements of the period, and by this time had reproduced work by Carrà, de Chirico, Fattori, Gino Severini, Giorgio Morandi, Georges Braque, Pablo Picasso, Juan Gris, Jacques Lipchitz, and Fernand Léger. Its aim, like that of much of the Italian avant-garde of this time, was the "renewal of Italian painting." Its name, a borrowing from Berenson's idea of "tactile values," refers both to the essence of things and to the sculptural quality of objects that Giorgio de Chirico and Carlo Carrà tried to represent. *Valori Plastici*'s aesthetic focus shifted somewhat over time, following wider trends in the avant-garde culture of the period. It began by supporting the aesthetics exemplified by the paintings of Carrà and de Chirico in 1917–18, but by the time it stopped publication, it favored a stricter return to Italian classical tradition.[24]

Berenson's ideas about "tactile values" provided part of the basis for the dominant postwar aesthetic of "plastic values." "Plastic values" summarizes, to use Emily Braun's language, "the innately

Italian style of solidly modeled, cubic forms that had its origins in the early Renaissance."[25] Artists working in this style turned away from the overdone, beaux-arts style that had come to dominate nineteenth-century Italian aesthetics (witness the aforementioned Vittorio Emanuele monument in Rome) and looked to such earlier innovators as Masaccio, Giotto, Paolo Uccello, and Piero della Francesca as models for their own innovation—not just because their figures were constructed using the formal qualities these modern artists emulated, but because they were Italian. This emulation was not conceived as a return to the past but rather as a model for innovation. "In order to overcome the pride of mere mechanical facility and technique—sad inheritance of the nineteenth century—there is nothing better than to study the teachings of a Giotto fresco," wrote Carlo Carrà in 1925.[26] That these painters were known for breaking aesthetic norms increased their appeal, and that Berenson addressed this aspect of their work increased his.

Sarfatti, like many Italian painters of the period, saw in Renaissance Italian works models for modern innovation that avoids novelty for its own sake. This combination of tradition and innovation, emulation and revolution, would define the cultural Nationalism that Sarfatti envisioned for a new, Fascist Italy. Throughout her championing of new art, she would ever look to Italy's glorious tradition, as seen particularly in the monumental architecture of ancient Rome and the paintings of the Italian Renaissance, as a signal of the innate greatness of Italy, arguing that Italians "have in their blood long centuries of refined aesthetic tradition."[27]

Other artists and writers agreed, using Renaissance works as models. In 1922, Ardengo Soffici commented that the work of Dante "is like the gospel and the paradise of our race, as well as the ledger where all of its rights have been recorded."[28] Giuseppe Bottai's journal *Critica Fascista* asked prominent figures in the Fascist cultural scene how a "Fascist art" should look, and in 1926–27 published their responses. Many answered that it should be traditionally Italian, with that tradition growing from the Renaissance. Alessandro Pavolini, journalist, editor, and militant *squadrista*, saw in the great centuries of Italian art—the fourteenth, fifteenth, and sixteenth—a "choral presence" of "the people." "Behind Giotto, as behind the irascible Michelangelo," he wrote, "entire citizenries burn with passion." He goes on to enumerate Florentine examples—Ghiberti's Baptistry doors, Brunelleschi's dome for the duomo, the base of Benvenuto's statue of *Perseus* (which now stands in the Piazza della Signoria)—which demonstrate for him that "Art is of general interest in these centuries." And artworks of such times, he argues, create a connection between the individual and his milieu:

> The work of art is a work of an individual, not a collective. But in our (Italian) works of art, one can sense that the artist, while his mind was reasoning on its own and his arm was moving freely in the ardor of his work, had his feet resting on solid reality, on a precise plane of reference. That plane of reference was his understanding of the people, of the thirst for beauty shared by men of the same race, with all their limitations yet with all of their incomparably fresh and deep intuitions.

Granted, artists generally connect themselves to a wider culture but, according to Pavolini, it is in *Italian* works especially that this happens: his parentheses may try to give that word lesser status, but they instead proffer importance. Although periods of Romanticism lead to decadence, and art cannot function as it should, the Fascist movement has brought Italy out of that decadence, and is again "bringing Italian artists to the spiritual conditions most befitting their work and faithful to our Italian tradition."[29] The Italian Renaissance represented how art can enrich a culture, and the Fascist government aimed to restore the conditions of this great age, thereby recreating its productive environment.

But the Renaissance's traditional appeals were not enough to ensure its primacy in the vision for a new Italian art during the Fascist era. Cipriano Efisio Oppo, painter and art critic as well as Secretary General of the National Fascist Trade Union for Artists, and one of the artistic directors of the Mostra della Rivoluzione Fascista, addressed other aspects that made it distinctive. He wrote in 1927 that the new Italy should avoid Imperial Rome as an image of its great past, as even Napoleon, a foreign conqueror of Italy, had taken that ancient empire as a model. Instead, Oppo asserted, Italy must draw on its whole rich history, a history which uses the Renaissance as its nascent moment. He said, "Fascist art must mean Italian art in the same traditional sense," and to gloss this he listed members of an Italian cultural pantheon—Giotto, Dante, Masaccio, Alberti, Michelangelo, Jacopo della Quercia, and others—who in turn birthed "a thousand others," who, he noted, were "revolutionary and traditional at the same time, new and old together like the magnificent acceptable contradiction that is the history of Italian art."[30] Although those others included artists and thinkers of later periods—Caravaggio, Leopardi, Verdi—even they seem to spring from the sense of Italianness that originated in the Renaissance.[31]

As might be expected, Oppo's definition of Italian art stresses the elements already praised by the Fascists:

> Italian art is primarily order, tough discipline, good faith and awareness; hermetic art that does not need to proselytize. It is joyous candor and sincere anguish, not born of intoxication or intellectual and artificial torment; roughness, not frivolity and pedantry; simplicity, not verbosity and foolish luxury. It is intelligence, not cleverness and theory; originality of substance, not originality of form; technical jealousy of every art, not the unnatural coupling of painting, music, poetry, etc. Finally it is the ambition to be of the people and universal, in contrast with the (sectarian) spirit of elites and schools.[32]

While not every artist agreed with Oppo's ideas about the direction that Italian art should follow, this harkening back to the Renaissance extended further than Oppo. In his book on Giotto, published in 1925, Carrà noted that for numerous reasons the work of Giotto "has special interest for us to-day":

> First of all, this work constitutes one of the most spontaneous efforts of the plastic genius of the Italian people, who in the field of figured arts were the pioneers of all western painting. Secondly, because in the so-called formal incapacity of Giotto, we find a precious hint to teach us to be in our turn genuinely sincere toward ourselves. Finally, the best contemporary artists exhibit a not very different formal incapacity.[33]

He goes on to list Cézanne and Fattori—artists emulated by many members of the Italian avant-garde of the day—as specific examples of this tendency. In the months after the First World War, Carrà wrote of feeling "an absolute need to reattach myself to our purest traditions"—found in the work of Giotto and Paolo Uccello.[34] His national pride in Giotto, then, combines with a sense that this artist of the *trecento*, so crucial to the *quattrocento*, still defines the formal experimentation of the *novecento*.

This sense of influence occurs particularly in the work of the group of artists known as the "Novecento," or "Novecento italiano," which included painters Mario Sironi, Achille Funi, Leonardo Dudreville, and Pietro Marussig, and benefited from the intellectual sponsorship of Margherita Sarfatti. Her vision of cultural Nationalism saw something innately artistic in Italians, going back to the High Renaissance masters and ancient Romans.[35] Part of her interest in the Novecento painters was rooted in their ability to draw on this tradition and bring out the innate balance and harmony that she thought defined Italian culture.[36] As Cannistraro and Sullivan have shown, she celebrated the Novecento painters' "modern classicity," which went well beyond the copying of earlier styles. In 1920, in the catalogue for an exhibition of Achille Funi's work, she specifically likened his style of portraiture to that of Piero della Francesca:

> Look at the slender figure of the lady, cut unevenly—in fact you could say engraved—in profile upon the shining azure of the sky, with its well-drawn symmetrical little clouds, as in those famous portraits of the fifteenth and sixteenth centuries by Piero della Francesa and Ambrogio de Predis, even with the lock of parted hair over the ears, a touching and delicious detail, embroidered in the profile portrait of Beatrice d'Este. And yet she is a lady, a modern girl of today not so much because of today's clothing and hairstyle but because of the gait, the attitude, the glance, and the smile; just as much of the indefinable that is the seal of the present, fugitive and light, but sapid, characteristic, and precious, more than the eternal humanity of every time.[37]

Her analysis shows that Funi's art bears some characteristics of that older work, but not at the expense of expressing a sense of modernity. In all this work, tradition and modernity come together to make something new, modernist.

In choosing the name "Novecento italiano," the group echoed the use of the term "quattrocento" (or "fifteenth century") used to describe such artists of the early Italian renaissance as Piero della Francesca, Paolo Uccello, and Masaccio, seen as crucial innovators and prominent figures in the history of Italian art. Inherent in the name was a Nationalist move, perhaps overemphasized by the word "italiano." As the painter Anselmo Bucci noted in a letter to Sarfatti, the "italiano" was not really needed, because "Novecento" (or "twentieth century") might in itself indicate that the group was Italian:

> [Novecento] is Italian just like "Quattrocento," like "Cinquecento," like "Settecento." The French with their

Cattrosentó Senchesentó mean well and only refer to the Italian fifteenth and sixteenth centuries; better to say: centuries of *Italian art*. Don't you think?[38]

Sarfatti did, because as late as 1930, in catalogue copy for another exhibition of paintings by artists of the Novecento, she made a similar argument:

> Having been assumed into the heaven of art, the Trecento, the Quattrocento, the Cinquecento are names designating not merely the chronology of a century or a period, but rather a style and a characteristically Italian plastic glory. To name an artistic movement "Novecento Italiano" seemed, in the gray years between the wars, a rash omen for the greatness of our era and for the artistic supremacy of our nation. It was a creation of energetic faith and of anticipatory pride that we reclaim proudly.[39]

This "characteristically Italian plastic glory" dominated the Novecento's aims and connected their art tightly to the political objectives of the Fascist regime.

The painters of the Novecento wanted to be distinctly Italian, and also modern and innovative while valuing the emphasis on form that they saw in the earlier masters. Emily Braun has demonstrated the extent to which Mario Sironi borrowed stylistically from *quattrocento* masters in such paintings of 1922–24 as *The Architect*, *The Student*, and *Venus*: "the figures are rendered as massive and immobile, cloaked by heavy mantles of drapery that cast shadows like the flutes of a classical column." The works incorporate features showing "the influence of the Quattrocento primitives," and "the sharp angles with which Sironi defined the planes of the facial features and the treatment of the brows and ridge of the nose in one continuous line owe directly to Masaccio." In *The Architect*, she highlights the presence of a

Corinthian capital, "a traditional attribute found in Renaissance emblem books," used to forge a connection between the figure of the painting and "the painter-architect or *pictor-artifex* of Alberti's *De re aedificatoria*."[40] While some of these stylistic choices pay simple respect to important predecessors, the elements that Sironi borrowed also serve their own political purpose in his works. For instance, Braun notes that, "in the urban landscapes, Sironi empowers the representation of the workers' domain and, by extension, their political role by using a pictorial language of heroic dimensions: his reference to the prestigious style of the fourteenth century acknowledges the dominant status of the masses in the twentieth."[41] Art of the Renaissance, then, not only represented a glorious Italian past but also offered aesthetic solutions for modern Italian artists and their shaping of modern Italian citizens.

As Pound had looked to the Italian Renaissance as a model for an American *risvegliamento*, so did these modern Italian artists emulate the Renaissance, adding a Nationalist note. Pound could see in their cultural work the beginnings of the kind of relationship between a state and the arts that he had advocated for so many years: artists could help a nation make sense of, enrich, and love its culture. Granted, without moving to Italy and discovering Italian cultural Nationalism, Pound could still have maintained his respect for Italian culture—and it would likely have continued to be important to him. But engaging in the contemporary Italian scene—so different from the tourist vision of the country—rendered his sense of the Italian Renaissance not as something museal, but vibrant. In fact, he shifted the focus of his own writing about the Renaissance in order to converse with contemporary Italian ideas. To see this happening, we must turn to his Italian edition of *Guido Cavalcanti Rime*.

"Polishing off the rust": *Guido Cavalcanti Rime*

In 1932, when Ezra Pound's friend Francesco Monotti received a copy of Pound's edition of *Guido Cavalcanti Rime* (1932), he wrote back, "Re Cavalcanti, I have been wondering if it would not be a good opportunity for you to visit Il Duce, and present him with a copy. Have you thought of it?"[42] That Monotti, editor of the English section of *Bibliografia Fascista* during the 1930s and later involved in the state-run exhibitions in the 1940s, would read this book as a suitable calling card to Benito Mussolini suggests that he found in Pound's work the same celebration of Italian cultural heritage as in Mussolini's Fascist regime. Marking the tenth anniversary of the Fascist revolution, 1932 saw significant cultural reflection in Italy. Artists and politicians alike were keen to combine elements of Italy's heteroclite past to forge an enduring Fascist nation. Pound agreed with the many artists and intellectuals who saw the Renaissance, and specifically the early writers and artists of Florence, as central. In 1933 he wrote of Italy's promise as a well-governed modern nation: "I dream for Italy an epoch, and that little by little, *mutatis mutandis*, will resemble somewhat the 14-century, an epoch in which the highest culture and modern science, functions at maximum. In the 14-century the very apex of power coincided with the apex of culture."[43] By diving into Italy's cultural heritage, and emerging with Cavalcanti in his teeth, Pound would offer to modern Italy pieces of its past that could well serve its present. In short, he was following the directives that Sarfatti had offered modern Italian artists—that they should find modern means of innovation in the artifacts of tradition, taking time to "polish off the rust" and allow the old pieces to shine through new uses.

Certainly for Pound the act of breathing life into the scattered limbs of cultural heritage was hardly new. His "I Gather the Limbs of Osiris" (1911–12) had laid out his methodology of venturing into the past to show modern readers a forgotten gem. In the third section of this series, he offered five translations of Cavalcanti's sonnets and *ballate*, meant to stand as emblems of his pre-Dante Tuscan aesthetic. Pound wrote that Cavalcanti's poetry "is interesting, apart from its beauty, for his exact psychology, for an attempt to render emotions precisely; emotions, uncommon, perhaps, save in a land of sun, where the soul and the senses are joined in a union different, may be, from that which occurs in other countries."[44] Already, here, he echoes claims made around the same time by the members of the *Vociani*—that the artistic products of a region, and especially of Tuscany, derive largely from the climate and land in which they are made. And for Pound, these translations were part of his program of "seek[ing] out the luminous detail and present[ing] it," in the hopes that by "hanging his own gallery" of such details, he might recharge the arts of the present.[45] This weaving the beautiful elements of the past into the fabric of contemporary artistic production was Pound's early modernism, his way, as a young poet in London, of negotiating the complicated relationship between tradition and innovation.

Being in a nation that, en masse, was looking to its cultural heritage as a means of enlivening its modernity must have seemed like a dream to Pound. As he had gestured to the *quattrocento* as the source of hope for modern America, so did contemporary Italian thinkers and artists find in that period ideals, artistic innovations, and political structures that would help modern Italy define a national identity. And accustomed as he was to finding his own intellectual work an upstream journey—against the resistant mainstream of Britain and the United States—being a part of a large movement in Italy would have been a relief. It is no wonder he looked around him and declared Italy "the only country of the world that I feel is governed better than I could suggest."[46] Having had difficulty securing a British publisher for his edition of Cavalcanti's poems, he was quite willing to transform his edition into a book that could help Italy in its cultural Nationalist mission.

GUIDO CAVALCANTI RIME

EDIZIONE RAPPEZZATA
FRA LE ROVINE

GENOVA
EDIZIONI MARSANO S. A.
VIA CASAREGIS, 24
ANNO IX.

1. Ezra Pound, title page of *Guido Cavalcanti Rime* (Genova: Edizioni Marsano S. A., [1932]). (Beinecke Rare Book and Manuscript Library) Copyright © 1935 by Ezra Pound. Reprinted by permission of New Directions Publishing Corp.

68 *Fascist Directive*

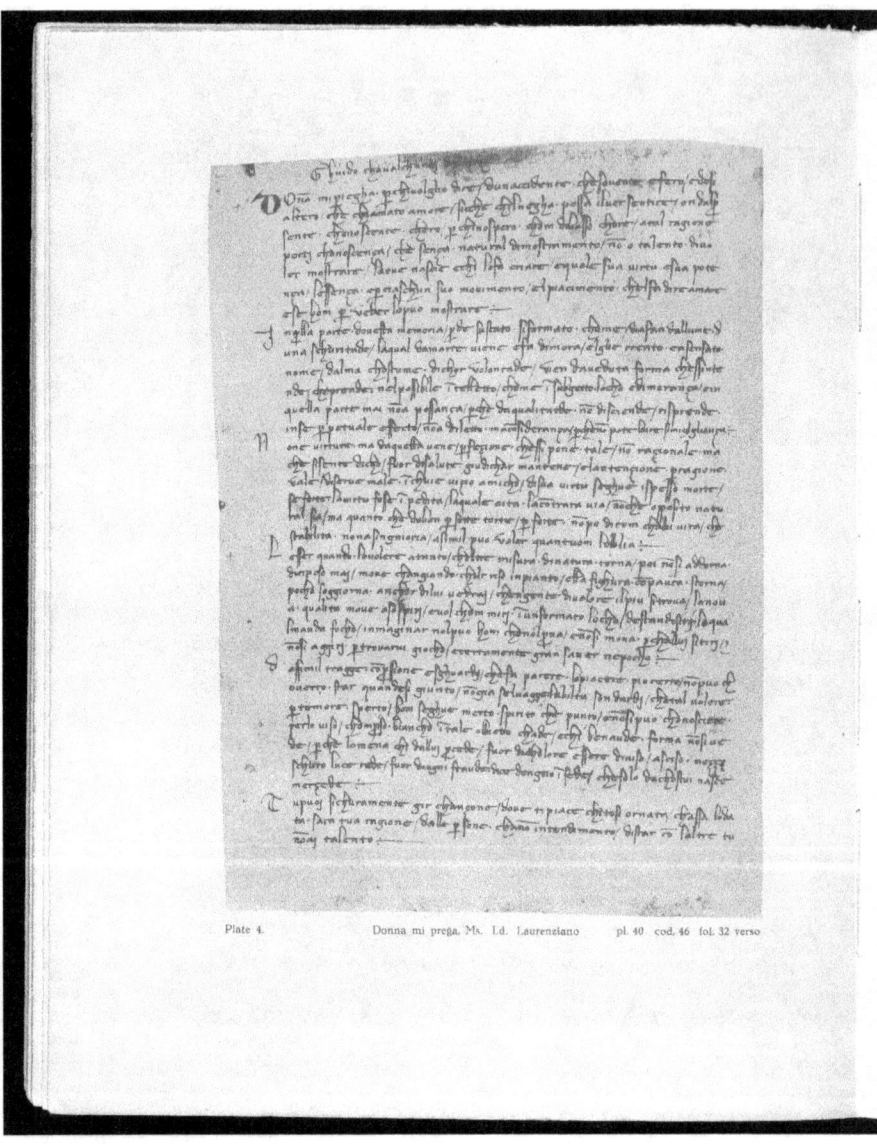

2. Ezra Pound, *Guido Cavalcanti Rime* (Genova: Edizioni Marsano S. A., [1932]), Plate 4, "Donna mi prega," Ms. Ld. Laurenziano. (Beinecke Rare Book and Manuscript Library) Copyright © 1935 by Ezra Pound. Reprinted by permission of New Directions Publishing Corp.

Though not conceived as an Italian Nationalist project, Pound's *Guido Cavalcanti Rime* became one when it was published in Genoa and read by Pound's friends involved in the cultural projects of the Fascist regime (Fig. 1). Such a reception allowed Pound to use its Nationalist associations to support his own literary objectives. He had been working on translations of Cavalcanti since the mid-1910s, but the leads he had in 1928–29 on publishing an edition in England fell through. He finally published it in 1932 in Italy, under the auspices of Edizioni Marsano in Genoa, all at his own expense.[47] In so doing, he transformed the book. In England it would have been an edition of a little-known foreign poet. In Italy, however, it could be a scholarly edition of a national poet, a predecessor to Dante and the kind of figure who appealed to the cultural Nationalism important to Mussolini's Fascism. Strands of Pound's celebration of Cavalcanti concurred with Italian intellectuals' sense of their glorious past. Pound's turning the book into an Italian edition let it be read in the context of this cultural Nationalism. Pound's positioning of this book within conversations about using culture to construct Italian identity prefigures his more dramatic affiliations with Mussolini's regime, as he comes to believe more and more in the rhetoric—often at the expense of the reality—of Italian Fascism.

Pound's book, like much of the cultural work done in Italy during the first decade of the Fascist regime, makes a shift from regional identity to the national identity crucial to the Fascist regime. The tropes through which the Florentine avant-garde had, circa 1907, delineated a Tuscan identity for themselves— valorization of Dante, celebration of the rural peasantry, interest in Florentine painters of the Renaissance—made their way into the attempts, circa 1932, to strengthen the Italian nation by celebrating its cultural heritage. The Florentine avant-garde had admired Giotto, Masaccio, Piero della Francesca, and Leonardo as Florentine and Tuscan painters who made great innovations. These same artists, now reimagined as Italian rather than Tuscan, served as the basis of innovative art and thought during the Fascist era. As Cipriano Efisio Oppo had said that "Fascist art must mean Italian art in some traditional sense," so Pound made connections between modern Italy and the Italian pre-Renaissance, Mussolini, and Cavalcanti. Pound's celebration of Guido Cavalcanti—himself a Tuscan poet contemporary with Dante—blends Tuscanness into Italianness. Those elements of Cavalcanti's Tuscanness that Pound admired became, by the time he finished his edition, a hope for a rejuvenated Italianness.

Pound's transformation of his Cavalcanti project into an Italian product required significant changes to his original conception.[48] His title page calls the book an "Edizione rappezzata tra le rovine," or an "edition patched from the ruins." The Table of Contents for the new edition is, of course, in Italian. The contents are divided into three sections: a scholarly edition (in Italian) of Cavalcanti's poems, a series of photostatic plates of the poetry as found in manuscripts, and English material—essays and translations. This strange structure led the collector and scholar of English literature Mario Praz to deride it as "an exquisitely Poundian amusing jumble."[49] That Pound positions the Italian scholarly material first betrays his attempt to attract an Italian audience. Second come the photostatic reproductions of the sources of Cavalcanti's poems, testimony to the archival digging that Pound had done to breathe life into the limbs of Cavalcanti's work and an expensive stumbling block to publishing the book in England (Fig. 2).

The edition's English essays position Cavalcanti in the literary world of thirteenth-century Tuscany, explaining to English readers why they should read Cavalcanti although they may never have heard of him. The bulk had been published before, mostly in the late 1920s, and mostly in *The Dial*.[50] Here they are relegated to a third section called "Frammenti dell'edizione bilingue," or "Fragments of the Bilingual Edition," as if the material in English were left-overs, something beyond which he had moved. And whereas Pound dedicated his first attempt at a publication of Cavalcanti's work, a book published in 1912, to Violet Hunt and Ford Maddox [*sic*] Hueffer, here his dedication is to Manlio Dazzi, the librarian at the Malatestine Library and reviver of Italian culture who, Pound wrote in 1936, "brought to light Mussato, curated the library, found a way to have first-rate music in a small town, and improved the structure of the Querini gallery."[51] Stefano Maria Casella has demonstrated how important the "Paduan pre-humanist" Albertino Mussato (1261–1329) was to Pound—Pound stressed on numerous occasions the importance of Mussato's Latin tragedy *Ecerinis* and often lamented its neglect by readers and scholars— and the extent to which Pound linked Dazzi and Mussato in his mind.[52] Furthermore, the first ancillary text in the edition, titled "Ad Lectorem—E. P." is in Italian, and Pound signs it "Rapallo, Maggio – Anno IX," thereby positioning himself as an author in Italy, in the Italian language, and within the Fascist dating system.[53]

Pound situates Cavalcanti with respect to well-known Italian writers—writers also significant to the sense of Italian identity developing in 1932. In his Italian introduction, Pound calls Cavalcanti "the father of Tuscan poetry," arguing for his supremacy over Dante, if only because Cavalcanti was Dante's elder by fifteen years. But Dante for Italians of this time represented not merely a great poet, but The Great Italian Poet, the father of the Italian language, and the beginning of Italian modernity—as well as the subject of numerous birthday celebrations, architectural plans, and deluxe editions.[54] Thus, by association with Dante, Cavalcanti can be central to the Tuscan cultural milieu that would generate the Italian Renaissance—a period in Italian history that had accumulated great significance. "Cavalcanti's glory needs no further support," Pound asserts in Italian. "There has always been a tradition among those who claim to know, that 'outshined by Dante, he has become like a moon to the sun.'"[55] But Pound then turns this relationship around, emphasizing Cavalcanti's poetic influence on Dante and his philosophical innovations.[56] He suggests that, philosophically, Cavalcanti was far "more 'modern' than his young friend Dante Alighieri, *qui était diablement dans les idées reçues*, and whose shock is probably recorded in the passage of Inferno X where he finds Cavalcanti's father and father-in-law paying for their mental exertions."[57]

Much of Pound's introductory material roots Cavalcanti in his philosophical context, showing what he could have read, to demonstrate the value of his thought and art. He says Cavalcanti made a great contribution to the psychology of emotions, exhibiting in his poems "keen ... understanding" and "precise ... explanation":

> we have in him no rhetoric, but always a true delineation, whether it be of pain itself, or of the apathy that comes when the emotions and possibilities of emotion are exhausted, or of that stranger state when the feeling by its intensity surpasses our powers of bearing and we seem to stand aside and watch it surging across some thing or being with whom we are no longer identified.[58]

Although Pound includes biographical details about Cavalcanti, he does not offer them up until the reprinting of "Sonnets and Ballate: Introduction to Edition of 1912," the last section of the book. He summarizes the events of Cavalcanti's life—his birth, betrothal, political work, and death—emphasizing his involvement in the factional struggles of Florence during the late thirteenth century and his relationship with Dante, in matters of politics and poetry.[59] All this information and valuation, then, combines to situate Cavalcanti as crucial to the moment leading to the Italian Renaissance, a moment also associated with Dante.

Although Pound relates Cavalcanti's value to Dante's, he systematically distinguishes Cavalcanti from Petrarch's flaws. "The difference between Guido and Petrarch," he says in his English essay "Mediaevalism," "is not a mere difference in degree, it is a difference in kind."[60] He explains that difference in terms of the forcefulness of Cavalcanti's language:

> In Guido the "figure," the strong metaphoric or "picturesque" expression is there with purpose to convey or to interpret a definite meaning. In Petrarch it is ornament, the prettiest ornament he could find, but not an irreplaceable ornament, or one that he couldn't have used just about as well somewhere else.[61]

This distinction between Petrarch and Dante/Cavalcanti plays on Pound's larger preference for poetry without unnecessary verbiage or ornament. And, in distinguishing Cavalcanti thus from Petrarch, he agrees with the Florentine avant-garde of the 1900s in preferring Dante over Petrarch. As Walter Adamson has shown, this group favored "the 'plebeian,' 'realist,' and 'masculine' tradition of Dante" in opposition to "the 'elegant,' 'empty,' and 'feminine' tradition of Petrarch," which they had come to associate with decadence and D'Annunzianism.[62] That Pound saw strength and purpose in Cavalcanti's figurative language, compared with the empty elegance of Petrarch, positions Cavalcanti firmly in Dante's camp, with extra clout based on the very categories employed by the cultural figures active in defining Italy's cultural identity.

Dante was but one piece of a larger emphasis on *Toscanità*, discussed previously. For Pound, *Toscanità* was the most appealing of the regionalisms prevalent during the period. He already had tremendous interest in the activities of particular Tuscan poets—having written about Dante and Cavalcanti in *The Spirit of Romance* (1910), and having tried there to identify the importance of the language used by Tuscan poets. His conclusions at the time, however, were not overly sympathetic to the Tuscan troubadours—hardly surprising given his profound admiration of such Provençal poets as Arnaut Daniel and Bernart of Ventadorn. There the Italian poets Guido Guinicelli, Cino da Pistoija, and Guido Cavalcanti are clustered together as the "Tuscan bookworms," and he notes that "the Tuscan poets gambol through the complicated Aquinean universe with an inconsequent preciseness which bewilders one accustomed to nothing more complex than modern civilization."[63] In 1910, he called Cavalcanti a "spirit more imperious and less subtle than Dante." By 1929, however, he had retracted the expression, seeing Cavalcanti in a more favorable light.[64] By this point, then, Cavalcanti was central to his celebration of a medieval Tuscan aesthetic.

Defining this medieval "Tuscan aesthetic" was as important to Pound as to Italian critics of the early twentieth century, but while they focused on painting, he sought an aesthetic pertinent to poetry. In "Medievalism," Pound emphasizes the uniqueness of the Tuscan poets: their qualities do not appear in Greek, Roman, or Troubadour poetry—nor has he seen them in modern poetry. He distinguishes medieval Tuscan art from ancient Greek art, whose aesthetic he sees existing "wholly in plastic." By contrast, "The Tuscan demands harmony in something more than the plastic."[65] Pound's poetic aesthetic insists there is something in the art that supersedes tangibility, and he thereby shifts the terms of prevailing discussions of the early Renaissance.[66] Instead of plasticity, he concludes that the crucial element is "an interactive force: the *virtù* in short."[67] This ethical quality which, Dasenbrock has shown, Pound learned from Machiavelli and would also apply to Mussolini, "means activity and innovation," the ability to "avoid depending upon any set of preconceptions and face the newness of any situation newly."[68] Pound was not alone in looking to Machiavelli as a source of inspiration for modern Italy. In 1870, literary critic Francesco De Sanctis imagined a new age grounded in Machiavelli's ideals—in which action and ideals could be driven by liberty, equality, fatherland, state, and nation.[69] And, of course, thanks in part to Sarfatti's guidance, Mussolini himself was a fan of Machiavelli, often seeing him as a guide to his own political maneuvers.[70] Throughout the Fascist period, the Florentine philosopher was often named—along with the likes of Michelangelo, Dante, Petrarch, and Galileo—among glorious Italians worthy of revival and emulation in the modern era.

Like the Florentine artists, who saw something vital in the Tuscan landscape, Pound argues that the Tuscan aesthetic and ethics rely on a climate distinct from that of northern Europe:

> The senses at first seem to project for a few yards beyond the body. Effect of a decent climate where a man leaves his nerve-set open, or allows it to tune in to its ambience, rather than struggling, as a northern race has to for self-preservation to guard the body from the assaults of weather.
>
> He [the artist] declines, after a time, to limit reception to his solar plexus. The whole thing has nothing to do with taboos and bigotries. It is more than the simple athleticism of the *mens sana in corpore sano*. The conception of the body as perfected instrument of the increasing intelligence pervades. The lack of this concept, invalidates the whole of monastic thought. Dogmatic asceticism is obviously not essential to the perceptions of Guido's *ballate*.[71]

His sense that living in Tuscany allows a particular relationship with the world—the ability to shift one's approach based on the needs of any given situation—leads to the sense that Tuscan art is spatially rooted, that Tuscan identity is about living in Tuscany and breathing *Toscanità* (whether climatic, geologic, literary, or sculptural) one's whole life. The relationship between artwork and idea, then, is about the body as a highly tuned instrument, capable of sensitive readings. Such a conception intertwines the physical and mental, suggesting that denying either dulls the instrument.

Pound was hardly the only writer during this period making claims about the relationship between artist and environment. Margherita Sarfatti, in *Segni, colori e luci* (1925), made a similar point, but rather than distinguishing Italian from non-Italian, she used it to distinguish among the artistic productions of different regions:

> And climate, the appearance of the country in which he lives, has an influence on the artist. Leonardo himself, naturalist and scientist, enamored of the true and beautiful, pursued the line of contour consecrated by Tuscan tradition. He lived, looked, and worked in the dry air of Tuscany, where the transparent lucidity belongs to the Tuscan atmosphere as it does to the Attic hills. The thick mists of Lombardy, the atmosphere morbid and wrapping up the Po Valley with its own affectionate lights, gradually persuading it to replace the sign with the stroke. Instead of the precise line, little by little, he chooses volume and a degrading shadow. After him come the northern painters of the plains, lakes, and lagoons, Correggio and Luini, the Lombards and the Venetians, masters of the symphonic tonality of color and light; and the Bolognese who model the fury of shadow in a full range of colors.[72]

Sarfatti argues here that each of these artists or schools paints light based on the way it appears in their particular regions, and that the dramatic climatic differences even among Tuscany, Lombardy, Emilia-Romagna, and the Veneto account at least in part for the great stylistic differences among these schools. Such an assertion aims to account for the variety in artistic styles of Italian painters during the Renaissance, and upholds those regional differences even now that "Italy" exists as a nation. Just as the Po and the clear light of Tuscany persist, so do regional differences among Italians. The new Italy had to recognize these differences—and incorporate them—to succeed as a nation.

For Pound to make a similar assertion, however, he must translate pictorial to verbal representation. For Pound, art—be it literary or visual—is not merely about replicating what is seen, but rather about communicating an experience. The work of art must contain something of the original experience. One way for Pound to translate pictorial to verbal might have been to suggest that dialectal differences sent literary production in different regions in different directions. Instead, he insists that weather makes the difference—weather in which a person can stand not to shiver. He thus implies an even stronger connection between bodily experience and mental processes, because a pen writing words, unlike a paintbrush creating a scene, cannot hope to trick the eye.

As Pound continues to build his argument, he engages with other extant theories about the Renaissance and its art. He says that *quattrocento* sculpture contains something beyond physical form, and compares it with Egyptian sculpture: "The best Egyptian sculpture is magnificent plastic; but its force comes from a non-plastic idea, i.e. the god is inside the statue."[73] This comparison echoes wider attempts to understand the relationship between Italian Renaissance painting and ancient works. In his writing about Paolo Uccello, Carlo Carrà established the importance of Uccello's innovations by tracing a lineage back through earlier masters of the Renaissance all the way to Egypt:

> The rule of succession of the spiritual form became more and more uncertain in the irregularities of styles exhumed beyond Egypt; and the contribution of Masaccio, like that of Giotto before him, had become drained of its substance. Cunning charm prepared the fields and the seed to create the pleasant ambiguity characteristic of the *cinquecento*.[74]

Carrà is likely referring to recent excavations of Egyptian and Assyrian monuments, which were highly publicized and influential for many artists, including Mario Sironi.[75] That Pound, like Carrà and Sironi, could see something relevant to an understanding of the Italian Renaissance in recently recovered ancient works from an entirely different place suggests his awareness of ongoing conversations about Renaissance art. He adds later, "This sculpture with something inside, revives in the quattrocento portrait bust. But the antecedents are in verbal manifestation."[76]

He thereby creates continuity not only between the visual arts and poetry of medieval Tuscany, but also within the contemporary discourse of the Nationalist importance of the visual arts of the early Renaissance.

Pound's insistence that this Tuscan aesthetic involves something beyond the plastic is crucial to his championing of poetry. While the notion of tactile values may explain why these early Renaissance paintings look different from their predecessors, it cannot make sense in the context of literary arts. Nevertheless, for Pound, who wanted to draw attention to Cavalcanti, the connection to early Renaissance arts of Italy, those works in high vogue, is crucial. He insists that revolutions in the verbal arts always precede those in the visual arts. "Nobody can absorb the *poeti dei primi secoli* and then the paintings of the Uffizi without seeing the relation between them, Daniel, Ventadorn, Guido, Sellaio, Botticelli, Ambrogio Praedis, Cosimo Tura."[77] Margherita Sarfatti also saw the importance of poets to the larger Nationalist project. In 1928, she wrote, "An ideal (yet very real) unity in the spirit, in the words, and in the genius of Italy's poets existed long before Italian unity was achieved in life and in history."[78] But Pound's comment explicitly links the verbal to the visual arts.

This emphasis on the visual arts of the Renaissance marks a shift in Pound's thinking of that period. As Reed Way Dasenbrock has noted regarding Pound's writings from the 1910s about the Italian Renaissance, "Pound's Renaissance is not the Renaissance of Botticelli, Fra Filippo Lippi, and Andrea del Sarto, but the Renaissance of Italian humanism."[79] By the 1920s and 1930s, however, his view of that period of Italy's glorious history has shifted to include valorization of the artists central to contemporary Italian thinking. And in his return to the troubadour poets, Pound demonstrates the relevance of his own work even further: not only is his *Guido Cavalcanti Rime* important to the Nationalist cultural work of the regime, but such critical works as *The Spirit of Romance* and poetic books like *Exultations* (1909) matter too. He reimagines himself as having always been a cultural agent of the Italian state.

By 1932, regional identities in Italy were coming together to forge a common Italian identity. The Fascist regime employed artists and intellectuals in the work of revitalizing national culture, incorporating some of the avant-garde projects of cultural rebirth of the previous decades. In so doing, artists and intellectuals were transformed from outliers to state agents. An art critic like Margherita Sarfatti could have tremendous influence in this new regime, and her vision of regionally differentiated artistic production coming together under the umbrella of the Fascist state was tremendously influential. As a part of this project, the work done to construct such regional identities as *Toscanità* was redirected to the definition and celebration of *Italianità*.

In Pound's Italian preface to *Guido Cavalcanti Rime*, he uses a discussion of orthography to acknowledge the work that has still to happen for the pieces of Italy to come together:

> From the plates, one discovers that orthography is a question of taste rather than of historical truth. Suppose that Guido wrote in the Florentine dialect of his epoch, etc. For a bilingual edition, an oldish orthography would have been of little use, as it would distract the attention of the reader from the poetry itself, returning it to the particularities of spelling. Here and there I gave the spelling of an old manuscript, and from it one can judge how much it serves the modern Italian public. Printed orthography always conformed to a certain norm, while in manuscripts of differing provenance are found different archaisms that were known to Guido or sometimes unknown or unusual. They serve better to display the origin of the manuscript than to understand the poetry.[80]

Pound appreciates the particularities of Cavalcanti's language—and how that language was transformed by manuscript copyists—but he is ultimately more interested in a modern Italian appreciation of Cavalcanti's *poetry*. He shares with the Florentine avant-garde writers a disdain for pedantry and philology.[81] And although a celebration of *Toscanità* might benefit from attention to the intricacies of the medieval Florentine dialect, he wants now to reach a wider Italian audience, and a modern-day Sicilian or Neapolitan would have enough trouble with modern, let alone old, Tuscan.

As we have seen, then, part of the Italian national cultural project of the 1920s and 1930s was defining a sense of *Italianità*, and Pound contributes with his presentation of Cavalcanti. His edition, while of interest to scholars, imagined itself making Cavalcanti accessible to a variety of audiences: it gives printed, modernized versions of the poems, and its plates allow a curious reader to look at where the poems as texts come from. English translations of the poems make Italian cultural heritage accessible outside Italy, and the ancillary essays illuminate the poetry's contexts. Moreover, in case the material he presents are not sufficient, Pound offers lists and tables showing a curious and mobile reader how to find the texts in libraries all over Italy. As Cavalcanti's manuscripts appear in libraries throughout the nation, so should his poems have wide appeal. Pound says on his title page that his edition is "rapprezzata tra le rovine," or "patched from the ruins": this patching action represents a textual equivalent of the "polishing off the rust" that Sarfatti advocates for modern Italian painters.

What this book became, then, was one of Pound's earliest contributions to the Fascist cultural projects in Italy. It barely preceded the celebration of the Fascist Decennio, marked by the Mostra della Rivoluzione Fascista, or the Exhibition of the Fascist Revolution, spectacular celebrations throughout Italy, groups of postage stamps, and special postmarks. Like the painters of the Novecento movement who looked back to Italy's *quattrocento* artists for inspiration, and intellectuals and government officials who saw Dante as the father of Italian vernacular literature and a great supporter of

Empire, Pound celebrated Cavalcanti's role in the history of letters. While Pound's interest in Renaissance Italian humanism was not new, in moving the publication of *Guido Cavalcanti Rime* from London to Genoa, Pound blended his cultural enterprise with Italy's, putting his scholarship into the cultural Nationalist mix.

When Pound later seeks to define the future of the Italian regime in his draft of an unpublished essay, "Italy: The Second Decennio," written in 1935 or 1936, he returns to ideas he had laid out in describing this Tuscan aesthetic. There he asserts that the reason for the success of the Fascist government during its first ten years was "Mussolini's objection to the inhumanity of mechanization, to his distaste for an incomplete man or an incomplete philosophy, the general sparse and shaggy state of American civilization."[82] Pound, like so many Fascist Italian artists and thinkers of the period, roots Mussolini's insistence on a complete person in medieval Tuscany. In his opening of the Centro di Studi sul Rinascimento in Florence in 1937, Giovanni Papini similarly saw a connection between the Renaissance and Fascism, highlighting especially the "equilibrium between body and spirit, the harmony between physical and intellectual education, youthful leadership, the celebration of adventurous and heroic lives, the concordance between patriotic love and respect for the church, and the renewal of the idea of Rome as the active force behind the conception of the doctrine of the state."[83] As Tuscan art insisted on a union of mind and body that could make a person a "perfected instrument," so Mussolini insists that Italian citizens be complete beings. Pound continues, "Fascism refused to debase Italian values, it refused to limit all merit to profit motive. It demanded mens sana in corpore sano and the muscular activity recently shown in East Africa is in no way superior to the Italian mental athletics anno XIV of THIS ERA."[84] This return to the same trope of sound mind in sound body to address this completeness, shows how his scholarly work on Cavalcanti shaped his later political thinking about Mussolini.

Once Pound entered the Italian debates about cultural Nationalism in the early 1930s, he remained convinced by the regime's objectives and was drawn deeper into its rhetoric. As a public intellectual he wanted to shape the regime's direction, whether through the curricula for the study of Italian literature that he sent to Mussolini or through his numerous contributions to Italian, English, and American periodicals about cultural events in Italy. As an American, he lacked the *personal* national identity that would open opportunities for determining Italian cultural identity, but as a writer publishing in Italy and devoted to reviving an important but neglected writer from Italy's glorious past—and publishing in Italy—he made opportunities to speak, creating a sense of literary citizenship that would become particularly complex during the Second World War. All through the Fascist period, as more and more cultural Nationalist projects were unfolding in Italy, Pound admired intellectuals' and artists' involvement in the regime's activities. As we shall see in the next chapter, these activities increasingly became subject matter for his prose and began to shape his literary style.

CHAPTER 3

The Bundle and the Pickax: Fascist Cultural Projects

And the disappearing medieval squalor! I will use the word "rubbish" [*spazzatura*] precisely. The rubbish of fifteen centuries neglected the Roman glory—try to find the sonnets of Joachim du Bellay, adapted by the Latinists of the Renaissance, translated into English by Spenser, etc. From last April, when I was in Rome, to December, Mussolini has done more toward clearing out this glory than had all the popes from the seventh to the nineteenth centuries.

—Ezra Pound[1]

Once Ezra Pound discovered the cultural Nationalist projects of Mussolini's regime, they became crucial to his work. The more he looked, the more he found worthy of his attention. All around him, the regime was finding ways to use Italy's cultural heritage to construct a Fascist modernity. Whether we think of the vast archaeological excavations that revealed more of Rome's ancient history, adaptation of ancient icons to modern purposes, or the modern building projects that borrowed from the architectural elements discovered during these excavations, Italy's past was becoming a more prominent inspiration for its future.

Pound's own investment in cultural heritage was similarly forward-looking, as he sought ways of using the past to create a rich and flexible future. This chapter demonstrates that the Fascist investment in a similar—and similarly modernist—goal helped to inspire Pound's own thinking and making of art.

Such critical works as Tim Redman's *Ezra Pound and Italian Fascism*, Peter Nicholls's *Ezra Pound, Politics, Economics and Writing*, Alec Marsh's *Money and Modernity: Pound, Williams, and the Spirit of Jefferson*, and Leon Surette's *Pound in Purgatory: From Economic Radicalism to Anti-Semitism* have revealed a number of the important ideological shifts that allowed Pound to become so invested in Mussolini and Fascism. Because these works' treatment of Pound's increasing economic, political, and racial thinking during the 1930s is so rich and well handled, they may inadvertently give readers the mistaken sense that Pound abandoned cultural interests altogether during this period. Certainly, the mass of his economic writings is sizable, but in the mix of these writings shines a continuing—and perhaps strengthening—interest in the role of culture as a means of fomenting national identity and bolstering political regimes.

This chapter explores an array of Fascist cultural Nationalist projects and icons—including the *fascio littorio*, the cult of Mussolini, the employment of modernist art in state-sponsored exhibitions, the cultivation of tropes of *Romanità*, or "Romanness," and the vast archaeological excavations in Rome and complementary building projects. Pound's responses to these projects appear throughout his work of this period. I focus especially on *The ABC of Reading* (1934) and *Jefferson and/or Mussolini* (1935), and on periodical contributions published in both English and Italian. This range of works shows the pervasiveness of Pound's interest in Italian Fascist cultural projects. Pound's responses to these projects and icons show how his thinking about the role of the arts and culture changed during this period—and his responses to these projects shape his shifting modernism.

The *Fascio Littorio* and Cultural Unification

Pound appreciated the way that Mussolini's Fascism brought together an array of cultural elements to build a greater whole. The regime consistently sought the involvement of artists, intellectuals, writers, and architects to help shape Italy's Fascist mission. As a result, the political and cultural project that became "Fascism" drew on a variety of prewar ideas about rejuvenating Italy culturally—including those from the Milanese Futurists and the Florentine group around the journal *La Voce* (1908-1914). Walter Adamson notes that *La Voce* focused on the "cultural implications of Italian political issues... and looked literally everywhere for the political meanings of art, literature, music, journalism, and other cultural practices." He describes its offspring *Lacerba* as "a much more narrowly literary journal aimed at an experimentalist rapprochement with Milanese futurism."[2] That Fascism was able to interest both the *Vociani* and the Futurists was important to its potential to unify the Italian nation. Art critic and early member of the Fascist Party Margherita Sarfatti emphasized this in 1928 in her essay "Art and Fascism":

> The renovation of Italian culture initiated by Gabriele d'Annunzio was completed by two conflicting forces and temperaments: on the one side, by Futurism; on the other, by Benedetto Croce and by the cultural movement that gave rise to the reviews *La Voce* and *Lacerba*. Within the spheres of the spirit and culture, both contributed (though in contradictory ways) to creating the great Italy of today: an independent Italy, able to stake out firm positions, planted right at the center of international life. Tomorrow, after the war and thanks to Fascism, she will be greater still.
>
> However unlike one another, *La Voce* and Futurism were working so single-mindedly toward a common goal that a moment of convergence and collaboration was inevitable.[3]

But the Futurists and the *Vociani* could not agree on the means of achieving a Fascist culture, or even each other's right to participate in such a thing. Writing in Giuseppe Bottai's journal *Critica Fascista*, F. T. Marinetti claimed in early 1927:

> The *Vociani*, almost all of whom are offspring or followers of Croce, have no right to speak on the question of fascist art. Like their mentor, they were ruthless deprecators of the creative genius of our race. They howled relentlessly against us futurists when, before anyone else, we imposed Italian literary artistic political pride in theaters and in the streets, taking on mockery and derision and debating with fists and blows.[4]

Unsurprisingly, Ardengo Soffici, co-founder of *La Voce*, noted that "this futurist tendency has been followed and glorified, logically enough, by Russian Bolshevism," which "fact alone suggests that this cannot be the optimum manner to achieve the general goals of fascism."[5] Despite such differences, artists from an array of persuasions participated in these discussions of how a Fascist art might look.[6]

The realm of political and social thought had similarly conflicting groups. Italy's strong Socialist Party focused on problems facing the nation's growing working class, and in the more agricultural southern regions, the Sicilian *Fasci* (not directly related to the Fascist Party formed later in Milan) took on the plight of farm workers.[7] As in the arts, many thinkers looked to ideas developing elsewhere in Europe. Italian Syndicalists, following a model from France, modified Socialism with an emphasis on strong trade unions as a means of developing workers morally and psychologically, and as a place of organization and identification.[8] Italian Nationalists, on the other hand, wanted a strong conservative political system to bolster national identity and strengthen the nation after centuries of foreign domination.[9] While these various

The Bundle and the Pickax 87

3. Antonio Floridi posing with a *fascio littorio* made from ears of wheat. Farm owned by Camillo Frizzoni, in Morengo in the province of Bergamo; on the *fascio*, a photograph of the Duce, 1926. (Alinari Archive, Florence)

groups did not always agree about the means, they all wanted to build a stronger Italian nation, and the Fascist Party found ways to use their talents.

Members of Mussolini's Fascist Party came from an array of backgrounds. He could hardly embrace all the tenets of Futurism, for instance, for fear of alienating members of the Florentine *La Voce* group. And while Fascism certainly took on a Nationalist bent, many party members still had strong loyalty to their own origins—to particular regions, or to cities, or the countryside. The Fascist Party was heterogeneous from the start, including anarchists, republicans, Catholics, and *Arditi*.[10] Some factions were interested in international modernism, while others explicitly rejected it, wanting a modern Italy free of foreign contamination. Some "Fascists of the first hour" were deeply anti-Semitic, others were Jews. The easiest way for the party, and later the regime, to achieve wide participation was to allow diversity of background and belief, and therefore not determine a narrow political program for the party.

The *fascio littorio* proved an eminently useful symbol for this new party (Fig. 3). As Simonetta Falasca-Zamponi has summarized, the *fascio* derived from the ancient Roman *fascis*, carried by *lictores*, or minor Roman officials. This symbol of authority is composed of "a bundle of equal rods tied together and to an ax." Used since the early 1890s in the names of workers' organizations and interventionist groups, it was co-opted by Mussolini in 1919 in his founding of Fasci Italiani di Combattimento and maintained in 1921 in the name of the Partito Fascista Italiano.[11] Although Mussolini was not the first to use this iconographic symbol, the *fascio* became the emblem of the new Italian state in 1926. Its representation of unity, force, justice, and discipline provided a model for Italian citizenship.[12] Important twigs in this bundle were the intellectuals and artists explicitly working for the regime, often as administrators. They modeled the behavior befitting a Fascist intellectual, and as such played a crucial role in bolstering the regime's cultural richness. In the *British Union Quarterly* in March 1937, Pound wrote:

> There are not six men in England who have the faintest shadow of an adumbration of an approach to an idea of the terminology now current in Italy in discussion of the different elements that were bound together in the FASCIO, or bundle, in and before 1922, Nineteen twenty two. A great and superstitious horde attacks a vague residue of tendencies inherent in the velleity of the early Italian *nazionalisti* and which, if untempered and uncombined in the "bundle," would have died dead in reaction. There are not 40 men in England who have taken thoughtful note of the decoration which hung over the stairs in the Decennio exposition five years ago: Blue, Black and Red mingled together.[13]

Reflecting on the history that he would learn in the Mostra della Rivoluzione Fascista, discussed in more depth below, Pound emphasizes his own understanding of the pre-Fascist Italian Nationalisms and modernisms that were absorbed into Mussolini's vision for the Fascist state.

Pound recognized that the problems of accessing the cultural heritage in Italy were even greater than he had found in Anglo-American society. He commented in a chapter of *Jefferson and/or Mussolini* devoted to "Intelligentsias" that "on the whole the gap between the old civilization, the specialized cultural heritage of the educated Italian and the uncultured Italian is probably greater than exists anywhere else or at least, one finds it in sharper contrast" (*J/M*, 25). He understood that all Italians had a strong and long-lived sense of culture—in the broadest sense, encompassing not just high culture but also the "habits of civilization" he had identified following C. H. Douglas and Leo Frobenius. "In one sense," he wrote, as we have seen, "they've all got some sort of culture, milleniar, forgotten, stuck anywhere from the time of Odysseus to the time of St. Dominic, to the time of Mazzini" (*J/M*, 25). The difficulty, though, is that what that culture is, precisely, varies so much, and in such small spaces. "In twenty minutes I can walk into a community with a different language, the uphills speaking something nearer Tuscan and the downhills talking Genovesh. I have heard an excited Milanese cursing the Neapolitan for an African" (*J/M*, 25). Like Mussolini, and others before him, Pound recognized that this difference made it nearly impossible to unify Italy with one culture or even language. The various cultures and "conservatisms" in Italy, Pound says, are "All of 'em carved in stone, carpentered and varnished into shape, built in stucco, or organic in the mind of the people" (*J/M*, 32).

Problems of communication and identity aside, Pound acknowledges that this difference matters more than an outside observer might expect, because "under it lies the fact that truth in Milan is anything but truth down in Foggia" (*J/M*, 26). This awareness of Italy's fragmented culture convinces Pound that it is not possible—or even desirable—to take one piece and impose it on the whole. He enumerates details of marvelous conversations he had about the economics of modernity and the "respective merits of Horace and Catullus," calling them "Subject matter for two dozen Italian Prousts, who don't exist because each segment of the country is different" (*J/M*, 30). To aim for national sameness would take from Italy what was distinctly Italian—its variety. Mussolini knows this, Pound argues: in discussing the Duce's oratorical style, he emphasizes that it "differs from town to town" and "The speech at Forlì was at Forlì and not at Torino" (*J/M*, 65). Pound's awareness of the diversity and complexities of the Italian situation was one of the reasons that he believed that Fascism and Mussolini—who shared that awareness—had the ability to do something revolutionary in Italy.

This idea of combining disparate elements into a bundle, in order to make each them stronger by association with the others, appealed to Pound not just politically, but aesthetically. In poetry, the *fascio* resembles Pound's ideogrammic method, described in *Guide to Kulchur* (1938) as "presenting one facet and then another until at some point one gets off the dead and desensitized surface of the reader's mind, onto a part that will register" (*GK*, 50). This bundling also drives Pound's "totalitarian" sense of culture, and his explanation of how different aspects of a culture impact one another. The ability to recognize connections among an array of fragments or strands—an ability he identifies with Mussolini, but also with himself—is a particularly modernist ability, in that it sees a way to forge a new, forward-looking way of life from old parts that had been shattered by the forces of modernity. It is Fascism's modernism that appeals to Pound, and Pound was hardly the only person to transfer this sense of Fascism as a movement onto Mussolini the man.

Mussolinismo

Like many other Fascists, Pound bought into the myth of Mussolini—sometimes also called "the myth of the Duce" or *Mussolinismo*—which historian Emilio Gentile has shown to be one of the most popular myths of the interwar epoch. For many Italians, Mussolini had an almost mythic quality, and he was approached with admiration, enthusiasm, loyalty, and manifestations of genuine devotion and fanatical dedication.[14] Prominent cultural critics of the regime considered the Duce the ultimate embodiment of a Fascist art—such that painters and sculptors needed to emulate the masterpiece he represented.[15] Pound's descriptions of the Duce, in both his poetry or prose, share these characteristics.

Gentile notes that such a myth of a leader is typical of modern mass movements, and that even in Italy this mythic image did not originate with Fascism. He identifies tropes of "great men" or powerful leaders in the writings of Nietzsche (the idea of the "superman"), Thomas Carlyle (who wrote of "great men" and a "cult of heroes"), Jacob Burckhardt (who emphasized the leadership of "great men" in history, and especially during the Italian Renaissance, which he called "the age of despots), Gustav Le Bon (whose theories of the working of crowds allowed for domination by powerful leaders), Max Weber (whose sense of the phenomenon of leadership emphasizes the power of charismatic persons). In periods of civil crisis, there is room for a "genius" or "superman" figure to rise to power. Socialism imagines such a charismatic leader figure as a means of bringing about revolution, and Mussolini's role within the Italian Socialist Party certainly allowed for some of these associations to gather around him.[16] Even before the March on Rome, such intellectual and cultural Nationalists as Giuseppe Prezzolini (writing in *La Voce* in Florence), Gaetano Salvemini (contributor to *Unità* of Milan), and painter Carlo Carrà supported Mussolini, highlighting his courage and passion, and calling him the leader for a new generation. Fascist mythology imagined Mussolini as a "new man" and a "national renewer," and added the idea of the Duce as a "savior of the fatherland" and "great artist [*artifice*] of its glory and future greatness." More ordinary Italians, Fascists or not, were fascinated by this new leader who was young, energetic, dynamic, possessed of Napoleonic or Caesarian traits, and who spoke in a simple oratorical style.[17] Mussolini's appeal a range of Italians made him powerful: Fascism frequently faded behind his impressive personality. As one parliamentary deputy put it,

> In order to understand something of Fascism, one must consider the *personality* of its founder and its leader: Benito Mussolini. ... The leaders of Fascism who surround him express the most bourgeois mediocrity and nothing more. ... Mussolini emerges above them in a conspicuous, absolute way, not as much for his intellectual vigor, his cultural, technical and concrete preparation, as for the 'insolence' of his personality. ... what counts is his personality ... the only theory that fascism has is one person: Benito Mussolini.[18]

This emphasis on "personality" transformed Mussolini from man into myth. He was rumored never to sleep, and the light in his office was left on at all hours to support this legend. He frequently posed for photographs that suggested youthful vigor and superhuman power—whether expressed by his ability to tame beasts, his love of flying airplanes, or his willingness to ski shirtless.[19] His birthday was not celebrated (lest people remember he was aging), any illnesses were concealed, he was supposed to be impervious to accidents and assassination attempts, and he was imagined to be capable of being in several places at once.[20] His speeches became spectacular performances and he was frequently compared to such illustrious historical figures as Socrates, Julius Caesar, Washington, Napoleon, and Lincoln.[21] Embodying Fascism in this one man allowed necessary simplifications that could widen the movement's appeal.

Pound's vision of Mussolini shares these mythic qualities but emphasizes certain traits. Like many Italians, he saw Mussolini and the Fascist state as interchangeable, and frequently preferred to think of "il Capo" over the state itself. This kind of back and forth is frequently found on the grammatical level in Pound's prose. Here is a typical formulation:

> But note that *Mussolini* is NOT a fanatical statalist wanting the state to blow the citizen's nose and monkey with the individual's diet. IF, when and whenever the individual or the industry can and will attend to its business, *the fascist state* WANTS the industry and the individual to DO it … (*J/M*, 69; emphasis added)

Pound emphasized that Fascism could not exist without Mussolini: "This is not to say I 'advocate' fascism in and for America, or that I think fascism is possible in America without Mussolini, anymore than I or any enlightened Bolshevik thinks communism is possible in America without Lenin" (*J/M*, 98). Mussolini *was* Fascism.

Mussolini's qualities made the Fascist state in Pound's view. Mussolini's intelligence exists outside the universities—indeed Pound says that "If Mussolini had committed the error of getting into an Italian university there would have been no Fascist decennial" (*J/M*, 59–60). Mussolini's practical and active intelligence solves problems that stymie others: "The Duce who never tries to put in a wedge butt end forward" (*J/M*, ix). Pound called Mussolini "the great debunker" because "The DUCE sits in Rome calling five hundred bluffs (or thereabouts) every morning" (*J/M*, 35). He associates this quality with Mussolini's career as an editor, "who will see through their bunkum and for whom they will go to the scrapbasket just as quickly as an incompetent reporter's copy will go to the basket in a live editorial office" (*J/M*, 74). It is no surprise that this quality should attract Pound, who rhetorically positioned himself as a debunker of British or American misconceptions about Fascism.[22]

For Pound, Mussolini's genius requires "the capacity to see ten things where the ordinary man sees one, and where the man of talent sees two or three, PLUS the ability to register that multiple perception in the material of his art."[23] A crucial part of that genius is his ability to "*get things* DONE" (*J/M*, 89)—a characteristic which requires an "essential dynamism," and which, Pound emphasizes, distinguishes the Duce from most intellectuals. For this reason, he can measure Mussolini by his achievements, not his ideas: "When Mussolini has expressed any satisfaction it has been with the definite act performed, the artwork in the civic sense, the leading the Romans back to the sea, for example, by the wide new road into Ostia" (*J/M*, 100).[24] Gentile's point that to succeed, a political myth must conform to collective desires and aspirations certainly pertains here:[25] Pound learned to admire aspects of the Duce, but to a great extent he was drawn to Mussolini because the leader possessed qualities that Pound already championed.

In Pound's view, Mussolini's power came not from a quest for power but from a "very different passion, the will toward *order*"

(*J/M*, 99). Pound emphasizes Mussolini's own choice of title—his refusal "to be called anything save 'Leader' (Duce) or 'Head of the Government'"—noting that "dictator" is not among them but rather a term "applied by foreign envy" and "not represent[ative of] the Duce's fundamental conception of his role" (*J/M*, 110). In *ABC of Economics*, Pound adds that "Mussolini as intelligent man is more interesting than Mussolini as the Big Stick."[26] Pound closes *Jefferson and/or Mussolini* by analogizing Mussolini as a "lover of ORDER" with *tò kalón*, or "the beautiful" (*J/M*, 128)—a term that reflects Pound's Neoplatonic conceptions of beauty as something that goes beyond the eye to call on the soul.[27] This love of the beautiful and of order separates Mussolini from the despots, or lovers of power. Emilio Gentile has shown that Mussolini was admired by many as a revolutionary and dictator who demonstrated the qualities of an administrator—realism and a sense of measure.[28] In this way, Pound's perceptions of the Duce were part of a larger, more orchestrated construction.

Mussolini's oratorical style contributed to the power of his personality. As Simonetta Falasca-Zamponi has noted, the fact that he traveled throughout Italy to make speeches distinguished him from previous leaders: many Italians had not seen any head of government before Mussolini.[29] Mussolini's style of oratory—informed by his work as a journalist—was crucial, too. His speech was direct, his word choice simple, syntax unadorned, and his eloquence came not from overblown expressions but from rhythm and tone.[30] Margherita Sarfatti compared Mussolini to the Nationalist poet Giosuè Carducci, claiming that he "writes with his nails when engaged in polemics," eliminating humor and employing "Irony and sarcasm without subtle undertones so as to better jump on the opponent, to smash him with insolence after the debate, and to bring the scoffers over to one's own side." This style, Sarfatti argued, brought him success as a journalist and an orator.[31] Her architectural metaphors solidify the notion of Mussolini as a builder or *artifice*. For Sarfatti, this style helped "to explain the powerful hold that Mussolini's personality has exercised over the Italian populace, especially over the youth who make up the new class of intellectuals."[32]

Pound loved Mussolini's rhetorical simplicity. The Duce's style became a good example in Pound's crusade to clarify language—a goal that united his poetry and his poetics. In *ABC of Reading* (1934), Pound stressed the connections between language, governance, and literature:

> Good writers are those who keep the language efficient. That is to say, keep it accurate, keep it clear. It doesn't matter whether the good writer wants to be useful, or whether the bad writer wants to do harm.
>
> Language is the main means of human communication. If an animal's nervous system does not transmit sensations and stimuli, the animal atrophies.
>
> If a nation's literature declines, the nation atrophies and decays.
>
> Your legislator can't legislate for the public good, your commander can't command, your populace (if you be a democratic country) can't instruct its "representatives," save by language. (*ABCR*, 32)

Pound's emphasis on efficient, accurate, and clear language echoes that of Sarfatti, with whom he corresponded and whose biography of Mussolini he studied. In a non-democratic country, the language of the leader is even more important. In *Jefferson and/or Mussolini* he notes, "Mussolini as an ex-editor uses oratory, and by comparison with Italian habits of speech ('these damned Eyetalyan intellexshuls that think they are still contemporaries of Metastasio'), that oratory is worth study" (*J/M*, 65).

Mussolini's straightforward, simple style—which Pound associates with his ability to put ideas into action—opposes the overburdened approach to "culture" that Pound sees elsewhere in

Italy. He says that "culture in the serious sense"—associated with "the scholarly class" and "sensitive kindly professors" and "people still browsing on the hang-over of the Renaissance"—is a problem rather than a boon, because it slows the country down. The professors are "too cultured to make an affirmation." He continues: "They have never asked anyone else to change an opinion and had never expected to change one of their own," noting that "Scholarship has led them into a realm of uncertainty, or to a remote grove where contradictions are needless" (*J/M*, 59–60). Pound claims, "*Fascism is probably the first anti-snob movement that has occurred in this peninsula since the days of Cato the younger.*"[33] He calls Mussolini's directness, whether in his speaking style or general manner, "The secret of the Duce," and notes that it allows him "to pick out the element of immediate and major importance in any tangle."[34] This ability, Pound claims in his essay "Ave Roma" (1933), is what makes an "authentic genius."[35] Such rhetorical style is intimately linked to Mussolini's use of the *piccone*, as we shall see in the next section.

Within the party, Margherita Sarfatti was one of the most important builders of *Mussolinismo*. In the years from 1927 to 1934, she wrote articles for publication in the United States, but they were signed by the Duce.[36] Most importantly, however, she wrote a biography of Mussolini, published first in London as *The Life of Benito Mussolini* (1925) and then in Italy as *Dux* (1926). The book sold 200,000 copies in Italy, was printed in seventeen editions, and translated into eighteen languages.[37] Cannistraro and Sullivan read this biography as the starting point for *Mussolinismo*, which they call "the regime's most enduring and systematic propaganda campaign." No other Fascist leader—besides the Duce himself—is mentioned by name in the book, accentuating the impression that Mussolini *was* Fascism. Sarfatti used Macchiavelli's directions for princes to describe Mussolini's leadership, and argued that the entirety of Italian tradition filled Mussolini with joy and inspiration.[38]

Sarfatti quoted from Mussolini's *juvenilia* celebrating Nietzsche's ideas of the "superman" and the "will to power." The concept of the superman, as she said Mussolini was coming to understand it, "miraculously brings back to life the prince of the Renaissance," exemplified by Cesare Borgia and Sigismondo Malatesta.[39] Pound, of course, favored this latter analogy:

> Mussolini is the first head of a state in our time to perceive *quality* as a dimension in national production. He is the first man in power to publish any such recognition *since*, since whom?—since Sigismond Malatesta, since Cosimo, since what's-his-name, the Elector of Hanover or wherever it was, who was friendly with Leibnitz?[40]

Additionally, Cannistraro and Sullivan suggest that she was one of the early proponents of *Romanità*, which as we will see below was both central to the regime's self-image and highly responsible for the urbanistic and archaeological projects undertaken in Rome. In *Dux*, Sarfatti makes biographically significant connections between Mussolini and ancient Rome—young Mussolini relaxing, reading in Latin the "memories of Caesar, the wisdom of Tacitus, the poem of Aeneas"—and suggests that all these things "fascinated him as a sort of myth," such that "Rome was, for him, mother and lover."[41]

Sarfatti's biography helped shape Pound's understanding of Mussolini. Pound wrote to her in February 1934, "Despite your not keeping yr / promise to send it me, I read yr "Dux" and found it a much better book than you had led me to xpect."[42] Then on 9 October of that year, he wrote again, "I hope to send you my Cantos 3I/4I in a few days. I believe they were published yesterday in New York. If you have patience to read enough of them you will find a few familiar passages, for which my rascally thanks."[43] Indeed, in Canto 41, Pound borrowed at least two passages from *Dux*.[44] This Canto participates explicitly in a celebration of *Mussolinismo*, beginning with Mussolini's remark, oft quoted by Pound, about a volume of Cantos, "Ma qvesto è divertente," and emphasizes the draining of the swamps to make new towns, and numerous other stories about the Duce, taken from *Dux* and elsewhere.

Pound could not have chosen a more appropriate source for his mythologizing of Mussolini. As Cannistraro and Sullivan note, "When the writer Curzio Malaparte asked Margherita why she had fabricated an event related in *Dux*, she replied with perfect sincerity, 'To create the legend.'"[45] In his thinking about Mussolini, the regime, and its projects, Pound profoundly trusted the Fascist propaganda machine, so that he frequently offered the regime's own formulations and views as his own. And if Mussolini himself dominated Pound's thinking about Fascism as a political movement, the regime's cultural projects transformed his approach to his own literary work, and therefore his sense of modernism.

Modernism and Fascist style

Pound panted over the ways Mussolini's Fascist regime employed various forms of modernism in its architecture, propaganda art, exhibition design, and mural decorations. From the beginning, the Fascist regime presented itself as young, daring, innovative, and forward-looking, invested in *la rivoluzione continua*, or a continuous revolution. A modernist aesthetic perfectly emblematized these qualities, and the presence in the party of a number of avant-garde artists and thinkers only cemented the role that modernism would play, particularly during the first decade of the Fascist era. Furthermore, the Fascist regime sponsored numerous art prizes and offered arts patronage to employ modernist artists in building a Fascist infrastructure. For Pound, this Fascist practice embodied his vision of how state-sponsored arts patronage could make and sustain a rich artistic culture.

Pound's writings on Italian modernist art are not extensive. Indeed, we are left to piece together his thoughts from remarks about Marinetti here, or a comment about an exhibition there. What we do know, however, is that in the cultural conflicts of the 1930s between a more innovative and internationally engaged vision of modern art and a more Nationalistic vision focused on Italian tradition, he favored the former. He never relinquished his celebration of those artists, like Wyndham Lewis, Henri Gaudier-Brzeska, and Jacob Epstein, whom he had championed in his London days. In his writings about music and his organizing of concerts of modern music, Pound frequently pointed to the virtues of Stravinsky, Bartók, and Hindemith. He was no fan of the Venice Biennale, and its tendency to showcase academic Italian art, rather than modernist works.[46] And in the realm of architecture, Pound celebrated the designs and architectural writings of P. M. Bardi, who was interested in Rationalism, the Italian version of the International Style.

David Barnes has demonstrated the importance of Marinetti to Pound's interest in the Futurist architect Antonio Sant'Elia, who died during the First World War and became a kind of martyr during the Fascist period, his work garnering renewed interest.[47] Pound envisioned the building of a Casa Littoriale in Rapallo as a part of a program to make his town a center of culture, and he hoped it might follow a design by Sant'Elia. Rationalist P. M. Bardi was also partly responsible for Pound's interest in Sant'Elia. In his *Rapporto sull'Architettura* (1931), Bardi wrote, "Let us go back to the beginning of this creative enterprise: to Sant'Elia who, with characteristic Italian audacity, arrested the direction of an architecture headed for the cemetery."[48] In 1934, in an announcement of Bardi's *Belvedere della architettura Italian d'oggi*, Pound celebrated the significance of steel for the designs of the Futurists, and especially of Sant'Elia: only such a modern building material would allow such daring designs.[49] Bardi's volume, Pound argues, "demonstrates amply the progress of fascist civilization" and "the arrival of modern architecture in Italy," and he hopes that the dissemination of these designs will bring "the end of the nineteenth century, of a fluffed-up taste for the nineteenth century style."⁵⁰ In 1932, when the PNF had announced the competition for the Palazzo del Littorio on the now finished via dell'Impero, the Futurists had argued for a project selected from among Sant'Elia's designs, saying, "We futurists, faithful interpreters of the great art of Sant'Elia, propose to build the 'Casa del Fascio' and its connected buildings by realizing his prophetic architectural dream, choosing from among his most typical projects those which are more consonant with our aims."⁵¹

Perhaps these activities were still in Pound's mind in 1936, when he concocted a plan for Rapallo to become an "international center of culture." He hoped the city would offer resources for serious scholars and curious foreign travelers. Pound worried that tourists were unable to appreciate the "vibrant life of the new epoch":

> Tourists, after this trip to Rapallo (once it becomes an international center of culture) could travel in Italy better prepared to understand not just the delectable Italy of the *quattrocento*, but the new Italy, the Italy that travelers would not understand if they saw only the antiquities without seeing the Decennial Exhibition [Mostra della Rivoluzione Fascista] or who, seeing Rome for the first time, would have believed the city mourned by Joachim du Bellay to be that which is found today along the Lungotevere.
>
>   A Casa Littoria in Rapallo could perfectly contain at least a library accessible to dilettante foreigners or travelers, helping them to immediately understand the New Italy.⁵²

For Pound, the structure that would allow Rapallo to become such a center was the Casa Littoriale, or Casa del Fascio, the headquarters of the local Fascist Party and often a center of culture and government. For Pound as for other devotees of Fascist culture, it was crucial that these buildings often be new constructions and frequently modern in design—emblems of how new building could come from a creative deployment of the Italian cultural heritage.

Pound hoped that Rapallo would choose a design by Sant'Elia. In so doing (if one were suited to Rapallo's distinct geography, of course), the city could build a Fascist center of culture that would serve both as a monument to this great architect and a sign of Rapallo's investment in the modern epoch.[53] That Pound is thinking about the cultural implications of such a project—both its educational and monumental aims—demonstrates the extent to which he had taken the practices of cultural administration to heart, and wanted to contribute to this larger Fascist project. In his argument for making Rapallo a cultural center, he offers as a striking example his own "musical research" in the Tigullian Studies venture, the subject of Chapter 5.[54]

Pound consistently urged the Fascist regime to build its modern Italy upon modernist monuments. And he argued time and again that painting be made a part of architecture, rather than something "vendible" or "collectible"—something not integrated into the being of a building and therefore subject to the whims of the market. "A few bits of ornament applied by Pietro Lombardo in Santa Maria dei Miracoli (Venice) are worth far more than all the sculpture and 'sculptural creations' produced in Italy between 1600 and 1950" (*ABCR*, 151). A building whose very design incorporated decorative elements—such things as mosaic decoration, or fresco murals, or sculptural elements—represented the culmination of his vision for Fascist culture. Mural arts were especially popular during the Fascist period, as a means of incorporating architecture and paintings—making painting an integral part of a building.[55] "Mural painting is social painting par excellence," painter Mario Sironi wrote in the "Manifesto of Muralism" (1933). "It works upon the popular imagination more directly than any other form of painting, while directly inspiring the decorative arts."[56] Pound's sense of the importance of decorative arts in architecture aligned with that of the architects of the regime's iconography

Pound touted the Mostra della Rivoluzione Fascista (or "Exhibition of the Fascist Revolution") as a model for how history should be told. The exhibition, which opened in Rome's Palazzo delle Esposizioni on 29 October 1932, employed avant-garde artists to construct history as a collaboration of artifacts, artistic intervention, and visitor investment. It was the first of many exhibitions put on by Mussolini's regime employing avant-garde artists in the "communications service" of the regime, as Pound would later argue all writers and poets should work.[57] Displayed objects—newspaper clippings, letters, flags, and bloody shirts—were integrated into the monumental and dynamic structures devised for display. As Jeffrey Schnapp summarizes, "It narrated the history of Fascism from 1914 through 1922, not according to the conventional methods of museum display, but rather via a kaleidoscopic fusion of Rationalist architectural schemes, a Futurist-inspired aesthetic of collage and photomontage, and an emergent mythico-heroic architectural Classicism."[58] The show was wildly successful, drawing 3.8 million visitors over two years.[59] Pound visited in late December 1932, and called the show, in a letter to Olga Rudge, "rather impressive, if one have of <u>senso storico</u>."[60] By 1932, the Pound who would fresh-facedly narrate in letters the events of his day—who he had met and what they had to say, details about ideas or poems he was working through, places he had visited and what made them interesting—had changed into a Pound who preferred short hand, brief descriptions of events in a language of abbreviations and phonetic spellings, a language that his correspondents tended to mimic when writing to him. Brief though it is, this remark about the exhibition contains the germs of the more extensive commentary he would give the exhibition in print. Pound would continue thinking about this exhibition, emphasizing that he learned far more from it about the years 1921–24 in Italy than anywhere else.[61]

To keep the Fascist revolution vibrant, its designers chose temporary over permanent display. The catalogue clarifies the exhibition's difference from museums: "This Exhibition does not have the arid, neutral, alienating quality that museums usually do. Instead, it appeals to fantasy, excites the imagination, restores the spirit."[62] The Futurists' distrust of museums—the sense that they, like libraries, represented a tendency to entomb art—led Fascist cultural administrators to look for alternatives.[63] Furthermore, by employing prominent avant-garde artists, the regime solidified its commitment to revolution and change. Visitors were not to be passive observers but active participants in the experience of history—and thus party to the project of Fascist Italy.[64] Pound commented in 1933 that the history told there was one told by Italians themselves, *not* by foreigners—a crucial distinction, given the Nationalist emphasis of Fascist cultural production and historicism and the regime's desire to make the exhibition one that told the people's history, for Italians and foreigners.[65] The participatory exhibition appealed to Pound's pedagogical spirit, and his sense that by actively engaging readers he could make them better thinkers. As late as March 1937, when he was writing *Guide to Kulchur*, Pound would still be thinking about the Nationalist and Fascist iconography of the MRF.[66]

For the exhibition, the Palazzo's Beaux Arts visage (Fig. 4) was concealed behind a simple red and gray façade, its columns turned into a row of four *fasci*, all in a design by Rationalist and sometime Futurist Adalberto Libera and architect Mario De Renzi (Fig. 5).

Architectural historian Libero Andreotti describes the façade:

> The design was simple in the extreme: a red square block, symbolizing the blood of the martyrs, flanked by two lower wings in gray, with four giant fasci standing several meters from the wall and connected by a horizontal slab supporting the letters MOSTRA DELLA RIVOLUZIONE FASCISTA. Centered symmetrically on the arched opening, the scheme offered a modern reinterpretation of a triumphal arch, with the metal fasci substituting for a giant order of columns. In Rome, needless to say, the reference would have been directly to the nearby classical ruins, a main point of attraction for visitors to the capital. In this

way the façade expressed a major theme of the decennial celebrations, the link between Fascism and Italy's Roman heritage. Continuity was also reflected in the way the design combined a rough "Roman" treatment of the back wall, which according to the guidebook evoked the color and texture "typical of Roman housing," with the slick and "modern" expression of the pilaster-fasci and connecting slab.[67]

This façade exemplifies new design growing out of Rome's cultural heritage. We have already seen how important the *fascio* was to Pound, in his description of this façade quoted earlier. Although Pound is here writing mostly about the functioning of the Fascist state, the imagery of the "Decennio exposition"—Pound's almost phonetic translation of "esposizione" yields a word that combines the notions of revelation and explanation—has become interchangeable with the history it sought to represent.

In *Jefferson and/or Mussolini* and "Ave Roma," Pound emphasizes that he learned much about the years 1921–24 in Italy from the "Exposition del Decennio," that he had not known before.[68] Giuseppe Terragni's design for Sala O, representing January to October 1922, shows how the artists involved took the raw material of history and transformed it into a spatial experience in which visitors could participate and learn (Fig. 6).[69] Terragni began with a lengthy chronicle, written by Enrico Arrigotti, of events from the period of 1922 leading up to the March on Rome.[70] Terragni's solution for expressing the tumult of the period spatially brought together montage representations of important moments in the move toward October 1922, overlaid with layered structures—often overlapping planes of images that break the uniform plane of the gallery wall, blurring the line between structural elements and exhibited objects.[71] Similarly, Guido Mauri and Esodo Pratelli's design for Sala N, depicting the year 1921, built a dynamic historical vision (Fig. 7). Combining objects in glass cases with explosive

4. Palazzo delle Esposizioni, Rome. (Photograph by the author)

5. Façade of the Palazzo delle Esposizioni, covered for the Mostra della Rivoluzione Fascista, according to a design by Adalberto Libera and Mario de Renzi, Rome (c. 29 October 1931–21 April 1932). (Alinari Archive, Florence)

6. Giuseppe Terragni, The Year 1922 leading up to October (Sala O), Mostra della Rivoluzione Fascista, Rome. (Alinari Archive, Florence)

7. Guido Mauri and Esodo Pratelli, The Year 1921 (Sala N), Mostra della Rivoluzione Fascista, Rome. (Alinari Archive, Florence)

and abstracted depictions of important events, their highly layered design joins text and image, mimicking the books of Alessandro Melchior for young people, which presented Fascist culture as "steeped in the mystique of violence and sacrifice."[72] In short, these artists employed their own modernist aesthetic to represent this tumultuous period and create for visitors a sense of experiencing these events.

Ezra Pound noted that the first impression of this exhibition was "confusion," but that out of that feeling grew greater knowledge. When visitors were confronted by the material in Sala O, they had to make sense of the various pieces—how they fit together and what they were to represent. For instance, the image of the speeding locomotive used to represent the break-up of the strikes in early May was not immediately legible:[73] a visitor had to contemplate how that visual image worked, why it could signify the strike break-up, and what the break-up of the strike meant for the continued progress of the Fascist revolution. Additionally, the room's design could carry great emotional power than could a more staid exhibition of artifacts in cases, thereby reaching visitors not only intellectually but also emotionally—an intellectual and emotional complex in a moment of time. The final part of the room represented mass demonstrations, giving the impression of Mussolini's will being transformed into action.[74] By presenting the artifacts that testify to the history leading up to the March on Rome in such a dynamic environment—in which wall surfaces are disrupted by overlapping, often transparent layers of text and image alike are spread along diagonal surfaces (long associated with motion), and a visitor must move through the room to decipher the representations of events and actions—the exhibition itself brings ideas into action.

The exhibition's organizers looked to the leaders of Italy's avant-garde artistic movements to construct the MRF. The artistic directors were Cipriano Efisio Oppo (who, in addition to being an artist and critic, had been general secretary of the Rome Quadriennale in the late 1920s and early 1930s) and Futurist poet Filippo Tommaso Marinetti. Oppo and Marinetti doubtless disagreed on aesthetic issues: where Marinetti valued the modernist innovations associated with the Futurists—abstraction, dynamism, glorification of power and violence—Oppo was one of the main advocates of a "national style" in the tradition of nineteenth-century realism, a style he described as having "clarity in narration, dignity, healthy sensuality," "the evocative power of nature," "not a cold or analytic copy … but neither the horrid, the deformed, or the monstrous."[75] In a period in which the identity of a national style was truly up for grabs, it was appropriate to have artistic directors with such different tastes.

In part because of Marinetti's influence, the exhibition's artists included such Futurist painters as Gerardo Dottori and Enrico Prampolini. Even before he visited it, Pound wrote about the importance of the Futurists' presence there as indicative of the exhibitions modernness:

> It is frankly impossible today in Italy, that is in the New Italy, to make a truly contemporary exhibition or public monument, that is not dominated by the Futurist movement, that is, in a more widespread sense, either directed by the Futurist group, or impregnated by one or a lot of contemporary "schools." We are not indiscreet boys anymore; we leave private activity to sincere passeists [*passatisti*]; but a modern-day public monument must be modern.[76]

In addition, the exhibition contained several rooms designed by the leaders of the Novecento movement, Mario Sironi and Achille Funi. The nativist *Strapaese* faction, rural in origin and associated with the hard-line *squadristi* of the provinces, was represented by Mino Maccari, Amerigo Bartoli, and Leo Longanesi.[77] The pioneer of industrial design Marcello Nizzoli devised innovative solutions for displaying artifacts without cases, relying instead on structural

110   *Fascist Directive*

distinctions between objects and their support mechanism.[78] Additionally, the prominent architects Mario de Renzi, (whose work on federal buildings and exposition pavilions resulted from his work on the MRF), Adalberto Libera, and Giuseppe Terragni (both Rationalists associated with the Gruppo 7) brought to bear ideas about spatial design on the design of exhibition galleries.[79]

There were two rooms dedicated to Mussolini in the exhibition, both playing on his role as editor of *Il Popolo d'Italia*. From Pound's Canto 46 (published in 1936), we know that he remembered at least one of these rooms

> That office?
> Didja see the Decennio?
> ?
> Decennio exposition, reconstructed office of Il Popolo.[80]

One of these rooms was the Sala d'Onore (Sala R, Fig. 8), designed by Mario Sironi, a leader of the Novecento movement. Emily Braun has called this room "the inner sanctum of the Fascist cult," featuring as it did a huge warrior sculpture of Mussolini and a Gallery of the Fasces.[81] The room emphasized Mussolini's power with the word, as the four walls of the small modern tabernacle at the back are joined by rollers from the printing press for *Il Popolo d'Italia*, and the colossal statue of Mussolini holding a book in his left hand, almost levitating above the word "DUX" in massive letters.[82] Architectural historian Libero Andreotti describes the recreation of Mussolini's office in Sala R, accessible through a door under the statue of the Duce:

> Among the sparse furnishings were his desk, with three hand grenades, his pistol, and a copy of *Roma Futurista*. Behind the desk stood the black flag of the Arditi, with skull and dagger. This was the Duce's command post during the revolution; it stood at the center of three-sided "exedra" whose lateral walls were shaped like enormous stylized fasci. The blades

carried the Duce's mottoes, "Credere Obbedire Combattere" (believe, obey, fight) and "Ordine Autorità Giustizia" (order, authority, justice). Below, on either side, were the dates marking the beginning and the end of the revolution.[83]

This is man become myth. The combination of the highly realistic office space with the more typically Sironi-ish monumentality adds to the sense of a struggle between the desires to document the artifacts of the past and to represent the past more timelessly.[84]

Despite shared subject matter, Leo Longanesi's Sala del Duce (Sala T) could not have been more different. The gallery was understated in the extreme, framing photographs and documents in small wall cases, themselves framed by painted lines. The simple white trim delineated sections of the room—emphasizing authenticity over monumentality. In sum, the room emulated traditional museum design, where objects are kept completely separate from the architecture of the room.[85] Where Sironi was associated with one of the modernist avant-garde movements in Italy, Longanesi's affiliation with *Strapaese* meant that he rejected such movements as threats to the more authentic culture and tradition of rural Italy. The sober appearance of his Sala del Duce, resembling more traditional museums of the late nineteenth and early twentieth century, does not come from any lack of imagination on Longanesi's part, but rather from his "strategy of the past," which was rooted in the bourgeois virtues of simplicity, honesty, and decorum that he associated with the nineteenth century. He therefore updated nineteenth-century display strategies to present a more genuine image of the Duce. Like Sironi, he brought design elements borrowed from the world of printing—old-fashioned book-binding materials, use of the "Longanesi" typeface, also employed in *L'Italiano* and based on types found in Gian Battista Bodoni's *Typographical Manual* (1818).[86] This room reconstructs Mussolini's second office at *Il Popolo d'Italia*, a more managerial space with a poster of Dante behind the desk (Fig. 9). Mussolini had "personally supervised the selection and arrangement

8. Mario Sironi, Salone d'Onore (Sala R), Mostra della Rivoluzione Fascista, Rome. (Alinari Archive, Florence. Sironi: © 2016 Artists Rights Society (ARS), New York / SIAE, Rome)

The Bundle and the Pickax 113

9. Reconstruction of Mussolini's office at the headquarters of *Il Popolo d'Italia* on the via Lovanio, Sala del Duce (Sala T), Mostra della Rivoluzione Fascista, Rome. (Alinari Archive, Florence)

of the material for display," including objects representing his cultural work and "three recent attempts on his life."[87]

Where Sironi's Salone d'Onore created an environment of struggle, Longanesi's Sala del Duce highlighted consolidated power, the objects around the Duce's desk testifying to his connection with Italian history and his powerful status. Within the MRF, Longanesi's more traditional mode of exhibition could be as surprising as the more radical design elements of Terragni and Sironi.[88] So which room of the exhibition was Pound remembering in Canto 46? We cannot be certain—or even know whether he had not combined the two in his mind, merging the dynamic struggle and avant-garde engagement with tradition of Sironi with Longanesi's emphasis on the genuine and investment in revitalizing the recent past. Either way, Pound's image of the Duce, shaped by the MRF, is not unlike the *fascio* itself, made stronger by the combination of many strands of contemporary Italian culture.

Modernism did not dominate Italian cultural Nationalism throughout the Fascist period. As the "Great Debate on Fascism and Culture," published in Giuseppe Bottai's *Critica Fascista* during the mid-1920s, makes clear, there were always voices opposing international European modernism as a style for the Fascist state. Even as they advocated an innovative use of tradition, members of the Novecento movement Massimo Bontempelli and Ardengo Soffici denounced foreign influence, saying that Fascist art needed to be rooted in Italian soil.[89] By the mid-1930s, critics like Roberto Farinacci and Ugo Ojetti, who opposed a modernist aesthetic, were on the rise. In 1933, Farinacci denounced the Novecento group, accusing the artists of "technical poverty, spiritual vapidity, [and] imprudent pro-foreign, Masonic tastes."[90] By 1937, as a result of Italy's growing relationship with Germany, where modernism had been denounced as "degenerate," anti-modernist (and anti-Semitic) factions like Farinacci's gained greater prominence, and modernist artists and architects were increasingly labeled "Jewish," regardless of their faith.[91] Despite the fact that much of Italian modernism drew on Italian tradition—from Etruscan tomb sculpture, to Byzantine mosaics, Romanesque sculpture, and early Renaissance fresco painting—modernist art, and its attempt to unite Italian culture with contemporary European art, waned in favor of revived interest in the monuments and aesthetics of imperial Rome.

Romanità

A crucial aspect of Fascist iconography—particularly from the later 1930s—is what Romke Visser has called the regime's "cult of *Romanità*." We have already seen how the *fascio littorio*, borrowed from ancient Roman iconography, became an important symbol early on but over time Roman imperial iconography became more wide-ranging and prevalent. The dating system of the new "Era Fascista" was marked with Roman numerals, the March on Rome on 28 October 1922 marking its beginning. This calendrical reform no doubt appealed to Pound in part because he already considered 1922 the birth-year of modernism, thanks to the publication of T. S. Eliot's *The Waste Land* and James Joyce's *Ulysses*. Roman titles of the Fascist Militia became government symbols.[92] The *lupa* (the she-wolf who mothered Romulus and Remus), deified Roma, triumphal arches and recognizable archaeological monuments, famous statues of Julius and Augustus Caesar, the acronym "S.P.Q.R." (for the Latin, *Senatus Populusque Romanus*, or "Senate and People of Rome")—not to mention the more showy and at least partly invented elements like the *passo romano* and Roman salute—all these icons of ancient Rome were employed as symbols of the new regime, which portrayed itself as an inheritor of the greatness of Rome.[93] As an example, a lamppost planted on the via dell'Impero in Rome (now via dei Fori Imperiali) combines images of an imperial eagle, the *lupa*, "S.P.Q.R.," and *fasci* (the heads of the axes were broken off after the war) (Fig. 10). These same images appeared in carvings, on coins and stamps, in cover designs for magazines. As Joshua Arthurs has demonstrated, this deployment of Roman imagery and excavation of the Roman past represented "an essential aspect of the regime's program of revolutionary modernization."[94] This systematic emphasis on Romanness would become a prominent trope in Pound's writing, too—a surprise given his earlier disdain for Roman literature and culture.

An interest in Rome as a model for Fascist Italy had begun in the late 1910s, before Mussolini took power. As Cannistraro and Sullivan have shown, Margherita Sarfatti tried to persuade Mussolini early on to emulate classical aesthetics and rebuild the civilization and empire of Rome.[95] On 20 September 1922—before the March on Rome—Mussolini emphasized the importance of Rome to a spiritual regeneration of Italy: "We aim to make Rome the beating heart, the galvanizing spirit of the imperial Italy of which we dream."[96] Writing in 1937, Giuseppe Bottai would remember the proclamation of 21 April 1921 as the birthday of Rome and a national holiday, and Mussolini's declaration in

10. Lamppost featuring Romanizing imagery, via dei Fori Imperiali, Rome. (Photograph by the author)

Perugia in 1923, on the anniversary of the March on Rome, that Rome was the "predestined sign of the race, to which our destiny as a people binds us."[97] And on 31 December 1925, when Mussolini installed the senator Filippo Cremonesi as the first governor of Rome, the Duce stood in the Palace of the Conservators in the Capitoline Museums, in the Hall of the Horatii and Curiatii (one of several rooms whose decor celebrates important moments in the history of ancient Rome), and argued for "The New Rome." "In five years," Mussolini said, "Rome must appear marvelous to all the people of the world: vast, ordered, powerful, as it was in the time of the first empire of Augustus."[98] He spoke of plans to liberate the ancient monuments and build a third Rome on the banks of the sacred Tiber.

Visser demonstrates that while some historians have read Fascism's employment of Roman imagery as shallow and opportunistic, it was instead part of a larger attempt to foment an imperialist Italian identity around already powerful points of national pride.[99] Peter Aicher has noted that while the notion of *Romanità* was not an invention of the Fascists, it had been important to the underpinnings of Italianness sprouting from the Risorgimento, "The sheer intensiveness of the fascist attempt to link itself with ancient Rome, promulgated in wide sectors of the population using all media—print (both popular and academic), architecture, archaeology, public ceremony, stamps, symbols, cinema, school instruction—constituted a new distinctive phase of the myth of Rome."[100] During the second decade of the Fascist era, Mussolini's speeches and writings increasingly exploited the myth of Rome.[101]

Whether we think of the more showy aspects or the more historical aims that appealed to educated Italians (and foreigners), the cult of *Romanità* was a powerful source of Italian identity and Fascist propaganda, and "useful to support the claims that fascism was making history."[102] It appealed to educated and uneducated Italians alike.[103] We can see from titles of Pound's periodical publications of the 1930s—such works as "Ubicumque Lingua Romana," "Ave

Roma," and "Europe MCMXXXVI"—that he employed the trappings and flourishes of *Romanità* as well as its rhetoric. Crucially, the elements of *Romanità* on display in the Mostra Augustea della Romanità—or "Exhibition of Augustus and Romanness"—would become a part of Pound's ideas about acculturation; this subject is discussed at greater length in Chapter 6. One result of this state use of *Romanità* was that "many of the scholars who, like a large number of their university colleagues, were deeply involved in the politics and administration of the young Italian state, welcomed fascism as a means to make their patriotic and colonialist dreams come true."[104] In this sense, these scholars were not so different from Pound. While Pound's initial attraction to Fascism's cultural mission may have had more to do with his sense of Mussolini as a modern Renaissance patron prince, and his sense that the artistic awakening of that earlier era of Italian glory could be repeated, thanks to the valorization of Italy's cultural past and the promised institutional support of modern artists, this celebration of the classical past came to be more important to him as the 1930s went on.

Visser documents how numerous state-sponsored scholarly institutions contributed to the proliferation of *Romanità* as it was subsumed into Fascism. The relationship between the Fascist regime and these institutions was never unidirectional. Antonio Cederna makes clear in *Mussolini urbanista* that the so-called Fascist vision for a reconstructed Rome was as often determined by the fellows of the Istituto di Studi Romani as by government officials.[105] In this way, the power and breadth of the Fascist iconography and cultural projects come to light: in Pound's mind, too, these projects were not undertaken solely by people with designated government posts, but also by any and all who tied their work to the regime. This means that archaeologists like Corrado Ricci—who will feature prominently in the next section—were as much a part of his Fascist *Gerarchia* as Giuseppe Bottai or Margherita Sarfatti. As we will also see in the next section, both the erection of the Stele of Axum and the building of the Foro Mussolini are examples of the wider importance of *Romanità* to the Fascist regime. Indeed, the excavation of so many of the imperial Roman monuments of Rome were consistent with the "cult of *Romanità*," a cultural concept important to Romans and Pound alike.

Archaeology and new building

All through the Fascist period in Italy, ancient architectural monuments were restored to help provide the relatively young nation with a coherent cultural identity—and Ezra Pound was paying attention. Particularly during the later 1930s, as interest in *Romanità* superseded other Italian cultural models, the rediscovery of ancient Roman monuments took on a politicized tone. Together with this archaeological work came new building projects based on older models. At the time, Albert W. Van Buren of the American Academy in Rome noted the new enthusiasm in Italy for archaeological recovery: "Now as never before in modern times is the heritage of antiquity felt to belong to the Italian people as a whole; and the recovery, preservation, and interpretation of that heritage is recognized as one of the most essential and noble functions of the government."[106] This is what Pound called Italy's cultural heritage, manifested archaeologically not just in the sites themselves, but also in museum exhibitions, improved transportation to archaeological sites, and government publications about excavations. The examples discussed in this section contributed to Pound's sense of Italian Nationalism—crucial to his writings of the 1930s. Pound found in these archaeological restorations and urban projects a model for how one might approach the culture of the past and employ that cultural heritage for contemporary purposes.

In *Jefferson and/or Mussolini*, Pound identifies two signs of an "Italian awakening," associated with a new ability to find what is valuable amidst the culture of the past. First, bookshop windows, where he could see a wider variety of books—classics and modern texts, Italian and translated—and at cheaper prices. Second, "The restauri," or architectural "restorations." Archaeological recovery of an ancient past in Italy had been important since the Risorgimento, when Nationalist ideology looked for a strong secular past, separate from the Roman Church. Additionally, the passage of laws virtually forbidding foreign excavation on Italian soil insured that Italian archaeological projects frequently had a Nationalist stamp.[107] Not surprisingly, given Pound's long-standing interest in medieval culture and such medieval monuments as San Zeno in Verona, he focused on traces of the Romanesque:

> From Sicily up to Ascoli, from one end of the boot to the other, the blobby and clumsy stucco is pried loose from the columns; the pure lines of the Romanesque are dug out, the old ineradicable Italian skill shows in the anonymous craftsmen. Three whole columns, six fragments, a couple of capitals are scratched out of a rotten wall and within a few months the graceful chiostro is there again as it had been in the time of Federigo Secondo.[108]

Discovering the true remnants of the past, long hidden by later interpretation and additions, represented for Pound a particularly modern way of engaging with heritage. He cheered Mussolini's archaeologists' removal of later "encrustations"—despite their own significance and his own admiration of similarly late additions to Rimini's Tempio Malatestiano.[109] In other words, Mussolini's archaeology, celebrated by Pound, chose one national past at the expense of others, and Pound's emulation signifies a marked shift in his own aesthetics.

Pound favors rebuilding when it uses cultural traditions—often local—and gives work to artisans. He says of the work being undertaken in Ascoli and Agrigento, "here a column, there an entire cloister—or a school of practical art, rising again and making new plinths, capitols, and ornamental pieces, with perfection equal to the ancient, when they are missing the originals."[110] Pound makes two points here about this rebuilding. First, it is more restrained than the fantastical rebuildings of the likes of Viollet-le-Duc, which often and without evidence added entirely new structures to existing buildings. Second, it allows for an ongoing practice of traditions of the fine arts—an employment of Italian cultural heritage by living modern artists. He notes in *Jefferson and/or Mussolini* that this restoration work "is not merely a matter of FILLING in the old gaps with concrete. It is a reconquest of an ancient skill, such as I saw the head artisan using in Teramo or in Ascoli Piceno up in the mountains over there by the Adriatic 'where nobody goes'" (*J/M*, 85). He uses the example of the Ligurian tradition of painting houses' exteriors with *trompe l'œil* architectural features. This tradition, he laments, is in danger of dying out with the "spread of reinforced concrete." He is eager to see it resuscitated as a way of improving the beauty of the countryside—overwhelmed, he says, by ugly advertising posters—and as a nod to Italy's rich local cultural traditions. "Would Ghirlandaio not have wanted to paint the great boundary wall of Florence?" he asks, pointing to "disciples of the schools of fine arts" who could be invited to beautify the landscape with their outdoor art—and for less money than the cost of advertising.[111] By drawing on the Renaissance practice of paying artists to build and decorate monuments that the entire citizenry could enjoy, Pound aims to use artisans and traditions to make Italy a stronger nation.

Despite his own admiration of international modernism, Pound emphasizes the danger of choosing international trends over local traditions. He notes the geological wisdom of "The old countryside of Liguria, in the form of a crescent moon among the crags in the valleys." Importing to that landscape "large and magnificent avenues, copied from Philadelphia or from some other country, would completely wreck the climate of swimming beaches and wholesome places" for which Liguria is known, letting in "the noxious winds from the mountains."[112] It makes sense, in other words, for urban design to fit its region rather than follow a one-size-fits-all model. Indeed, given the number of broad avenues being built to modernize Italian cities, Pound's attention to the problems of such modernization shows his engagement in the conversations going on about how Italy ought to change. And it reveals the complexity of his attraction to both localizing and internationalizing aesthetics—typically mutually exclusive during this period. Pound's seemingly incompatible views may indicate a desire not to commit to one side or the other in this debate, and it certainly marks one of the ways in which his own aesthetic views needed to shift to remain in accord with those of the Fascist regime.

Pound identifies other threats to the beauty of the Italian countryside. The greatest of these is the increase in advertising posters. His choice of particular Italian words is important: "But alongside this care for beauty, this reclaiming [*bonifica*] of artistic heritage, is to be noted the evil defacing [*malefica deturpazione*] of the countryside, caused by unrestrained invasion of commercial advertising, of posters."[113] Pound consciously uses the Italian word *bonifica*, literally meaning "reclaiming" or "drainage." But in a more ideological sense, as Ruth Ben-Ghiat notes, *Bonifica* or *Bonifica Integrale* referred to Mussolini's draining of the Pontine Marshes, a project begun in the 1920s which later came to be associated with other campaigns of reclamation, all seen as "different facets and phases of a comprehensive project to combat degeneration and radically renew Italian society by 'pulling up the bad weeds and cleaning up the soil.'"[114] This notion of cultural reclamation, of selecting the great elements of a culture and getting rid of the "weeds," became a crucial element of Pound's sense of how a person comes to culture.

Pound further plays with meaning. He also uses *malefica*, a word not typically used as a noun, but which in its feminine adjectival form (meaning "evil" or "maleficent" and modifying *la deturpazione* or "defacing") acts as a visual if not grammatical parallel to *bonifica*. In using the word *deturpazione*, Pound may also have been echoing Mussolini's speech on the occasion of the birthday of Rome—21 April—in 1924, in which he noted the need "to liberate all of ancient Rome from mediocre defacings" ("liberare dalle deturpazioni mediocri tutta la Roma antica").[115] Through this linguistic play, Pound contrasts the Fascist reclaiming of artistic heritage to the threat of advertising's defacing of the countryside. His evocation of the draining of the Pontine Marshes is no accident either: as he says in *Jefferson and/or Mussolini*, "from the time of Tiberius the Italian intelligentzia has been *talking* about draining the swamps" (*J/M*, 23)—but Mussolini actually did it. Through his rhetorical play, Pound suggests that the aesthetic threat of modern advertising posters is anti-Fascist, and anti-modernist.

Pound goes on argue that these posters threaten Italy's tourism industry. He writes that advertising "is also a damage to Nations, especially to those that make an industry of tourism; and we know that most tourists love the beautiful, and that the defacing of the scenery can foment unjust defaming of Italy."[116] By this time, Fascist Italy had identified tourism not only as a money-making venture, but also as a way of spreading the Fascist vision of the new nation. In January 1929, Van Buren commented that "The energy and capability of the present government have already made Ostia one of the most accessible archaeological sites of the Mediterranean by the opening of the excellent electric railway from the Capitol to the sea." Van Buren enumerates other important ways that transportation to the archaeological sites around Italy had improved, concluding, "all of which makes the archaeologist's journey an easier one."[117] The same was true for tourist travel.[118] We should remember here Pound's praise, discussed earlier in a different context, of this access in *Jefferson and/or Mussolini*: "When Mussolini has expressed any satisfaction it has been with the definite act performed, the artwork in the civic sense, the leading the Romans back to the sea, for example, by the wide new road into Ostia" (*J/M*, 100). And we shall see shortly the significance of the archaeological work at Ostia to the regime.

The most visible and important archaeological work undertaken by Mussolini's regime was the "liberation" of ancient Roman ruins in the modern capital city. Pound emphasizes Mussolini's role in these projects in the first passage about the *restauri*: "Where other regimes would have haggled and niggled the fascist regime has just gone ahead, without any fireworks whatever" (*J/M*, 85). (We can argue about the fireworks.) Pound's enthusiasm for all things archaeological placed him among a recognized group of Italian poets. Giuseppe Bottai opened his essay "Il rinnovamento di Roma" (1937, 1940) by asserting, "The renovation of the greatness of Rome is at the summit of Italian poets' aspirations, who—from Dante, to Leopardi, to D'Annunzio—foretold the triumphal events of the Empire, of which—the Duce, artifex—our generations are heroes." In accord with Mussolini's imperial aspirations in Africa, Bottai went on to imagine (and remember, this is 1940) that this archaeological work indicated a resurgence of Italian empire, and quoted from Mussolini himself to show the extent to which this archaeological work was Fascist work:

> The building expansion of the City, the isolation of the monumental areas, the improvement of the popular districts are the material signs that have hailed the resurrection [*risorgere*] of the Empire on our fated hills; and that will mark and comment upon, in marble and travertine, the new history. "Rome must appear marvelous to all the people of the world: vast, ordered, powerful as it was in the time of the Empire of Augustus."[119]

Many of these projects were very dramatic. The building of the via della Conciliazione in 1936–38 cleared out vast sections of the *borgo* to build a broad modern avenue connecting the Piazza San Pietro in the Vatican to the Piazza Pia beside Castel Sant'Angelo, which made the seat of the Roman Church more visible from areas outside the newly established independent Vatican City (Fig. 11).[120] Several projects were undertaken in 1938 for the bimillennium of the birth of Augustus, such as the "liberation" of the Mausoleum of

11. Demolition in St. Peter's Square for the construction of the via della Conciliazione, 1936. (Leoni Archive / Alinari Archives, Florence)

12. Men at work demolishing and leveling the Velian Hill, between the Colosseum and Piazza Venezia, for the construction of the via dell' Impero, Rome, 17 February 1932. (Istituto Luce / Alinari Archives Management, Florence)

Augustus (it had been transformed into a theater), the building of the Piazza Augusto Imperatore, and the reconstruction of the Ara Pacis Augustae, or the Altar of the Augustan Peace.[121] Beginning in the late 1920s and continuing until the events and costs of the Second World War brought them to a halt, these projects transformed the city of Rome and the ways in which Rome's ancient past could be viewed and understood.

Probably the most prominent of these works, and a project admired by Pound, was the building of the via dell'Impero in Rome and the adjoining restorations of the imperial *fora* (Fig. 12). Inaugurated by Mussolini on 28 October 1932, the tenth anniversary of the March on Rome, this project most visibly created a modern broad road linking the Colosseo and the Piazza Venezia, the site of the Palazzo Venezia, from which Mussolini governed and from whose balcony he made speeches.[122] Since the late nineteenth century, when Rome became the capital of the new Italy, Rome had been modernizing: its population had grown significantly, it was now the center of a sizable government bureaucracy, and it needed to funnel traffic more effectively.[123] The street had symbolic significance, too, as it formed a visible link between the seat of Mussolini's government and the most visible monument of the Roman Empire. This project was not an invention of the Fascist government—indeed it had been part of earlier plans for the city—but under Mussolini's regime it featured a parade route at its center.[124] As Spiro Kostoff has noted, the "true Haussmannization of the Third Rome comes under the Fascists": "According to fascist theory, straight and wide avenues were indispensable."[125] Pound had thought such a road unsuitable for Genoa, but this project in Rome garnered his praise.

Corrado Ricci conceived and oversaw this project's archaeological component. Ricci was well established in art and archaeological circles in Italy, having been a senator; director, or superintendent of art galleries in Parma, Modena, Ravenna, Milan, and Florence; Director General of Antiquities and Fine Arts; and president of the Institute of Archaeology and History of Art.[126] As Lawerence Rainey has shown, Pound was introduced to Ricci by the eminent archaeologist Giacomo Boni, whom Pound met by chance in the Roman Forum in the spring of 1923. Pound thus learned of Ricci's work from his monumental volume, published in 1925, about the Tempio Malatestiano in Rimini, which monument Pound had discovered in the summer of 1922.[127]

Pound may also have been familiar with Ricci's writings about the "liberation of the remains of the imperial fora," imagined by Ricci in 1911 but actualized under Mussolini's government. Pound acknowledges, "Someone mentions the Senatore Corrado Ricci and no one knows who else or how many other sensibilities have been employed" (*J/M*, 85). In other words, these are not projects undertaken by one man or one mind, but by a whole host—the archaeological component of the Fascist *Gerarchia*. That Ricci, himself a Romagnese born in Rimini, was considered by many an honorary Roman after his death—in recognition of his work to reveal "the divine majesty of ancient Rome"—shows the importance of these imperial *fora* to the wider project of re-establishing Rome's imperial history and potential future.[128] In July 1933, a bronze statue of Julius Caesar was installed on the via dell'Impero, and in a speech made on that day (and reproduced in *Il Popolo d'Italia*) Mussolini explicitly linked the March on Rome with Caesar's crossing of the Rubicon—an image that would return time and again in Fascist iconography.[129] Writing in *Capitolium* in November 1932, F. P. Mulè said of "the value of these excavations" that they "reconnect today with the past, thereby increasing our responsibility to the Patria."[130]

In the early twentieth century, only parts of the *fora* of Trajan and Augustus and the "Colonnacce" could be seen, but Ricci's excavation revealed substantial parts of the imperial *fora*, including the southwest half of the Forum of Caesar, the northeast part of the Forum of Augustus, parts of the Forum of Peace, the central and northeast sections of the Forum Transitorium, and sections of the Forum and Market of Trajan.[131] Although the Roman Forum had never disappeared, and had been opened up beginning in the late nineteenth century, many parts of the imperial *fora* had, like so many ancient monuments in the city, been dismantled so that their building materials could be reused. The remaining parts were hidden under newer buildings, as ancient ruins were frequently used as foundations for later structures.

Nevertheless, it often took archaeological work to discover the precise connections between ancient structures and the more modern buildings that reused their elements.[132] The building of the via dell'Impero, which required some leveling of areas of the Velian Hill adjoining the Basilica of Maxentius and Constantine, also allowed for new architectural additions.[133] The retaining wall for the basilica housed five marble maps: the first four, mounted in 1934, traced the various geographical spans of the Roman Empire (Fig. 13); the fifth, added in 1936 but removed after the war, celebrated the conquest of Ethiopia in that year and showed the extent of Mussolini's empire.[134] In this way the regime made prominent the connections it wanted seen between its own projects in modern Rome and the greatness of ancient Rome. The project was criticized at the time for building the via dell'Impero through the site of the imperial *fora*—it crossed over parts of the *fora* of Nerva, Trajan, Vespasian, and Augustus—but, as Mussolini reminded his critics at the time, the excavations were only half the project, beside the much-needed road.[135] The project has subsequently been widely criticized for the historical elements it irreparably destroyed.[136] But at the time, proponents ignored all but the project's overblown aspirations. G. Marchetti Longhi, writing in *Capitolium* in February 1934, used typically grandiose terms: the road, he said, "is connected to Rome's fated predestination to universal and eternal dominion; and it is this profound significance that the Via assumes in the present and in the future, for us and for our descendants."[137] In the Fascist period, archaeology rarely existed outside of modern building projects of one kind or another.

The Bundle and the Pickax   129

13. Marble maps celebrating the extent of the Roman Empire, Basilica of Maxentius and Constantine, via dei Fori Imperiali, Rome. (Photograph by the author)

Pound observed the success and speedy completion of the project. In an essay of 1933, he celebrates the clearing away of "medieval squalor" in projects like this one, thereby adopting the rhetoric of the regime for the work of the *piccone*, or pickax. Documentary photographs of the work for projects like this one frequently feature Mussolini himself or other workers wielding a pickax in service of the demolition work, getting rid of a later building that traps and disguises the ancient ruins (Fig. 14).[138]

Pound likens the "rubbish" [*spazzatura*] of fifteen centuries that had hidden the "Roman glory" of sites like these to the difficulties one faces in trying to get to an old text: "try to find the sonnets of Joachim du Bellay, adapted by the Latinists of the Renaissance, translated into English by Spenser, etc." In adopting derisive terms for the structures demolished—which included medieval and Renaissance neighborhoods, churches, and a

14. Benito Mussolini, on the roof of a house on vicolo Soderni near Ripetta, inaugurates the demolition in the piazza Augusto Imperatore, for the bimillennium of Augustus, 22 October 1934. (Istituto Luce/Alinari Archives Management, Florence)

sixteenth-century garden—Pound echoes the regime's language, devaluing the monuments destroyed in the name of liberating a desirable past.[139] He thereby revises and redeploys his own positions on aesthetics and history in order to agree with the regime. Pound then notes that between his two visits to Rome in April and December 1932, Mussolini had more progress "toward clearing out this glory than had all the popes from the seventh to the nineteenth centuries." And Pound echoes the phrasing of numerous Italian Fascists, concluding his essay with the assertion that while modern machines had certainly aided the process, "What has cleared out the Via dell'Impero is the WILL [*VOLONTÀ*]."[140]

For Pound, of course, this idea of "directio voluntatis," direction of the will, is crucial to Mussolini's success; he denies "that *real* intelligence exists until it comes into action" (*J/M*, 18). Pound hereby adopts tropes of *Mussolinismo* and echoes the Fascist "Actualism," an ethical system outlined by Giovanni Gentile in 1916. In the words of Claudio Fogu, actualism "aimed at affirming the absolute immanence of theory and practice in the 'pure act,' against all transcendental components of idealist as well as materialist thought."[141] Roger Griffin notes a connection between Gentile's actualism and Fascism's "conception of history as a dynamic, living, futural reality that is to be proactively 'made' through the exertion of effort, vision, and will-power, and not just reconstructed *post hoc* in the university library."[142]

We might also return to the popular Fascist motto: *Il fascismo fa la storia, non la scrive*—"Fascism makes history, it does not write it."[143] Pound admires Mussolini's "capacity to pick out the element of immediate and major importance in any tangle," a quality that Pound was determining to be crucial to intelligence, to making sense of the wider world. In other words, Fascism's distillations can help a person see. Mussolini, Pound claims, "found himself in the cluttered rubbish and cluttered splendour of the dozen or more strata of human effort" (*J/M*, 66), but his *virtù* allowed him to sift through and pick out what was important. Pound likens the accrued rubbish to "the Romanesque cluttered over with barocco": his use of this archaeological metaphor demonstrates how much he had internalized Mussolini's *piccone*. In an image in *Jefferson and/or Mussolini*, he reads that same pickax or, as he calls it, "fascist axe," into ideograms from Confucius representing "La rivoluzione continua" or, more literally, the meaning "renovate, day by day, renew" (*J/M*, 113; Fig. 15).[144] Like the periplum or the Chinese ideogram, the *piccone* had become for Pound an emblem of a way of reading and a model for his prose writing. That he here combines his long-held directive to "make it new" with Confucian ethics and Fascist ideology shows how readily Pound would redeploy and adapt his aesthetics to coincide with his changing beliefs.

As William L. MacDonald has demonstrated, the archaeology supported by the Fascist regime cannot be fully separated from the building projects undertaken at the same time. Not only were many of the same people involved in excavations and building

Confucius on " La rivoluzione continua."
King Tching T'ang on Government. Part of the inscription on the king's bath-tub cited by Kung in the Ta Hio II. I.
The first ideogram (on the right) shows the fascist axe for the clearing away of rubbish (left half) the tree, organic vegetable renewal. The second ideograph is the sun sign, day,
" renovate, day by day renew."
The verb is used in phrases: to put away old habit, the daily increase of plants, improve the state of, restore.

15. Ezra Pound, *Jefferson and/or Mussolini* (London: Stanley Knott, 1935; New York: Liveright, 1936), p. 113.Copyright © 1935, 1936 by Ezra Pound; renewed 1963 by Ezra Pound. Reprinted by permission of Liveright Publishing Company.

The Bundle and the Pickax   133

16. Shops around the courtyard of House of the Lararium, Ostia Antica,
c. 1920–30. (Alinari Archive, Florence)

design, but recently revealed ancient sites and their reconstructions (whether on paper, in plaster models, or in some cases on the sites themselves) had substantial impact on the design of modern monumental structures.[145] One of the most interesting cases for our purposes, interested as Pound was in the relationships between the discovery of the past and the building of the present moment, is the excavation of Ostia Antica (begun 1909) and the building of the Foro Mussolini (now the Foro Italico). In ancient times, Ostia had been Rome's seaport at the mouth of the Tiber. The city was gradually demolished—first, as a result of earthquakes, tsunamis, and the dumping of potsherds; then, at the fall of the empire, thanks to pirates and invaders; and still later, by cathedral

17. Detail of the mosaic pavement of the frigidarium in the Baths of the Cisiarii, Ostia Antica, c. 1920–30. (Alinari Archive, Florence)

builders and baroque-era architects seeking materials for new structures. The excavations at Ostia, like many projects around the city of Rome, accelerated in 1938, and in the four years from 1938–42, about half of the buildings visible today were unearthed by Guido Calza and his team.[146] The excavations at Ostia revealed ancient Roman structures very different from the classically ornamented Vitruvian structures that had survived in Rome. At Ostia were found apartment buildings, markets, warehouses, and other quotidian buildings designed almost exclusively in the plain style (Fig. 16)—unadorned brickwork, uncomplicated shapes—and elaborate black-and-white floor mosaics (Fig. 17). Now that these architectural elements were known, architects were eager to imitate them in new residential and civic architecture throughout Italy.[147]

Perhaps the most striking instance of borrowing from Ostia appears in the Foro Mussolini, in the north of the city beside the Tiber. This modern forum, a clear analogue to those unearthed in the via dell'Impero project, consists of vast open space decorated with mosaic pavement, lined on both sides by inscribed marble slabs, and flanked by modern buildings designed for athletic pursuits.[148] The Foro was inaugurated with the erection of Mussolini's obelisk on 28 October 1932, the tenth anniversary of the March on Rome.[149] About this monument Van Buren wrote in late 1929, before it was erected:

> The transportation from the quarries of Rome of the huge monolith which is to serve as a monument in honor of the head of the government is a striking event as maintaining the continuity of practice which Imperial Rome inherited from Egypt: for Rome is a city of obelisks.[150]

As Augustus had carted obelisks back from Egypt, and Pope Sixtus V had moved them to the sites of prominent churches, so Mussolini erected his own modern obelisk. At the other end of the Foro is the Fountain of the Sphere, and along the sides, rows of inscribed marble slabs mark important events in the history of the Fascist era (inscriptions were added later, after the war, to mark the end of Fascism). The vast black-and-white mosaics at Ostia find echoes in the mosaics adorning the pavement through the center of the Foro (Fig. 18).[151] These mosaics celebrate significant events, achievements, and goals of the Fascist regime—thereby creating parallels between Mussolini's archaeological endeavors and Augustus's transformation of Rome from a city of brick to one of marble.[152] In 1937, Pound mailed a postcard of the Foro Mussolini to Olga Rudge, singling out that image for her notice among others he had purchased for their daughter Mary, an indication of his interest (Fig. 19).

Drawing on a common trope of *Mussolinismo*, Pound's emphasized a sense of the Duce as builder. "I don't believe any estimate of Mussolini will be valid until it *starts* from his passion for construction," Pound famously claimed in *Jefferson and/or Mussolini*. "Treat him as *artifex* and all the details fall into place" (*J/M*, 33–34). Pound hardly invented this analogy; indeed, it was a significant part of Fascist ideology.[153] In an interview of 1932, Mussolini said:

> When I feel the masses in my hands, since they believe in me, or when I mingle with them, and they almost crush me, then I feel like one with the masses. However there is at the same time a little aversion, much as the poet feels towards the material he works with. Doesn't the sculptor sometimes break the marble out of rage, because it does not precisely mold in his hands according to his vision? … Everything depends on that, to dominate the masses as an artist.[154]

Artist, sculptor, poet—all combine under Pound's Latin "artifex"—usually rendered as *artifice* in Italian. Pound similarly highlighted the notion of Mussolini as an artist in the "Autumn Letter" (1934) printed at the front of *Jefferson and/or Mussolini*: "The more one examines the Milan Speech the more one is reminded of Brâncuși, the stone blocks from which no error emerges, from whatever angle one look [*sic*] at them" (*J/M*, ix). By comparing Mussolini to this esteemed modernist sculptor, Pound makes him not just an *artifex*, but a modernist. As numerous scholars have noted, this view of the Duce allowed Pound to ignore any number of inconvenient or undesirable aspects of the regime and its activities, but it also expresses the importance to Pound of the urbanism and construction undertaken by the regime. Such projects signify by their completion (see *J/M*, 100). Mussolini's modernist vision goes into action to modernize Italy.

18. Black-and-white mosaics from the Foro Mussolini, now Foro Italico, Rome. (Photograph by the author)

138 *Fascist Directive*

19. Postcard of Foro Mussolini, Fountain and Monolith, Rome, mailed by Ezra Pound to Olga Rudge 18 June 1937. (Olga Rudge Papers, Yale Collection of American Literature, Beinecke Rare Book and Manuscript Library) Copyright © 2016 by Mary de Rachewiltz and the Estate of Omar S. Pound. Reprinted by permission of New Directions Publishing Corp.

Every historical era chooses the history that it will preserve, and the Fascist period was no different: archaeologists and architectural historians today mourn the loss of so many medieval and Renaissance buildings to Mussolini's *piccone*. At the time these demolished buildings were called slums and hovels, and the regime celebrated the way that citizens of the city were moved from homes with no running water to modern developments outside the city center. But these new structures were often no better and mass transit had not yet solved the problem of getting the relocated Romans to their jobs in the center.[155] Losses did not stop here: also demolished were later historical structures, seen as less important than those of ancient Rome to the image that Fascist Italy wanted to project of itself. The pace of the excavations, so admired by Pound, was part of the problem: in the interest of speed, material was dismantled, ignored, discarded, or destroyed.[156] At the same time, such contemporary commentators as Van Buren pointed out that many of the most important finds in Rome would not have been made without the intimate link between Fascist archaeology and urban renovation.[157] In a city as ancient and prone to flooding—and therefore to the burial of buildings over time—as Rome, it is frequently only in the destruction of the city fabric that new remnants of its ancient past become visible.[158] Pound, more poet than archaeologist, liked it this way. For him, the decision to select a cultural heritage and bring it to view mattered more than retaining all of the past's detritus. This approach therefore became his model.

For Pound, if not for more recent commentators, Mussolini's cultural undertakings offered a solution to the problem of Italy's disparate culture and distinct lack of unity. He says in *Jefferson and/or Mussolini*: "No one denies the material and immediate effect: *grano, bonifica, restauri*, grain, swamp-drainage, restorations, new buildings, and, I am ready to add off my own bat, AN AWAKENED INTELLIGENCE in the nation and a new LANGUAGE in the debates in the Chamber" (*J/M*, 73). Pound emphasizes that this solution does not eclipse Italy's varied and complicated language, culture, and history; nor does it lay yet another layer of "rubbish" on the pile. Instead, it recognizes elements of value in Italy's disparate culture and unites them.

Out of the rubbish, Pound believed, Fascism brought lost pieces of the past back to sight. It solved problems that had plagued Italians for centuries and made available resources that had been trapped. It began to provide Italy some economic independence. And it brought cultural thinking out of the quagmire that Pound had seen preceding it. For Pound, who was during this period working to identify new models for making the cultural heritage of the past useful to the present, these cultural solutions became a prominent metaphor for how to read and write. In reading, as with archaeology, one must learn how to find what matters. A writer, like a drainer of marshes, might clear dreckish material in order to reclaim fertile soil. A writer, like an exhibition designer, might make a radical new thing by combining the artifacts of the past and innovative modernist techniques. And a writer, like a builder, must consider the wider context into which he is writing. Like Mussolini, readers and writers make choices appropriate to the circumstances in order to forge a connection with the past or with other minds.

CHAPTER 4

Ezra Pound and/or the Fascist *Gerarchia*

> The most intelligent men in Italy are in office or vividly interested in official process, and in government work, they are to be found in the *Gerarchia*, or milling about it.
>
> —Ezra Pound[1]

Although Ezra Pound idolized Benito Mussolini, and very much identified Italian Fascism with Mussolini himself, he also watched the staff of intellectuals who helped make the Fascist regime. In a letter to Margherita Sarfatti in February 1934, he wrote that the present era, more enlightened than any since the Risorgimento, is "inhabited by DUX ipse, and almost no one else that one hears of, tho' there must be a staff of aviators and architects."[2] Certainly the regime was designed to foreground Mussolini himself, but Pound's recognition of the staff reflects his desire to be among those responsible for designing and piloting the regime. Indeed, this "staff" included important intellectuals, architects, archaeologists, critics, and others who, in the words of Philip V. Cannistraro and Brian Sullivan, "brought cultural respectability to a movement that otherwise appeared to be nothing more than a gang of violent, anti-intellectual thugs."³ We have already seen how Pound noticed the nationalizing cultural projects of the Fascist regime, engineered by the likes of Margherita Sarfatti, Giuseppe Bottai, Roberto Farinacci, P. M. Bardi, F. T Marinetti, Mario Sironi, and Corrado Ricci. Pound's investment in their work went beyond mere observation, however, in that he sought ways of collaborating with them and even becoming a cultural administrator of Mussolini's regime. The correspondence presented in this brief chapter—most of it previously unpublished—demonstrates Pound's attempts to become a part of the Fascist *Gerarchia* rather than settling for writing about them.

Ezra Pound first published *Jefferson and/or Mussolini: L'Idea statale, Fascism as I Have Seen It* in London in 1935, with the publisher Stanley Nott. Thirty copies were printed. On the verso of the title leaf, Pound included a note dated April 1935:

THE BODY OF THIS MS. WAS WRITTEN AND LEFT MY HANDS IN FEBRUARY 1933. 40 PUBLISHERS HAVE REFUSED IT. NO TYPESCRIPT OF MINE HAS BEEN READ BY SO MANY PEOPLE OR BROUGHT ME A MORE INTERESTING CORRESPONDENCE.⁴

Critics believe the number forty to be an exaggeration, but there is no doubt that Pound had trouble finding a publisher for this text. In an April 1934 letter to Galeazzo Ciano (the Undersecretary for Press and Propaganda for Mussolini's regime, and also Mussolini's son-in-law), Pound claimed that Routledge's was the "thirty-fifth rejection" of the book, and that the editor said "The chief trouble is Pound's indiscriminate admiration of Mussolini, which he is not able to back up with much evidence, and which wd. be a far from popular doctrine to preach in this country at the moment."⁵ Pound dismissed the editor's assessment as "the Effect of ten years British newspaper slop," but he was clearly proud to be able to prove his admiration of Mussolini to Ciano.

Pound compensated for the interval between writing and publication by disseminating the ideas of *Jefferson and/or Mussolini* through other means. Indeed, the "Letter" included at the front of the first American edition (and originally published in British literary magazine *The Criterion*) testifies to his use of periodical publishing as a means of doing so. We can see from the articles collected in the eleven-volume periodical archive edited by Lea Baechler, Walton Litz, and James Longenbach the extent to which Pound repeated ideas in different articles, refining them in the process and getting them out to different audiences—probably a much wider audience than could have been reached by the thirty-copy first British edition of *Jefferson and/or Mussolini*.

It was just as important, though, that he used those ideas as the basis of letters to influential members of the Italian Fascist *Gerarchia*, those government officials and intellectuals who were employed in various ways by the regime to enrich and disseminate Mussolini's vision for Italy. This concept of "hierarchy" had become crucial to the workings of Fascism early on. In 1917, Mussolini had written in *Il Popolo d'Italia*:

> He who talks of "hierarchy" [*gerarchia*] means a scale of human values; he who talks of a scale of human values means a scale of responsibility and duties; he who talks of "hierarchy" means discipline. Above all, he who talks of "hierarchy" in reality takes up a fighting position against all those who tend—in spirit or in life—to lower or destroy the necessary ranks of society.[6]

This hierarchical structure was crucial to Fascist organization—of the government itself and of the corporations that integrated capital and labor.[7] It required a strong cadre of leaders within the government but below the "Capo," since "A hierarchy ought to culminate in a pin's point."[8] That the monthly review of political commentary published by *Il Popolo d'Italia* from 1922 to 1943 was titled *Gerarchia* shows that this concept could be used as a means of structure, valuation, and control in a wide range of cultural and bureaucratic matters.⁹

For Pound, the concept of *Gerarchia* proved immensely useful. In Chapter XXII of *Jefferson and/or Mussolini*, called "C'est toujours le beau monde qui gouverne," Pound closes a discussion of the cultural evidence of the reawakening in Italy by saying that "The term 'gerarchia' is perhaps the beginning of a critical sense, vide the four tiles and the dozen or so bits of insuperable pottery, pale blue on pale brownish ground, in the anteroom of the Palazzo Venezia."¹⁰ He refers here to newly recovered and recognized fragments of Italy's past cultural greatness, reclaimed by the Fascist government of the present and displayed in the seat of Mussolini's regime, evidence that "the conventionally recognized 'classic,' or accepted great works of the past" have been set aside in favor of "a greater exigence and precision with regard to antiquity" (*J/M*, 84). These newly treasured objects match the regime's selection of a new cadre of persons to form the *Gerarchia*, the new "beau monde." In May 1936, Pound wrote in the *Saturday Review*:

> The strong men AROUND Mussolini get very little attention and I have seen no attempt to understand the quality of their strength. In fact no one in England seems to understand that strength is perfectly compatible with respect for the opinions of the Head of the Government.¹¹

Similarly, in his essay "Ubicumque Lingua Romana" (1938), Pound emphasized that "the *best intellect* and the most straightforward human energies in Mussolini's Italy are *not* to be found among the provincial intelligentzia": rather, "The most intelligent men in Italy are in office or vividly interested in the official process, and in government work, they are to be found in the *Gerarchia*, or milling about it." He notes "a reserve of energetic Italians wholly unguessed by foreigners unfamiliar with Italy" who are "*interested* in corporate organization."[12] These men's involvement in government is crucial to Pound's conception of the Fascist regime, and it may be to his letters to members of the *Gerarchia* that Pound refers in his foreword when he notes, "NO TYPESCRIPT OF MINE HAS BEEN READ BY SO MANY PEOPLE OR BROUGHT ME A MORE INTERESTING CORRESPONDENCE." This correspondence continued even after the publication of *Jefferson and/or Mussolini*, but I suggest that the strategy Pound developed to compensate for the delays in its publication provided him a model of engagement with the Fascist hierarchs. By drawing together these various letters, showing their connection to Pound's developing ideas about the relationship between the state and culture, we can relate them to his growing comprehension of the role intellectuals played in Mussolini's government—a role he dearly wanted.

A selection of Pound's Italian correspondents from the 1930s and 1940s reads like a *Who's Who* of the Italian Fascist hierarchy. Correspondence with Camillo Pellizzi, contributor to *Civiltà Fascista*, professor at the University of London, and President of the National Institute of Fascist Culture (INCF), shows Pound working to disseminate his thoughts about Italian literature, but unwilling to change his program or his language to make himself better understood. There is also Margherita Sarfatti, art and cultural critic and biographer of Mussolini, leader and theorizer of the Novecento movement, editor (for a time) of the journal *Gerarchia*, and one of Mussolini's most trusted advisors (as well as his lover). Pound corresponded with her about developments in Italy's cultural mission and about ways of getting his ideas to Mussolini. Correspondence with Francesco Monotti, editor of *Bibliografia Fascista*, suggests connections between Pound's editing of Cavalcanti and the cultural projects of Mussolini's regime. In these letters, Monotti explained some of the workings of such Fascist-sponsored publications as *Gerarchia* and *Il Popolo d'Italia*. Pound wrote to Fascist journalist and minister Giuseppe Bottai, founder of *Critica Fascista*, minister of corporations in the early 1930s, and Minister of National Education from 1936 to 1943. Bottai was also the founder of the Bergamo Prize (awarded to artists working in modern styles) and the editor of the literary journal *Primato* (1940–43). To Bottai, Pound offered pedagogical suggestions about the teaching of Italian literature and the preservation of cultural monuments. Pound also corresponded with Roberto Farinacci, an important Blackshirt leader and advocate of *squadrismo*, as well as the editor of *Il Regime Fascista* (1926–33), an intermittent member of the Fascist Grand Council, and a leader of the brutal anti-Semitic crusade that followed the passing of the racial laws in 1938. Pound used their shared anxiety about the power of the Catholic Church and the Jewish "usuriocrazia" to begin a conversation about his willingness to serve the regime. Continuing attempts to get published in Italian papers led to correspondence (already mentioned above) with Galeazzo Ciano, and with Carlo Camagna, director of the press agency La Stefani. Pound even exchanged a few letters with Mussolini himself, and with Vito Mussolini, Benito's nephew and the editor of *Gerarchia* after Sarfatti's replacement. To all these people, active in the cultural aspects of Mussolini's government, Pound had plenty to offer. In offering ways of enriching the literary, musical, and historical culture of Italy, Pound shared with them the goal of building a culturally strong Italy, which he believed to be necessary not only to Italy's imperialist aims, but to peace and stability in Europe.

Many of Pound's letters express frustration that what he has to offer is rarely accepted. "I'd be perfectly willing to take orders," he noted in a letter to Ubaldo degli Uberti, editor of *La Marina Repubblicana*, "only as I am a damn yank, the Boss can't, and don't want to give me any."[13] In March 1935, he complained to economist Odon Por that "Mostly, when I try to write in Italian or give interviews[,] I come up against some local APE/[.] Gentile or Bottai might obviate that."[14] He tried to use Sarfatti's influence to secure a meeting with Mussolini in 1936, noting that "someone"—probably Por—had told him "that both the foreign office and the ministero Stampa 'are afraid' of me"—a prospect that seems to have pleased as much as frustrated Pound. He continued: "It is also suggested that I 'write direct' to the Capo del Gov. How the deuce CAN one write direct? When Polverelli was there, I had the feeling that IF I managed [to] say anything intelligent, it got through to the Capo."[15] Pound knew that Sarfatti understood the working of the Fascist hierarchy well enough to know "how to write direct," but he may not have known how tenuous was her position by this time, and that she was not likely to have burned what little capital she still had to get Pound's ideas to the Duce.[16]

Pound continued to seek access, complaining to Camillo Pellizzi in early 1937 that editors of Fascist publications "have ASKED for articles. I then write the articles, and the editors then relapse into SILENCE as so many pealess and terrified rabbits." He added, "Only thing of mine printed in TWO years in Italy, was bashed in Vita Italian[a] by Farinacci, just before he went to Africa."[17] In late 1939, Pound wrote directly to Farinacci, enumerating connections between his own cultural programs and those of Mussolini's government. Although Pound had acknowledged in April 1934 that "Farinacci is NOT the prevalent spirit" of Italian Fascism, he recognized his importance to the party and its ideology.[18] Pound understood Farinacci's strong anti-Semitic and anti-clerical views: his letters address the "usuriocrazia" dominating the American press, the recently republished *Jews at the Conquest of the World* by Osman Bey, and the relationships between Judaism and the Catholic Church.[19] About Farinacci's advocacy of *squadrismo* in the days before the March on Rome, Pound says, "Proclamations from Farinacci indicating that the proper way to remember the martyrs was to beat up all the working men in the district" (*J/M*, 53). Even so, Pound was disappointed not to secure an appointment with Farinacci, whom he believed to be a real man of action.

Pound wanted his own work towards raising the level of culture of the average "man on the street" to be useful in Italy, a part of Mussolini's plan for cementing national unity through culture. He wrote in "Ubicumque Lingua Romana":

> I can also tell the men of my own profession (that is students and writers) how I think they can and should form their guilds, or corporazioni, or whatever they wish to [c]all them. I have in my own way got results from associations, before one put a special name on them. I know as much as the next man about the nature of artists and writers and how it is possible to bring them together in the spirit of the fascio as I understand fascio, or union.[20]

In July 1934, Pound suggested to degli Uberti that he would be willing to translate his *ABC of Reading* into Italian if it would be published. He would make a translation *and* an Italian adaptation: "There is also my outline of the analogous list of essential authors for ITALIAN study/ that wd/ make a new chapter."[21] Expressing frustration to Sarfatti in February 1934 at his inability to get *Jefferson and/or Mussolini* published, Pound wrote, "My own educational campaign continues"—a campaign comprising the political and historical analysis of *Jefferson and/or Mussolini* and his writings on literature and economics. He suggested that his *ABC of Reading* could improve Italian schools:

> The ABC of Reading wd/ save a lot of TIME if it were put into USE. I mean in high schools and universities. (evidence of THAT; when it is printed, which is promised for April). Whether Italian Univs/ have entered the present epoch, or are any better than those in America, I must leave to people better informed than I am. The various diseases probably differ between countries.[22]

He hoped that Sarfatti, given her sense of Italy's cultural situation, would solicit a copy of his primer. As Redman has noted, that book (and the essay "How to Read" from which it is expanded) marks Pound's transition from poet to pamphleteer and "represents Pound's first systematic attempt to define the role of art in a well-ordered state."[23] It is important, then, that Pound recommended this book to Sarfatti, already his model of cultural administration: he wanted her to see that his writings about literature contribute to the functioning of the state.

Redman has noted that "precise verbal definition" provides the basis of Pound's sense of social order.[24] Indeed, Pound claims in *ABC of Reading* that "if a nation's literature declines, the nation atrophies and decays," and that:

> The man of understanding can no more sit quiet and resigned while his country lets its literature decay, and lets good writing meet with contempt, than a good doctor could sit quiet and contented while some ignorant child was infecting itself with tuberculosis under the impression that it was merely eating jam tarts. (*ABCR*, 32–33)

For Pound, "Good writers are those who keep the language efficient. That is to say, keep it accurate, keep it clear" (*ABCR*, 32). It is no surprise that his definition of good writing here accords with Sarfatti's own description of Mussolini's style, in her essay "Art and Fascism" (1928), where she emphasizes the Duce's spontaneity and clarity, as well as the sparseness and solidity of his language.[25] Mussolini exemplifies Pound's poetical equation, "Dichten = condensare," the idea that "Great literature is simply language charged with meaning to the utmost possible degree" (*ABCR*, 36). Exploiting the idea of *ABC of Reading* as a primer, Pound devotes exercises to teaching pupils to recognize the difference between needed and unnecessary words, as in this series of "Tests and Composition Exercises":

1. Let the pupils exchange composition papers and see how many and what useless words have been used—how many words that convey nothing new.
2. How many words that obscure the meaning.
3. How many words out of their usual place, and whether this alteration makes the statement in any way more interesting or more energetic.
4. Whether a sentence is ambiguous; whether it really means more than one thing or more than the writer intended; whether it can be so read as to mean something different.
5. Whether there is something clear on paper, but ambiguous if spoken aloud. (*ABCR*, 64–65)

If the book were adopted in Italy, as Pound recommended, these exercises should have led a critical student to appreciate and even emulate Mussolini's spare style and his sentences' hard edges, helping move the masses towards a Fascist style.

Given the connections Pound could see between literary language and its political usage, the elision of Mussolini and poetry is no surprise.[26] Sarfatti herself explains the political importance of such language, particularly in an era of change:

> Revolutions in every domain of religion, society, philosophy, and art are made by altering the watchword. They are made by launching a new watchword first within the governing elites and then by extending it to the mob: a watchword that stops them, surprises them, makes them reflect, and places them under the spell of action.
>
> Simplicity, concision, and clarity of thought and expression are the great watchwords for the artistic style of a new regime, of a renewed nation.[27]

Her sense of the crucial role of language in making an idea compelling is a more rhetorically focused version of Pound's remark in *ABCR* that "Your legislator can't legislate for the public good, your commander can't command, your populace (if you be a democratic country) can't instruct its representatives save by language" (*ABCR*, 32). Yes, Pound's statement assumes the working of a democratic society, while Sarfatti describes the working of hierarchical structure, whereby the linguistic power of the elite can shape the lower classes, but both recognize the power of language in a political context like that of Mussolini's Italy, and they value the role of the writer—be he a journalist, critic, or poet—in preserving language's power. It is no wonder that Pound thought his textbook could help the Fascist cause.

Similarly, in October 1934, Pound comments to Sarfatti, "In view of the Milan Speech on Saturday, mightn't it now be the time for translating my 'ABC of Economics' into Italian?"[28] That speech, Pound claimed, was a sort of obituary for Scarcity Economics, and it drew Pound's attention. He wrote numerous letters about it, one of which was published in *The Criterion* and then became a preface to *Jefferson and/or Mussolini*:

> On Oct. 6th of the year current (anno XII) between 4 P.M. and 4–30 Mussolini speaking very clearly four or five words at a time, with a pause, quite a long pause, between phrases, to let it sink in, told 40 million Italians together with auditors in the U.S.A. and the Argentine that the problem of production was solved, and that they could now turn their minds to distribution.[29]

From here he enters a lengthy discussion where, in addition to lamenting the fact that the ideas in *Jefferson and/or Mussolini* were falling out of date because of delays in its acceptance and publication, Pound declares Scarcity Economics dead, thanks to Mussolini's speech. Pound even gives a close redaction of Mussolini's speech, justifying himself by comparing Mussolini's speech to Brâncuşi's perfect sculpture, whose work he frequently celebrated.[30] Pound saw his own writings as a part of the Fascist project, and so wanted them available to a wide audience.

Pound had made a similar offer of educational reform to Mussolini himself in November 1933. A history of Italian literature had enraged Pound because of its old-fashioned tendency not to read Italian literature in an international context. Such an approach, he wrote in what Francesco Monotti called his "inimitable Italian," denies the real merits and importance of Italian writers. As a solution to this pedagogical problem, Pound offered the Duce a five-page curriculum of the history of Italian literature, which made explicit connections between works of important writers and larger cultural and international movements.[31] He does not seem to have received a response.

That lack of response did not hinder his enthusiasm. He continued to argue for literature, language, and the other arts as a crucial part of Italian—and Fascist—culture. "Confound it," he said to degli Uberti in May 1936, "Italian LITERATURE oughtn't to be the LAST department of Italian life to rub its eyes, sit up and take notice that something is going ON."[32] From his focus on the cultural projects of the regime, he knew that while Mussolini did not have time to focus on matters of culture and literature, he was wise enough to have others in his government who did. And Pound wanted to make sure that the regime's approach to culture and literature was a smart one, and not a replication of the problems of the American academy or of intelligentsia in general. Pound made a similar pitch to Pellizzi at about the same time, saying, "No sense in wasting ANOTHER decennio. You might do the job on yr/ own. but a FEW people cd. be gathered for a CONSCIOUS renovation of literature IN Italy."[33] It is no surprise, given Pound's investment in the notion of the cultural heritage, that he saw literary work and project of empire intertwined. "All very well to start an IMPERO," he commented to degli Uberti in May 1936, "But what about having some art AND letters DEL IMPERO?"³⁴ As late as August 1940, he would still be lamenting in Italian to degli Uberti that the power of the Italian language was diminishing, having dropped off rapidly after the death of Dante: to allow the language so to stagnate hindered Italy and Italian power.³⁵ Given the attention that had been paid by the regime to cultural affairs, he was not wrong to hope that his concerns might be shared.

By the end of 1936, Pound was again thinking of a curriculum and was ready to send it off to Giuseppe Bottai, if Odon Por would establish a connection for him. "ANY use trying some of my CULTURAL work on him," he asked, going on to explain links between his edition of Cavalcanti and the regime's educational projects. "After all," he noted to Por, "I have 30 years work on that sort of thing behind me if you count from graduation in 1905." He offers:

Three ~~TWO~~ items for Bottai/
1. ~~Decent~~ Modern system for study of inedited mss/ in Italian libraries/
    CULTURAL HERITAGE
    Valorization of cultural heritage.
2. Real history of the U. S. A. ; not the capitalist fakes now in use. from fasc. views pt. including econ. hist
3. AS BEFORE submitted to that dumb bunny on Civ.Fas. a reorganization of literary criticism ; hist. etc. on basis that the Italian peninsula need not FEAR comparison with product of other geographic areas or tribal uniks.

yr deevoted Kulturmench Ez. P.³⁶

Here is a continuation of Pound's emphasis on the preservation and *use* of the Italian cultural heritage—literature, history, architecture, and music. He noted in December 1935 in a letter to Carlo Camagna that Olga Rudge, whom he credits as "the real founder of our Rapallo concerts … has started a work for the valorization of the Italian heritage in music, analogous to that which I have done in my edition of Guido Cavalcanti."[37] As his *Guido Cavalcanti Rime* had been a foray into the Fascist cultural Nationalist project, his work on Vivaldi made a similar contribution: both could be models for bringing Italian archival materials into a modern Fascist Italian culture.

Because of his work with unpublished musical manuscripts, musical heritage was a focus of Pound's letters. In the spring of 1937, he wrote letters to Benito Mussolini and to his son Vito, by then the editor of *Gerarchia*, arguing for the necessity of microphotographic editions of musical manuscripts—an issue central to his revival of Vivaldi. In his letter to Vito, Pound notes that this enormous cultural treasure of Italian music lies buried in libraries, citing the 309 concerti of Vivaldi that Rudge had catalogued in Turin.[38] Part of the issue for Pound is the preservation of these unique materials, in case of fire or other damage to the repository in which they are stored. He would continue his discussion with Bottai in 1939, noting the importance of preserving unique materials and suggesting transatlantic conversations with archivists at the Library of Congress.[39] But it was just as important, he argued, that this heritage not lie dormant in archives. Instead, it should be employed by actual musicians in actual performance—both so that it could be known by those interested in Italian culture and so that it could contribute to the making of new music in a modern, or even Fascist style.[40] For Pound, the rediscovery of this Italian musical heritage is analogous to the unearthings in the regime's archaeological projects. If Mussolini's people could reassemble the pieces of the Ara Pacis—and build a modern structure to house it—then why could they not do the same for Italy's musical heritage? As he noted to Por in July 1940, Pound was all in favor of this clearing out:

> … the sooner Rome is beautified by the removal of that other square building last eye sore down towards S.Maria in Cosmedin, the better.

>   on pewerly AESTHETIC grounds.
> no I cant draw it. you know the one I mean. = defect in architectural sense. It is not OF the Era fascista.⁴¹

The revival of valuable parts of Italy's heritage must go hand in hand with a rejection of those ugly structures that block the view of the glorious past and the building of the Fascist present. That Pound was making the same claims in his correspondence that he made in his prose shows how determined he was to be heard.

Pound hoped that the publication of *Jefferson and/or Mussolini* could serve as credential, making clear to his Italian Fascist correspondents his seriousness about enriching Italy's cultural and economic situation. Writing to Carlo Camagna, director of the press agency La Stefani, in February 1935, Pound noted that *Jefferson and/or Mussolini* was now out in America, and that he had written in that book that "Jefferson's political CONSTRUCTION outlasted Napoleons by over a century BECAUSE Jefferson was thinking those things contained in Chapter XXX of my Jeff/Mussolini."⁴² In that chapter he emphasizes that Jefferson's writing about the political and economic situations of his time demonstrate a "well-developed sense of the *gerarchia* (hierarchy) in nature" (*J/M*, 116). That Pound uses the Italian term for "hierarchy," also the label for the regime leadership, shows that he is thinking not just of the vertically hierarchical structure of Fascism, but also of the centrality of a cadre of intelligent and well-equipped leaders. These are the people Pound wants to join.

Pound had some difficulty getting his writing published in the Italian press. Editors insisted that he make it comprehensible to a broad Italian audience, but Pound vehemently refused to simplify his ideas. In January 1937, Camillo Pellizzi offered Pound an opportunity, noting that the young and intelligent in Italy are "rather provinciali and apt to think worlds of the Bloomsbury and similar sets." Pellizzi worried that such thinking made them vulnerable to ideas from Moscow, and suggested that Pound could offer an alternative by telling Italian readers what he thinks based on his experiences in modern Italy.

Pellizzi believed that such an essay would encourage people, because Pound would be expressing his views honestly.[43]

Three years later, Por even tried in 1940 to get Pound an opportunity to publish an article in *Civiltà Fascista*, but Pellizzi would not publish the article that Pound submitted. Por explained that he did not think what Pound had submitted was something a broad set of readers could understand.[44] Pound responded with irritation:

> Pel/ asks me to write down my IDEAS. I send a syllabus or catalogue, and ask which PART of the subject he thinks can be useful.
>
> 'A clear article "people" can understand' !! WHAT people ?
>
> I am not a kindergarten department.
>
> A 'CULTURA' is made up of various elements. A curriculum is ordinarily DIVIDED into various subjects. BUT in a CULTURE these subjects have some relation to each other, in fact they all emerge from a basic philosophy; which causes modifications, i.e. the life pushes out the dead parts of the decayed precedent condition. Of course IF the universities are NOT expected to change their bunk, it merely means that they, and the schools are NOT OF the present culture.[45]

Pellizzi wrote directly to Pound as well, explaining that the piece was too short and incomprehensible to the readers of *Civiltà Fascista*. He encouraged Pound to explain his ideas more clearly, and try to write more with Italian readers in mind.[46] Pound responded almost immediately, defending his approach and refusing to temper his message to any specific audience. He notes that what he is giving is a "FIRST draft or sketch for the pamphlet," and that "It is not a WHOLE curriculum." He adds, "Some, in fact most, of the items wd/ have to be studied by whatever Italian profs/ were to water 'em down, and get 'em into shape for the Italian class room/ THAT certainly is not my job." He likens his role to that of an artistic visionary who has apprentices to flesh out the details:

> Also (damn it) I am not expected to teach kindergarten but to stimulate a movement , i;e; five or six younger men who can fill in the design/ alle same 'school OF Nic. del Cossa' etc. somebody to design the fresco, and the pupils to putt on the pink=wash, blue=wash, green wash, inside the demarcations.

He finishes by expressing frustration at the ignorance of his anticipated audience, and wondering how he can bring them from that point to where he believes they need to go: "How the hell can I tell what THEY dont know? I dont want to tell 'em Cicero was a latin author and Columbus went to America."[47] He believed he could not succeed in "stimulating a movement" this way, but by refusing to modify his writings—to reach the "man on the street" he claimed to want to educate—he lost the chance to publish on these topics.

Pound did succeed in disseminating some of his ideas from *Jefferson and/or Mussolini* in the Italian press. In the 1930s, his ideas and writings appeared in *L'Indice* and *Giornale di Genova* (Genova); *L'Ambrosiano, Libro e Moschetto,* and *Almanacco Letterario* (Milan); *L'Avvenire d'Italia* (Bologna); *La Vita Italiana, Meridiano di Roma, AntiEuropa, Prospettive,* and *Rassegna Monetaria* (Rome); *Broletto* (Como); *La Stampa* (Turin), and of course *Il Mare* (Rapallo, where many of these publications concerned the Tigullian Studies concerts). He addressed the archaeological restorations being undertaken throughout Italy, the need for a refining of the Italian language, his sense of an Italian awakening and the importance of a pamphlet culture to that awakening, his understanding of the relationships between Jefferson and Mussolini, and the importance of state-sponsored exhibitions of art—and especially modern art—to the Italian scene.[48] Certainly Pound would continue to publish in Italy as long as he lived there, but the early 1930s represent a flurry of publications in Italian and for Italians, closely related to the ideas written, but not yet published, in *Jefferson and/or Mussolini*. By the early 1940s, Pound's Italian publications, especially in *Meridiano di Roma*, would skyrocket, far surpassing publications in English. Nevertheless, compared with what he would have liked to publish in Italy—and with the enormous number of English-language publications in the United States and Great Britain—his publications were hardly extensive enough to satisfy a hopeful *gerarch*.

Pound's correspondence, when read together, represents a clear and coordinated effort to become a part of the small corps of Fascist hierarchs, a cultural elite driving the entire Fascist project. We can further see from these letters—from the temerity of replies, from the rejection of articles, from the ignoring of published works—the growing frustration and intransigence that Pound felt in response to his work and ideas being rejected (or more often ignored) by the Party. This lack of success led him in interesting directions, however. One, of course, was his move to radio, once a broadcasting opportunity was offered. Through his broadcasts on Radio Rome, we know Pound thought he could reach not just audiences within Italy, but also abroad.

But this lack of success also led him to take on his own cultural endeavors, to become a real cultural administrator. We already saw his plan from 1936 to make Rapallo an international center of culture; he offered at that time, as the prime example of how this could happen, the Tigullian Studies venture. That project, of course, was his work with Olga Rudge (and sometimes Gerhart Münch and Alfredo Casella) to revive the music of Antonio Vivaldi. In some ways, it functioned as a consolation—a means of contributing to the Fascist revival of Italian cultural heritage, despite the lukewarm response he received from the actual Fascist *Gerarchia*. If Pound could not become an actual part of that *Gerarchia*, then he could expand its mission to include work under his own control. Whatever the motivation of the Tigullian Studies venture, it would represent his greatest contribution to the cultural heritage of Fascist Italy.

CHAPTER 5

The Fascist Cultural Nationalism of the Vivaldi Revival

> We lit our little spark four years ago during the days of the sanctions. We have mentioned a Vivaldi-Bach axis, and we could also, if necessary, proclaim a musical autarchy of our own.
>
> —Ezra Pound[1]

Through the music of Antonio Vivaldi, Ezra Pound could become a cultural administrator for Mussolini's Fascist regime, reviving modern Italian culture through its rich cultural heritage. Since the early 1930s, Pound had been working with German composer Gerhart Münch and American violinist Olga Rudge (Pound's lover and the mother of his daughter) to offer innovative concerts in Rapallo. They called these concerts "Tigullian Studies," after the Gulf of Tigullio on whose coast Rapallo lies, and the programs featured Münch and Rudge and whatever traveling musicians—often very well known—were in town. Pound helped to choose the music, produced publicity, and introduced the pieces and their history. As we shall see, he also produced much of the Vivaldi material the Tigullians performed. Originally, the Tigullians were interested in Vivaldi as a source of new material, but as they began to discover his unknown music, they invested in Vivaldi for his own sake.

As hard as it is to imagine the world of classical music without Antonio Vivaldi, his work was largely unknown until the 1930s. Now we know of over 770 works by him, but when Olga Rudge and Ezra Pound began looking for music to perform in Rapallo, only about 100 pieces were known. Thanks in part to the work of Stephen J. Adams, Anne Conover Carson, Giulio de Angelis, Archie Henderson, and R. Murray Schafer, we know a great deal about Rudge's and Pound's efforts toward reviving Vivaldi's work.[2] Pound's actual work with the music for these concerts and the significance of his investment in them to his larger attempts to become a part of the cultural Nationalist projects of Fascist Italy have not previously been addressed. We have seen how desperately Pound wanted to contribute to the Fascist project, and Italy's musical heritage offered the opportunity. Here I examine those efforts in the light of new archival material, a sense of composer Alfredo Casella's work with Vivaldi, and the wider context of Fascist cultural Nationalism, to demonstrate that for Pound, this work was the culmination of a decade's desire to act as a Fascist cultural administrator. Casella's own Nationalist musical aims offer important parallels to Pound's, so the first part of this chapter explores the conversation between his work and that of Pound and Rudge. The chapter's second half delves into the archive of Pound and Rudge's Vivaldi materials to demonstrate how involved Pound was in the musical aspects of the Tigullian Studies venture and how his musical work connected to his investment in Fascist cultural Nationalism.

Within a few decades of his death in 1741, Vivaldi had all but fallen into oblivion. His work was primarily known through keyboard transcriptions of about ten of his concerti by J. S. Bach: because Bach's reputation was firmly established, his interest in Vivaldi testified to the Italian composer's value.[3] The entry in *Grove's Dictionary of Music and Musicians* (1928)—replaced by Rudge's entry in the edition of 1940—made a common assertion:

"Vivaldi in fact mistook the facility of an expert performer (and as such he had few rivals among contemporaries) for the creative faculty, which he possessed but in a limited degree."[4]

But between the wars, Italians were eager to rediscover their cultural past, and Vivaldi started finding his way back into concert halls. The article "Una nuova antica gloria musicale italiana: Antonio Vivaldi" (1919) by Alceo Toni, mediocre composer and music critic for *Il Popolo d'Italia*, is considered by musicologist Michael Talbot to mark the beginning of the Italian Vivaldi revival.[5] Of particular interest was the music of the seventeenth and eighteenth centuries—music that had fallen by the way during the nineteenth-century symphonic explosion in Italian music. The earliest real initiator of this revival was Giovanni Sgambati (1841–1914), who through his composing and conducting worked not only to deprovincialize the Italian musical climate but also to bring older Italian music back into the repertoire. Vivaldi fared well in concerts given by the Accademia di Santa Cecilia and elsewhere during this period.[6] Still, the renditions of Vivaldi's music being performed in Rome were hardly philologically "accurate." As Cesare Fertonani has shown, Bernardino Molinari's sumptuous orchestrations (e.g., sixteen first violins) had many personal and modern twists to them, such as his rendition of the continuo by the combination of a harpsichord and an organ, or his rewriting of entire movements. Ultimately, performances of Vivaldi's music made the Venetian composer familiar to audiences, even if that meant adjusting his music to expectations of late nineteenth-century Italian opera audiences.[7]

In 1926, the number of known Vivaldi compositions grew dramatically when the National Library in Turin, with funding from Roberto Foà, acquired a large collection of Vivaldi manuscripts. Alberto Gentili, a composer, director, and musicologist lecturing at Turin University, had quickly identified them as half of Vivaldi's personal collection of his own music, and in 1930, with funding from Filippo Giordano, the library acquired the other half.[8] This is the collection of manuscripts that Olga Rudge began exploring in 1935, searching for music to perform in Rapallo and later for the purpose of cataloguing the manuscripts themselves.

In *Guide to Kulchur* (1938), Pound used this collection to lament how little of the musical past is presently known: "With 309 concerti of Vivaldi unplayed, lying in Turin as I write this, it is as useless as it wd. be idiotic to write of musical culture in Europe" (237). Elsewhere he offers similar concern: "Nobody, in 1938, knows anything of Vivaldi. A few (less than six) scholars have approximately respectable ideas of his compositions. Not one of them has even read through all of his compositions. You cd. probably read most of it in Turin and Dresden" (*GK*, 150). A response to *Guide to Kulchur*, published in the *Musical Times* in November 1938, affirms Pound's assessment. The writer "Feste" doubts Pound's count of 309 concerti and his belief in their quality: "Someone ought to look into this matter of Vivaldi's output. According to 'Grove' he wrote only about seventy concertos. And—*pace* Mr. Pound, who is a warm Vivaldian—most of us who know those that Bach arranged will say that seventy are probably sixty too many."[9] It would not be until well after the Second World War that scholars and musicians gained a real sense of Vivaldi's works.

Olga Rudge would later make important contributions to a separate venture celebrating Vivaldi's music. Called the "Settimana Celebrativa di Antonio Vivaldi," or "Vivaldi Week," this series of concerts was held at Siena's Accademia Musicale Chigiana in September 1939 under the musical direction of the composer Alfredo Casella. Rudge was working as secretary for the Accademia, and Stephen Adams has shown that she deserves some credit for the structure of the Siena concerts—their use of comparative material and their focus on many pieces by a single composer.[10] Additionally, on the occasion of this festival, she published the first thematic catalogue of Vivaldi's works in Turin—a project whose design and objectives will be discussed later in this chapter.[11] While Vivaldi had previously been known only as a composer of instrumental music, the Siena concerts included sacred choral music and the first performances of Vivaldi's opera *L'Olimpiade* (1734) since his death, as well as two keyboard transcriptions of Vivaldi's concerti by Bach. Casella insisted on presenting Vivaldi's music as faithfully as possible, to get a real sense of eighteenth-century musical norms and tastes. Because Casella's own engagement with Italy's musical heritage mirrors Pound's, the following section describes the contribution of his musical compositions and curatorial work to Fascist cultural Nationalism.

Alfredo Casella's musical nationalism

Like Ezra Pound's, Alfredo Casella's work to revive Antonio Vivaldi's music was motivated in part by his sense of cultural Nationalism. His interest in Vivaldi is no surprise, given his other attempts to revive earlier Italian musical culture in the name of creating an Italian musical modernism. Although Casella was often criticized by fellow composers for being anti-Nationalist, his motivations often align with those of Margherita Sarfatti, Mario Sironi, and Giuseppe Terragni, all of whom looked simultaneously to Italy's past and to a wider European culture to bring new energy to Italy's cultural scene. Sarfatti, who acted as an art critic, patron, and booster under Mussolini's regime, dreamed of a "second Italian Renaissance that would restore the supremacy of her nation's art and return the center of the art world from France to Italy."[12] She saw Italian modern art as part of a conversation that included artists from throughout Europe. At the same time, however, in an article supporting the objectives of the Novecento group, she wrote in 1921, "Originality and tradition are not contradictory terms. By returning to the purest traditions of Giottos, Masaccios, Paolo Uccellos, one does not renounce the originality of modern times, but only polishes off the rust and purifies our art of imitative alloys."[13] Gianfranco Vinay has argued that Casella's vision of modernism cuts a "third way" between a "conservative, traditionalist and provincial tendency towards melodrama" and an "international avant-garde modernism," as advanced by Schoenberg. That third way conjoined tradition (ancient, or at least pre-Romantic) with modernism (Italian, and therefore tempered).[14] Pound recognized in Casella a kindred spirit, writing in 1937:

> Back before the war Alfredo Casella started educating the Roman, and thence the Italian, public in modern music. At once the most competent of living Italian composers, an unrivaled teacher, an impeccable orchestral conductor and that far rarer thing a creative musician with a wide interest in other men's work and utter impartiality in judging it, Casella gave, first for a handful of Romans, the best modern compositions.[15]

Perhaps in part because of the similarity of their ambition, and in part because of their shared field of study, Casella became for Pound and Rudge a leading competitor.

Casella was a native of the Piemonte, born in 1883 in Turin, and his early cultural allegiances were more to Paris than Rome. He studied in Paris from 1896 to 1914, gaining exposure to the musical trends embodied by such composers as Maurice Ravel, Gabriel Fauré, Gustav Mahler, Claude Debussy, Béla Bartók, and Igor Stravinsky. He distanced himself from nineteenth-century Italian musical culture, as represented by Giuseppe Verdi and characterized by romanticism and melodrama. He was, however, aware of other artists' attempts to modernize Italian culture. About the publication of F. T. Marinetti's "The Founding and the Manifesto of Futurism" in 1909, he said, "It seemed the announcement of a new and greater Italy," adding that it "was the only Italian artistic movement between 1870 and 1914 which received world-wide attention and had universal influence."[16] Like the Futurists, he had originally wanted to separate modern music from its immediate predecessors: in 1913 he published an article rejecting the romanticism of Verdi.

He would later retract that rejection with the statement, "A truce has thus been made with the preceding century"—a statement not unlike Pound's reconciliation with Walt Whitman in "A Pact" (1913).[17] Casella's first explicitly Nationalist piece, *Italia* (1909), used national folk material as a way of creating national music, but he acknowledged that his 1913 setting of Giosuè Carducci's "Notte di maggio" borrowed from Claude Debussy and Igor Stravinsky, rather than Italian tradition.[18] Casella's engagement with Italian tradition and with a wider European musical avant-garde would come to define his particular style.

After the First World War, Casella returned to Italy, living in Rome. There was at that time a significant cultural distance between the Piemonte and Lazio regions—the kind that made unifying national identity difficult and which Mussolini's cultural ministers were trying to diminish. Casella emphasized the "ethnocentric pride" of the "Roman of Rome," noting that "Foreigners and even other Italians would collide with an atavistic indifference toward everything which was not Roman, for the simple reason that nothing greater could ever exist in the world." As a Piemontese, he "found it more problematical to come to Rome than to stay abroad, considering the differences in character, in customs, and in manners."[19] Aiming to revive Italian musical culture, he sought control of the Roman weekly *Musica*, attempting unsuccessfully to make it an agent of Italian musical change.[20] With composers Ottorino Respighi, Ildebrando Pizzetti, and Gian Francesco Malipiero, in 1917 he founded the National Music Society, later renamed the Italian Modern Music Society (Società Italiana di Musica Moderna or SIMM), whose goal was "performing the most interesting music of the young Italians, resurrecting our old forgotten music, printing the most interesting new compositions, publishing a periodical, and organizing a system of exchanging new music with the principal foreign countries." The group's detractors called it "a nest of 'futurists.'"[21] Casella's work toward cultural revival brought him in contact with many important artists and intellectuals outside the realm of music. In December 1917 he founded the "polemical journal" *Ars Nova*, whose contributors included Giovanni Papini, Carlo Carrà, Giorgio de Chirico, and Mario Broglio. That these writers had already embarked on their own missions to revive and modernize Italy demonstrates Casella's involvement in the same strains of cultural Nationalism already examined here. Although the journal had a brief run, Casella compared it to the Florentine journal *Lacerba*, literary offspring of *La Voce*, and concluded that it "accomplished in its field a much needed cultural advance."[22]

In September 1923, Casella and Malipiero joined with Gabriele D'Annunzio to form the "New Music Corporation" (Corporazione delle Nuove Musiche or CDNM), which would perform new music and revive old music, especially the work of Claudio Monteverdi. The organization lasted five years, bringing Béla Bartók and Paul Hindemith to Italy (composers Pound aspired to lure to Rapallo), performing Stravinsky's *L'Histoire du Soldat* and *Octet for Wind Instruments* for the first time in Italy, presenting a multi-city tour of Arnold Schoenberg's *Pierrot Lunaire*, and playing music by Maurice Ravel, Francis Poulenc, Respighi, Malipiero, Ernest Bloch, Ernst Křenek, Zoltán Kodály, and others.[23] Casella connected the CDNM to other internationalizing strands of Italian cultural Nationalism: "Futurism, *La Voce*, *Lacerba*, *Valori Plastici*, the New Music Corporation were the major attempts in the last quarter century to deprovincialize our art."[24] Casella's contextualization of his own work amidst the better-known cultural Nationalist work of a wider group of Italian artists and intellectuals demonstrates how interconnected these various cultural strands were in Italy at the time. Pound knew Casella's work, comparing it to his own in an otherwise unpublished press release he sent to Ethel de Courcy Duncan in November 1933:

> This determination [at Tigullio] to have nothing but the best coincides with a manifesto of Alfredo Casella written from the fascist angle and declaring that certain kinds of

bad music are no longer tolerable, Casella with usual tact refrains from being very specific and calls the condem[n]ed stuff 'music of the small bourgeoisie' which allows even Giordano and co. to suppose he doesn't mean them, but at any rate the demand for a tidying up of the Italian critical sense appears to be growing.[25]

Pound could emulate figures like Casella, who employed a Fascist stance to improve Italian culture, even though he was criticized by other Italian composers for being too reliant on foreign tendencies.[26] Nevertheless, Casella shared terms with Fascist cultural critics, and had openly declared Fascist sympathies by 1926. Like many artists of the period, he saw no conflict in belonging to the Fascist artistic hierarchy and musical avant-garde.

Building on the CDNM's work to revive Monteverdi, in 1926 Casella wrote two pieces that bring Italian tradition into modern music. *Scarlattiana* draws on motifs from sonatas by Domenico Scarlatti (1685–1787) to create "a divertimento for piano and small orchestra," which Casella considered "a product of the combination of the personalities of Scarlatti and a musician of two centuries later."[27] In one respect, Casella followed the directive of Fascist journalist and later Minister of National Education Giuseppe Bottai, who wrote in 1927 that "Fascist art" should look to "the great autochthonous traditions of Italian art," but Casella's music did not throw off the "incrustations of foreign artistic movements" that Bottai denounced.[28] The piece is a "recomposition" in the spirit of Igor Stravinsky's *Pulcinella* (1922)—the ballet commissioned by Sergei Diaghilev for the Ballets Russes and composed based on older pieces written by Giovanni Battista Pergolesi (1710–36) and other Italian composers.[29] In combining these elements, Casella was like many other Italian modernists who allied their aims with the Fascist regime's.

Written in the same year, *Roman Concerto* was Casella's "first attempt to achieve a style … baroque in its monumentality." For

Casella, the baroque—his way of naming the neo-classical—was an explicitly *Roman* form, given the predominance of baroque architecture in that capital city and the style's derivation from ancient models. He identified the baroque style with "musicians like Bach and Vivaldi, whose disciple I had been for so many years," but relied on a sense of the architecture to explain the style:

> That sense of relief in the masses, in the mouldings, in the chiaroscuro, which goes back directly to the greatest Roman art; that liberty and fantasy in interpreting the classic forms; the grandeur of this purely Italian art which became international through the enormous influence it exerted over all of Europe.[30]

Casella's explanation of historical models parallels the modern emphasis on neo-classical and baroque music that Fiamma Nicolodi describes as a means of creating a uniquely Italian modernism.[31] Although Casella called the baroque Roman—linking it to the long magnificent history of Roman architecture and its particular deployment during the Counter-Reformation—the style typifies the architecture of his native Turin as well, creating an *Italianità* that combines the two.

Roman Concerto combines features of the monumental baroque with elements borrowed from Stravinsky. As if deliberately imitating the opening of *The Firebird* (1910), the piece begins in e-flat minor with a progression of notes in the low strings that could very well have earned Casella his reputation for copying Stravinsky. As in *The Firebird*, those notes gradually rise into the higher string parts. Stravinsky's piece overlays repeating progressions of notes in regular rhythms, continuously and coherently building until the third section, about five minutes in, when the firebird appears in a burst of high strings, pursued by Ivan Tsarevitch. Casella's piece opens with a direct echo of Stravinsky's haunting beginning, albeit with more changes in time signature; by the twelfth measure he brings in high strings, building tension similarly to Stravinsky's piece. At the twenty-sixth measure, however, the piece shifts abruptly, changing to a bright E-flat major key signature, and introducing the solo organ part with a big E-flat major chord. That organ part distinguishes the *Roman Concerto* from such earlier compositions of Casella as the *Elegia eroica* (1916): the latter, written in memory of a soldier killed in the First World War, retains the Stravinskian idiom throughout. The *Roman Concerto* continues to blend the counterpoint and arpeggios of the baroque and the chordal and melodic progressions to which Stravinsky has accustomed modern ears. Nevertheless, Casella claimed that the piece had "an indisputably Italian style … in which is glimpsed, rather than the influence of this or that foreign master, the old ancestral shadows of Frescobaldi, Monteverdi, Vivaldi, Scarlatti, or Rossini."[32] The Rome that the piece imagines is a bright mixture of old and new, of ancient heritage and modern innovation.

Like the Mussolini's government's deployment of archaeology to connect Rome's classical heritage to the modern Fascist state, Casella made his music at once modern and traditional.[33] And, like the modernism practiced by the painters of the Novecento group, Casella's music looks both across the Alps and into the Italian past for source material. Moreover, like the Roman Empire, and Mussolini's ambitions, the baroque style that Casella championed was one that, he claimed, had originated in Rome and then spread throughout Europe. Casella continued his work toward reviving the music of the Italian baroque, researching in the summer of 1934 at the Library of Congress in Washington, DC, manuscripts of music by Luigi Boccherini (1743–1805), Muzio Clementi (1752–1832), Antonio Vivaldi (1678–1741), Giovanni Battista Sammartini (c. 1700–75), and Felice Giardini (1716–96), reproductions of which he took back to Italy.[34] Elsewhere, he celebrated Mussolini's imperial efforts in Ethiopia and the regime's backing of work toward musical renewal "through various ministerial portfolios, union enterprises, and subsidies and prizes of every type;

through assistance conceded to the operatic and symphonic arts; and through the rigorous control [he exercised] over musical 'exports.'" Like Pound, Casella thought Mussolini deserved much of the credit for the success of Fascism's cultural renewal, praising the leader for "having understood how to make each of us feel the worker's sense of proud noble awareness that each of us [is] adding his stone to the majestic edifice of the new fascist order."[35]

And as Pound did in Rapallo, Casella served as artistic director for the Vivaldi Week in Siena, preparing much of the music for the concerts. Cesare Fertonani calls Casella's Vivaldi transcriptions music some of the most ambiguous of the period, presenting conflicting desires to respect the original text while reviving them according to the best understanding of the time. The result is that Casella's transcriptions sometimes "restore" the music by adding elements, and sometimes adhere to the manuscript.[36] Casella was a pioneer in bringing to light unpublished and unknown pieces—such as the *Gloria* (RV589), now a centerpiece of the choral repertoire.[37] Thus, Casella served as a model of sorts and as something to push against. Pound could admire Casella's "third way" of Nationalist composition, and could appreciate that his music was made in service of the Fascist state. He could also envy Casella the greater recognition he received as a composer. This is not to say that Pound modeled the Tigullian Studies venture on Casella's work. Rather, Pound's awareness of Casella and his negotiation of the relationships between his own work and Casella's exemplify Pound's different approach to serving as a Fascist cultural administrator.

The cultural Nationalism of the Tigullian Studies venture

By the time the Vivaldi Week came together in Siena in 1939, Pound, Münch, and Rudge had been working for some time on the Venetian composer. The Vivaldi work grew out of their

20. Cover of program, "Concerto dalla Collezione Chilesotti," November 1933. (Olga Rudge Papers, Yale Collection of American Literature, Beinecke Rare Book and Manuscript Library, by permission of New Directions Publishing Corporation)

performances of Mozart's violin sonatas in 1933, and in 1934 of Münch's transcriptions of ancient music from the manuscript collection of musicologist Oscar Chilesotti.[38] The group was given access to the collection in the hopes that they could bring to light some of the sixteenth- and seventeenth-century music collected (largely in tablatures) by Chilesotti, who had died in 1916. Gerhart Münch arranged a number of important pieces, and among those performed in 1933 were Francesco da Milano's lute version of Janequin's *Chants des Oiseaux* and Jean Bésard's "Branle del villaggio," a piece Pound called "Stravinsky-like."[39]

The cover design of the program for these concerts incorporates the *fascio*, emphasizing that this exploration of Italian musical heritage was undertaken in service of Fascist art, and a Fascist nation (Fig. 20). Pound wrote that this work "has produced … a real addition to the whole body of existing music. In fact, we have a new sonata, obtained via Chilesotti's collection, which would have remained sterile but for Münch's discrimination and enterprise."[40] He refers here to Münch's violin transcription of the Janequin, whose score would become the bulk of his Canto 75. With this claim, Pound connects the Tigullians' work with that of cultural figures like Casella, who used older Italian cultural heritage to create new art for a modern Fascist state, the painters of the Novecento school emulating Giotto and Piero della Francesca, or architects imitating ancient Roman buildings discovered in excavations at Ostia. "We must not remain solely contemplatives," Mussolini had said to the students of the Academy of Fine Arts in Perugia in early October 1926. "We must not simply exploit our cultural heritage. We must create a new heritage to place alongside that of antiquity. We must create a new art, an art of our times: a Fascist art."[41] Through Münch's transcription, new music grew from the material in the Chilesotti collection. Pound was not the only person to see the Tigullians' work as a means of making new art from old traditions. Writing in the *Musical Times* in 1934, Basil Bunting comments:

21. Ezra Pound, "Studi Tigulliani," *Il Mare* (14 March 1936). (Olga Rudge Papers, Yale Collection of American Literature, Beinecke Rare Book and Manuscript Library) Copyright © 2016 by Mary de Rachewiltz and the Estate of Omar S. Pound. Reprinted by permission of New Directions Publishing Corp.

> musicians have as much to learn from such writers as Jannequin and Francesco da Milano as painters from Giotto and Duccio. However, this piece [Münch's violin transcription of da Milano's version of Jannequin's *Chant des Oiseaux*] has ceased altogether to be a museum antique, and is as accessible, as fresh and 'modern' (not only in its discords) as any violin sonata or 'poème' available.[42]

In the context of the Futurists' condemnation of museums, Bunting's comment emphasizes the vitality of this music. Pound echoed this distinction, saying that Münch could "recognize when a piece is of great *archaeological* value but unsuitable for a concert performance."[43]

The Tigullian Studies sessions consisted of a combination of performances, lectures, and discussions, and Pound's words of introduction were often printed in *Il Mare*. He celebrated the advantages that small towns like Rapallo had over "centers of usury" like London, which rarely devote extensive time to single composers, and only attend to the work of already respected masters. In this context, he argued, a real study of Vivaldi's work can begin. Pound framed the Tigullian Studies in an image of the Fascist state:

> The lesson of the fifteenth century, the Italian cultural heritage, teaches us that as far as high culture is concerned the small town is not or should not be a pale (sometimes even clumsy) imitation of the great city, but must do something of its own in its own way. This idea of the healthy, robust, dynamic cell works very well within the concept of the differentiated and well-developed body of the corporate state.[44]

Pound imagines the corporate state working like the disparate principalities of Renaissance Italy, each achieving its own ends. But within the framework of a modern unified nation, each town's work contributes to the betterment of the whole. The last paragraph of Pound's first "Tigullian Studies" article makes the venture explicitly Fascist (Fig. 21): "For further details and information write to: E. Pound, Albergo Rapallo. For identification, the card of the Fascist Institute of Culture."[45]

Underlying these study sessions was extensive research. Rudge found a number of Vivaldi manuscripts in Cambridge and at the British Museum during January 1936, and performed a few works while she was in London.[46] "The Vivaldi 2 violin and piano wot J. S. Bach trans[cribed] is a wow for 2 fiddles!," she wrote to Pound in January 1936. "[D]id it last night."[47] In autumn 1936, Rudge spent about a month in Turin, exploring the contents of the Foà and Giordano collections.[48] Almost immediately, she identified 131 instrumental concerti—a good bit shy of the 308 instrumental works she would eventually find.[49] Although Pound urged her to keep focused on the works for solo violin, she branched out, examining every volume she could, and making a list of cantatas and operas as well. "It is worthwhile looking at the operas," she wrote to Pound near the end of her stay. She continued, mixing in third person pronouns for self-reference, as she and Pound frequently did in their correspondence: "in fact I <u>should</u> if I had <u>thought commenced</u> by them, as they are mostly <u>dated,</u> & so from differences in handwriting [one can] get an idea of <u>date</u> of concerti which are none of them dated—However she thinks she is vaguely right in which came first."[50]

During her stay, Rudge compiled the material for her thematic catalogue of Vivaldi's music held in the Foà and Giordano collections. Pound believed that the "Catalog of Viv/ in of Foa Torino; wd. be great card in Dresden if/when we get there."[51] Furthermore, he was keen for her to get public credit for her research, and he said "that thaaar katterLOG is the best log she can float on for the moment."[52] Pound had begun urging her to compile such a catalogue when she was working in England in early 1936: while she was eager to find work to perform, he was trying to figure out exactly what of Vivaldi's work had been published, and what existed in unpublished form. At this point, the only catalogue of Vivaldi's music was that compiled by Wilhelm Altmann, which only listed published works. Knowing that there were manuscripts in Cambridge, Dresden, and Turin, at least, and perhaps some items held in the British Museum and elsewhere, Pound laid out a clear working method for Rudge:

> The FIRST thing to DO/ is to start your catalog/ of Viv/ with MUSIC PAPER, and , as we said orig/ wit the bits/ start, or themes or whatever/ cert/ the opening bars of the violin part/ so that you can know AT once whether a given mss/ or old edtn/ is the SAME or different to one's already in hand.
>
> [in pencil he provides an example of musical transcription]
>
> a SMALL note book, say half the size this sheet wd/ do BUT you might(suit yrself) make a copy that wd/ fotograph. And OV course accuracy is desirable.[53]

Her catalogue, finally printed in *Antonio Vivaldi: Note e documenti sulla vita e sulle opera* (1939)—the material documentation of the Vivaldi Week—is organized based on the bound volumes in which pieces appear: she has lists for Volumes I–VIII, numbering pieces first by their position in the volume of which they are a part, but also by their position relative to the entire collection (Fig. 22).[54] At the end of the catalogue, she included a list of sacred works, organized in the same way. This work was groundbreaking, and other musicians and musicologists—including Casella and Alberto Gentili at Turin—were eager to see what she had. Worried about losing the credit for her work and at Pound's urging, Rudge hesitated to share it until it was published.[55] Her catalogue remains important. As Peter Ryom notes in his monumental and widely used catalogue of Vivaldi's instrumental works, "Despite the publication of more

The Fascist Cultural Nationalism of the Vivaldi Revival

22. Olga Rudge, *Thematic catalogue of the instrumental works of Antonio Vivaldi in the Giordano and Foà Collections, National Library, Turin* (1936), microphotograph of first page. (Olga Rudge Papers, Yale Collection of American Literature, Beinecke Rare Book and Manuscript Library) Copyright © 2016 by Mary Rudge de Rachewiltz.

recent and more detailed lists of the Turin collections, O. Rudge's catalogue is still the only thematical index in existence of the principal collections of extant Vivaldi works." As a result, he included references to her catalogue "at the end of the individual descriptions of the manuscripts of this collection."[56]

Pound and Rudge used *Il Mare* to publish their discoveries. Pound's publications documented the research and performances of the Amici del Tigullio, while Rudge's gave a sense of Vivaldi's music, his position in musical history, and how recent studies were reframing the wider understanding of his significance. Given the collaborative nature of these writings, it is a shame that *EPM* does not include—and thus translate—Rudge's articles. The chronology of Pound's and Rudge's *Il Mare* Vivaldi publications is as follows:

> Ezra Pound, "Tigullian Studies," 14 March 1936 (*EPM*, 384–87)
> Olga Rudge, "Antonio Vivaldi: musico di violino," 4 April 1936
> Ezra Pound, "Tigullian Studies," 11 April 1936 (*EPM*, 387–89)
> Ezra Pound, "Tigullian Studies," 25 April 1936 (*EPM*, 390–92)
> Olga Rudge, "Vivaldi: la sua posizione nella storia della musica," 9 May 1936
> Ezra Pound, "Concerts of March 29 and April 1," 27 March 1937 (*EPM*, 424–26)
> Ezra Pound, "Tigullian Musical Life," 4 December 1937 (*EPM*, 426–29)
> Olga Rudge, "La rivista *Broletto* di Como e la Microfotografia," 26 February 1938
> Ezra Pound, "The Vivaldi Revival," 25 November 1939 (*EPM*, 450–51)

These writings were largely collaborative, in that there seem to be extensive conversations—both those recorded in letters and those of which we have no record—showing Pound's and Rudge's thinking intertwined.

As soon as Rudge started finding unpublished Vivaldi material, Pound wanted to broadcast their findings. He sensed that the time was ripe for a Vivaldi revival, and he wanted to make sure that he, Rudge, and Münch got credit for their work early on. Writing in *Il Mare* in December 1937, Pound noted the beginning of a Vivaldi Society in Venice, and said, "We don't want to call ourselves the 'forerunners' of the effort in Venice, but we would like to remind people that we were the first to seek a revival of Vivaldi's music."⁵⁷ While Rudge was in London in early 1936, Pound asked her for an article for *Il Mare*: "A note on VIVALDI in her best woptalian iz indicated," he said, adding, "Its defects needn't reach anyone save Mare readers but it is time she started a scriptorial style/ doggy as posszbl."⁵⁸ Rudge focused on the music, but Pound emphasized documentation. His letters from this period show him prodding her to write and finish articles. Having delivered one to *Il Mare*, he commented that he had said to the editor, "I had had to 'far il dentista' to drag it out of HER."⁵⁹ Pound seems to have been incapable of leaving Rudge to write the articles herself. Outlines he devised for her raise questions central to the Tigullians' study: What was Vivaldi's relationship to Bach? Can Vivaldi's influence on Bach explain why Bach's music is superior to Handel's? What is the significance of the differences between Vivaldi's and Bach's handling of the continuo part? How does Vivaldi's music compare with that of his contemporaries and precursors? How will the newly discovered material in Turin affect contemporary critical assessment of Vivaldi's compositions? and What about all these newly discovered operas?⁶⁰ Drawing in part on these letters, Rudge laid out a program of study to assess Vivaldi's place in the history of music:

> An adequate study of the Vivaldi problem must take into consideration the following questions:
> 1. The state of the cultural heredity as received by Vivaldi;
> 2. The stitching together done by him;
> 3. Vivaldi in relation to Bach; clarify if Bach's transcriptions of Vivaldi's works were executed only to facilitate more practical performance [i.e., with available instruments] or if they imply a development;
> 4. Whether Bach's selections represent the best of Vivaldi's corpus, or whether he made them from a particular part of Vivaldi's work, corresponding to a certain aspect or phase of Bach's own work;

5. An analysis and critique of the particular inherent qualities and attitudes of his music with precise attention to the concerto form that Vivaldi largely developed;
6. Vivaldi in his own era: whether he holds the position he merits, and if not, these would be the reasons of this neglect; it might be owing to the current editions of his music, which perhaps give a false idea of his value, consisting in large part of reductions made in a style and with a taste belonging neither to Vivaldi's epoch nor to ours, and so posing little interest for us.

This last problem, of Vivaldi in the present time, will be truly the most important and thrilling.[61]

Pound and Rudge's interest in the issue of the cultural heritage reveals itself from the very beginning of this list: concern about what Vivaldi could do with his "cultural heredity" corresponds to their interest in putting modern Italy's cultural heritage to use. Much of the material that appeared in Rudge's articles also seems to have provided content for the lectures Pound gave at performances of Vivaldi's music in Rapallo.

Even Rudge's Vivaldi entry for the 1940 supplement to *Grove's*, a piece we know she wrote on her own in 1939 while Pound was on his American tour, shares concerns with their earlier writings published in *Il Mare* and elsewhere. Rudge wrote to Pound twice in 1939 about the composition of this piece, once in May, to say that "yeow she will have to write it herself," and once in June, to say that she had received acknowledgement for it from editor H. C. Colles's secretary.[62] Rudge's entry in *Grove's* replaced the scant piece by Reginald Lane Poole (1928).[63] It lays out her knowledge of Vivaldi's biography, gives an extensive treatment of Vivaldi's choral music, which she notes "has been entirely forgotten," and includes a list of all the works in Turin attributed to Vivaldi.[64] The article was revised for the next edition of *Grove's*, adding treatment of

23. Example of one of Ezra Pound's microphotographs from Sächsische Landesbibliothek, Dresden. Actual photograph measures 4.5 inches wide by 3.5 inches tall. (Now in Olga Rudge Papers, Yale Collection of American Literature, Beinecke Rare Book and Manuscript Library) Copyright © 2016 by Mary de Rachewiltz and the Estate of Omar S. Pound. Reprinted by permission of New Directions Publishing Corp.

Bach's keyboard transcriptions of Vivaldi's works and a list (not prepared by Rudge) of Vivaldi's operas and published works.[65] This was probably the most important of the articles springing from their research and, until 1980, remained the introduction to Vivaldi in *Grove's*, one of the most authoritative sources for the study of music.[66]

The first Vivaldi article published in *Il Mare* notes that the group's "study-workshops" would examine "the Italian musical heritage of the period before Bach, beginning by reading all

Vivaldi's works for one or two violins and piano."[67] It is a surprisingly musicological article for a small-town newspaper—evidence that Pound knew they were covering new ground and wanted to leave flags along their route.[68] The article notes where they planned to begin their studies: he starred two sonatas, seven concerti for violin and piano, and two concerti for two violins; those pieces would be accompanied by "parallel references to Bach's music" and other compositions, including Janequin's *Chant des Oiseaux* as transcribed by Münch and Stravinsky's *Pulcinella*.[69] Pound saw Vivaldi not only as an *Italian* composer *preceding* Bach, but also as a composer whose rediscovery resonated with modern experimentation. In his correspondence with Münch, Pound proposed concert programs positioning Vivaldi in conversation with Hindemith, Bartók, Scriabin, and Stravinsky, thereby arguing for the same kind of modern Italian musical culture as Casella.[70] Rudge made similar comparisons in early 1938, likening Vivaldi's music to Stravinsky's and Casella's, and to the surrealist paintings of Joan Miró.[71] This connection between ancient sources and modern creation accords with Mussolini's, Sarfatti's, and Bottai's desires for Fascist art.

From the Pound-Rudge correspondence, from Rudge's collection of concert reviews, and from a comparison of the Pound-Rudge holdings of musical manuscripts with Peter Ryom's massive thematic catalogue of Vivaldi's instrumental work, I have been able to piece together a sense of the Vivaldi programs in Rapallo. Many of the performances were taken from unpublished works.[72] Performed in February 1938 was the Concerto in A with echo for two violins, orchestra, and continuo (RV552), one of the first pieces transcribed by Pound. Thanks to the work of Gerhart Münch, in 1937 Pound got hold of a trove of microphotographs (11.5 cm by 8.6 cm) of manuscripts from the Sächsische Landesbibliothek (Dresden), which he set about copying into scores that could be performed in Rapallo (Fig. 23).[73] Pound wrote to Münch in August 1938: "some of the photos are of complicated pages/ hard on the eyes if you haven't a good magnifying glass. I use two sets of glass, wearing one; and using the other for things hard to see."[74] Pound was most interested in preparing scores of unpublished works, those not already available for performance.[75] He had written to Rudge, "What is shut up in a single printed copy in a bibbyteker is just as hard to git at as if it wuz in mss," and wrote in another letter:

> Constructive suggestion// Performers shd/ be ASKED to go to libraries and PLAY the stuff if not for music lovers; at least for a few competent judges/
> That wd/ stimulate the publication of old music that said PERFORMERS WOULD play.[76]

We already see here a distinction between usable and unusable cultural heritage—a distinction that would come to dominate Pound's thinking about culture in *Guide to Kulchur*.[77] There he writes:

> Bach had a perfect right to reset Vivaldi for his organ. He wanted a USABLE version of magnificent compositions. Münch is, to date, his most serious successor in the recurring decimal of good Vivaldi presentation. (*GK*, 251)

In music, this distinction is even more clear than in literature: where material in archives can easily be transformed into a poem—which Pound did when he was working in the British Museum Library in the first decade of the century—it cannot be used in performance, and so is not usable for music.[78]

Microphotography represented a solution. In a sense, the Tigullian concerts aimed not only to revive Vivaldi's music, but also to advertise the microphotographic process, seen by Pound and Rudge not only as a means of making music available, but as the latest development in musical notation. Pound counts microphotography as a crucial part of "The New Learning" as he describes it in *Guide to Kulchur*: he urges that "The microphotographic edition of music shd. NOT be delayed."[79] Lest readers miss the claims made at the performance, Rudge published the article "The *Broletto* review of Como and Microphotography" in *Il Mare*. Therein she noted that much of Italian musical heritage was unpublished, and that microphotography offered a solution for students and for publishers seeking to produce perfect but cheap editions.[80] Writing about the Rapallo Vivaldi concerts, English painter and priest Desmond Chute, part of Rapallo's expatriate community, shows the emphasis on microphotography in the discussions surrounding the music:

> The concerts finished with a most interesting evening, during which Ezra Pound spoke of the aims of the Amici del Tigullio, explaining the development of musical notation from the primitive accentual system up to the more modern microphotographic process and illustrating them with recited poetry and ancient music played on the violin, with the display of prints, reproductions, films, etc. Microphotography permits having editions of irreproachable authenticity; it needs only be publicized in order to bring an end to the anomaly of limiting available music to a few editions of dubious value, while the greater part of the musical patrimony of the world lies buried in libraries. Fruit of this research was the delicious *Concerto in A* for violin and echo by Vivaldi (performed with infinite grace by Olga Rudge and Luigi Sansoni), recently found in the Dresden Museum by the studious Tigullians, and provided by them, with admirable economy of means, with a piano part strictly conforming to the original score. *O si sic omnes.*[81]

Not surprisingly, Chute's emphasis on pulling the cultural heritage out of libraries to make it available echoes Pound's thinking about how people should be able to engage with their heritage.

The Fascist Cultural Nationalism of the Vivaldi Revival   185

In order to perform Vivaldi's vast corpus of instrumental music, the Tigullians had to make transcriptions themselves. Pound copied numerous scores from the Dresden microphotographs. He even created his own thematic catalogue, listing twenty distinct works (see Appendix).[82] Not all these scores are complete: one trails off after a page and a half (RV241), and others have only the solo line filled in. But for some scores, such as the Concerto in A, there are multiple drafts that demonstrate Pound's working process. First is an initial draft in ink, with pencil corrections in Rudge's hand (Fig. 24). Then Pound prepared a new fair copy, incorporating Rudge's corrections, and from that copy he prepared partitions for performance (Fig. 25).

Pound's scores were used in the program for 5 February 1938, for instance. The write-up in *Il Mare* shows that three pieces were performed that evening. First was the concerto in A, "reduced and drawn from manuscript using the microphotographic system … and adapted in the Tigullian studio to available instruments." Next, a concerto in D, in "free interpretation made by Gerhart Münch, with less liberty than that used by Stravinsky in adapting various passages and movements of music by Pergolesi to make the new work, *Pulcinella*." In comparing Münch's transcription with Stravinsky's *Pulcinella*, the announcement positioned this concert in the wider context of modernist adaptation of older work—including Casella's work with Scarlatti. It also established Münch's transcription as more loyal to tradition than Stravinsky's piece—notable since Stravinsky was criticized for claiming *Pulcinella* as a new work, given its closeness to the original source material. The performance "set Vivaldi's music in relief"—and completed the circuit of modern and ancient music—by closing with a sonata for violin and piano by Debussy.[83] The *Il Mare* write-up notes that music of Vivaldi's time assumed a certain amount of improvisation, and that modern performers can "sometimes create more effectively by taking this license, in the spirit of the twentieth century and of the new and Fascist era."[84] At play is a distinction between

24. Ezra Pound, transcription of "Concerto in La" (Vivaldi's Concerto in A for violin, 3 violins "per eco," strings and harpsichord, RV 552), draft copy. Pound's work is in ink and Rudge's corrections are in pencil. (Olga Rudge Papers, Yale Collection of American Literature, Beinecke Rare Book and Manuscript Library) Copyright © 2016 by Mary de Rachewiltz and the Estate of Omar S. Pound. Reprinted by permission of New Directions Publishing Corp.

The Fascist Cultural Nationalism of the Vivaldi Revival 187

25. Ezra Pound, transcription of "Concerto in La," violin part. (Olga Rudge Papers, Yale Collection of American Literature, Beinecke Rare Book and Manuscript Library) Copyright © 2016 by Mary de Rachewiltz and the Estate of Omar S. Pound. Reprinted by permission of New Directions Publishing Corp.

two kinds of modern intervention in ancient music. The Tigullians condemned modern *editions* that blunted the spirit of older music, but they celebrated *performers'* attempts to revive that music's spirit. Such interventions represented the blending of ancient and modern, the desire to make the old scores live in accord with Fascist modernizing and revitalization.

Pound did more than merely copy these pieces, however. For instance, he arranged Vivaldi's Concerto in D minor, originally for viola d'amore and lute, orchestra, and continuo (RV540), for violin and keyboard. Doing so required combining the parts originally written for violin, viola d'amore, and lute into one solo line. Pound's letters to Rudge demonstrate his complex engagement with the music itself. On 7 July 1938, he wrote to her acknowledging that his ambitions might exceed his ability:

> have YOU any ideas whether ALL the filling in shd/ be uniform arabesque / repeating in the middle voices EVERY possible line that can be repeated/ wich I spekk Johnnie B/ wd/ have// or whether one shd/ try mainly to keep the show MOVINK erlong ... or both.
>
> not that advice is likely to make up fer my iggurunce.[85]

Thinking about Johann Sebastian Bach's reinterpretations of Vivaldi's music for keyboard, Pound wonders how to condense a piece for solo instrument, orchestra, and basso continuo into an easily (and cheaply) performed violin and piano arrangement. He is making choices about how much of the original score can be retained and where it might appear in the new transcription. In other words, he is transforming the music—interpreting it, reimagining it for a new context, making it into a modern recomposition. But he acknowledges his basic musical ignorance in June 1938, saying that he has "gt/ difficulty rememberin wot key has three flat. AND so forf."[86] In June 1938—and speaking of himself in the third person as he often did in letters to her—he

The Fascist Cultural Nationalism of the Vivaldi Revival 189

complained to Rudge that the concerto on which he was working did not offer much excitement:

> and he haz just finished page I. of a bdy 3 flats/ concl/ wot is a tooty part and nowt much to do but cawpy the bloomink parts onto the PYanny wich is DULL doing. esp as it all goes GGGG CC etc. However he is chewink along on legible fotos.[87]

Reductions for violin and keyboard were common ways to produce Vivaldi's music during this period, giving a sense of a piece without an orchestra and conductor. In fact, Alceo Toni's reduction of Vivaldi's *Four Seasons* for four-hand piano had brought those now famous concerti into bourgeois households, building their popularity.[88] And the same situation that motivated other reductions pertained to Rapallo—lack of both money and access to a variety of instruments.[89]

Pound quickly found himself yearning for a wider array of instruments to employ for his transcriptions. Writing in August 1938 about a score with two sharps, Pound commented, "[I] think it is prob/ shd/ be done with quartet and [Desmond] Chute's old pyanny// I mean wiff regard to local resources/ Cello, viola and acc/ violin; with spinet or harpsichord wd/ give all there is to it."[90] In another case, he suggested adaptation for a trio of violin, cello and piano to accommodate notes that would otherwise be difficult to produce:

> waaal he haz begun another Viv/ looks like a autografo/ and I aint sure but wot Johnnie Bachh picked it/ can't see if its da Pisandel or da Federico/ da Vivaldi or <u>PER</u> (i;e; made for somebody by Viv/) anyhow I will larn somfink copying it out/ lokkz to meh azil it wd/ make a nice trio wiff cello/ otherwise some of the nuts gotter be shifted soz PYannyist can play yem// all.[91]

Pound was right that this piece, the Concerto in C major for violin, orchestra, and continuo (RV 172), exists in autograph in Dresden, but it was not source material for one of Bach's keyboard concerti.[92] About the Concerto in C minor for solo violin, orchestra, and continuo (clavecin) (RV 198), Pound wrote to Rudge in July 1938, "I don't think adapted to reduction/ but worth doing so as to try out and probably shd/ be done wiff cello and VYoler/ at least for slow mov/ marked senza cembalo// Pizz of the two. wiff wot I fink izza nize lil violin choon."[93] The more time he spent with these scores, and the more musical situations he confronted, the more convinced he became of the difficulty of simplifying these pieces to produce a violin-piano transcription. Perhaps if he were a trained and accomplished composer as Münch was, he would have trusted his own ability to interpret Vivaldi freely, but instead his adaptive work seems more limited to the movement of notes among parts. In September 1938, he wrote that he had adapted a concerto in a new way:

> He is vurry fond of her// an he haz begun anuthr Viv/ and she WONT like it BUT he haz allus said that it are NOT obliGATory to putt the one top line on the fiddle and the rest on the PIE.yano when trying to git the deSIgn or forrum of a conc/ an nif she dont like playing two strinks on the fiddle where he haz putt it/ she can play the PYANNY line instead and leave them TWO nuts fer the PY/
>
> only till he hearz it he cant tell wot it soundz like EITHER waye and thazzatt.[94]

Recognizing that this set up might not work—or perhaps, more importantly, might not please Rudge—he takes the chance at his adaptive move. He continued work on this adaptation, adding a couple of days later, "Hiz next page of Viv/ looks O.K. to HIM ; ef she don't eggsplode: and if she hazza po' di PAZiHENza fer to try one or two bars different ways to see which."[95] We can only

The Fascist Cultural Nationalism of the Vivaldi Revival 191

regret that her response to the piece—"explosion" or not—has not survived, and must instead rely on the score itself.

The existence of so much musical transcription in Pound's hand indicates that despite what other critics have believed, his contribution to the Rapallo revival of Vivaldi goes beyond the role of organizer to active musical participant.[96] In August 1938, Pound came to a point in his reading of Vivaldi that suggested a real affinity between his own musical compositions and those of the baroque composer:

> Blarst me halyards ef here aint ole Viv in his second movmink doing wot I invented fer meself in Villon/ eight vs/ 9. vurry intelligint COMposer. …
>
> Have finished second movmunk// melody seems very DIFFERENT from other Viv's concs/ up to yet/ no harm to lend a li(l VARiety.
>
> Valzer, wot OH!![97]

The second movement of this concerto is written in 3/4 time, although it is not exactly a "waltz," as Pound suggests. Nevertheless, that he relates this piece to his own music for *Le Testament* (1920–33) combines with his close engagement with the Vivaldi scores to demonstrate his musical involvement in the Tigullian Studies venture.

Meanwhile, Pound hoped that Gerhart Münch would conduct similar research in Germany. Despite Pound's ambitions to "put YOU on the map" with an album of Vivaldi reductions for piano and violin, Münch was less invested in the Vivaldi project.[98] He doubted the value of Vivaldi's work, noting that the concerto on which he was working "is a bit thin and the 'Virtuoso-parts' are sometimes empty." He said: "I'd like to cut out a lot, but I fear that will be considered a capital sin.------ Other proposition; I could get a lot of unknown Old German Stuff: Would that do?"[99] Pound responded that Vivaldi "is a GOING train" and that given the "mild Vivaldi boom" going on, it would be a shame to "let the kudos go to Casella."[100] By this time, of course, Pound knew Casella's and the Accademia Musicale's plans to revive Vivaldi in Siena, and worried that the Vivaldi Week would occlude the Tigullians' achievements.[101] Pound bristled at Münch's suggestion of switching to a German composer, responding dubiously, "Of course IF there is an equally diverse MASS of ONE German composer, that cd/ bebe boomed."[102] Given the competition between Italy and Germany for cultural primacy during this period, and Pound's interest in *Italian* cultural heritage, throwing off a newly rediscovered Italian composer in favor of a German composer would hardly do. In November 1939, he questioned the moniker "an Italian Bach" often applied to Vivaldi: "Vivaldi was a true Italian, who often had the self-assurance to leave his lines blank and unembellished wherever he or a contemporary would have immediately understood which notes needed to be added to his meagre indications."[103] Although Pound would just as soon have seen his Rapallo venture receive all the recognition for reviving Vivaldi, Rudge's involvement with the Accademia Musicale Chigiana meant that he could view their Vivaldi Week as a continuation of his own endeavors.

Even though that work was completed in Siena, with Casella at the helm, Pound subsumed the Siena concerts into his own. Indeed, his write-up of the Settimana Celebrativa di Antonio Vivaldi in *Il Mare* gives but a single sentence to that festival, devoting the remainder to his own Rapallo work, and claiming Siena's successes as an outcome of the Rapallo venture. In this essay, Pound assumes the pose of a true cultural administrator of Fascist Italy. His rhetoric borrows heavily from that of Fascist writings of the time: "We have mentioned a Vivaldi-Bach axis," he writes, echoing the Rome-Berlin axis (1936), "and we could also, if necessary, proclaim a musical autarchy of our own."[104] He positions the Tigullians' venture in the midst of Mussolini's dispute with the League of Nations over Italy's invasion of

Ethiopia, noting that their work began "four years ago during the days of the sanctions." He thus suggests that their interest in Vivaldi's music follows a desire to depend only on Italy's own resources, as Mussolini had urged in his initiation of the policy of *autarchia* in March 1936 before the Second National Assembly of Corporations. Although Mussolini claimed that the policy was a response to the League's sanctions, the move to economic self-sufficiency was also an ideologically driven method of building national consensus and closing ranks.[105] Despite the success of the Siena concerts, Pound argues, the work of reviving Vivaldi is not over: "A week of his music … has still left three hundred concerti unpublished and a quantity of sacred and operatic music untouched!" In Rapallo that work will continue, he notes, saying that they are busy "studying several dozen 'repatriated' compositions"—presumably those from Dresden. The article's final paragraph expands "Italian musical autarchy" to include "enough unpublished music by Vivaldi and Boccherini to last for ten years of musical weeks and festivals."[106] In expanding his focus thus, Pound had his eye on other cultural administrators, like Alfredo Casella, Margherita Sarfatti, and Giuseppe Bottai, who sought cultural means to make Fascist Italy strong. Although Pound's writings from the 1930s suggest that he had long seen himself as a cultural administrator for Mussolini's Italy, his Vivaldi venture was the first concrete product of his ambitions.

Coda: the Vivaldi Revival after 1939

Pound's and Rudge's contributions to the Vivaldi Revival did not end in 1939, but continued even after the Second World War. In 1941, in a Settimana Celebrativa della Scuola Veneziana, Vivaldi's work again appeared at the Accademia Musicale Chigiana under Casella's artistic direction.[107] Of the six concerts, four featured work by Vivaldi, three of them exclusively devoted to his work.[108] As was the case in 1939, the program emphasized Vivaldi's unpublished works, drawing liberally on the collection at Turin. The oratorio *Juditha triumphans* (RV 644) was performed twice, again demonstrating the wealth of choral compositions by the Venetian. As Anne Conover argues, "This epic masterwork, which had been lost to the world, was saved by Olga's diligence and curiosity when she discovered the score at Cambridge University's Fitzwilliam's Library."[109] She also notes that this piece, probably because of its discovery by Rudge, merited discussion from Ezra Pound in a radio broadcast given in October 1941. He speaks there of wanting "the clean and decent Americans to hear the Vivaldi Oratorio Juditha Triumphans; which makes ole pop Handel look like a cold poached egg what somebody dropped on the pavement." The occasion of the 1941 festival elicited memories of their Tigullian work on Vivaldi, of the Sienese Vivaldi Week of 1939, and of Vivaldi's place in European musical history:

> Mozart when he came down to Italy did NOT set the public crazy. And part of the reason was, as I conjecture, that the Italian had then had an earful of Tony Vivaldi. That is guess work. But there are things to set against Bach. In fact things Bach took hold of and rearranged; without as I think improvin' 'em.
>
> I had a chance to hear both together two years ago in Siena, in a good orchestral concert, one up to Casella, the way the program was built.
>
> Man named Guarnieri conductin', been doing three years now in Siena, at this summer fest. And I would by god rather hear Guarnieri conductin' Vivaldi than hear Toscanini conductin' Beethoven in Salzburg. An idea which occurred to me, durin' the Juditha performance.
>
> I tell you that Italy is carryin' ON. *La rivoluzione continua.* This is the kind of thing Italians go on doing, despite that dirty mugged bleeder and betrayer of his allies, Winston babyface Churchill.[110]

The Fascist Cultural Nationalism of the Vivaldi Revival 195

Pound considers Vivaldi together with Mozart and Bach, finding the non-Italians lacking—and similarly defends Italian performances of Italian music in Italy over other performances elsewhere. This brings us back to his notion of "musical autarchy." That he links the renewed performances of Vivaldi's music to the Fascist revolution—the same continuous revolution that he celebrates in *Jefferson and/or Mussolini* (see Fig. 15)—emphasizes that this musical work ultimately had a political objective—that of helping Italy to "carry on," to make itself new using Fascist tools.

Pound's thinking about Vivaldi and Bach together comes in part from the Tigullian Studies programs, in part from the 1939 Siena festival, and in part from the 1941 festival, which similarly paired works by Vivaldi and Bach. In one multi-composer concert of instrumental and vocal chamber music, there were two Bach keyboard transcriptions (BWV 593 for organ and BWV 972 for harpsichord), gesturing to the influence of Vivaldi's music. One evening's performance consisted entirely of two transcriptions of Vivaldi concerti, one by Casella (Concerto in A minor, RV 523) and the other by the musicologist Fausto Torrefranca (Concerto in G minor, RV 576).[111] As Fertonani has shown, Torrefranca's edition of this concerto differed greatly from all those discussed thus far: because Torrefranca worked as a musicologist and not as a musician or composer, he aimed for a prototype of a "critical edition," and his published text (1937) includes an introductory note more like an apparatus, complete with a statement of criteria for revision and directions for execution. In substance, the transcription he created was a sort of hybrid between a true critical edition and a practical edition, constructed according to the interpretive methods of the early nineteenth century, and his version of this piece did not sound substantially different from Casella's version of the Concerto in A minor.[112] Listeners in Siena in 1941 would still have heard Vivaldi as translated through the musical tastes of that period. After the Second World War, as a result of the work of the Armenian conductor Angelo Ephrikian and the Italian composer

Gian Francesco Malipiero, the editor for the complete works series published by Ricordi, the music of Vivaldi started to be heard in a manner more akin to that of Vivaldi's own time.[113]

After the Second World War, research into Vivaldi's life and work took off. The collaboration of businessman Antonio Fanna and composer Gian Francesco Malipiero led to the founding in 1947 of the Istituto Italiano Antonio Vivaldi in Treviso. Starting at its founding and continuing to 1985, the Istituto, with Ricordi and under Malipiero's direction, published performing editions of all of Vivaldi's instrumental music—549 volumes in all.[114] Performance of Vivaldi's work continued too, most notably by Angelo Ephrikian's Orchestra della Scuola Veneziana (founded 1947), Renato Fasano's Virtuosi di Roma (1948), and I Musici (1952).[115]

In 1950, Olga Rudge edited two of Vivaldi's concerti, based on the Dresden microphotographs, published as *Due Concerti Manoscritti*.[116] The volume reproduces from Dresden manuscript 2389/O/4 numbers 1 and 2: Concerto in C major for two violins "in tromba," two flutes, two trumpets, two mandolins, two salmoè, two theorboes, cello, orchestra, and continuo (RV 558) and Concerto in A major with echo for violin and echo, orchestra, and continuo (RV 552). In editing these pieces, Rudge worked not from the manuscripts themselves, but from Pound's collection of photographs, which he had donated to the Accademia in 1938.[117] At the time of the publication of the *Due Concerti Manoscritti*, Rudge believed that the Dresden Vivaldi manuscripts had been destroyed during bombing raids in the Second World War but, as Schafer and Adams have noted, this was not the case. Although some of the collection was damaged by water used to put out fires in the library, the Vivaldi collection fared rather well.[118]

Scholars have continued the work of assessing the significance of Vivaldi's work and cataloguing his compositions. Mario Rinaldi published his *Antonio Vivaldi* (1943) in Milan, and French musicologist Marc Pincherle's *Antonio Vivaldi et la musique instrumentale* (1948) was published in Paris. Later, Walter Kolneder's *Antonio*

Vivaldi: His Life and Work (1970) was added to the mix. Scholars to the present day continue the work of refining our understanding of Vivaldi, still adding a great deal to the understanding of his operas and continuing to discover new works. Various catalogues have appeared over time, after those published in conjunction with Siena's Vivaldi Week, including Mario Rinaldi's *Catalogo numerico tematice delle composizioni di Antonio Vivaldi* (Rome 1945), Marc Pincherle's *Inventaire-thématique* (volume 2 of his *Antonio Vivaldi et la musique instrumentale*, 1948), Antonio Fanna's *Antonio Vivaldi: Catalogo numerico-tematice delle opere strumentali* (Milan 1968, second edition 1986), and the Danish scholar Peter Ryom's widely used *Thematisches Verzeichnis der Werke Antonio Vivaldi: kleine Ausgabe* (Leipzig 1974/1979) and large version, *Répertoire des œuvres d'Antonio Vivaldi: les compositions instrumentals* (Copenhagen 1986).[119] While the earlier catalogues have been superseded by Ryom's masterwork, their dates acknowledge the duration of the project to make sense of the entire collection of Vivaldi's music. That the history of this revival is so fresh makes it in itself a topic of study among Vivaldians, as may be witnessed in the treatment of the matter in Michael Talbot's *Antonio Vivaldi: A Guide to Research*, which deliberately—and in opposition to the usual practice of the book's series—catalogues scholarly treatments from the late nineteenth century in order to facilitate study of Vivaldi interpretation over the last century. A central piece of this musicological work was the Tigullian Studies venture, in which Pound and Rudge made their own contribution both to rekindling interest in Vivaldi's music and to invigorating Italian cultural Nationalism in the Fascist era.

We can see from Pound's work with Vivaldi's music and from his continuing interest in other efforts to revive Vivaldi's reputation how invested he had become in the work of using cultural heritage to enrich the Fascist nation. Indeed, his contributions to the Vivaldi Revival mark his first real Fascist cultural Nationalist achievement. What we cannot yet fully see here is how allying himself to the Fascist cultural Nationalist mission would impact Pound's own writing, but *Guide to Kulchur* reveals the degree to which Pound's modernism was shaped by his investment in Mussolini's regime.

CHAPTER 6

Italian Fascist Exhibitions and Pound's Fascist Directive

> I can also tell the men of my own profession (that is students and writers) how I think they can and should form their guilds, or corporazioni, or whatever they wish to [c]all them. ...
>
> Among other things I should treat literature as communications service, not as the quantitative production of merchandise.
>
> —Ezra Pound[1]

By linking his cultural and critical work to Mussolini's Fascist regime, Ezra Pound found new ways to immerse himself in the government's Nationalist project. But in his odd textbook *Guide to Kulchur*, we see Pound employing Fascist tropes, rhetoric, methods, and ideals to make a very different kind of critical book than he had in the past. Indeed, although his writings of the late 1920s and early 1930s contain echoes of Mussolini's rhetoric, or draw on Fascist ideals to make their arguments, or contain sections built around Fascist tropes, *Guide to Kulchur* is his first prose work to exemplify a truly Fascist methodology. Many of Pound's prose works preceding Mussolini's declaration of empire in 1936—works as early as *Spirit of Romance* (1910) and as late as *ABC of Reading* (1934)—rely on an exhibitionary method, in which he lays out texts for readers to explore: he wants his readers to access the materials through which he comes to his conclusions. In these earlier works, Pound frequently asserts that criticism is not a viable substitute for first-hand reading and critical thinking. He famously comments in "How to Read, or Why" (1929) that "I have been accused of wishing to provide a 'portable substitute for the British Museum,' which I would do, like a shot, were it possible. It isn't."[2]

Guide to Kulchur claims, on the other hand, that such a substitute is not only possible but preferable. In a letter to Frank Morley of Faber & Faber in London, written during the early stages of the book's inception, and as if negating this earlier claim, Pound calls the book "Wot Ez knows, or a substitute (portable) fer the Bruitish museum."[3] This dramatic reversal exemplifies Pound's new imagining of culture, and mirrors the contemporaneous shift in Fascist propaganda: instead of gesturing to the complexity of culture and teaching a reader how to approach it, he gives a digest and insists on an interpretation.

The prompting for *Guide to Kulchur* came in February 1937, from Morley, who sensed a market for such a popular textbook, and who gave Pound rein to work in his own way.[4] Pound's outline matches the completed *Guide*'s three parts: method (based in Confucius's *Analects*), philosophy (a history of thought), and history (a history of action). A week and a day after his initial letter to Pound proposing the guide, Morley wrote again, worried that the public would not take a "guide to kulchur" seriously—but his initial suggestion stuck. Imagining himself as a propagandist, Pound turned to the propaganda methods of Mussolini's regime.

Pound wrote *Guide to Kulchur* quickly in March and April 1937, during the height of Fascist-sponsored cultural production in Italy. By this time, Pound was well aware of the imperialist ambitions and achievements of Mussolini's government. In October 1935, Mussolini invaded Ethiopia, part of the Abyssinian Empire, thereby solidifying his drive for a militaristic empire and inviting hostility from the League of Nations. On 9 May 1936, Italy took Addis Ababa and Vittorio Emanuele III was declared emperor. Ezra Pound saved in his personal papers a copy of *Il Popolo d'Italia* from 10 May, with its banner front-page headline, "The Duce Announces to Italy and the World the Constitution of the Fascist Empire," and numerous articles, including the text of Mussolini's declaration, titled "Italy finally has its empire."[5] In September 1937, several months after Pound had written *Guide to Kulchur*, the Mostra Augustea della Romanità opened in Rome's Palazzo delle Esponsizioni, celebrating the bimillennium of the birth of the Emperor Augustus, classical Rommanness, and connections between the Augustan era and Mussolini's Rome.[6] *Guide to Kulchur*, published in 1938, was written and published in the historical context of these Fascist attempts to shape Italian and world culture through imperial expansion and state-supported artistic production.

Pound's idea of culture grew primarily from his favorite economist C. H. Douglas, whose notion of "cultural heritage" Pound summarized thus in 1934:

> The source of value is the cultural heritage; that is, the whole aggregate of mechanical inventions, their correlations and possible correlations, the improvement of seed and farming methods, and the customs and habits of civilization (subject to some selection and horse-sense, but, at any rate, treated as a potential and as a level of demand and perception).[7]

The paradox that people might need a guide to this habitual culture demonstrates that Pound's culture includes both ordinary habits and a more Arnoldian vision of the best that has been thought and said.

Part of the appeal of this sense of culture derived from its centrality to the Nationalist vision of Mussolini's Italy. Pound

26. Tempio Malatestiano, Rimini. (Photograph by the author)

asserted in the *New York Herald* in 1934 that whereas many modern leaders ignore their nations' rich pasts in addressing modern economic problems, "Mussolini has taken his rank as the First European by a solid refusal to sabotage the cultural heritage."[8] Indeed, Mussolini relied on this notion of "cultural heritage" as an important tool for social change.[9] As we have seen, the Fascist regime used a series of mass exhibitions to communicate its vision, celebrating wide-ranging aspects of Italian culture: aeronautics, children's camps, the history leading up to the March on Rome, technical institutions, even the problems with using the pronoun *lei* for formal address.[10] As Ruth Ben-Ghiat has argued and earlier chapters of this book have noted, many Italian intellectuals felt that a lack of national identity had left Italy vulnerable to cultural colonizing by other nations and saw the advent of a dictatorship as a chance to build a unified Italian culture.[11]

Italy represented a microcosm of all culture for Pound: if reconciling the myriad pieces of Italian culture was a challenge, then how might one collect all the parts of 2,500 years of world culture? Pound rejected a "great man" approach, as culture must be something shared, not personalized. When Frank Morley asked in June 1937 to add the subtitle "The Book of Ezro" to *Guide to Kulchur*, Pound declined, saying "it is TOO pussnl."[12] Such an objection may shock readers of Pound's London poetry and criticism, accustomed to his sense that "it is the artist's job to express what is 'true for himself,'" and that "the man who tries to express his age, instead of expressing himself, is doomed to destruction."[13] Pound's new vision of culture, however, followed the Fascist conception of totalitarian culture, where no single element is valued over the whole. Fascism explicitly repudiated the bourgeois individualism that it associated with liberalism. *The Doctrine of Fascism* (1932), signed by Mussolini but written in part by Giovanni Gentile, asserts: "Anti-individualistic, the Fascist conception of life stresses the importance of the state. It affirms the value of the individual only insofar as his interests coincide with the state's, which stands for the conscience and the universal will of man in history."[14] Many artists working for the Fascist regime agreed. In December 1933, Mario Sironi, Massimo Campigli, Carlo Carrà, and Achille Funi published "The Manifesto of Muralism," a defense of mural art written by Sironi and positioned in the context of both Italy's long traditions of public art and Fascism's conceptions of citizenship. "Every individual artists faces a moral challenge," the manifesto claims, "that of renouncing an egocentrism that renders his spirit infertile; that of becoming a 'militant,' an artist in the service of a moral ideal who subordinates his individuality to the collective task." The signers noted that "Literal anonymity is not the issue here (for it is at odds with the Italian temperament), but rather a sense of intimate dedication to the collective enterprise." This idea that the artist must become "an ordinary man among men" would prevent subjectivity and originality for their own sake, and thus allow art to function in service of collective benefit rather than enhancement of the individual ego.[15] In this way, mural art could be Fascist art, and the significance of Fascist art could surpass the work of any individual.

Despite his earlier tendencies, Pound, too, no longer simply celebrated individuals who stood too far apart from their culture: now his assessments are more complex. The Tempio Malatestiano, commissioned by Sigismundo Malatesta and treasured by Pound, is in *Guide to Kulchur* both an "apex of what one man has embodied in the last 1000 years of the occident," and a "monumental failure" (Fig. 26): although Sigismundo "registered a state of mind, of sensibility, of all-roundedness and awareness," he did it "*against* the current of power" (*GK*, 159). As a result, the Tempio cannot truly be considered *part* of its culture. And whereas most of Beethoven's music, and even Pound's own *Cantos*, are "records of personal struggle"—particular to the person who composed them and requiring a fair amount of effort to understand or appreciate—other works, such as Pietro Lombardo's carvings of mermaids in Santa Maria dei Miracoli (Venice), belong to the domain of culture (Fig. 35, discussed in more detail later). About such works Pound writes, "the perception of a whole age, of a whole congeries and sequence of causes, went into an assemblage of detail, whereof it wd. be impossible to speak in terms of magnitude" (*GK*, 136). They grow not out of the work of an individual genius, but a confluence of forces. Pound wanted, in other words, to move away from art as a private, personal practice toward art as public property: art must benefit an entire state, an entire population, in order to enter the realm of culture. Although he admired such great men as Mussolini, he wanted to distribute that greatness more widely. In Fascist exhibitions, he found methods for communicating his ideals to the masses.

In Chapter 3, we saw how Pound admired the Mostra della Rivoluzione Fascista (1932), an exhibition that made its way into

Italian Fascist Exhibitions   205

27. Façade of the Palazzo delle Esposizioni, modified for the Mostra Augustea della Romanita, under the direction of G. Q. Giglioli, Rome, photographed on the occasion of the official visit of Adolph Hitler, 3–9 May 1938. (Leoni Archive / Alinari Archives, Florence (AVQ-A-003696-0112))

his *Cantos* and about which he was still thinking as late as March 1937, when he was writing *Guide to Kulchur*.[16] This exhibition celebrated the Fascist ideal of *la rivoluzione continua*—so important to *Jefferson and/or Mussolini*—and embraced an array of avant-garde styles as an emblem of this "continuing revolution." As the 1930s went on, however, Pound became more invested in the rhetoric and iconography of Italy as a finished state. The monumental Romanizing architecture of the later 1930s, for instance, suggests not perpetual change but a sense of solid completion. As Marla Susan Stone has written, "Fascist culture after 1936 challenged the eclecticism and modernism of the early and middle 1930s with an imperial and increasingly racial and militarist aesthetic."[17] These concepts are visible in the Mostra Augustea della Romanità, or Exhibition of Augustus and Romanness, which opened in Rome's Palazzo delle Esposizioni on 23 September 1937, marking the bimillenium of Augustus's birth. The exhibition transformed the Palazzo's façade into a faux stone triumphal arch, resonating with the triumphal arches in Rome's Forum, and the military victories they celebrated (Fig. 27, and see Fig. 4).[18] Jobst Welge calls the triumphal arch "the quintessential symbol of *romanità*," and further notes that these arches—common elements of Fascist-era buildings—were the "most emblematic and self-reflective element of architectural translation in this period."[19] While the exhibition celebrated Augustus and his empire, it everywhere honored Mussolini's Rome as well: Mussolini's triumph, the façade tells us, is that he has returned Italy to the splendor of the Rome of the *Pax Augustea*, through his cultural and economic programs at home and his imperial successes abroad. Atop the four podia that covered the façade's columns stood four casts, two each of two colossal Roman statues of barbarian prisoners, the originals of which stand in the Palazzo dei Conservatori on the Capitoline (Rome).[20] Those figures combined with a cast of a Victory found at Metz to emphasize the imperial quality of Mussolini's triumph. To each side of this triumphal arch were wide swathes of faux stone walls, decorated only with inscriptions from such Latin writers as Livy, Cicero, Pliny, and Augustine, translated into modern Italian, and above them a seemingly stone-carved "DVX" (a Latinate version of the more common *Duce*) repeated four times on each side.

Casts of ancient sculptures and reconstructions of ancient structures dominated the exhibition (Fig. 28). Relying on casts rather than originals meant that the organizers could bring together far more works than would have been possible in their original form. As Claudia Lazzaro notes, using reproductions instead of originals also freed the objects from their roles as "art" and "enabled the monuments to serve a more ideologically burdened narrative of the past."[21] The locations in which the originals were displayed—Ankara, Bucharest, Provence, Vienna, Florence, and of course Rome itself, to include only those works which stood in the two "Rooms of the Empire"—testify to the broad scope of the Roman Empire and Mussolini's ambitions. The objects themselves, then, mattered less than the image of Rome they assembled and the geographical space they represented. Yet, these objects were grouped thematically, rather than geographically, thereby gesturing to the universality and continuity of the ideals they represented.[22]

Mirroring Pound's sense of cultural heritage, the exhibition joined high cultural elements with common life. Some exhibits focused on the Roman Empire itself—its origins, its history preceding Augustus, the later stages of the empire's history and its self-defense, and the rise of Christianity. Several rooms centered on Augustus and the monuments associated with him (Fig. 29). But while the exhibition celebrated the range of Rome's architectural projects, it made explicit space for ancient Roman daily life—industry, religion, schools and youth organizations, family life, arts and letters, libraries, agriculture, medicine, economic life, and games. The organizers' definition of culture, then, was far wider than Arnold's "the best which has been thought and said."

Augustus's relevance to the Fascist present was most explicit in the final room, "The Immortality of the Idea of Rome: The Rebirth of the Empire in Fascist Italy."[23] The exhibition's catalogue asserts the regime's revival of the idea of Rome after a period of dormancy:

> The imperial Roman idea was not extinguished with the fall of the Western Empire. It lived in the heart of the generations, and the great spirits testify to its existence. It endured the mysticism of the Middle Ages, and because of it Italy was able to experience the Renaissance and then the Risorgimento. From Rome, restored capital of the united Fatherland, colonial expansion was initiated and achieved the glory of the Vittorio Veneto with the destruction of

28. Exhibited reliefs and casts, Mostra Augustea della Romanità, Rome, 23 September 1937. (Archivio Storico Istituto Luce)

the empire that had opposed the unification of Italy. With Fascism, by the will of the Duce, every ideal, every institution, every Roman work returns to shine in the new Italy.

Thanks to Italian soldiers' epic enterprise in Africa, the Roman Empire is rising again on the ruins of a barbaric empire.

Such a miraculous event permeates the speech of the great, from Dante to Mussolini, and the restoration of great Roman works.[24]

This explicit linking of Mussolini and Augustus permeated the Mostra Augustea for the Augustan era had become a useful past

29. Reconstruction of the temple of Augustus and Ancyra, made for and exhibited at the Mostra Augustea della Romanità, Palazzo delle Esposizioni in Rome, 1937–38. (Alinari Archive, Florence)

30. Stele of Axum, Rome, 2003. (Photograph by the author)

to glorify.²⁵ The arrangement of the room clarified its significance: around the curved walls appear block-letter inscriptions quoting Mussolini. Images connect ancient and modern works. For instance, the catalogue sets two obelisks side by side, brought back as symbols of imperial conquest. Titled, "Romanness and Fascism," the two pictures are explained by the caption: "On the left: Obelisk formerly in the Circus Maximus (now in the Piazza del Popolo), brought to Rome by Augustus and commemorating the Roman conquest of Egypt—On the right: Obelisk of Axum, brought to Rome to commemorate the Italian conquest of Ethiopia" (Fig. 30 gives an image of the Stele of Axum, called an obelisk in the catalogue to emphasize its connection with Rome's ancient past).²⁶ As the Egyptian obelisk represented the glories of Egypt, conquered by Rome, so did the Stele represent Axum, the ancient and powerful capital of Ethiopia, conquered by Mussolini.²⁷ Where the Mostra della Rivoluzione Fascista might have asked visitors to interpret these two images, the Mostra Augustea della Romanità told visitors explicitly that the ancient objects justify Mussolini's imperial project.

Similarly, although Pound had previously bemoaned Rome's decadence, in the late 1930s he followed a wider Fascist valorization of that ancient empire.²⁸ His earlier writings see Rome as a pale imitation of Greek greatness: an article of 1922 had commented that "Athens had a civilization, Rome had an empire, and the greatest virtue of that empire was to act as a carrier for Athenian civilization."²⁹ In sculpture, he condemned the "empty copy of empty Roman allegories that are themselves copies of copies" (*GB*, 110). Conversely, in 1937, Pound applauds Rome. Addressing conversations about a United States of Europe and suggesting that there are more important trends in the European situation, he says, "there is an older dream based on perceptions and instincts far more vigorous than rough analogy with the U.S. Constitution and the Articles of Confederation." That dream is Italy's renewed Roman Empire, but it is not "merely Italian":

> The watchful reader should not fall into the error of supposing this dream to be purely, or merely, Italian. The Roman Empire civilized the occident as we know it. The IDEAL was so solid that it persisted in Constantinople for centuries. It persisted in German Europe, in the very terminology of the Rulers. It was an ideal of ORDER, not of bunk, not of humanitarian illogicality but of a POSSIBLE ORDER functioning amid very perfect human beings without any calculation being made on their sudden and/or total amelioration before next Saturday fortnight.
>
> Obviously no man will be able to THINK the revival of the Roman Empire clearly unless he have some fairly clear and articulate idea of what the old Roman Empire was and how it came into being.[30]

Gone is Pound's concern about Rome's decadence and its empty copies of copies. Like the writers of the catalogue copy for the Mostra Augustea, he asserts the continuity of the Roman ideal through centuries in which it seemed to slumber, in the context of the dream of a new Rome—much as the Mostra Augustea justifies Mussolini's new empire. He explains Rome's successes and the reasons for a Roman sense of order in the economic terms that had become his structure for understanding the history of ideas, civilizations, and art:

> Dr. Walton [Brooks] McDaniel [professor of Latin at the University of Pennsylvania] writes to me, "Few people realize what a disease usury was in the (Roman) Republican period." My own hypothesis is that the Roman Empire became possible when the Greek (maritime) usury system gave way to the more moderate agrarian usury of the Romans.[31]

In other words, Rome's true glories came with the empire—beginning with the reign of Augustus and continuing through Constantine and

Italian Fascist Exhibitions 213

RAPALLO, ITALY

There is no use in writing about Europe as if it had been founded by the Pilgrim Fathers in 1620, nor in seeing it second-handed through the eyes of English weekly reviewers. And there is certainly no use in my writing about it if I am merely to tell GLOBE readers what they already know or believe.

If I am to write for GLOBE we may as well understand each other. I have been right several times in the past. Plenty of people have thought me crazy. But they always think me crazy for what I am actually saying at the moment, not for what I SAID fifteen or twenty years ago.

EZRA POUND

31. Ezra Pound, "EVROPE—MCMXXXVI," *The Globe* 1:2 (May 1937): 106. Copyright © 2016 by Mary de Rachewiltz and the Estate of Omar S. Pound. Reprinted by permission of New Directions Publishing Corp.

32. Envelope mailed by Ezra Pound to Olga Rudge 19 October 1937, featuring a stamp celebrating the bimillennium of Augustus, 1937. (Olga Rudge Papers, Yale Collection of American Literature, Beinecke Rare Book and Manuscript Library) Copyright © 2016 by Mary de Rachewiltz and the Estate of Omar S. Pound. Reprinted by permission of New Directions Publishing Corp.

Justinian—and relied on economic shifts. Lest the reader miss Pound's correlation between the future of Europe and the greatness of ancient Rome, the article is printed with a large Roman-style triumphal arch above the text, the title—"EVROPE—MCMXXXVI"—chiseled across its face (Fig. 31). Although the iconography doubtless resonated differently in distant Minnesota than in Rome, Mussolini's Romanizing imperial aspirations frame Pound's ideas.

Although I cannot be sure that Pound visited the Mostra Augustea, he was aware of it and encountered its ideology and

33. Envelope mailed by Ezra Pound to Olga Rudge 22 October 1937, featuring stamps celebrating the bimillennium of Augustus, 1937. (Olga Rudge Papers, Yale Collection of American Literature, Beinecke Rare Book and Manuscript Library) Copyright © 2016 by Mary de Rachewiltz and the Estate of Omar S. Pound. Reprinted by permission of New Directions Publishing Corp.

iconography on such mundane objects as postage stamps. While Fascist Italian stamps had long used the Italian past to represent the present culture and government, the imagery shifted after Mussolini's declaration of empire. The Roman past, which appeared only occasionally on stamps in the early 1930s, became dominant by 1937 as the regime embraced its imperial symbolism.[32] The stamps commemorating the bimillenium of Augustus's birth used the imagery developed during his reign to consolidate power as emperor, and we see them on Pound's correspondence. For instance, one uses the statue of Augustus of Prima Porta, which depicts Augustus in his role as emperor, a spear in his left hand and his right raised as if addressing troops, wearing the famous breast plate bearing representations of conquered territories, the god Mars, and the chariot of the sun god. (Fig. 32). Another stamp uses the monumental statue of Augustus as Pontifex Maximus, also known as the "Via Labicana Augustus," together with temple facades to honor his role in the restoration of temples and in Roman religious life (Fig. 33). Those stamps celebrating Augustus's power on the seas depict the gilded Columna Rostrata Augusti—a gilded column decorated with the beaks of ships—placed in the Roman Forum to celebrate Augustus's return to Rome after his defeat of Sextus Pompey in 36 BCE (see Fig. 33).[33] Such use of booty to represent victory mirrors the statues of barbarian captives affixed to the façade of the Mostra Augustea. The airmail stamps marking the bimillenium use details from specific Augustan monuments with significance to modern Italy: a detail from Rome's Ara Pacis, for instance, marks Augustus's consolidation of Roman authority throughout the empire. Pound himself linked the Ara Pacis to the Mostra Augustea: in a letter to Olga Rudge from October 1938, he wondered whether the exhibition had closed (it had not), and called the Ara Pacis "the grand finale."[34] One stamp reproduces the entire Ara Pacis, and another shows a detail of a relief depicting a procession of the imperial family, including three children. This latter stamp represents the prosperity of the Romans, and likely celebrates Augustus's social legislation, designed to encourage upper-class Romans to procreate.[35] The Ara Pacis, not seen for thousands of years, was discovered in parts beginning in the sixteenth century and completely excavated in 1937–38, on Mussolini's watch.[36] The Fascist government ordered that previously unearthed pieces, scattered among museums inside and outside of Italy, be returned to Rome for the reconstruction.[37] The very presence of the reliefs testified to Mussolini's power in restoring the past glories of Rome.[38] As common objects used by ordinary people, these stamps, like the Augustan coins that combine an image of his head on one side with a monument to his victories on the other, communicated the regime's ideology even to those who might not visit the spectacular exhibitions in Rome.

Pound's sense of modern Italian culture similarly shifted to emphasize the drive for empire. In an article from July 1936, he wrote in the Rapallo newspaper about the donation of a Stradivarius violin by Rapallo to Rome. While many Rapallesi were saddened at the loss, Pound read this donation as a symbol of small towns' contributions to the imperial project. Using the rhetoric of empire, he argued:

> Now that the Empire exists, we must consider the relationship between center, periphery, and minor nuclei of the State. An Empire needs a Center in which the intelligence and the strength of the race are concentrated, but from which in turn the light of its civilization spreads across and penetrates the lesser nuclei. This diffusion depends not only on the undefined will of the lesser cities but also on their sensibility and perception. It is not enough to be sensitive to the passive reception of benefits alone; it is necessary to show ourselves ready to seize the opportunity for constructive work.

Still speaking of a return to Roman order, he traces the movement of ideas in an imperial context: "The New Order will spread from Rome in ways neither understood nor dreamed of, in ways foreseen only by a few people who have an 'ardent imagination,' and it will spread not only 'geographically' in space, but will also grow in depth of development and concept."[39] His plan for lesser cities follows the regime's vision for a new Roman empire.

As Ben-Ghiat has shown, the Fascist notion of the nation as an organic entity derived both from liberal-era ideas about national development and from the Nationalist movement's approach to imagining state goals.[40] As early as 1923, in an essay entitled "The Italian Empire," F. T. Marinetti used analogies to the human body to imagine that an "Italian empire, because our slender peninsula—elegant backbone with a hard head of heavy and domineering Alps, epitome of all the beauties of the earth and bursting with creative genius—has the right to govern the world."[41] In 1928, Margherita Sarfatti, an early proponent of a new Italian empire with Rome as its heart, said that Benito Mussolini "is making Italy aware of its unity and moral greatness through her capital's architectural unity and material greatness." She acknowledged that such "centralization imposes painful sacrifices, defacements, and decapitations on the other cities of the 'Italic folk endowed with many lives.' But these are necessary and fruitful."[42] Pound agreed. Lesser cites were not rivals of Rome, but rather part of its organic whole:

> In the magnificent body of the Fascist state no one is excluded, but everyone must function according to his abilities, according to his imagination and perception. ... Rome's power did not cease with the fall of the Empire of the Caesars, it was not the creation of Julius alone, its order was perpetuated in the action of Antoninus, Constantine, and Justinian, and later with the canon law of the Middle Ages.[43]

His organic image of the empire rests on Fascism's corporate state, and his image of this body-state grows from the idea of empire in ancient Rome: ancient cultural heritage enables modern success.

Pound's description, like the imperialist propaganda of the time, replaces the reality of colonized bodies with a classicizing image of a Roman body of state. As Ben-Ghiat has shown, in the conquest of Ethiopia,

> the Italians combined old-fashioned savageries (decapitations, castrations, and burning and razing of civilian quarters) with industrial killing methods (aerial gas

34. Front of dust jacket, Ezra Pound, *Guide to Kulchur* (London: Faber and Faber, 1938). Copyright © 1938 by Ezra Pound. Reprinted by permission of the New Directions Publishing Corp.

bombings and efficient open-grave executions) that are more commonly associated with Hitler and Stalin's soldiers than with Mussolini's rank and file ... the slaughter in Ethiopia was so out of keeping with Italians' self-perception as the more 'humane' dictatorship that it has been edited out of popular and official memory. Until 1995, the Italian government, and former combatants such as Indro Montanelli, denied the use of gas in East Africa.[44]

But this denial of the reality of colonized others is hardly limited to Italy's colonial conquests, as Fredric Jameson has suggested. Instead, it is part of a larger "strategy of representational containment" characteristic of this period of imperial literature. Jameson argues that during the period from the late nineteenth century through the Second World War or so, the "radical otherness of colonized, non-Western peoples" was systematically made invisible in favor of "others" rooted in other imperial nation-states.[45]

Guide to Kulchur follows this trend. Although it demonstrates a pervasive concern with empires (Roman, Macedonian, British), noting their rise and fall and what they offered civilization, its discussion is deeply rooted in the metropolis. Pound's writing about the condition of the British Empire may be shaped partly by the fact that by this time Mussolini's commentary on Britain had soured, emphasizing its limitations rather than strengths.[46] Pound's analysis in *Guide to Kulchur* follows suit:

> Never in all my 12 years in Gomorrah on Thames did I find any Englishman who knew anything, save those who had come back from the edges of Empire where the effect of the central decay was showing, where the strain of the great lies and rascalities were beginning to tell. (*GK*, 228)

Even in such passages, where Pound makes reference to the colonial situation at "the edges of Empire," it is a returning Englishman whose opinion he repeats. In so representing the British Empire, he is replacing the colonized other with what Jameson calls the "Imperial type," the Englishman who has benefited from the imperial conquest and whose views stand in for the reality of the colonial situation.[47] There is no engagement in *Guide to Kulchur* with the brutal realities enabling Italian empire.

At the same time, Pound's sense that the empire's condition is more visible at its peripheries than in its metropolis reflects the complexity of his own geographical position, in remote Rapallo rather than urban Rome, but engaged nonetheless in the cultural work of the empire. That so much of Pound's thinking about empire comes in a chapter of the *Guide* entitled "Losses" indicates his anxiety that the falls of empires bring a loss of culture: by extension, the Italian empire must thrive that its cultural programming might educate those who need it. To counteract the loss of cultural heritage—not in Italy, where work is already underway to recover it, but in the United States and Britain, where people have not understood this loss—Pound uses Fascist methods to bring his vision of culture to a decadent populace.

Pound's purpose in *Guide to Kulchur* is to counteract the overwhelming cultural ignorance of "the man in the street in England and the U.S.A. 1938" (*GK*, 26). Even the book's jacket design acknowledges the way that Pound represents himself as the pinnacle of culture by pedestalizing a profile bust of him made by Gaudier-Brzeska to represent "Wot Ez knows" (Fig. 34). The colors echo the symbolism dominating the façade and interior of the Mostra della Rivoluzione Fascista, with its blood-red and gray.[48] Pound himself had noted the "Blue, Black and Red mingled together" in this exhibition.[49] The red lettering of the book's title combines with the gray of the illustration and of "Faber & Faber," with just a bit of blue-green shading for the column, to present an image of the kind of culture to which Pound will guide his readers.

Pound's writings throughout this period emphasize the importance of curiosity to cultural growth. "There can be no doubt that the Renaissance was born of wide-awake curiosity," he wrote in 1937.[50] The *Guide* laments, however, the general lack of curiosity in American and English thought.[51] A common rhetorical gesture in *Guide to Kulchur* is explicit reference to his reader's curiosity: "If a man have sufficient curiosity to look for a basis in fact …" (*GK*, 24) or "Can I direct the reader's curiosity by prodding him …" (*GK*, 25). Such prodding, Pound suggests, is the work of the critic: "It is the critic's BUSINESS *adescare* to lure the reader," he notes, and soon adds: "He is not there to satiate" (*GK*, 161). Providing his readers with fishing line and lures instead of fish is a way to ensure not only that they will follow his advice but rather that they will promulgate his sense of culture beyond the works he mentions, thereby deepening their own indoctrination. The *Guide*'s principal purpose, therefore, is the stimulation of readers' curiosity. The first chapter draws from Confucius to discuss the "six becloudings," in which each action—which might seem good in itself—becomes confused when performed without "the love of learning."

Pound believed he could bring readers to culture by stimulating their curiosity. Culture, to the totalitarian mind, produces understanding. Pound, therefore, wanted to create a "total man" whose understanding would permit him to converse with the greatest philosophers (*GK*, 47). The new learning would focus on where ideas "weigh in"—where they *matter* (*GK*, 44). This integrated sense of knowledge and appreciation would lead to a greater understanding of such important issues as economics: "the one thing you shd. not do is to suppose that when something is wrong with the arts, it is wrong with the arts ONLY" (*GK*, 60). Being able to understand art and culture—to recognize quality, to distinguish works from one period from those of another—is not merely a matter of connoisseurship, or asserting highbrow standing. It can rectify larger social problems. "I suggest that finer and future critics of art will be able to tell from the quality of a painting the degree of tolerance or intolerance of usury extant in the age and milieu that produced it" (*GK*, 27). Those critics, like Pound's intended audience, could thus contribute to the projects imagined when Mussolini addressed the need for a new cultural heritage: by knowing their past they could build a brighter future.

From his long-held focus on creating new works of art—art which, he now emphasizes, must be integrated into a larger totality rather than isolated in museums—Pound extends his sense of cultural heritage to the creation of good government. "When the vortices of power and the vortices of culture coincide, you have an era of brilliance," he says in *Guide to Kulchur* (266). Early in the book, he lays out a parable of good government, showing that clear terminology is crucial to that realm. He translates Confucius's idea that "If the terminology be not exact, if it fit not the thing, the governmental instructions will not be explicit, if the instructions aren't clear and the names don't fit, you can not conduct business properly" (*GK*, 16). Reading is no mere contemplative act, but one with a purpose: "Properly, we shd. read for power. Man reading shd. be man intensely alive" (*GK*, 55). That power is not merely personal, but civic. In *Jefferson and/or Mussolini*, Pound claims in Arnoldian terms that "A good government is one that operates according to the best that is known and thought. And the best government is that which translates the best thought most speedily into action" (91).[52] He also addresses the role he imagines for citizens:

> "The art," says my venerable colleague once Vorticist W. Lewis, "of being ruled"! The art of not being exploited begins with "Ch'ing Ming"! and persists invictis, uncrushable on into Gourmont's *Dissociation d'idées*. If the affable reader (or delegate to an international economic conference from the U.S. of A.) cannot distinguish between his armchair and a bailiff's order, permitting the bailiff to sequestrate that armchair, life will offer him two alternatives: to be exploited or to be the more or less pampered pimp of exploiters until it becomes his turn to be bled. (*GK*, 244)

The very aspects of culture that Pound has been celebrating appear here as remedies against exploitation. Italian Nationalists and intellectuals had recognized since the time of the Risorgimento that Italy's lack of a coherent national identity had made it vulnerable to conquest by other nations.[53] Similarly, Pound wants the citizens of the United States to be strong, to resist exploitation. He shows time and again his esteem for the constitutional basis of the United States, even if he lamented that nation's recent decline: "The specific lesson (1938) might be to recognize the U.S. Constitution as an innovation, and to hesitate for a very long time before scrapping it in favour of expedients and experiments oft tried and oft proved ineffective" (*GK*, 275). At the same time that he thinks about those governing, however, he wants his imagined "man in the street" to be able to resist similar exploitation on a more local level. Culture is as essential to good citizens as it is to good leaders.

Pound presumes that tidbits of culture, rather than swathes of text, best pique readers' curiosity. He relies, therefore, more on the remembered gist of works than on quotations from the works themselves. "In the main, I am to write this new Vade Mecum without opening other volumes," he tells his reader, "I am to put down so far as possible only what has resisted the erosion of time, and forgetfulness."[54] As Michael North has noted, knowledge that has become part of a person's being need not be looked up: it resists forgetting.[55] In determining that he does not need the "original" works themselves, Pound rejects also his older method of letting quoted text speak for itself. Such earlier works as *The Spirit of Romance* or *Guido Cavalcanti Rime* show off the results of his vast archival research. By the time he wrote the *Guide*, however, Pound was dubious of how the act of archival digging can be privileged over the significance of its results: "Naturally there is nothing duller than the results of such digging, UNLESS the searcher have some concept to work to. Not the document but the significance of the document" (*GK*, 220–21). In *Guide to Kulchur*, Pound's

Italian Fascist Exhibitions 225

35. Base of a pillar, 1481–89, Tullio and Pietro Lombardo, Santa Maria dei Miracoli, Venice. (Alinari Archive, Florence)

value judgments speak without archival evidence, and the pieces to which he gestures matter less than the whole he creates.

In valuing the newly created whole over its pieces, Pound made the same choice as the designers of the Mostra Augustea, who used casts and models to represent the Fascist interpretation of Augustus's empire. For this reason, the Mostra Augustea communicated not despite the use of casts but because of them: an assembly of so many authentic pieces might distract the public, absorbing them in seeing "the real thing"; an assembly of casts allows a more sweeping look, taking in the regime's whole image of the ancient Roman Empire. Pound, too, blends the works to which he refers into "culture." For instance, when he sets out his distinction between culture and records of personal struggle (as discussed above), he references Pietro Lombardo's carvings of mermaids at Santa Maria dei Miracoli in Venice (see Fig. 35). This church's carved exterior includes stone decoration and paneling in a variety of colored marbles, and its interior contains beautiful stone inlay, carved banisters, figures of saints, and pilasters with intricate reliefs. In such a setting, these reliefs—forming the bases of two pilasters—could easily pass unnoticed, a testament to the integration into the whole of which they are a small part. As such, they are important examples for Pound. These same carvings appear in an earlier review of Adrian Stokes's *The Quattro Cento* (1932), where they feature in a story about the inadequacy of criticism when faced with works of remarkable beauty:

> The Quattrocento abounded in partial works, time and again a bas relief contains one or two figures illuminated by the artist's contact with the deeps, and beside these figures are others that are nothing but a recollection or botch or some Greco-roman *porcheria*. The highest highbrow will do no better than the old *custode* in Santa Maria dei Miracoli saying, "There it is. For four centuries they have been trying and they cannot get anything as good as these mermaids."[56]

Pound suggests that not everything has equal aesthetic value. The critic's job is to help a less knowledgeable observer find the beautiful and culturally significant thing, and the inability of criticism to surpass simple pointing argues for a better approach to culture.[57] The *custode*'s pointing tells interested onlookers that there is beauty to be seen and asks them to work to see it.[58] The anecdote recurs in *Guide to Kulchur*, but abbreviated to such a degree that only a reader already familiar with it would understand:

> The old guardian at Sta Maria dei Miracoli says of the carving "It just seems that nobody *has* been able since ..."
> That refers to a culture. (*GK*, 136; Pound's ellipsis)

Taken at face value, this story has become a potentially impenetrable stand-in for his new sense of culture. It leads up to the chapter's definition of culture—"the perception of a whole age, of a whole congeries and sequence of causes" (*GK*, 136). Yet as a story that teaches, it risks failure because not enough of the story is given to show its point. By so dramatically abbreviating the story—by hacking away at it with Mussolini's *piccone*—Pound prevents his reader coming to the same conclusion as he does. Instead, they have two options. First, they could rely on his definition, where he *tells* rather than *shows* what culture is. Although in giving his readers an example of a meaningful cluster of statues, he may be trying to emulate the way the Mostra della Rivoluzione Fascista brought visitors into the work of history, Pound's tendency to abbreviate mimics the Mostra Augustea, less inviting his reader to learn with him than simply passing on what he believes. Alternatively, however, an engaged reader could do the work—the *substantial archaeological* work—of discovering what those ellipses represent, thereby gaining a real power over the text at hand.

36. Model of the Roman Empire during the time of Emperor Constantine, exhibited in the Mostra Augustea della Romanità, 1937–38, Rome. (Alinari Archive, Florence)

In the same way that the individual sculptures copied in the Mostra Augustea pale in comparison with the ideological message of the entire exhibition, or the individual places that compose the new Italian Empire matter less than an organic whole, individual paraphrased ideas pale before the larger image of "culture" in Pound's *Guide*. In earlier periods, Pound was willing to showcase individual "luminous details"—small pieces that somehow speak to larger trends—or to celebrate the works of isolated geniuses, but by this time his thinking was far more totalitarian, constantly examining the relations among the various elements of a culture.

One exhibit in the Mostra Augustea gives a visual model for such an approach: a specially commissioned model (scale 1:250) reconstruction of imperial Rome at the time of Constantine, the moment of its greatest extension (Fig. 36). Based on the work of Rodolfo Lanciani, but drawing on more recent excavations executed during the Fascist period, the model's scale allows the viewer to understand imperial Rome more comprehensively than visits to any individual monument around the city permit.[59] Unencumbered by the architecture of more recent centuries, the model gives a more holistic—dare I say totalitarian—view of Rome as Mussolini's government wanted to remember it. As Simonetta Falasca-Zamponi has shown, the Fascist view of ancient Rome was selective, highlighting such aspects as its superior power. Excavations were conducted "in search of the ruins of 'its' Rome," and usually involved destruction of newly discovered medieval buildings "in order to let ancient Rome predominate as the original witness of fascism's glorious destiny."[60]

Similarly—as emphasized in Chapter 3—Pound repeatedly advocates the clearing away of unnecessary material that occludes the real culture of ancient Rome. He asserts, "culture (damned word if there ever was one) ought NOT to be a blighted haystack of knowledge so heavy it crushes or smothers" (*GK*, 183). Chapter 3 considered Pound's discussion of the Fascist archaeological restorations in *Jefferson and/or Mussolini*, where he emphasizes the removal of later encrustations that hid ancient monuments and beauty from view. Italy, Pound claims, is sensibly clearing out sediment that has beclouded its cultural heritage, and he cheers Mussolini's ability to bring what lies beneath to light. What Pound was seeing, of course, were visible traces of the larger emphasis on *bonifica*, or reclamation, in Fascist concepts of modernity. As Ben-Ghiat has shown, this term referred not only to such concrete manifestations as the "conversion of swampland into arable soil" but also to more abstract attempts at human reclamation and cultural reclamation, and even, by 1938 or so, to the anti-Jewish laws.[61] If the image of Isis rejoining the divided limbs of Osiris represents Pound's earlier sense of himself as a cultural leader, then this image of Mussolini clearing away the accumulated burden of intervening time to access the cultural heritage of Italy represents Pound's newer vision of cultural work. In *Guide to Kulchur*, he expresses this ability to see in a fascinating mix of metaphors: "We may know that whole beams and ropes of real history have been shelved, overclouded and buried."[62] This clearing away involves the elimination of "dead catalogues" once understanding is achieved. He uses a metaphor from bookkeeping to explain how education should work: "The loose leaf system is applied in effective business. Old accounts, accounts of deceased and departed customers formerly blocked the pages of ledgers" (*GK*, 56). So, too, should students of culture excise old accounts from their cultural ledgers, incorporating living ideas but disposing of dead ones. Other nations, he implies through his carefully chosen terminology, need to learn from the Duce's example. England—"a mere bog or clog in the world's sub-sewer" (*GK*, 249)—or the United States—a "mind-swamp," where "swamp = mud plus stagnant water" (*GK*, 246)—need to do some clearing out of their own terrain, much as Mussolini cleared Italian swamps, or Pound was clearing a way for "culture."

Coupled with this clearing away is the building of new cultural heritage so that culture does not stagnate. Speaking again of Confucius, he writes, "The dominant element in the sign for learning in the love of learning chapter is a mortar. That is, the knowledge must be ground into a fine powder" (*GK*, 21). As mortar, culture cements new construction, and again Mussolini is the model. The Fascist state emulated ancient Roman building. Mussolini made this parallel clear in his famous comment from May 1922: "Fascism constructs its ideal and material edifices in the Roman way, stone by stone, and like the Roman ones, they will challenge time."[63] As Emily Braun has shown, Italian artists were given the role of master builders under the Fascist regime, using edifying myths to articulate a sense of *Romanità* for a classless society.[64] As we saw in Chapter 3, modern Italian architecture drew on elements of ancient buildings discovered in

Fascist excavations. Pound similarly aspired to be such a builder, constructing a new future from a usable past.

To this end, Pound emphasizes useful knowledge—that aspect of culture that allows a person to achieve something new. Useful knowledge is not about "load[ing] up your memory with the chronological sequence of what has happened, or the names of protagonists, or authors of books, or generals and leading political spouters," he suggests, but rather about "understand[ing] the processes biological, social, economic now going on" (*GK*, 51). This difference between a memorized list and a sense of process is the difference between knowledge and understanding. Understanding those processes, being able to embrace "ideas going into action" is what gives one a sense of culture for "the history of culture is the history of ideas going into action" (*GK*, 44).

Finding a way to bring these ideas into action dominates Pound's thinking about culture. By 1937, he had rejected art made only for exhibition, preferring "art made for USE—that is painting to have painted into the plaster and stay while one lives there" and also "music for who can play it and distinct from music made for the least common, and most vulgar, denominator of the herd in the largest possible hall."[65] Following the Futurists' belief that museums are cemeteries, Pound wanted art integrated into the public sphere, not sequestered in designated exhibition spaces.[66] Good art is usable art, art that accomplishes something. Similarly, as Marla Stone has demonstrated, the Mostra Augustea's purpose was "recruiting the past for the present."[67] When one possesses useful knowledge and is connected to one's culture, then one can engage successfully with new texts, experiences, and statal needs. "When one knows enough one can find wisdom in the Four Classics," Pound says about the cryptic declarations of Confucius. "When one does not know enough one's eye passes over the page without seeing it" (*GK*, 17).

The problem for Pound is that the west has made its vast collection of cultural heritage inaccessible. As we saw in Chapter 5, this problem had inhibited his revival of early Italian music—the scores now trapped in archives, hindering performance. As if revisiting his own tendency to rely on the archive as the storehouse of knowledge, Pound sets his realization of this problem in the British Museum Library's Round Reading Room (London), where he had spent two decades making modernism:[68]

> About thirty years ago, seated on one of the very hard, very slippery, thoroughly uncomfortable chairs of the British Museum main reading room, with a pile of large books at my right hand and pile of somewhat smaller ones at my left hand, I lifted my eyes to the tiers of volumes and false doors covered with imitation bookbacks which surround that focus of learning. Calculating the eye-strain and the number of pages per day that a man could read, with deduction for say at least 5% of one man's time for reflection, I decided against it. There must be some other way for a human being to make use of that vast cultural heritage. (*GK*, 53–54)

What he prefers now is the more Fascist, corporate model in which all contribute to the cultural work of empire. It is not enough for the elect to have access to this vast repository. Instead, Pound wants to make the cultural heritage widely available. Presenting a "totalitarian" sense of culture—one that makes sense of the whole rather than the pieces—is no easy task.

Pound's inability to achieve synthesis reveals itself in his various approaches. At one point, he wants to guide his reader to the important tidbits of the last 2,500 years, to "provide the average reader with a few tools for dealing with the heteroclite mass of undigested information hurled at him daily and monthly and set to entangle his feet in volumes of reference" (*GK*, 23). At another, he tries to take his accumulated knowledge and "reduce it all to one principle" (*GK*, 15). These different desires make the reader wonder whether culture is heteroclite or unified. Pound's objection to Aristotle's *Nicomachean Ethics* lies in its lack of uniform argument or quality: "It is heteroclite, a hodge-podge of astute comment and utter bosh" (*GK*, 308). He recognizes, however, that he too might be accused of this tendency: "Let the reader be patient," he protests, "I am not being merely incoherent. I haven't 'lost my thread' in the sense that I haven't just dropped one thread to pick up another of a different shade. I need more than one string for a fabric" (*GK*, 29). He uses various metaphors to express his desire for a larger structure on which to hang individual pieces of culture: "a bracket for one kind of ideas, I mean that will hold a whole set of ideas and keep them apart from another set" (*GK*, 29), a "card-index" or "set of cubby holes whereinto one can sort one's values and make them into a schema" (*GK*, 305), or "some sort of provisory scaffold, hat-rack or something to work from" (*GK*, 260). He wants to emphasize "the new synthesis, the totalitarian" (*GK*, 95), but it seems he has set himself an impossible task.

The cultural tool on which Pound ultimately settles for conveying the totality of culture is poetry, an art form that seems to him to solve the problem of how to make sense of modernity's—and especially colonial modernity's—heteroclite pieces. Pound offers poetry as a totalitarian synthesis. Poetry, he argues, can contain the vastness of an artist's culture and use aesthetic pleasure to pique the reader's curiosity. It can carry a powerful message, like the propaganda art for which Pound argued in "Ubicumque Lingua Romana" and his letter to C. H. Douglas. Pound acknowledges that he was neither the first nor greatest person to think so: "The Duce and Kung fu Tseu equally perceive that their people need poetry; that prose is NOT education but the outer courts of the same. Beyond its doors are the mysteries" (*GK*, 144–45). The problem, he suggests, is that the Anglo-American art-for-art's-sake model of modernist poetry—which he himself helped construct with such comments as "art never asks anybody to do anything, or to think anything, or to be anything"—hinders poetry's synthetic and rhetorical abilities. Unlike prose critique, poetry makes from the cultural heritage a new work, a new whole.[69] Where prose writers may tend to organize different pieces of that heritage into categories and thereby hinder knowledge by separating them, poets, and even playwrights writing in verse, are more totalitarian in their approach: "Shakespeare gets TO the far orientals because he does not shut his meaning into egg-shells" (*GK*, 165). Because of the integrated artistic structure he created, Shakespeare can reach even those who do not necessarily make sense of the world through the same systems of order. For Pound, the greatness of Thomas Hardy's verse shows why poetry can be so powerful: "No man can read Hardy's poems collected but that his own life, and forgotten moments of it, will come back to him, a flash here and an hour there. Have you a better test of true poetry?" (*GK*, 286). But poetry also draws out those forgotten parts of the larger cultural past that can allow the creation of great new things. "Man gittin' Kulchur had better try poetry first," he suggests, because "poetry is totalitarian in any confrontation with prose. There is MORE in and on two pages of poetry than in or on ten pages of any prose save the few books that rise above classification as anything save exceptions" (*GK*, 121). The concision of poetry, its formal organized qualities, and its powerful imagery and language make it the right means of acculturation. But much as the Fascist excavations in Rome cleared away any artifacts hindering a vision of Rome as a coherent, imaginable whole—understandable as the Fascist regime desires—the poetry to which Pound would guide his reader excludes many models of the cultural heritage in favor of others.

Nevertheless, what *Guide to Kulchur* argues for is a new kind of modernist poetry—new to Pound at least. He no longer wants art that "exists as the trees exist."[70] He argues for "literature as communications service, not as the quantitative production of merchandise."[71] Like the Mostra Augustea, this kind of poetry is as valuable for its rhetorical potential as for its beauty. As Pound's *Cantos* demonstrate, this poetry is neither simple nor straightforward. It requires an active and engaged reader, capable of grappling with its difficulty. Mark Wollaeger has argued that "Modernist narrative makes reading difficult; it requires that we slow the process down, become more conscious of the choices we make as we establish provisional networks of meaning." Using Roland Barthes's categories, he claims that where readerly texts are written for easy consumption, writerly texts—modernist texts—are "designed to solicit the self-conscious engagement of readers in the production of meaning."[72] Or, as Pound says in *Guide to Kulchur*, a person reading must be "intensely alive" (*GK*, 55). Poetry, in Pound's conception, requires an active reader: it engages that reader in a more active kind of citizenship. We might think of his indignant response to editors' asking him to make his writings simpler: "I am not a kindergarten department."[73] In his earlier prose, Pound was willing to provide readers with the tools to make discoveries, but now he wants them to work for it. He wants to reach the masses, but he is done holding their hands. If readers will not do the *work* of reading—"read for power"—they will miss the chance to become empowered citizens. And poets, too, must consider their affiliations as they produce poems to serve as "communications service."

Moving away from our tight focus thus far on Pound's prose, Chapter 7 considers how Pound's *Pisan Cantos* negotiate a role as "communications service" to the regime, and to the larger ideals for which Pound argued across genres.

CHAPTER 7

Propaganda Art: Can a Poet be a Traitor?

I said when I first heard of Ezra's freedom, that he walked out of the gate of St. Elizabeths alone, into another dimension. I was wrong. He walked out into the same dimension; that is, he seems to have walked out into life as he left it, 12 years ago. He goes on with "all the clichés," as Norman calls them, picking up the cudgels where he was forced to lay them down.

Who are these dummies, these ogres of a past age, these fearful effigies that wrecked our world, these devils, these dolls? Who are they? We put away childish things. It is we who walked into another dimension. Did they ever exist? Did Ezra ogre-ize himself by his association with Radio Rome? Joan laughed immoderately when I told her of Ezra's broadcast! Hitler and Mussolini flung at this late date into the very teeth of the British Lion!

It is funny. It isn't even sad.

No. It isn't sad. There is a reserve of dynamic or daemonic power from which we may all draw. He lay on the floor of the Iron Cage and wrote the *Pisan Cantos*.

—H. D.[1]

H. D.'s *End to Torment* is a memoir of Ezra Pound, and of her lifelong and complex relationship with him. As youths, the two fell in love, despite the opposition of H. D.'s father. They were poets together in London during the Imagist movement, and then pursued different poetic careers, H. D. exploring Freudian psychoanalysis while Pound invested in Mussolini's Fascism. H. D. lived through the Blitz in London, writing *Trilogy* as a testimony to that experience's relationship to her interests in mythology, occult knowledge, and psychoanalysis. Pound, as we have seen, published "textbooks" aimed at teaching neophytes about reading, economics, and culture. He wrote poems for *The Cantos*, including a couple in Italian in support of Mussolini's Salò government. He further effaced the line between poetry and propaganda in his broadcasts on Radio Rome, urging the UK and US not to fight against the Axis powers.[2] His writing used anti-Semitic language to rage against what he perceived to be an international Jewish banking conglomerate. The combination of his Fascist sympathies and anti-Semitic rhetoric have led many to dismiss his poetry. It has led others to try to make a clean break between his politics and his poetry, in the hopes that the latter can be redeemed from the former. In this closing chapter, I use H. D.'s memoir together with some important passages from Pound's *Pisan Cantos* to trace how Pound's modernism transformed through his affiliation with Fascism, emphasizing how this transformation plays out in his prose and poetic methods. These reflections will take us to the question that I believe most vexed H. D.: Can a poet be a traitor?

From January 1941 to July 1943, Pound made broadcasts on Radio Rome that were sent by shortwave to the US and the UK. H. D. writes in *End to Torment* that although she did not hear them herself, she was told that "the effect was baffling, confused, confusing, and she didn't feel that the 'message,' whatever it was, was doing any harm or any good to anybody."[3] Listening to recordings of these broadcasts makes clear that they were both loaded with allusions and incredibly difficult to hear. Even the monitoring unit of the Federal Communications Commission, whose transcriptions were used to assess whether Pound was acting against his country, mistranscribed entire swaths of text (*EPS*, xii). Nevertheless, as James J. Wilhelm has demonstrated, taken in the context of wartime events, these broadcasts could have discouraged American troops and citizens, and offered consolation to the Axis powers.[4] And Pound's vitriol and anti-Semitism is shocking.

In July 1943, Pound was indicted for treason, and when Italy fell in 1945, he was arrested and, at age fifty-nine, incarcerated at the Disciplinary Training Center at Pisa, where he was held for three weeks in a cage, constantly lit and exposed to summer heat. Here, as H. D. emphasizes, he wrote the *Pisan Cantos*. When Pound experienced severe anxiety, confusion, and fatigue, he was moved to the medical compound, where he stayed five more months before being sent to Washington, DC, in a shaky mental state. Indicted for aligning himself with America's enemies, he was declared unfit for trial by reason of insanity and committed to St. Elizabeths Hospital, where he was incarcerated from late 1945 to 1958. This time at St. Elizabeths was particularly painful given Pound's comment in a radio broadcast: "Whom God would destroy, he first sends to the bug house" (*EPS*, 27).

H. D. wrote of Pound "ogre-izing himself by his association with Radio Rome"—by his direct engagement with the propaganda mission of Mussolini's government, and the second indictment issued by a Federal Grand Jury on 26 November 1945 charged that Pound, "in violation of said duty of allegiance, knowingly, intentionally, willfully, unlawfully, feloniously, traitorously and treasonably did adhere to the enemies of the United States." He was further charged with "giving to said enemies of the United States aid and comfort within the United States and elsewhere" by "accepting employment from the Kingdom of Italy in the capacity of a radio propagandist." The indictment charged that "the purpose of said messages, speeches, and talks was, among other things, to create dissension and distrust between the United States and its military allies," "to create racial prejudice in the United States," to create the impression "that Italy is the natural ally of the United States." Pound's broadcasts "urged the people in the United States to read European publications rather than the American press and to listen to European radio transmissions." He was also charged with:

> counseling and aiding the Kingdom of Italy and its military allies and proposing and advocating to the officials of the Government of the Kingdom of Italy ideas and thoughts, as well as methods by which such ideas and thoughts could be disseminated, which the said defendant, Ezra Pound, believed suitable and useful to the Kingdom of Italy for propaganda purpose in the prosecution of said war.[5]

Pound called himself a propagandist. No surprise: he had long admired Mussolini's propaganda methods, and his interest in using the arts for propaganda purposes. He wanted to contribute his counsel, ideas, thoughts, and writings to Italy's political mission throughout his time there, and his radio broadcasts were part of the same project. Pound conceived of his role on the radio as combating anti-Axis propaganda (*EPS*, 146), "punk propaganda" (*EPS*, 76), "Fleet Street propaganda" (*EPS*, 152), "hebe propaganda" (*EPS*, 253), and "usury propaganda" (*EPS*, 388). These forms of propaganda, he argued, obscured the truth, threatened Europe, and carried the United States and Britain into an ill-advised and unjust war; as he would conclude Canto 78, "there / are / no / righteous / wars" (*C*, 78:503).

As Mark Wollaeger has demonstrated, the precise meaning of "propaganda" was in flux at this time. During the First World War, and continuing through the second, "propaganda" was beginning to take on its contemporary meaning of "tendentious persuasion by interested parties," but to a great degree it still carried its older meaning of "persuasive information or mere boosterism." Wollaeger notes:

> The information propagated might come from interested sources, but its integrity or reliability was not necessarily suspect. That would change over the first half of the twentieth century, when two world wars helped link "propaganda" to lies and deception without completely erasing the notion that "to persuade" might simply mean "to inform."[6]

Based on his defenses of his action on the radio, it seems that Pound understood "propaganda" in the more positive sense of informing or educating the listening public—a goal that so many of Pound's writings of the time share. In a letter written upon learning in 1943 that he was under indictment, he wrote:

> The whole basis of democratic or majority government assumes that the citizen shall be informed of the facts. I have not claimed to know all the facts, but I have claimed to know some of the facts which are an essential part of the total that should be known to the people.
>
> I have for years believed that the American people should be better informed as to Europe, and informed by men who are not tied to a special interest or under definite control.
>
> The freedom of the press has become a farce, as everyone knows that the press is controlled, if not by its titular owners, at least by the advertisers.
>
> Free speech under modern conditions becomes a mockery if it does not include the right of free speech over the radio.
>
> And this point is worth establishing. The assumption of the right to punish and take vengeance regardless of the

area of jurisdiction is dangerous. I do not mean in a small way; but for the nation.[7]

Pound emphasizes his radio role as informing the American citizenry of "facts" to which he did not believe they had access through the American press. His argument here is in accordance with his belief—expressed through the publication of his pedagogical prose of the 1930s—that education makes a stronger citizenry.

In his broadcasts, Pound was quick to distinguish between "Axis propaganda" and "mankind propaganda," suggesting, despite his advocacy of Italian and German policies, that his message was of the latter variety.[8] He argued against war as a means of creating scarcity and destroying heritage, and repeats that the United States and Britain had no reason to be at war with Italy. He opposed an alliance with Bolshevism. He tried desperately to reveal the dangers of what he saw as Jewish domination of the American and British economies, and he suggested that if these nations returned to their respective and interrelated cultural heritages, they could find a way out of this mess without spilling more blood, bombing more monuments, or further destroying their own or their enemies' economies. Or, as he would still be arguing in Canto 74, "gun sales lead to more gun sales / they do not clutter the market for gunnery / there is no saturation" (*C*, 74:449). He proudly claimed the title of propagandist on 19 March 1942, saying "I was runnin' this SAME propaganda, back before Hitler became Chancellor of the Reich" (*EPS*, 64).

We know, of course, that his radio career began well after January 1933, so it is not only to his broadcasts that he refers in this statement, but also to his prose and poetry. He noted in the same broadcast that he had for some time been talking about "how the old show was runnin'. Runnin' DOWN. ... I began to say that in my poetry" (*EPS*, 64). In an earlier broadcast of 7 December 1941, he pointed his readers to Cantos 14 and 15 to see "what I had to say about the state of MIND in England in 1919" (*EPS*, 20). He read entire cantos as broadcasts—Canto 45 sometime in

1941 and Canto 46 on 12 February 1942. Usury is hardly the only topic shared by his poetry and propaganda. We find significant repeated material in the radio speeches and *The Cantos*—such as the ideas and writings of Mencius and Confucius; the foundation of the Monte dei Paschi bank in Siena; the American ideals represented by Thomas Jefferson, John Adams, and Martin Van Buren; the relationships between economic conditions and artistic production; the relationships between Mussolini and Sigismundo Malatesta; the *directio voluntatis*; the difficulty of beauty; Mussolini's clearing of the Pontine Marshes; Henri Gaudier Brzeska's art and war's threat to it; and the poetry and thought of Guido Cavalcanti. Pound even linked *The Cantos* and broadcasts through phrasal structures. The same phrase with which he ends Canto 1—"So that:"—recurs in his script for the broadcast of 16 May 1943 as a transition between a statement about the benefits of Italy's colonial aims and a discussion of arguments made about Germany's alliance with Italy (*EPS*, 309; *C*, 1:5). If in the poem the phrase seems an odd ending and perhaps an assertion of the connections between cantos—"things have ends and beginnings"—here it appears in its more typical usage of asserting a logical link between ideas. But the emphasis brought by all capitals—and presumably by Pound's tone in the broadcast—invites listeners who know his poetry to see the connection. Similarly, in his broadcast of 6 July 1942, he recounted a conversation between W. B. Yeats and Aubrey Beardsley about the role of ugliness in good art and the problems of making art to be sold, including Beardsley's remark, "Beauty is so DIFFICULT" (*EPS*, 193). This same conversation, of course, would figure prominently in the *Pisan Cantos*, where it seems to argue for a synthesis of those poems' lyrical beauty and raw emotion.

In the *Pisan Cantos* Pound remains concerned about how best "to get the meaning across," a notion he expresses several times and in different ways. He writes in Canto 80: "To communicate and then stop, that is the / law of discourse / To go far and come to an end" (*C*, 80:514). In Canto 79, he makes a similar claim, but poetically, he couches it very differently. "4 birds on 3 wires, one bird on one," he begins, continuing:

> the imprint of the intaglio depends
>   in part on what is pressed under it
> the mould must hold what is poured into it
>   in
>   discourse
>   what matters is
> to get it across e poi basta
>   5 of 'em now on 2;
>   on 3; 7 on 4
>   thus what's his name
> and the change in writing the song books
>   5 on 3   aulentissima rosa fresca

(*C*, 79:505–06)

37. Ezra Pound, extract from Canto 79, *Cantos* (New York: New Directions, 1993), p. 506. Copyright © 1934, 1937, 1940, 1948, 1956, 1959, 1963, 1966 and 1968 by Ezra Pound. Reprinted by permission of the New Directions Publishing Corp.

This polyphonic passage is hard to read because alongside the text in Latin script appears the same idea in ideograms, whose literal meaning of "words, speech, meaning" + "to apprehend" Pound translated as "Get the meaning across. Stop."[9] But he embeds this discussion of how discourse works—and presumably, therefore, how good propaganda should work—in a description of birds' movement among wires, which evokes for him the movement of notes on musical staves. And because he begins the thought with a reference to Clément Janequin, whose "Le Chant des Oiseaux" he presents in Canto 75 (in the form of Gerhart Münch's transcription of Francesco da Milano's single-voice version of the piece), this whole image of birds and wires and notes and staves literalizes the representational beauty and power of art (*C*, 75:470–71). So where to draw a line between medium and message? Are the birds the medium or the message? Do they represent Janequin, or does he represent them? Is the poem a medium for making a claim about discourse, or does the claim about discourse metaphorically tell us something about how to read the poem? That Pound sees such clear connections between his poetry and propaganda means that his readers cannot continue to insist on their separation.

H. D., who was less interested in Pound's political and economic message than in some relationship between his lyrics and hers, had far more difficulty reconciling Pound's poetry and propaganda than did Pound. In this respect, she can stand in for many of Pound's readers—for whom his political and economic ideas seem not just uninteresting but even embarrassing. What reader has not been vexed by the problem of Pound's politics, his anti-Semitism, his vitriol? Pound's friend W. B. Yeats described him in his Introduction to *The Oxford Book of Modern Verse* (1936) as "an economist, poet, politician, raging at malignants with inexplicable characters and motives, grotesque figures out of a child's book of beasts."[10] We can understand Yeats's concern about Pound's rage and the vehemence of his beliefs—not all of which we can stomach. Since so much of the anti-Semitism of the radio broadcasts has been recounted before, here is an example from the correspondence. Pound's friend and translator Lina Caico wrote to him in March 1937 about the situation of a young Jewish woman living in Berlin, begging Pound to offer her a place in the concerts he was organizing in Rapallo; Nazi law only allowed the musician to teach Jewish pupils and perform for Jews, but none of the Jews in Germany could pay her.[11] Pound's response was unequivocal and merits quoting at length:

> I know ALL about jews/
> Let her try Rothschild and some of the bastards who are murdering 10 million anglo saxons in England.
> I know there are jews and jews/ BUT until they will accept the responsability for governing at least Palestine

246 *Fascist Directive*

>   and defend at least ten acre of ground against savages AS all other races have done/
>
>   and until they accept the fact that all other races have suffered/ and until they at least participate in study of and attack on usury system NO. I am not having any more.
>
>   I have for 25 years known almost EXCLUSIVELY musicians crushed out by the damn system WHICH the jews NEVER attack. New York ist ganz verjudet. Let her go to N York or palestine where they have the "greatest" orchestra in the woild; vide Toscanini, 83 jews and one wop/ Jews are always longing to leave. I rescued one here, and and he H fliurished.
>
>   They are the GREAT destroyers of value/ the obliterators of all demarcations/ the shifters of boundary stones.
>
>   Occasionally a good one has to suffer for the sins of the race.[12]

This statement—made before the implementation of the Italian racial laws in July 1938—calls foul on any claim that Pound's anger at Jews was *purely* economic. Given an opportunity to separate out an individual from a race, he declines. That he does so in the context of his own musical work—one of the great contributions that he made to the revival of Italian culture—makes even clearer that he draws no distinction between politics and art. So even if we want to imagine the poet as separated from the material challenges his world, Pound will not let us. This issue has led scholars to a variety of mental gymnastics—sometimes arguing for a complete separation of poetry and politics, and at others devising elaborate theories to allow their reconciliation. H. D. makes this conflict explicit: Pound *did* "ogre-ize himself by his association with Radio Rome," but, and in part as a result, "He lay on the floor of the Iron Cage and wrote the *Pisan Cantos*." Using language steeped in a mysticism that seems incompatible with radio propaganda, she conceives of this latter act as one that could only result from access to "a reserve of dynamic or daemonic power from which we may all draw." But Pound's story challenges her conception of poetry as belonging to a realm distinct from politics and propaganda. Both the ogre-izing and the writing happened, and to insist on their separation does injustice to his story.

H. D. notes that this confluence challenges her sense—and, I would argue, our sense—of what poets are, as she realizes that Pound's story somehow implicates all poets:

> It is the *feel* of things rather than what people do. It runs through all the poets, really, of the world. One of *us* has been trapped. Now, one of *us* is free. But we, the partisans of world-thought, of the myth, shiver apprehensively. What now?[13]

Pound's captivity was her captivity, the captivity of all poets. Likewise, his freedom freed all poets, but it brought with it a larger problem: his ogre-izing was all poets' ogre-izing, just as all poets hope to access that "reserve of dynamic or daemonic power." If one poet can be "indicted" (a word over whose precise meaning she puzzles, seeming to wonder whether it has implications beyond its legal definition) for treason, then all poetry can be treasonous. And is madness the only or even a satisfactory escape? Elsewhere in *End to Torment* she writes, "I can not say that any of us are satisfied with the equation, Fascist-party-line-by-short-wave-to-America + Poet = *Senilität*."[14] Nor should we. Indeed, critical treatments of Pound's work which suggest that he could not but go mad, given the ways that he tried to separate his poetry from his propaganda, cannot do justice to the complexity of Pound's encounter with Fascism, and especially with Fascist cultural Nationalism. What we find when we look closely at Pound's literary work in the context of his investment in the cultural practices of Mussolini's regime is that this investment transformed both his literary work and his modernism.

On the simplest level, Pound employed methods central to the Fascist regime's approach to constructing Italian national identity. Pound's broadcasts on Radio Rome are, of course, the most notorious example of his turn away from the elite audience of his earlier modernism and instead to mass culture. Fascist mass exhibitions, parades, youth camps, and spectacles were crucial means of reaching a wide public, deemed an even more important audience than elites. By involving the masses in Fascism's nationalizing work, Mussolini's government aimed to make Italian national identity something that grew out of everyday practices as well as highbrow endeavors. Pound's own turn to mass culture, however, reached beyond these infamous radio broadcasts. Most importantly, his numerous textbooks—*ABC of Economics*, *ABC of Reading*, *Guide to Kulchur*, and so forth—all envisioned a larger public of readers not already trained in methods of encountering these subjects. Thanks in part to the cultural practices of Mussolini's regime, Pound was convinced of the relationships between cultural heritage and engaged citizenship, so learning how to read well, or about economics, or how to participate in one's cultural heritage all contributed to a larger project of creating citizens—whether Italian or American—who were better equipped to contribute to their nation. In a radio broadcast of 18 May 1943, Pound stressed that "a new concept of civics has been built up in Europe," and he traced this concept to Italian Nationalist Giuseppe Mazzini, who emphasized the importance of individuals immersing themselves in a spiritual sense of the nation (*EPS*, 313). Whether we think of Pound's attempts to collaborate with the cultural administrators of Mussolini's regime, of his work to bring pre-Bach Italian music to a wide audience, or his approach to such works as *Guide to Kulchur*, Pound saw the importance of cultural heritage to making strong and contributing citizens.

Also important to Pound was the Fascist structuring idea of *corporazioni* or *sindicati*—hierarchical and self-governing organizations of labor and capital, seen as alternatives to Socialism and

Capitalism. Involved in an acceptance of the importance of these guilds or syndicates was a renunciation of egocentrism in favor of a collective task, or a sense of working for a larger collective good. Most literally, we see Pound mulling over this idea in his essay "Ubicumque Lingua Romana" (1938), where he considers how he would organize such a syndicate of writers:

> I can also tell the men of my own profession (that is students and writers) how I think they can and should form their guilds, or corporazioni, or whatever they wish to call them. I have in my own way got results from associations before one put a special name on them. I know as much as the next man about the nature of artists and writers and how it is possible to bring them together in the spirit of the fascio as I understand fascio, or union.
>
> These are particular problems, and I think I am sufficiently in the spirit of the time to feel that it is almost useless to discuss them in the abstract. If at a given day in a given place I am asked to organize a sindicato of men of my own profession, I know how I should start doing it.
>
> Among other things I should treat literature as communications service, not as the quantitative production of merchandise.[15]

For Pound, the structure of the *corporazioni* was inherently linked to the "union" of the *fascio* and the sense of collective strength which that symbol implies. He emphasizes his clear sense of both how one organizes a collective and the "nature of artists and writers," figures who might not automatically recognize the benefit of such a collective. In Canto 80, he imagines sculptor Henri Gaudier-Brzeska advocating a similar confederation:

> when Gaudier had said he wd/ fight for la Patrie if war came
> but that anarchy was the true form of government

> (meaning, so far as I cd/ make out, some form of
> sindical organization. (*C*, 80:524)

Pound's backreading of Fascist structures onto Gaudier-Brzeska's patriotism emphasizes the connection he has come to see between artists and regimes. Most importantly, we find his new sense that poetry and other arts should be made in the service of a regime, and therefore valued more for their message than for any sense of them as a thing made. As I noted in the introduction to this book, such a claim flies in the face of his *ars gratia artis* aesthetic of the 1910s, but would now remain a part of his poetics to the end. It is important that in "Notes for CXVII et seq.," part of *Drafts and Fragments*, Pound writes "Let the Gods forgive what I have made," and *not* "Let the Gods forgive what I have said" (*C*, "Notes":822).

This change in aesthetic mission would of course also affect his own artistic and cultural project. In his writings of the Fascist period, Pound wants to shift, as he says in *Guide to Kulchur*, from a "record of personal struggle" (as he describes a variety of artworks, including his own *Cantos*) to "the domain of culture." In other words, he knows he needs to move away from his own issues, ideas, and history in order to represent a shared culture that can speak to a wider, or even mass, audience. If his *Cantos* are, on one level, a "record of personal struggle," they also aspire to represent history to a wider public and employ that history to effect political change in the present. We must go back to his claim to the title of "propagandist" in a radio broadcast in 1942 (*EPS*, 64). Whether he initially wrote his more politically and economically driven cantos with a propaganda purpose in mind, we know that by the start of the war, he had come to think of them that way, adding them to the mission of serving as a "communications service" for the regime. And, as H. D. noted, his poetry left the realm of the personal to implicate all poetry, so that even the highly indiosyncratic writing context of the *Pisan Cantos* represented the new poetic modernism to which Pound came through his engagement with Fascism.

Pound adopted and adapted numerous techniques and practices from Mussolini's regime. I have already shown how inclined he was to employ the rhetoric and imagery of the Fascist regime—using tropes of *Romanità* in titles and illustrations for articles, employing the myth of the Duce in his prose and poetry, and drawing on depictions of Fascist history presented in Fascist exhibitions. Most centrally, he came to employ Mussolini's *piccone* (or pickax) as a compositional method not unlike his ideogram. A selective and destructive impulse, the *piccone* cuts through layers of detritus to find a buried treasure, clearing away mess so that this treasure can be discovered by others. For Pound, the archaeological work of the *piccone* and the urban renewal of *bonifica* were crucially linked for both clear away hindrances to new projects. On a more personal level, finding the valuable piece amidst all the clutter was crucial, given how much learning he had himself amassed. Pound's compositional method for *Guide to Kulchur* emphasized this necessity for anyone who wanted to employ the cultural heritage of the past in the present moment. Crucially, the *piccone*—and the excavations it engendered—worked to rouse wider curiosity. "I'm not trying to sell you anything," he claimed in a radio broadcast of 12 June 1943, "I'm trying to open up a chink for the light to come through."[16]

This work, Pound suggests, cannot be his alone. He wants to teach others to employ their own pickaxes. In his radio broadcast of 16 March 1943, he even encourages his listeners to undertake their own searches for pieces of the cultural heritage that have been hidden in archives and treasury departments. "Well damn it all," he says, "go start diggin'. You will find it as tough as Babylonian excavations. As crabbed as the clay tablets in Nineveh, but you may as well start excavation" (*EPS*, 251). Pound had done his share of such digging by this point—most recently, bringing to light lost pieces of Baroque music, unearthing crucial elements of American cultural heritage for the Adams Cantos—and both his prose and poetic writings modeled how these treasures of the past could be made into new works in the present. In short, his project of employing the cultural heritage in service of present ideas and new art drew directly on the cultural practices of Mussolini's regime.

Similarly, he borrowed from the idea of *autarchia* in his writings. If Mussolini's policy grew in part out of the economic strictures imposed by the League of Nations' sanctions, then Pound's own cultural autarchy resulted from both his own geographical distance from libraries like the British Museum and his growing belief that what stays in a person's memory ultimately matters more than what might be available in books. Whether we think of his revelation of a vast Italian musical heritage that could be employed during the period of *autarchia*, or of his valorization in *Guide to Kulchur* of what "resists forgetting," the notion of a personal intellectual autarchy grew increasingly crucial in Pound's writings of this period. Perhaps the most dramatic example of this tendency, of course, is in his *Pisan Cantos*, written, as was *Guide to Kulchur*, in a situation that precluded frequent reference to sources. These poems, even as they mourn ends of eras, are a celebration of an "autarchic method," where Pound's heritage—as he has absorbed it into his being—becomes the basis of new and powerful art. As he writes in Canto 76, "nothing matters but the quality / of the affection— / in the end—that has carved the trace in the mind / dove sta memoria" (*C*, 76:477). Everything in these poems—the anecdotes, persons, comments, regional accents, literary references, personal associations, cultural implications, political references, economic grandstanding—can be here because it was already in Pound when he was captured and then imprisoned in the iron cage. To make poetry in this situation of incarceration, he has to draw on his own memory and resources. In this way, the *Pisan Cantos*' method of composition is as much an insistence on the survival of the Fascist dream as the image of Mussolini's bloated hanging body in Canto 74 is a lamentation of its end (*C*, 74:445). Even if Mussolini as an embodiment of the Fascist dream is dead, the cultural practices that he enabled live on, maintaining his project.

Permeating Pound's borrowings and adaptations of Fascist approaches to culture is his new sense of a link between art and propaganda. Indeed, it is this link that gives Pound's readers the most trouble. At the same time that Pound was learning from Mussolini's regime new ways of eliding art and propaganda, Anglo-American literary critics were fighting to keep the two apart. In 1939, Cleanth Brooks wrote that a poet writing propaganda poetry incurs particular risks:

> Because he is intent on the truth of his statement and preoccupied with the inculcation of a particular message, his poetry may easily take the form of a poetry of exclusion, leaving out of account the elements of experience not favorable to the matter in hand, and thus oversimplifying experience.

Brooks quoted—and amended—I. A. Richards's assertion that

> The question of belief or disbelief never arises when we are reading well. If unfortunately it does arise, either through the poet's fault or our own, we have for the moment ceased to be readers and have become astronomers, theologians, or moralists [and one may add "or economists"], persons engaged in a quite different type of activity.[17]

The kind of reading that poetry invites, Brooks suggests, is impossible when a poem has a "message" as well as being a product. In so arguing, he has a wholly different sense of art from Pound's, even though his sense would drive New Critical approaches to Pound's work for many decades. That Brooks would insert the category "economist" into the list—a class into which Yeats had placed Pound in his Introduction to *The Oxford Book of Modern Verse*—attests to the degree to which Pound stretched the boundaries of poetry as conceived by both men. Pound—in opposition to many of his critics—requires that his readers become not just economists, but historians, translators, musicians, philosophers, politicians, and even propagandists. And his insistence on communicating a believed-in message through poetry means that his poetry could aspire to the condition of his prose, testing the limits of the genre as surely as his breaking of the pentameter.

Still, Brooks was hardly unique. As critic Toby Clark has shown, Clement Greenberg, beginning in 1939 and continuing through his career,

> warned against the corrupting effects of what he called "kitsch," which he saw both in American mass culture and in the populist official art of Nazi Germany and the Soviet Union. To defend true art against this, artists should attend to purely artistic concerns; to make, in effect, abstract art which would be immune to political exploitation.[18]

Clark shows, however, that this "pure and free art," the post-Cold War Abstract Expressionism that dominated the New York art world by the 1950s, was itself employed in exhibitions by such institutions as the Museum of Modern Art—exhibitions, it turned out later, that were funded by the CIA—as exemplary of the "mark of freedom" of American painting, as opposed to the "regimented kitsch of Soviet communism."[19] The blind eye that many American art critics have turned to American propaganda's employment of high art is only one part of this story's importance: it also demonstrates the extent to which people are generally less inclined to try to see through the workings of advertisements or messages with which they agree. At the same time, however, we must remember how Fascist employment of avant-garde art in its service called foul on Greenberg's assertion that abstract art cannot be used propagandistically. Only by excluding propaganda art from our definitions of "true art" can we conclude, like Richard Wolin, that "modern art, from romanticism to art for art's sake, has assumed a predominantly effete, private, and self-referential character," that "It has thereby forfeited that monumental quality that once suffused Greek architecture and tragedy, and that was capable of spiritually uniting the polis and its citizens."[20]

As architectural historian Libero Andreotti has emphasized in his study of the Mostra della Rivoluzione Fascista, this exhibition and Fascist cultural projects generally forged an important kind of propaganda art—art whose main purpose was the "effective communication of ideas" and which may offer "unique opportunities for individual expression and experimentation." This public art serves a crucial social function—sometimes even becoming a cult object and participating in a collective ritual—and "may help to disseminate a new style and make it acceptable to a wider audience."[21] In short, propaganda art equally stresses message and material, social and artistic function. For Pound, this interest in the relationship between art and propaganda is a clear result of his encounter with Fascist cultural Nationalism. He could never have written his Italian Cantos (72 and 73) in 1913, when he claimed that "art never asks anybody to do anything, or to think anything, or to be anything" and that "It exists as the trees exist."[22] It is impossible to read the Italian Cantos without an awareness of their propaganda function and their espousal of ideas that scholars would prefer not make their way into Pound's poetry. Yet, a crucial part of these poems' value is their attempt to function propagandistically. That critics cannot agree on how to read these poems in the larger context of the *Cantos* projects makes clear what an artistic challenge they are. But for Pound, they are a clear result not just of his investment in Mussolini's ideology, but also of his new thinking about how poetry could function as propaganda and about the relationships between culture and politics.

During the Fascist period, Pound increasingly employed political ideology in support of his cultural administration of Vivaldi's music. He emphasized art's educational, social, political, and national function. He argued for the importance of cultural heritage in strengthening citizens. For such a man, these poems are the critical next step. That their aesthetics deviates from that of many of the other cantos, and their subject matter digresses from the poems' larger narratives, demonstrates how his poetry had to change to accommodate his new understanding of propaganda art. Returning to the expanse of *The Cantos* in the light of the Italian Cantos, it is easy to see their propagandistic workings, whether we think about Canto 45's diatribe against usury, Canto 41's participation in the myth of the Duce, Canto 46's thinking about the Mostra della Rivoluzione Fascista, the long examination of Jefferson and Adams in *Eleven New Cantos*, rumination on the founding of the Sienese bank in *The Fifth Decad of Cantos*, the bringing of all these ideas together in the *Pisan Cantos*, or the continued return to the corruption of history and economics in the Adams Cantos. *The Cantos* may not always serve as a "communications service" for Mussolini's regime or for Fascism per se, but they certainly and consistently argue for those ideals Pound came to espouse through his encounter with Fascism.

It was largely through his confrontation with Mussolini's Fascist modernism that Pound's own version of modernism was transformed. This new alliance between art and propaganda is a part of that shift, as Pound moves from an "art for art's sake" style of modernism to one that is extremely politically engaged, though of course he was hardly the only Anglo-American modernist writer to assume such engagement during the 1930s. During that decade, however, Pound was not really as involved in Anglo-American modernism as he was in Italian modernism, Just as the language in the cantos of the 1930s shows a disconnection from American or British colloquial English, his late modernism looks more Italian than British or American. Many Italian modernists who allied themselves with Mussolini's regime (Casella, Sarfatti, Sironi, Terragni) adopted a "third way" that combined elements of a national cultural heritage with an openness to the innovation of European modernism, thereby making and supporting new art that was at once national and international. Similarly, Pound's method of patronizing culture and creating art during this period was rooted heavily in cultural heritage, and he looked at Italian Nationalist models to open up a similar veneration of American cultural heritage. Later, he expanded his view, so that cultural heritage was less nationalized than internationalized, so that the teachings of Confucius and Mencius could be as important as those of Jefferson or Adams. And he consistently looked to other innovative European artists—Brâncuși, Gaudier Brzeska, Lewis, Bartók, Stravinsky, Joyce—for ways of making this cultural heritage new. His own *Cantos*, which challenge existing poetics and aesthetics, pushed the boundaries of how the new might draw on the old in a way that both revives the old and allows something new.

During his early years in London, Pound devised a modernism that would be transformed by his affiliation with Fascist modernism. In London, he returned over and over again to the library to make modernism—finding old texts to translate, reviving earlier literary characters in his own poetry, and consistently reading inspiration for his art in the texts of the past, even if that art was intended for a fairly small audience. In Fascist Italy, his methods changed, so that he came to question the institution of the library, worrying about how it hides and silences cultural heritage rather than letting it sing. But in the various cultural projects of Mussolini's regime, Pound saw models for how to bring cultural heritage into the public sphere, so that it could be accessible to a wide—even mass—public. This striving to make monuments accessible can be seen over and over—in his insistence that old music be brought out of hidden manuscripts and performed, so that people could hear it in the present day; in his many textbooks intended to make complex ideas and important cultural monuments known to a wide public; and even in his broadcasts on Radio Rome, which aimed to disseminate the ideas learned in Fascist Italy to American and British audiences. Pound wanted cultural heritage—a heritage necessary to have educated and engaged citizens—out there.

Perhaps most importantly, Pound saw in Fascist modernism a forward-looking vision of how to transform society into a desired future. Roger Griffin has emphasized that Fascist modernism was not a rejection of modernity, but rather a means of "using the built environment to lay the cultural foundations of an alternative modernity."[23] In this respect, Fascist modernism looked forward to a grand future rather than lamenting the collapse of the known world.[24] When Pound wrote *Hugh Selwyn Mauberley* (1920) as a farewell to London, he was mourning the loss of a world he had known—or had believed to be knowable. The poem's opening, "E. P. Ode Pour L'Election de son Sepulchre," famously emphasizes how "E. P." found himself "out of key with his time," working to "resuscitate the dead art / Of poetry" in conflict with an age more interested in simple paraphrase and plaster molds than in the "Attic grace" of new creation.[25] The poem memorializes dead friends and lost dreams—or the collapse of a known world. In contrast, works like *ABC of Reading* and *Guide to Kulchur* are filled with hopes of a grand future in which a new kind of citizen who, through rich involvement in his or her cultural heritage, is able to make a new modernity. Even Pound's radio broadcasts look at the surrounding destruction of war and usury and offer an alternative. They are thus, despite frustration at the current moment, full of hope for the future and willing to invest in bringing that future to bear. While the *Pisan Cantos*, like *Hugh Selwyn Mauberley*, are acutely conscious of "ends of eras" and the loss of friends, monuments, and even a dream for the future, they continue the process of forging an alternative, continuing to use the methods and forms Pound learned from Fascist modernism to create afresh in the face of seemingly impossible odds. The *Pisan Cantos* are everywhere focused on the passing on of a tradition. And it is the responsibility of the poet to enact these kinds of transmission and transformation. He writes in Canto 80:

> before the world was given over to wars
> Quand vous serez bien vieille
>   remember that I have remembered,
> mia pargoletta,
>   and pass on the tradition
> there can be honesty of mind
>   without overwhelming talent. (*C*, 80:526)

Similarly, in Canto 79 he combines his own preservation and the conservation of a different tradition:

> O Lynx keep watch on my fire.
> So Astafieva had conserved the tradition
> From Byzance and before then
>   Manitou remember this fire
> O lynx, keep the phylloxera from my grape vines.
>   (*C*, 79:509)

Though these acts of conservation may be separated temporally by centuries, their impulse and significance are the same. Pound's own remembering becomes the means of creation, and his own preservation requires also the assistance of another, thus becoming a communal act. This creation, which is also a transmission, represents the ability of Fascism's cultural methods to survive Mussolini's death.

In Canto 76, Pound aligns himself with the insects he sees at work around him, writing "As a lone ant from a broken ant-hill / from the wreckage of Europe, ego scriptor" (*C*, 76:478). This act of writing from the ruins—of continuing to create in the face of nearly overwhelming destruction—sets the sequence in defiance of the war that he has watched threaten culture in Europe and around the world. Fundamentally, whether that transmission occurs via poetry or radio broadcasts is irrelevant. Throughout the *Pisan Cantos* one finds powerful statements of defiance and persistence. In Canto 74, for instance, Pound says: "I surrender neither the empire nor the temples plural / nor the constitution nor yet the city of Dioce" (*C*, 74:454), and "What you depart from is not the way" (*C*, 74:445). Though he has lost much, he has not lost his way. While the sequence says, "well those days are gone forever" (*C*, 83:554), it also argues that "what thou lovest well remains" (*C*, 81:540). The sequence enacts a transformation of personal memory into shared culture and tradition. It is to this continued insistence on "laying the cultural foundations of an *alternative* modernity" that H. D. refers when she concludes, even in the face of Pound's very ugly politics, that "He lay on the floor of the Iron Cage and wrote the *Pisan Cantos*."

A critical reading of propaganda art requires that we acknowledge and wrestle with the propaganda *and* the art. In a critical context in which we acknowledge that any aesthetic has—or is—an ideology, then all art might be read as propaganda art. Certainly, the propagandistic workings of a great deal of art was foremost in the justification of its making—at least on the part of its patrons—even if those workings are not always visible to us today. If, for instance, we become attuned to the overwhelming presence of Fascist architecture, public art, and urban design, we recognize how numerous were Mussolini's imprints on the city of Rome. Granted: this mission is not always easy, given how many efforts were made after the Second World War to erase or downplay these Fascist fingerprints. Many places' names have been changed, an effort to reduce the visible Fascist presence. But like the lampposts from which ax heads have been removed, and fountains still bearing shadows of "removed" *fasci*, the structures and many of the intended functions of these places remain (see Fig. 10).

Mussolini was hardly the first to transform Rome. Whether we think of Augustus changing a city of brick to one of marble, or Pope Sixtus V's radical Counter-Reformation revision of the city, or Napoleon's looting of important antiquities, Rome has always been ripe for remaking. When it became the capital of the new Italian nation, Rome lacked the infrastructure necessary to maintain the government, commerce, and population that came with its new role. In many ways, Mussolini's work is a continuation of this vision of Roma Capitale, though the Fascist imagining emphasized the connection between ancient sites and modern power. Today, moving through the city of Rome allows a tour through various eras of propaganda art—starting perhaps with that of Augustus's imperial period, including various popes' work to enforce the power of the papacy, venturing into the self-promotion of wealthy families, pausing at projects designed to tout Rome as the capital of a newly unified nation, and incorporating the way that Mussolini's projects allowed a new vision of the city. In these ways, the city of Rome offers a perfect context for thinking about Fascist propaganda art, as it requires us to view Fascist art's arguments in and amidst so many others.

The city's numerous obelisks afford an excellent example of these arguments and counterarguments. Erected originally in Egypt, they were toted back to Rome by Augustus, who re-erected them in various places around the city as a sign of his imperial power. The obelisk now in the Piazza del Popolo, brought from Heliopolis and placed in the Circus Maximus, bears hieroglyphs detailing the glories of pharaohs Rameses II and Merenptah, whose successors Augustus vanquished. As a part of the new urban plan implemented by Pope Sixtus V, Domenico Fontana moved it to its present location in 1589.[26] Throughout Rome, these obelisks became a sign of the power of the Church, set up in the piazzas of important churches and usually topped with a cross or a papal symbol, in an attempt to Christianize the object and its presence in Rome. These same obelisks became a model for Mussolini, whose capture of the Stele of Axum was explicitly linked to Augustus by Fascist propaganda—a sign of the imperial connections between the two men, and an erasure of the papal appropriations. Becoming a good reader of Rome's urban fabric requires knowledge of this history and ideology, and how they shape a contemporary experience in the city. In this sense, we may use these obelisks as representative of the kind of reading that propaganda art generally, and Pound's writings specifically, requires.

Not surprisingly, the art and architecture of different periods contains different kinds and amounts of value for the living citizens of a city. It would be an understatement to say that papal propaganda and ancient Roman propaganda fare better in our contemporary moment than that of Mussolini's era. Indeed, many of the buildings and sites designed to celebrate the ideals and deeds of the Fascist government have fallen into relative disrepair. Our critical difficulties with propaganda art are partially to blame. For postwar Romans, the ax head that made a Fascist bundle so recognizable was an appalling sight, so it is no surprise that many ax heads and *fasci* were defaced, in order to reduce the Fascist imprint on structures that could not be demolished. And perhaps it is a similar impulse that leads to the neglect of areas like the Piazza Augusto Imperatore—where the Fascist-era mosaic-adorned facades of the buildings look particularly dingey in contrast with the nearby churches of San Rocco and San Girolamo degli Illirici, and the brilliant white travertine of the new Ara Pacis Museum. Perhaps such an impulse creates an unwillingness to protect the frescoes adorning the cortile—now a parking lot—of the Casa Madre dei Mutilati, a monument celebrated in its time for the integration of architecture and decorative arts. Now janitorial carts and bicycles typically lean against the paintings (Fig. 38). The big white blocks of the Foro Mussolini—now the Foro Italico—are perhaps too much of a temptation for graffiti artists, whose own work is far from ideologically neutral (Fig. 39).

To let these places decay, however, is to lose an era, and to lose cultural heritage. Just as no one can choose her own DNA, a community cannot choose its heritage. Of course, it might decide to privilege some periods, historical events, or personages over others, but even the shameful parts remain, exerting their influence on the present, and a culture ignores them at its peril. We need not celebrate those historical or cultural moments that deviate from contemporary

Propaganda Art 263

38. Frescoes celebrating the imperial wars in Addis Abeba and Somalia with cleaning supplies, courtyard of Casa Madre dei Mutilati di Guerra, Rome, 2004. (Photograph by the author)

39. Graffiti on marble markers in the Foro Mussolini, now Foro Italico, Rome, 2004. (Photograph by the author)

ideals; we need not leave odious names attached to prominent buildings or forums. At the same time, when we demolish them, we engage in the same selective history-making that Mussolini undertook with his *piccone*. To what degree are graffiti and neglect also a part of that heritage and history? What does it mean to curate cultural heritage? Or to make new art from engagement with it?

The relationships between Pound's poetics and politics beg the question that most vexed H. D.: Can a poet be a traitor? Legally speaking, yes, and perhaps only Pound's insanity defense saved him. But, from another angle, H. D. hoped not, because despite whatever political misgivings she might have had about Pound's actions, there is that refrain, "He lay on the floor of the Iron Cage and wrote the *Pisan Cantos*." For H. D., Pound's confinement confines all poets—"One of *us* had been trapped."[27] And perhaps H. D. feared the contamination of Pound's entrapment because she read it through her own confinement:

> They say I must go into Zürich for another X-ray. This terrifies me. This is the terror one can not speak of, *that walketh by night*. They might ask me to stay in the Klinik again. It is the fear of being caught, caged, confined—*a confinement*.[28]

Given Pound's ability to draw from that "reserve of dynamic or daemonic power from which we may all draw," we know that she *wanted* Pound's poetry to come from a different place than his ogre-izing. "There is no *reason* to accept, to condone, to forgive, to forget what Ezra has done," she wrote, reflecting on Pound's actions in the context of her friend Sylvia Beach's internment during the war. Still, when Beach asserts that Pound should not have been awarded the Bollingen Prize, H. D. can only respond, "But …" As she explains: "I said, 'But.' There is no argument, pro or con. You catch fire or you don't catch fire."[29] Even as she acknowledges the problems of Pound's actions—and the impossibility of ignoring or forgiving them—she says the poetry matters in a different way. What is she seeing?

It has never been more important to read, study, and teach writers like Pound. What do we, as contemporary critical thinkers, gain by relegating a poet or a philosopher to the trash-dump, just because we find their politics reprehensible? Pound's case, of course, is not so different from that of philosopher Martin Heidegger. To apply H. D.'s language, Heidegger ogre-ized himself by his association with Hitler. *And* he wrote *Being and Time*, widely considered one of the most important works of twentieth-century philosophy. Many of Heidegger's readers have sought a way around that confluence. It is just as painful to realize that a wise philosophy cannot save someone from poor political choices as it is to acknowledge that art is no prophylactic. But, as Philippe Lacoue-Labarthe has noted, Heidegger's association with Nazism was "completely consistent with his [philosophical] thought."[30] Or, despite attempts to embrace the philosophy while rejecting the politics, there can be no real split. Heidegger's idea of Being-in-the-world and his thinking about the relationships between "being" and "time" are not such a far reach from Pound's conception of *The Cantos* as "a poem including history." And Maurice Blanchot has shown that the consistencies between Heidegger's political and philosophical thought exist on many levels. He says that Heidegger's political speeches

> were frightening in their form as well as in their content, for it is the same writing and very language by which, in a great moment of the history of thought, we had been made present at the loftiest questioning, one that could come to us from *Being and Time*. Heidegger uses the same language to call for voting for Hitler, to justify Nazi Germany's break from the League of Nations, and to praise Schlageter.[31]

Like Heidegger, Pound used "the same holy language" to condemn a Jewish pianist to pay "for the crimes of her race" as he did to beg in Canto 80, "Pull down thy vanity." Heidegger and Pound matter not because we can cleanse their writing of their politics, but because we cannot.

As Lacoue-Labarthe said of Heidegger, Pound's political arguments and his poetic constructions come from the same place, and are consistent with one another. And, as Blanchot has said of Heidegger, the same language infuses both Pound's ugliest radio broadcasts and his most beautiful poetry. To the degree that Pound's poetry can function as propaganda, and to the degree that the United States government objected to his propaganda for giving aid and comfort to the enemy during time of war, then his poetry—at least in time of war—was treasonous.[32] Those, like Sylvia Beach, who thought that no line could be drawn between the rants and the raves, had a point. According to the definitions established in the indictment, the poetry should be no more celebrated than the broadcasts.

Still, it is crucial to Pound's case that Nationalism carries its own assumptions about identity—assumptions that Pound's writings do not share. One is that national identity trumps all. While a national identity might subsume other identities—religious, linguistic, geographic—it also creates a dichotomy around itself. Or in familiar wartime lingo, you're either with us or against us. Mussolini made great use of this notion, particularly after Italy was sanctioned by the League of Nations, but so did the language of Pound's indictment for treason. It did not matter whether the ideas Pound espoused on Radio Roma were good or bad, but that they were perceived to be offered in opposition to American power. According to this model of Nationalism, a person could put forward Italian propaganda, or American propaganda, but not—as Pound claimed he was doing—"mankind propaganda." Because Pound was legally an American citizen, his propaganda (in which we must include his poetry) was treasonous.

Pound's engagement with Italian cultural Nationalism led him to reject such tenets of Nationalism. He watched both American and Italian Nationalist projects in action, and identified with both nations, even though the ideology of Nationalism requires that a person be a citizen of one nation, not many. His poetry—his propaganda art—opened up a critique of Nationalism. There he made the traditional political categories seem alien: he refused to operate within the Axis-Allies binary dominating the discourse of the period, looking instead for ways to challenge the stability of all kinds of identity. As he claimed in a letter quoted above, "The assumption of the right to punish and take vengeance regardless of the area of jurisdiction is dangerous. I do not mean in a small way; but for the nation."[33] He is thinking there of the implications of his case to the boundaries of national power and citizenship. H. D. was right when she suggested in *End to Torment* that Pound's poetry requires readers to walk "into another dimension." The poems—their various voices, their sometimes conflicting ideas, their donning of identity positions—were already operating—in terms Homi K. Bhabha applies to theory—as places of hybridity, "where the construction of a political object that is new, *neither the one nor the other*, properly alienates our political expectations, and changes, as it must, the very forms of our recognition of the moment in politics."[34] This is what poetry does, what art does—and why it can become such a powerful propaganda tool, and why so many critics would insist on its absolute separation from message. Or, as Terry Eagleton has written about the aesthetic, Pound's poetry "provides an unusually powerful challenge and alternative to these dominant ideological forms, and is in this sense an eminently contradictory phenomenon."[35] The combination of political commitment and the unstable positioning of citizenship in lyric challenges both. Taking a position in a poem is not about some sense of fixed identity. Rather, it involves a constant renegotiation of vying identities, and reading them enacts the conflict. To encounter Pound's poetry *and* his politicized punishment is for readers to enter "another dimension" where suppositions about citizenship and creativity are unsettled. And H. D. is also right that Pound "walked out into the same dimension," since his poetry was, in this sense, already operating in this way. For him, nothing had really changed in the time he spent incarcerated at St. Elizabeths.

To make this claim, I know, flies in the face of those who would like to view Pound's time in St. Elizabeths as a sort of atonement. It is popular to suggest that at some point—whether at Pisa or "in the bughouse"—Pound realized his wrongs, and came to believe that he deserved punishment. I disagree—and not just because he flashed a sweaty Fascist salute when, after his release, he disembarked in Naples, never to return to the United States. It is rather that I think this view allows us too easy an escape from the complexities that Pound's writing presents. To believe he was atoning for his sins allows us to dismiss his political commitments as, to use Lacoue-Labarthe's terms, either an accident or a mistake. And we like that, because we can turn away from the "erroneous chapter" of Pound's life, and fix our glance instead on those poetic remnants we have cleansed of what some have called his "obstinate heresy." But to do so makes us miss the real accomplishment of Pound's work, for in ignoring the darker and offensives parts of his work, we dismantle the "struggle of identifications" that Pound's literary work enacts.

But if H. D. was right in her assessment of the ways in which Pound's poetry forces us to walk "into another dimension," she was wrong in suggesting that his poetry—or all poetry—draws from a "reserve of dynamic or daemonic power." She suggests that this realm from which poetry comes is somehow outside the realm of the political, or the day-to-day, or the engaged. But the power of Pound's work—which may be dynamic and often even seems daemonic—emerges from within its engagements. Rather than offering a critique from outside, Pound's challenge is entwined in the struggle, and it pushes at the boundaries of that struggle. Because his work was so invested in the cultural Nationalism of the Fascist regime, and in the Nationalistic struggles that drove the Second World War, his poems can complicate a sense of national identity from a variety of subject positions at once. Continuing to read his poems enables a rethinking of the very Nationalist identity categories on which definitions of treason are based.

APPENDIX

Vivaldi scores in Pound's hand in the Ezra Pound and Olga Rudge Papers

This table includes those Antonio Vivaldi scores that I have been able to identify in the Ezra Pound Papers (YCAL MSS 43), Ezra Pound Additions (YCAL MSS 53), and Olga Rudge Papers (YCAL MSS 54) in the Yale Collection of American Literature, Beinecke Rare Book and Manuscript Library. The Beinecke catalogue numbers identify the manuscript collection, box number, and folder number of the item in question.

The table uses Ezra Pound's own catalogue of his and Rudge's Vivaldi works as its basis (see p. 185). The first three items in the table do not appear in Pound's catalogue, but the remaining items are organized following his numbering system, which is also often used in his labeling of scores. While most items in his catalogue represent discreet and complete concerti, items #2 and #10 are parts of the same concerto (RV 198). The second column lists each concerto's name as given in Peter Ryom's standard catalogue of Vivaldi's works, *Répertoire des œuvres d'Antonio Vivaldi: les compositions instrumentales* (Copenhagen: Engstrøm & Sødring, 1986). The third column gives Ryom's catalogue number, the standard method of identifying Vivaldi's works. The fourth column identifies the location of the original manuscript that Pound and

Rudge were transcribing, whether the Sächsische Landesbibliothek (Dresden) or the Biblioteca Nazionale (Turin), including the library cataloguing numbers. A description of the scores and/or other items in the Beinecke collection follows in the fifth column, and the sixth and final column identifies correspondence in the Olga Rudge Papers pertaining to the piece.

EP's Cat. No.	Name	RV Cat. No.	Location of original manuscript	Description of score(s) in Beinecke	Mention in correspondence between EP and OR?
	Sinfonia in G major for string orchestra	RV 149	Dresden, SL, 2389/0/4	**YCAL MSS 43-Ov5-31:** out of order: pages 7–12, pages 1–6; page 1 includes full score; after that, violin part filled in, space left for keyboard accompaniment.	
	Concerto in D minor for solo violin, orchestra, and continuo	RV 241	Dresden, SL 2389/0/76	**YCAL MSS 43-Ov5-33:** very beginning: one and a half pages of EP's hand in ink and pencil, trails off on page 2; may be mislabeled? Score erroneously marked "Dresden 2389/0/57" (RV 224).	
	Concerto funèbre in B-flat major, for violin, oboe, salmoè, 3 "Viole all'Inglese", orchestra, and continuo	RV 579	Turin, Bibl Naz, Foà vol. 32, fol. 349–60	**YCAL MSS 54-154-3634:** No score, but photographs. One envelope of images of scores: 15 photographs, score has 2 flats, photo paper is 7 cm wide and 5 cm tall; image on paper is 6.2 cm wide by 4.6 cm tall. Photos are numbered on back. One photo is of an allegro movement, the basis of identification, but it is not clear whether all the pages go with it.	
1	Concerto in A major with echo for solo violin, echo, 3 solo violins, orchestra, and continuo	RV 552	Dresden, SL 2389/0/4 no. 2 (pp. 69–116)	**YCAL MSS 54-159-3723:** Full score, 2 drafts, also parts for first and second violins; **YCAL MSS 54-154-3634:** microphotograph of 2 pages of MS; **YCAL MSS 54-160-3731:** "LARGHETTO": 3 pp in EP's hand, black and red ink, red pencil; **YCAL MSS 54-160-3733:** "ECO Concerto / A.V.": another version of the Eco concerto (RV 552): EP's hand, 15 pages, black and red; written beside this entry in EP's catalogue: "* echo."	3 July 1938 (YCAL MSS 54-18-486)

Appendix   271

EP's Cat. No.	Name	RV Cat. No.	Location of original manuscript	Description of score(s) in Beinecke	Mention in correspondence between EP and OR?
2		RV 198		No manuscript identified. This item in EP's catalogue is actually the third movement of item #10. See below.	
3	Concerto in D major for solo violin, orchestra, and continuo	RV 226	Dresden, SL 2389/0/104	**YCAL MSS 54-159-3726:** "Rap. Aug. / Con de / ## / (3)": 18 pages, in black ink with some pencil and red pencil for marking divisions and notes and then also some pieces of paper overlaid in order to correct faulty sections (sometimes a small piece and sometimes an entire sheet).	May be discussed in 7-8 August 1938 (YCAL MSS 54-18-490)
4	Concerto in B minor for solo violin, orchestra, and continuo	RV 384	Dresden, SL 2389/0/88	**YCAL MSS 54-159-3728:** "VIVALDI / ¾ / ## / TO DO / No. 17 / Tigullio / (4) / Siena e Rapallo": 20 pages, full score, black ink with red and blue pencil, overlay; **YCAL MSS 54-159-3729:** "Vivaldi Dresden No. O/88 No. 17 Cat R": violin part only in ink, OR's hand, 4 pages, first and second movements; **YCAL MSS 54-160-3730:** Full score (violin and keyboard) in OR's hand, 18 pages.	
5	Concerto in G minor for solo violin, orchestra, and continuo	RV 329	Dresden, SL 2389/0/105	**YCAL MSS 54-159-3727:** "VIVALDI / Allegro / G- / (5)": 16 pages, black ink with red pencil corrections and overlays.	
6	Concerto in D major for solo violin, orchestra, and continuo	RV 229	Dresden, SL 2389/0/106	**YCAL MSS 54-160-3731:** in EP's hand, dated Siena 28 August XVI: Allegro, Largo, Allegro; 13 pages.	May be discussed in 19, 21 August 1938 (YCAL MSS 54-18-492)

EP's Cat. No.	Name	RV Cat. No.	Location of original manuscript	Description of score(s) in Beinecke	Mention in correspondence between EP and OR?
7	Concerto in E-flat major for solo violin, orchestra, and continuo	RV 262	Dresden, SL 2389/0/91	**YCAL MSS 54-159-3726:** "VIVALDI / Siena Ag. XVI / (7) continued / bbb / 16": pages 16–18, end of third movement; **YCAL MSS 54-159-3727:** "Vivaldi bbb / (Siena) Aug / Amusin Treat / Allegro / Largo / Allegro / (7)": 16 pages, preceding other fragment, combined they make full score, lots of corrections and overlay; **YCAL MSS 54-159-3726:** "Vivaldi – Tigullio (7)" full score not in EP's hand and does not look like OR? 17 pages very clean copy.	
8	Concerto in D major for viola d'amore, orchestra, and continuo	RV 392	Dresden, SL 2389/0/84	**YCAL MSS 54-159-3727:** "VIVALDI / Re maj. / ## / Rapallo Sept XVI / (8)": 23 pages, complete score in black ink with red pencil corrections and additions, some green and blue pencil.	May be discussed in 8, 10 September 1938 (YCAL MSS 54-18-494)
9	Concerto in C major for solo violin, orchestra, and continuo	RV 172	Dresden, SL 2389/0/42	**YCAL MSS 54-159-3726:** "VIVALDI/ Do / 24 Sett. 1938 / vide lar. / [Reserve fancy] / (9)": 24 pages, black ink with lots of overstrikes in red and green pencil, paper laid over for corrections; written beside this listing in EP's catalogue: "Cucu."	24 Sept 1938 (YCAL MSS 54-18-498)
10	Concerto in C minor for solo violin, orchestra, and continuo (clavecin)	RV 198	Dresden, SL 2389/0/102	**YCAL MSS 54-159-3727:** "VIVALDI CONCERTO / [bbb] / Rap. Luglio / ALLEGRO / I / (10) / TO DO": 28 pages, full score; third movement marked with "(2)," matching EP's catalogue entry of the second movement as a separate piece (entry #2 above) from catalogue entry #10; written beside this piece in EP's catalogue: "Casella."	May be discussed in 4 & 12 June 1938 (YCAL MSS 54-18-485); or in 12–13, 15, 18 July? (YCAL MSS 54-18-488)

Appendix 273

EP's Cat. No.	Name	RV Cat. No.	Location of original manuscript	Description of score(s) in Beinecke	Mention in correspondence between EP and OR?
11	Concerto in C major for solo violin, orchestra, and continuo	RV 184	Dresden, SL 2389/0/90	**YCAL MSS 54-159-3727:** "VIVALDI / Concerto in C / Kompleat with cuckow (11)": 10 pages, one place where EP claims to have corrected errors in MS; **YCAL MSS 54-159-3727:** "VIVALDI C. III / Allegro III / 9 / Swing time": pages 9–16; **YCAL MSS 43-Ov5-33:** 6 pages of first movement, then Andante movement (2 pages).	May be discussed 3 July 1938 (YCAL MSS 54-18-486)
12	Concerto in A minor for cello, orchestra, and continuo	RV 422	Dresden, SL 2389/0/110	**YCAL MSS 54-159-2727:** "Do mag. con obl. / Concerto / Allegro // (12) / [pencil]: No. 28 Cat. R 2389/01 110": 20 pages, written in red pencil down right side of front page, Pound's hand: "Reject."	
13	Concerto in A major for 2 violins, orchestra, and continuo	RV 521	Dresden, SL 2389/0/54	**YCAL MSS 54-159-3726:** "Trio [13]": 22 pages, all three movements filled in.	May be discussed 8 September 1938 (YCAL MSS 54-18-494)
14	Concerto in C minor for solo violin, orchestra, and continuo, "Il Sospetto"	RV 199	Dresden, SL 2389/0/78	**YCAL MSS 54-159-3727:** "Vivaldi Dresden Ms. O/78": beginning of violin line of first movement, not in EP's hand (OR's?); **YCAL MSS 54-159-3728:** violin part with space left for keyboard accompaniment, 20 pages numbered in OR's hand, with 2 pages (unnumbered) in EP's hand with full solo and accompaniment filled in: perhaps OR and EP were working together on this one.	May be discussed in 4 & 12 June 1938 (YCAL MSS 54-18-485)
15	Concerto in D minor for solo violin, orchestra, and continuo	RV 237	Dresden, SL 2389/0/46	No score identified.	
16	Concerto in D major for solo violin, orchestra, and continuo	RV 213	Dresden, SL 2389/0/61	**YCAL MSS 54-159-3726:** only a few measures filled in: 3 measures of first movement, 7 measures of second movement.	May be discussed in 7–8 August 1938 (YCAL MSS 54-18-490), or in 19, 21 August 1938 (YCAL MSS 54-18-492)

EP's Cat. No.	Name	RV Cat. No.	Location of original manuscript	Description of score(s) in Beinecke	Mention in correspondence between EP and OR?
17	Concerto in A minor for viola d'amore, orchestra, and continuo, with 2 solo violins and 2 solo altos in 2nd movement	RV 397	Dresden, SL 2389/0/82	**YCAL MSS 54-159-3726:** "VIV / Am. / marzo 31 ? allo anno XVII / (?17)": 19 pages, incomplete: only has the solo violin line written in for all three movements.	
18	Concerto in A minor for solo violin, orchestra, and continuo, Op. 9, No. 5	RV 358	Dresden, SL 2389/0/114	**YCAL MSS 54-159-3727:** "[untitled] (20)": Adagio (2 drafts) and Allegro (18); 18 pages in black ink with red and green pencil, overlaid corrections; **YCAL MSS 54-159-3727:** "Adagio" (OR's hand), violin line only.	
19	Concerto in C major for 2 violins "in tromba," 2 flutes à bec, (2 trumpets?), 2 mandolins, 2 solmoès, 2 théorbes, violoncello, orchestra, and continuo	RV 558	Dresden, SL 2389/0/4 no. 1 (pp. 5–68)	**YCAL MSS 43-Ov5-32:** "Concerto Do / A Vivaldi": 15 pages, first movement: full violin part with spare bassline, places where bassline not in at all; second movement fully developed; **YCAL MSS 54-154-3634:** photographs (not scores); 21 photos of a section of manuscript (11.5 cm wide by 8.6 cm tall). First page: "Concerto / con / Due Flauti / Due Tiorbe / Due Mandolini / Due Salmò / Due Violini in Tromba Marina / et un Violoncello"; **YCAL MSS 43-Ov5-33:** "Con mandolini": second movement, developed for solo part and accompaniment, 5 pages in EP's hand; **YCAL MSS 53-46-1018:** 2 pages of first movement, ink and pencil, EP's hand; written beside this entry in EP's catalogue: "first films"	

Appendix 275

EP's Cat. No.	Name	RV Cat. No.	Location of original manuscript	Description of score(s) in Beinecke	Mention in correspondence between EP and OR?
20	Concerto in F major for violin, 2 hautbois, 2 cors, bassoons, orchestra, and continuo	RV 568	Dresden SL, 2389/0/47	**YCAL MSS 54-159-3726:** [untitled] #20: partial only, pages 6–16; all of second and third movements, but only part of first: EP seems to have devised a keyboard part here from various parts in this concerto; **YCAL MSS 43-Ov5-33:** violin line plus bassline, with 2 separate pages of fragments—from this piece or something else?; **YCAL MSS 53-46-1018:** 55 pp MS of part of this piece (first movement) on front of which Pound has written "very doubtful"; written beside this entry in EP's catalogue: "1st films"	
21	Concerto in D minor for viole d'amore and lute, orchestra and, continuo	RV 540	Dresden, SL, 2389/0/4 no. 3 (pp. 117–44)	**YCAL MSS 54-159-3727:** out of order sections of item #21 (21 pages): fragment of #21 (pages 14–17); fragment of #21 (pages 8–13); #21 Allegro con Sordine (pages 1–3); #21 (pages 4–7).	

Select Bibliography of Archival and Historical Materials

Archivio Centrale dello Stato. Rome, Italy.

Archivi Alinari. Florence, Italy.

Ezra Pound Miscellany. Yale Collection of American Literature. Beinecke Rare Book and Manuscript Library. New Haven, Connecticut.

Ezra Pound Papers. Yale Collection of American Literature. Beinecke Rare Book and Manuscript Library. New Haven, Connecticut.

Manoscritti Vivaldiani, Raccolte Foà e Giordano. Biblioteca Nazionale di Torino. Turin, Italy.

Olga Rudge Papers. Yale Collection of American Literature. Beinecke Rare Book and Manuscript Library.

Accademia Musicale Chigiana, *Antonio Vivaldi: Note e documenti sulla vita e sulle opere. Settimana Musicale, sotto gli auspici della R. Accademia d'Italia, Siena 16–21 settembre 1939–XVII* (Rome: S. A. Arti Grafiche e Fotomeccaniche Sansaini, 1939).

Berenson, Bernard, *Italian Painters of the Renaissance* (Milan, 1936).

———, *I Pittori Italiani del Rinascimento*, trans. Emilio Cecchi (Milan: Biblioteca Universale Rizzoli, 2001).

Bottai, Giuseppe, *Politica Fascista delle Arti* (Rome: Angelo Signorelli, 1940).

Carrà, Carlo, *Giotto* (London: A. Zwemmer, 1925).

———, "Paolo Uccello Costruttore," *La Voce* (30 September 1916): 377–84.

Casella, Alfredo, *21 + 26* (Rome and Milan: Augustea, 1931); ed. Alessandra Carlotta Pellegrini (Florence: Leo S. Olschki, 2001).

———, *I Segreti della Giara* (Florence: G. C. Sansoni, 1941).

———, *Music in my Time: The Memoirs*, ed. and trans. Spencer Norton (Norman: University of Oklahoma Press, 1955).

Cecchi, Emilio, "Bernhard Berenson," *Valori Plastici* (Rome) 2 (July 1920): 86–88.
De Francisci, Pietro, *Augusto e l'impero*, Quaderni dell'Istituto Nazionale di Cultura Fascista Serie 7:3 (Rome: Istituto Nazionale di Cultura Fascista, 1937).
Fossati, Paolo, *"Valori Plastici", 1918–22* (Turin: Giulio Einaudi, 1981).
Gentile, Giovanni, *Fascismo e cultura*, Biblioteca di Cultura Politica a cura dell'Istituto Nazionale Fascista di Cultura 1 (Milan: Fratelli Treves Editori, 1928).
Gentili, Alberto, "La raccolta Mauroa Foà nella Biblioteca Nazionale di Torino," *Rivista musicale italiana* 3 (1927): 356–68.
Guzzi, Virgilio, *Pittura Italiana Contemporanea: Origini e Aspetti*, Quaderni dell'Istituto Nazionale Fascista di Cultura 3:3 (Milan and Rome: Casa Editrice d'Arte Bestetti and Tumminelli, 1931).
Hare, Augustus J. C., *Cities of Northern Italy, Volume 2: Venice, Ferrara, Piacenza, Parma, Modena and Bologna* (London: Smith, Elder & Co., 1884).
In memoria di Corrado Ricci: Un saggio ineditio nota delle pubblicazioni scritti di amici e collaborate (Rome: R. Istituto d'Archeologia e Storia dell' Arte, 1935).
Lavagnino, Emilio, *Fifty War-Damaged Monuments of Italy*, trans. Sara T. Morey (Rome: Istituto Poligrafico dello Stato, 1946).
Longhi, G. Marchetti, "La Via dell'Impero, nel suo sviluppo storico-topografico e nel suo significato ideale," *Capitolium* 10:2 (February 1934): 53–84.
Mulè, F. P., "MCMXXII—Ottobre—MCMXXXII: Le grandi arterie monumentali di Roma, Il Duce sulla via dell'Impero," *Capitolium* 8:11 (November 1932): 557–72.
Muñoz, Antonio, "La via dell'Impero e la via del mare," *Capitolium* 8:11 (November 1932): 521–56.
Mussolini, Benito, *La Dottrina del Fascismo, con una Storia del Movimento Fascista di Gioacchino Volpe*, Biblioteca della Enciclopedia Italiana 1 (Milan and Rome: Edizioni Fratelli Treves, 1932).
——, *Fascism: Doctrine and Institutions* (Rome: Ardita, 1935; New York: Howard Fertig, 1968).
——, *Opera Omnia*, ed. Edoardo and Duilio Susmel, 36 vols (Florence: La Fenice, 1951–63).
Partito Nazionale Fascista, *Mostra della Rivoluzione Fascista: Guida Storica a cura di Dino Alfieri e Luigi Freddi* (Rome: Officine dell'Istituto Italiano d'Arti Grafiche di Bergamo, 1933).
Prezzolini, Giuseppe, *Fascism*, trans. Kathleen Macmillan (London: Methuen, 1926).
Reale Istituto d'Archeologia e Storia dell'Arte, *In Memoria di Corrado Ricci: Un saggio inedito, nota delle pubblicazioni, scritti di amici e collaboratori* (Rome: 1935).
Ricci, Corrado, "Il Foro di Cesare, I," *Capitolium* 8:4 (April 1932): 157–72.

———, "Il Foro di Cesare, II," *Capitolium* 8:8 (August 1932): 365–90.
———, *Il Tempio Malatestiano* (Milan and Rome: Bestetti and Tumminelli, 1925). Reprinted with the appendix "Cinquant'anni di studi sul Tempio Malatestiano" by Pier Giorgio Pasini (Rimini: Bruno Ghigi Editore, 1974).
———, *Via dell'Impero* (Rome: La Libreria dello Stato, [1933]).
Rudge, Olga, "Music and a Process," *Townsman* 1 (January 1938): 21–22.
———, "Venice and Vivaldi," *Delphian Quarterly* 21 (January 1938): 7–10, 56.
Sarfatti, Margherita G., "Architettura, Arte e Simbolo alla Mostra del Fascismo," *Architettura: Rivista del Sindacato Nazionale Fascista Architetti* 12:1 (January 1933): 1–22.
———, *Dux* (Milan: Mondadori, 1926).
———, *The Life of Benito Mussolini*, trans. Frederic Whyte (New York: Frederick A. Stokes, 1925).
Strong, E[ugénie Sellers], "'Romanità' through the Ages," *Journal of Roman Studies* 29 (1939): 137–66.
Torrefranca, Fausto, "L'Italia musicale del Settecento: Una gloria ignorata della scuola veneziana," *Nuova Antologia* 5:926 (16 July 1910): 243–53.
———, "Modernità di Antonio Vivaldi," *Nuova Antologia* 77:1689 (1 August 1942): 179–87.
Turcotti, Erminio (ed.), *Fascist Europe, Europa Fascista: An Anglo-Italian Symposium*, 2 vols, 2nd ed. (Milan: Salesian, 1939).
Van Buren, A. W., "News Items from Rome," *American Journal of Archaeology* 44:3 (July–September 1940): 376–97.
———, "Art Activities in Italy," *Parnassus* 1:1 (January 1929): 4–6.
Venturini, Domenico, *Dante Alighieri e Benito Mussolini* (Rome: Nuova Italia, 1927).

Notes

Notes to Introduction

1. On the distinctions separating northern and southern Italy, see Christopher Duggan, *The Force of Destiny: A History of Italy since 1796* (Boston and New York: Houghton Mifflin, 2008), 220–77.
2. Spiro Kostof, "Review: The Third Rome: The Polemics of Architectural History," *The Journal of the Society of Architectural Historians* 32:3 (October 1973): 241.
3. Ezra Pound, "Ubicumque Lingua Romana" (1938), in Erminio Turcotti (ed.), *Fascist Europe, Europa Fascista: An Anglo-Italian Symposium*, 2nd ed. (Milan: Salesian, 1939), 1:45.
4. Ezra Pound to C. H. Douglas, 18 November [1937], Ezra Pound Papers, Yale Collection of American Literature, Beinecke Rare Book and Manuscript Library.
5. Ezra Pound, "The Serious Artist" (1913), *LE*, 46.
6. John Whittier-Ferguson, *Framing Pieces: Designs of the Gloss in Joyce, Woolf, and Pound* (New York and Oxford: Oxford University Press, 1996), 116.
7. A. David Moody, *Ezra Pound: Poet: Volume 2: The Epic Years* (Oxford and New York: Oxford University Press, 2014); and *Ezra Pound: Poet: Volume III: The Tragic Years 1939–1972* (Oxford and New York: Oxford University Press, 2015).
8. Matthew Feldman, *Ezra Pound's Fascist Propaganda, 1935–45* (Basingstoke and New York: Palgrave Macmillan, 2013).
9. David Barnes, "'Ct/ Volpe's Neck': Re-approaching Pound's Venice in the Fascist Context," in John Gery and William Pratt (eds), *Ezra Pound, Ends and Beginnings* (New York: AMS Press, 2011), 17–30; Barnes, "Fascist Aesthetics: Ezra Pound's Cultural Negotiations in 1930s Italy," *Journal of Modern Literature* 34:1 (Fall 2010): 19–35.
10. Tim Redman, *Ezra Pound and Italian Fascism* (Cambridge: Cambridge University Press, 1991).

11 Luca Gallesi, *Le origini del Fascismo di Ezra Pound* (Milan: Edizioni Ares, 2005).
12 Redman, *Ezra Pound and Italian Fascism*; Leon Surette, *Pound in Purgatory: From Economic Realism to Anti-Semitism* (Urbana and Chicago: University of Illinois Press, 1999); Luca Gallesi, *Le origini del Fascismo di Ezra Pound* (Milan: Edizioni Ares, 2005); Luca Gallesi (ed.), *Ezra Pound e l'economia* (Milan: Edizioni Ares, 2001); Peter Nicholls, *Ezra Pound: Politics, Economics and Writing* (Atlantic Highlands: Humanities Press, 1984); Alec Marsh, *Money and Modernity: Pound, Williams, and the Spirit of Jefferson* (Tuscaloosa and London: University of Alabama Press, 1998); Paul Morrison, *The Poetics of Fascism: Ezra Pound, T. S. Eliot, Paul De Man* (New York and Oxford: Oxford University Press, 1996).
13 Surette, *Pound in Purgatory*; Robert Casillo, *The Genealogy of Demons: Anti-Semitism, Fascism, and the Myths of Ezra Pound* (Evanston: Northwestern University Press, 1988); Wendy Stallard Flory, *Ezra Pound and* The Cantos*: A Record of Struggle* (New Haven and London: Yale University Press, 1980); Flory, "The Pound Problem," in *Ezra Pound & William Carlos Williams: The University of Pennsylvania Conference Papers*, ed. Daniel Hoffman (Philadelphia: University of Pennsylvania Press, 1983), 107–27.
14 Reed Way Dasenbrock, *Imitating the Italians: Wyatt, Spenser, Synge, Pound, Joyce* (Baltimore and London: Johns Hopkins University Press, 1991).
15 Lawrence Rainey, *Ezra Pound and the Monument of Culture: Text, History, and the Malatesta Cantos* (Chicago and London: University of Chicago Press, 1991). See also Peter Robinson, "Ezra Pound and Italian Art," *Pound's Artists: Ezra Pound and the Visual Arts in London, Paris and Italy* (London: The Tate Gallery, 1985), 121–76.
16 Niccolò Zapponi, *L'Italia di Ezra Pound* (Rome: Bulzoni, 1976).
17 Anne Conover, *Olga Rudge and Ezra Pound: "What Thou Lovest Well…"* (New Haven and London: Yale University Press, 2001).
18 Stefano Maria Casella, "To Adjust the Spelling of Guido," in *Ezra Pound 1972/1992*, ed. Luca Gallesi (Milan: Greco & Greco, 1992).
19 Omar Pound and Robert Spoo, *Ezra and Dorothy Pound: Letters in Captivity, 1945–1946* (New York: Oxford University Press, 1999); R. Murray Schafer, *Ezra Pound and Music: The Complete Criticism* (New York: New Directions, 1977); Massimo Bacigalupo, "Ezra Pound's Cantos 72 and 73: An Annotated Translation," *Paideuma* 20 (1991): 10–41; Leonard W. Doob, *"Ezra Pound Speaking": Radio Speeches of World War II* (Westport: Greenwood Press, 1978); Lawrence Rainey (ed.), *A Poem Containing History: Textual Studies in* The Cantos (Ann Arbor: University of Michigan Press, 1997); C. David Heymann, *Ezra Pound: The Last Rower: A Political Profile* (New York: Viking, 1976).
20 Massimo Bacigalupo, *The Forméd Trace: The Later Poetry of Ezra Pound* (New York: Columbia University Press, 1980); Bacigalupo, "The Poet at War: Ezra Pound's Suppressed Italian Cantos," *South Atlantic Quarterly* 83:1

(Winter 1984): 69–79; Ronald Bush, '"Quiet, Not Scornful?': The Composition of the *Pisan Cantos*," in Rainey, *A Poem Containing History*, 169–211; Bush, "Modernism, Fascism, and the Composition of Ezra Pound's *Pisan Cantos*," *Modernism/Modernity* 2:3 (September 1995): 69–87; Patricia Cockram, "Collapse and Recall: Ezra Pound's Italian Cantos," *Journal of Modern Literature* 23:3–4 (2000): 535–44. Additionally, Ron Bush's recent editorial work on the *Pisan Cantos*, while not yet published, has significantly informed my thinking about those poems.

21 Joshua Arthurs, *Excavating Modernity: The Roman Past in Fascist Italy* (Ithaca and London: Cornell University Press, 2013); Ruth Ben-Ghiat, *Fascist Modernities: Italy, 1922–1945* (Berkeley and Los Angeles: University of California Press, 2001); Giorgio Ciucci, "Italian Architecture During the Fascist Period: Classicism between Neoclassicism and Rationalism; The Many Souls of the Classical," *Harvard Architecture Review* 6 (1987): 76–87; Simonetta Falasca-Zamponi, *Fascist Spectacle: The Aesthetics of Power in Mussolini's Italy* (Berkeley, Los Angeles, and London: University of California Press, 1997); D. Medina Lasansky, *The Renaissance Perfected: Architecture, Spectacle, and Tourism in Fascist Italy* (University Park: The Pennsylvania State University Press, 2004); Harvey Sachs, *Music in Fascist Italy* (New York and London: W. W. Norton, 1987); Jeffrey T. Schnapp, *Staging Fascism: 18 BL and the Theater of Masses for Masses* (Stanford: Stanford University Press, 1996); Marla Susan Stone, *The Patron State: Culture and Politics in Fascist Italy* (Princeton: Princeton University Press, 1998).

22 Emily Braun, *Mario Sironi and Italian Modernism: Art and Politics Under Fascism* (Cambridge: Cambridge University Press, 2000); Philip V. Cannistraro and Brian R. Sullivan, *Il Duce's Other Woman: The Untold Story of Margherita Sarfatti, Benito Mussolini's Jewish Mistress, and How She Helped Him Come to Power* (New York: William Morrow and Company, 1993).

23 See, for instance the pieces compiled and translated in Jeffrey T. Schnapp (ed.), *A Primer of Italian Fascism* (Lincoln and London: University of Nebraska Press, 2000); the documents assembled in Schnapp, *Anno X: La Mostra della Rivoluzione fascista del 1932* (Pisa and Rome: Istituti Editoriali Poligrafici Internazionali, 2003); the translations of Futurist works in Lawrence Rainey, Christine Poggi, Laura Wittman (eds), *Futurism: An Anthology* (New Haven and London: Yale University Press, 2009); the contents of *Il Mare: Supplemento Letterario 1932–1933*, ed. Società Letteraria Rapallo (Comune di Rapallo, 1999); and the writings by Margherita Sarfatti in Catherine E. Paul and Barbara M. Zaczek (ed. and trans.), "Margherita Sarfatti and Italian Cultural Nationalism: Five Articles from *Il Popolo d'Italia*," *Modernism/modernity* 13:1 (January 2006): 889–916.

24 Matthew Affron and Mark Antliff (eds), *Fascist Visions: Art and Ideology in France and Italy* (Princeton: Princeton University Press, 1997); Richard J. Golsan (ed.), *Fascism, Aesthetics, and Culture* (Hanover and London: University Press of New England, 1992); Claudia Lazzaro and Roger J.

Crum (eds), *Donatello among the Blackshirts: History and Modernity in the Visual Culture of Fascist Italy* (Ithaca and London: Cornell University Press, 2005); Henry A. Millon and Linda Nochlin (eds), *Art and Architecture in the Service of Politics* (Cambridge and London: The MIT Press, 1978).

Notes to Chapter 1

1 Henry James, "Venice," *Italian Hours*, ed. John Auchard (State College: The Pennsylvania State University Press, 1992; New York and London: Penguin, 1995), 7. James began writing the essays of *Italian Hours* in the 1870s and they were published collectively in 1909.
2 John Ruskin, "Venetian Index," *The Stones of Venice* (New York: Peter Fenelon Collier and Son, 1900), 3: 381. David Barnes has argued compellingly that Ruskin's reading of Venetian architecture is far from apolitical and rather inflected through his experience of Daniele Manin's 1848 revolution ("Historicizing the Stones: Ruskin's *The Stones of Venice* and Italian Nationalism," *Comparative Literature* 62:3 (2010): 246–61). I have discovered no evidence that Pound would have understood this during his early visit to the city.
3 Ezra Pound to Isabel Pound, 10 August [1908], *Ezra Pound to his Parents: Letters 1895–1929*, ed. Mary de Rachewiltz, A. David Moody, Joanna Moody (Oxford and New York: Oxford University Press, 2010), 127.
4 Lawrence Rainey notes Pound's reliance on the late-Romantic tradition for his early understanding of the Tempio Malatesta in *Ezra Pound and the Monument of Culture: Text, History, and the Malatesta Cantos* (Chicago and London: University of Chicago Press, 1991), 14–23, 42. For a breezy summary of American literary responses to Venice during the eighteenth and nineteenth centuries, see Marilla Battilana, "Venice and its Region in American Literature (18th and 19th century)," in Luigi Monga (ed.), *Americans in Italy*, special edition of *Bolletino del C.I.R.V.I.* 15–16 (January–December 1987): 1–20. For a very complex examination of the city in literature from many periods, see David Barnes, *The Venice Myth* (London: Pickering & Chatto, 2014).
5 Augustus J. C. Hare, *Cities of Northern Italy, Volume 2: Venice, Ferrara, Piacenza, Parma, Modena and Bologna* (London: Smith, Elder & Co., 1884), 7–11.
6 William Dean Howells's *Italian Journeys* (1867), Horatio F. Brown's *Life on the Lagoons* (1884), and the ubiquitous Baedeker guides created similar impressions of the city to that gained from Hare.
7 Ezra Pound, "Three Cantos: I," *Poetry: A Magazine of Verse* 10 (June 1917): 117.
8 James, "Venice," 10.
9 James, "Venice," 12.

10 Pound, "Three Cantos: I," 113.
11 Ezra Pound to Homer Pound, [early mid-May 1908], *Ezra Pound to his Parents*, 110.
12 Margaretta M. Lovell, "Modernist Interrogations of an Old World: John S. Sargent's Venice," in Luigi Monga (ed.), *Americans in Italy*, special edition of *Bolletino del C.I.R.V.I.* 15–16 (January–December 1987): 117–43.
13 Hare, *Cities of Northern Italy, Volume 2*, 48.
14 James, "Venice," 21.
15 Ezra Pound to Homer Pound, [early mid-May 1908], *Ezra Pound to his Parents*, 110.
16 Ezra Pound to Homer Pound, May something near the end [1908], *Ezra Pound to his Parents*, 112; Ezra Pound to Isabel Pound, [19–25 Jun 1908], *Ezra Pound to his Parents*, 117.
17 Walter L. Adamson, *Avant-Garde Florence: From Modernism to Fascism* (Cambridge: Harvard University Press, 1993), 86.
18 Alexander J. De Grand, *The Italian Nationalist Association and the Rise of Fascism in Italy* (Lincoln and London: University of Nebraska Press, 1978), 9–13.
19 De Grand, *The Italian Nationalist Association*, 20.
20 Pound may have recognized this shortcoming later on, when he wrote in 1936 that American travelers who see only the antiquities and not the contemporary arts projects of the new Fascist Italy cannot fully understand Italy. See Ezra Pound, "Rapallo centro di cultura," *Il Mare*, 2 May 1936; *CI*, 283. I treat this piece in more detail in Chapter 3. On Pound's more engaged sense of Venice in the late 1920s and 1930s, see David Barnes, "Fascist Aesthetics: Ezra Pound's Cultural Negotiations in 1930s Italy," *Journal of Modern Literature* 34:1 (Fall 2010): 23–25.
21 Guido Perocco, *Origini dell'arte moderna a Venezia, 1908–1920* (Treviso: Canova, 1972), 31; trans. Barbara M. Zaczek, Catherine E. Paul, and Angelo de Giudici, "Venezia Passatista?: Luigi de Giudici and a Broader Futurism," *Visual Resources: An International Journal of Documentation* 26:4 (December 2010): 344. For further discussion of the role of Ca' Pesaro in the fomenting of avant-garde art in the Veneto, see Willard Bohn, *The Other Futurism: Futurist Activity in Venice, Padua, and Verona* (Toronto, Buffalo, and London: University of Toronto Press, 2004); and Zaczek, Paul, and de Giudici, "Venezia Passatista?," 331–66.
22 Umberto Boccioni, Carlo Carrà, Luigi Russolo, Giacomo Balla, and Gino Severini, "Manifesto of Futurist Painters" (11 February 1910), trans. Umbro Apollonio, quoted in Emilio Gentile, "The Conquest of Modernity: From Modernist Nationalism to Fascism," trans. Lawrence Rainey, *Modernism/modernity* 1:3 (September 1994): 64.
23 Mussolini, "Un grande amico dell'Italia: Augusto von Platen," *Il Popolo d'Italia* (3 July 1909) reprinted in Mussolini, *Opera Omnia di Benito*

Mussolini, ed. Edoardo e Duilio Susmel (Florence: La Fenice, 1957), 2:172; quoted in Gentile, "The Conquest of Modernity," 64.

24 Alexander J. De Grand notes that after *Il Regno* ceased publication in 1906, the movement would not regain momentum until after 1909 (*The Italian Nationalist Association*, 16–23).

25 Ezra Pound, "I Gather the Limbs of Osiris" [II] … A Rather Dull Introduction," *New Age* 10:6 (7 December 1911), 130–31; *P&P*, 1:44; *SP*, 22.

26 Claudio Fogu, *The Historic Imaginary: Politics of History in Fascist Italy* (Toronto, Buffalo, London: University of Toronto Press, 2003), 5.

27 Christopher Duggan, *The Force of Destiny: A History of Italy since 1796* (Boston and New York: Houghton Mifflin, 2008), 224–41.

28 On pre-Fascist attempts to define a secular "patriotic religion," see Emilio Gentile, *The Sacralization of Politics in Fascist Italy*, trans. Keith Botsford (Cambridge and London: Harvard University Press, 1996), 1–18. On the range of divisions in Italy at this time, see Duggan, *The Force of Destiny*, 228, 293, 385–86.

29 Duggan, *The Force of Destiny*, 16–17.

30 This variation in the reckoning of time among Italian regions is the basis of Henry James's title *Italian Hours* (Auchard, "Introduction," in Henry James, *Italian Hours*, x).

31 Duggan, *The Force of Destiny*, 102–15.

32 Duggan, *The Force of Destiny*, 211. As historian Claudio Fogu has noted, the adoption of the very term *risorgimento* in capitalized form "encoded this founding event not just as a metaphor, value, or rhetorical figure, but also as a proper *imago* of resurrection that not only resisted and overshadowed any conventional historical narrativization but also affected any such attempt." Indeed, it was not really until the period of the First World War that the "nationalizing myth of the Risorgimento" was born—meaning that the Risorgimento was understood as much in the context of that war as in itself alone (Fogu, *The Historic Imaginary*, 199–201).

33 Duggan, *The Force of Destiny*, 35–37.

34 Quoted and translated in Duggan, *The Force of Destiny*, 93. Reed Way Dasenbrock has shown how the early nineteenth-century poet Giacomo Leopardi's interest in the Italian lyric tradition of Dante and Petrarch was crucial to Pound's return to the work of early Italian poets Dante and Cavalcanti. See *Imitating the Italians: Wyatt, Spenser, Synge, Pound, Joyce* [Baltimore and London: Johns Hopkins University Press, 1991), 114.

35 Duggan, *The Force of Destiny*, 129–30, 176–77. The crucial components of Mazzini's regenerative myth included, in the words of historian Emilio Gentile, "The ethical concept of life as service to the fatherland; the messianic vision of politics as a new lay religion; the belief that only a collective palingenetic experience, through struggle, sacrifice, and martyrdom, would foster the birth of a new Italian people". See "The Myth of National Regeneration in Italy: From Modernist Avant-Garde to Fascism," in Matthew

Affron and Mark Antliff (ed.), *Fascist Visions: Art and Ideology in France and Italy*, trans. Maria Tannenbaum (Princeton: Princeton University Press, 1997), 28.

36 Giovanni Gentile, *Mazzini* (Caserta 1919), quoted in Duggan, *The Force of Destiny*, 413–14.

37 Benito Mussolini, *Opera Omnia*, 23:523, quoted in Duggan, *The Force of Destiny*, 455.

38 Duggan, *The Force of Destiny*, 450.

39 This distinction was framed by Italian statesman and novelist Massimo Taparelli d'Azeglio. On the use of this distinction in nineteenth-century discussions, see Gentile, *The Sacralization of Politics in Fascist Italy*, 6–7. Similarly, Roger Griffin has described Fascism as "a heroic attempt to complete the Risorgimento by integrating all Italians within the dynamically modernizing, demographically and territorially expanding, technologically powerful, culturally vital Great Italy". See *Modernism and Fascism: The Sense of a Beginning under Mussolini and Hitler* (Basingstoke and New York: Palgrave Macmillan, 2007), 225. On Mussolini's employment of this notion, see Duggan, *The Force of Destiny*, 435.

40 Pound agreed with respect to his own culture. He lamented in 1929 that what kept him in the 1910s from getting to the heart of Guido Cavalcanti's poems was not "Guido's Italian" but "the victorian language," "the crust of dead English, the sediment present in my own available vocabulary," and he noted that to make poetry, a poet must "make his own language"—something which he himself had not done in 1910. See his "Guido's Relations," *Dial* 86:7 (July 1929): [559]–68 (*P&P*, 5:166), which also appears as part of the English-language section of *Guido Cavalcanti Rime*.

41 Writing in *Valori Plastici* (Rome) in 1919, Giorgio de Chirico looked forward to a day when Italy could embrace a modern aesthetic, when "possibly we shall be able to avoid the repugnance of finding ourselves pushed aside in favor of monstrous apotheoses of bad taste and invading imbecility, such as the white monument to the Great King in Rome, otherwise known as the Altar of the Fatherland ..." See "Sull'Arte Metafisica," *Valori Plastici* (Rome) 1:4–5 (April–May 1919): 15–18, trans. Joshua C. Taylor in Herschel B. Chipp (ed.), *Theories of Modern Art: A Source Book by Artists and Critics* (Berkeley and Los Angeles: University of California Press, 1968), 451–52. Emilio Gentile called the Italy of this era "a state without a soul," where the people had no faith in "the religion of the fatherland" and Italy "was leading a mediocre existence among the great powers that were conquering the world and transforming it through industrialization" ("The Myth of National Regeneration in Italy," 29).

42 Duggan, *The Force of Destiny*, 28–29.

43 Duggan, *The Force of Destiny*, 88–89, 94.

44 Duggan, *The Force of Destiny*, 258.

45 Lazzaro, "Forging a Visible Fascist Nation," in Claudia Lazzaro and Roger J. Crum (eds), *Donatello among the Blackshirts: History and Modernity in the Visual Culture of Fascist Italy* (Ithaca and London: Cornell University Press, 2005), 27.
46 Gentile, "The Myth of National Regeneration in Italy," 28. Part of this move toward national regeneration entailed what Emilio Gentile called the "sacralization of politics": "This term does not refer to the political mobilization of traditional religions, but rather to the political ideologies and movements which adapted religious rituals to political ends" (27).
47 Walter L. Adamson, *Avant-Garde Florence: From Modernism to Fascism* (Cambridge and London: Harvard University Press, 1993), 79.
48 Fogu, *The Historic Imaginary*, 6.
49 For a rich treatment of Pound's many borrowings from Douglas, see Redman, *Ezra Pound and Italian Fascism*, esp. 51–75. Redman also notes Pound's joining of Douglas and Mussolini in his writings of the 1940s (199).
50 Pound, "Individual and Statal Views: Mr. Ezra Pound's Views," *Plain Dealer* (Brighton, England) 13, n.s. 1 (July 1934), supplement: 3; *P&P*, 6:185. Pound states this idea in many places during this period, sometimes restating the concept in these terms, and sometimes inserting slight variations. Elsewhere, he defines "cultural heritage" in more economic terms, as "the increment of association, and the possibilities inherent in a right proportion in the issue of fixed money and Schwundgeld, monnaie fondante, stamp scrip …" (*SP*, 276).
51 Ezra Pound to Odon Por, April [1934], Ezra Pound Miscellany, Yale Collection of American Literature, Beinecke Rare Book and Manuscript Library. Pound repeats this assertion in similar terms in another letter to Por, dated 15 April [1934] (*EPEC*, 94).
52 Ezra Pound, "Trees without Roots," *New York Herald* (Paris, 1 November 1934): 4; *P&P*, 6:207.
53 Quoted and translated in Jeffrey Schnapp and Barbara Spackman (eds), "Selections from the Great Debate on Fascism and Culture: *Critica Fascista* 1926–1927," *Stanford Italian Review* 8 (1990): 235; Mussolini, "Arte e Civiltà," *L'Assalto* (Perugia), 7 October 1926, vi; reprinted in *Opera Omnia di Benito Mussolini*, ed. Edoardo e Duilio Susmel (Florence: La Fenice, 1957), 22:230.
54 Schnapp and Spackman, "Selections from the Great Debate," 235.
55 Gentile, "The Myth of National Regeneration in Italy," 26.
56 Gentile, "The Conquest of Modernity," 59–60.
57 Richard Drake, "The Theory and Practice of Italian Nationalism, 1900–1906," *Journal of Modern History* 53:2 (June 1981): 214–15. As Drake notes, the party grew in the prewar period among the "right-wing literary men grouped around the Florentine cultural journal, *Il Marzocco*, and its political positions developed in opposition to Giolittian liberalism" (215).

58 Duggan, *The Force of Destiny*, 378–79. Walter L. Adamson has noted, "In social thought they were realists willing to reduce politics to the calculation of national interest and materialists ready to understand national pride in terms of wealth and territory." See "The Language of Opposition in Early Twentieth-Century Italy: Rhetorical Continuities between Prewar Florentine Avant-gardism and Mussolini's Fascism," *Journal of Modern History* 64:1 (March 1992): 22–51.

59 On the Nationalists' emphasis on these regions, see Alastair Hamilton, *The Appeal of Fascism: A Study of Intellectuals and Fascism, 1919–1945* (London: Anthony Blond, 1971), 4–5. These regions included Trieste, Trentino, and in some cases Istria, Fiume, and Gorizia. Not all Nationalists admired D'Annunzio, however, and some aspired to emphasize a vision of national glory that was less decadent than they thought D'Annunzio to be (Drake, "The Theory and Practice of Italian Nationalism," 223).

60 On the Nationalists' interest in Italy's international reputation, see Hamilton, *The Appeal of Fascism*, 5.

61 As Claudia Lazzaro notes, these groups "dominated the study of Italy's cultural heritage." See "Forging a Visible Fascist Nation," 13, 25.

62 Although some leaders of the Risorgimento had wanted to create Italians, Nationalists such as Enrico Corradini concluded that their remade products were not strong and solid enough, and they aspired to infuse Italians with the civic virtue that had made imperial Rome great (Drake, "The Theory and Practice of Italian Nationalism," 218).

63 David D. Roberts, *Historicism and Fascism in Modern Italy* (Toronto, Buffalo, and London: University of Toronto Press, 2007), 176, 182. On the absorption of Nationalist organizations into Fascism, see Duggan, *The Force of Destiny*, 437–38.

64 Adamson, "Language of Opposition," 36.

65 F. T. Marinetti, "Fondazione e Manifesto del Futurismo" (1909), in Lawrence Rainey (ed.), *Modernism: An Anthology*, trans. Lawrence Rainey (Oxford: Blackwell, 2005), 3–6.

66 Marinetti, "Fondazione e Manifesto del Futurismo," 49–53.

67 F. T. Marinetti, "La 'Divina Commedia' è un verminaio di glossatori" (1915), in Luciano De Maria (ed.), *Teoria e invenzione futurista* (Milan: Arnoldo Mondadori, 1968), 228–29; my translation.

68 F. T. Marinetti, "Contro Roma passatista" (1910), in Luciano De Maria (ed.), *Teoria e invenzione futurista* (Milan: Arnoldo Mondadori, 1968), 245–46; my translation.

69 F. T. Marinetti, "Contro Venezia passatista" (1910), in Luciano De Maria (ed.), *Teoria e invenzione futurista* (Milan: Arnoldo Mondadori, 1968), 30; trans. in Hamilton, *The Appeal of Fascism*, 8.

70 Pound, "[Interview]," *La Stampa* [between January and April 1932]; *P&P*, 5:334. As the editors of *P&P* note, this comment was widely reproduced, in *Stile Futurista* (Turin, 1934), in Luigi Colombo Fillia's *Il Futurismo:*

Ideologie, realizzazione e polemiche del movimento futurista italiano (Milan, 1932), and in Marinetti's "Art and the State—VI, Italy," in the *Listener* (1936).

71 See Adamson, *Avant-Garde Florence* and "The Language of Opposition."
72 Emily Braun, *Mario Sironi and Italian Modernism: Art and Politics Under Fascism* (Cambridge: Cambridge University Press, 2000), 22. On Mussolini's reading of *La Voce*, see Griffin, *Modernism and Fascism*, 205. Margherita G. Sarfatti discusses the early importance of *La Voce* in "Art and Fascism" (originally published as "L'Arte e Fascismo" in Giuseppe Luigi Pomba (ed.), *La civiltà fascista* [Torino: Unione Tipografico Editrice Torinese, 1928]), trans. Olivia E. Sears and Jeffrey T Schnapp in Jeffrey T. Schnapp (ed.), *A Primer of Italian Fascism* (Lincoln and London: University of Nebraska Press, 2000), 249.
73 See Antliff, "Fascism, Modernism, and Modernity," 148–69; Adamson, *Avant-Garde Florence*; Duggan, *The Force of Destiny*, 231–39.
74 As Walter Adamson has noted, "The worst of the D'Annunzian poses was that of the 'cosmopolitan' equally at home in Rome, Florence, or Paris, and thus truly at home nowhere," and many of these writers aimed deliberately to distinguish themselves from this tendency (*Avant-Garde Florence*, 92). Although Soffici had spent significant time in Paris, and his ideas about art were deeply influenced by the Parisian avant-garde, he returned home to Tuscany in June 1907 having determined that Tuscany was crucial to his work as an artist and to his project of renewing Italian culture (96). He even justified his interest in Paul Cézanne as a stepping stone between himself and Giotto. As Mark Antliff explains, "Soffici's avant-garde style also had an Italian genealogy; he drew comparisons between Cézanne's spatial distortions and those of the trecento 'primitive' Giotto, as both artists, wrote Soffici, rejected 'scientific' perspective for plastic forms based on 'spiritual' and emotive values." Soffici drew additional connections with Cézanne, likening his own move back to Tuscany in 1907 to Cézanne's regionalist retreat from Paris to his native Aix-en-Provence ("Fascism, Modernism, and Modernity," *The Art Bulletin* 84:1 [March 2002]: 158). A year later, Papini concurred, writing a letter to Giuseppe Prezzolini, his co-editor of the Florentine journal *La Voce*, saying that with Soffici he shared "a love of Tuscany—an idealized Tuscany, naturally—seen through Dante, cypresses and Carducci" (Giovanni Papini to Giuseppe Prezzolini, 18 May 1908, quoted in Adamson, *Avant-Garde Florence*, 98).
75 As Mark Antliff has noted, "Centered in the regions of Tuscany and Emilia-Romagna, the movement's proponents self-consciously allied themselves with the 'revolutionary' phase of Fascism (1919–22), when the Fascist squads brought their punitive campaign to rural Italy, thus facilitating Mussolini's rise to power in 1922" ("Fascism, Modernism, and Modernity," 158). As Emily Braun notes, "Here we find the origins of that distinctive character of the Italian avant-garde: militant in its politicization of culture,

modern in its conception of nation and masses, but not necessarily or exclusively modernist in its aesthetic forms" (*Mario Sironi and Italian Modernism*, 23).
76 Braun, *Mario Sironi and Italian Modernism*, 22.
77 Gentile, "The Myth of National Regeneration," 29.
78 Braun, *Mario Sironi and Italian Modernism*, 23.
79 Adamson provides a compelling and detailed rhetorical analysis of this merging in "The Language of Opposition in Early Twentieth-Century Italy."
80 Griffin, *Modernism and Fascism*, 216.
81 Ruth Ben-Ghiat, *Fascist Modernities: Italy, 1922–1945* (Berkeley and Los Angeles: University of California Press, 2001), 7.
82 Mussolini, "Per la nuova sede del Fascio di Milano," *Il Popolo d'Italia* (11 May 1922); quoted. and trans. in Braun, *Mario Sironi and Italian Modernism*, 103.
83 Ezra Pound, *Indiscretions; or, Une Revue de Deux Mondes* (Paris: Three Mountains Press, 1923), 10.
84 On the significance of the 1917 battle at Caporetto, see Griffin, *Modernism and Fascism*, 210; Duggan, *The Force of Destiny*, 391–400.
85 Matteotti was attacked by a group of five men, including Albino Volpi, a former Blackshirt leader and professional gangster who have been active in intimidating anti-Fascists. After a struggle, Matteotti was stabbed to death and buried in a ditch outside Rome. Mussolini denied being connected to the murderers, and succeeded in covering his involvement in the incident, although people continued to suspect him. When Matteotti's body was discovered in August 1924, anti-Fascists called unsuccessfully for Mussolini's dismissal.
86 On the Matteotti affair, Mussolini's involvement, and its relationship to his cultural endeavors, see Philip V. Cannistraro and Brian R. Sullivan, *Il Duce's Other Woman: The Untold Story of Margherita Sarfatti, Benito Mussolini's Jewish Mistress, and How She Helped Him Come to Power* (New York: William Morrow and Company, 1993), 289–99.
87 On the political use of literature and theater during the Fascist period, see Griffin, *Modernism and Fascism*, 236–39.
88 For an example of such celebration, see Sarfatti, "Art and Fascism," 242–45.
89 Braun, *Mario Sironi and Italian Modernism*, 103.
90 On the use of exhibitions to shape mass culture, see Stone, *The Patron State*. On the Mostra Anti-*lei* planned by Achille Starace in 1939 and the cultural context for banning the use of *lei* for formal address, see Simonetta Falasca-Zamponi, *Fascist Spectacle: The Aesthetics of Power in Mussolini's Italy* (Berkeley, Los Angeles and London: University of California Press, 1997), 106–09.
91 Lazzaro, "Forging a Visible Fascist Nation," 22.

92 On Rino Valdemeri's commissioning of an expensive edition of the *Commedia* illustrated by Amos Nattini, see Thomas L. Schumacher, *The Danteum: Architecture, Poetics, and Politics under Italian Fascism*, 2nd ed. (Princeton: Princeton Architectural Press, 1993), 58.
93 Jeffrey T. Schnapp, "Flash Memories (Sironi on Exhibit)," in Claudia Lazzaro and Roger J. Crum (eds), *Donatello Among the Blackshirts: History and Modernity in the Visual Culture of Fascist Italy* (Ithaca and London: Cornell University Press, 2005), 224.
94 Stone, *The Patron State*, 6.
95 Jeffrey T. Schnapp, *Staging Fascism: 18 BL and the Theater of Masses for Masses* (Stanford: Stanford University Press, 1996).

Notes to Chapter 2

1 Margherita G. Sarfatti, "Lettera da Berlino: Un'affermazione d'arte italiana," *Il Popolo d'Italia*, 30 April 1921, trans. Catherine E. Paul and Barbara M. Zaczek, "Margherita Sarfatti and Italian Cultural Nationalism," *Modernism/modernity* 13:1 (2006): 903.
2 Ezra Pound, "[Italy: The Second Decennio]," typescript (n.d.), leaf [11], Ezra Pound Papers, Yale Collection of American Literature, Beinecke Rare Book and Manuscript Library.
3 Pound, "The Renaissance," *Poetry* (1914), reprinted in *LE*, 218. See Reed Way Dasenbrock, *Imitating the Italians: Wyatt, Spenser, Synge, Pound, Joyce* (Baltimore and London: John Hopkins University Press, 1991).
4 Pound, "The Renaissance" (*LE*, 214–15).
5 Ezra Pound, *Patria Mia* (1913); *SP*, 128.
6 Margherita G. Sarfatti, "Art and Fascism" (originally published as "L'Arte e Fascismo" in Giuseppe Luigi Pomba [ed.], *La civiltà fascista* [Torino: Unione Tipografico Editrice Torinese, 1928]), translated by Olivia E. Sears and Jeffrey T Schnapp in Jeffrey T. Schnapp (ed.), *A Primer of Italian Fascism* (Lincoln and London: University of Nebraska Press, 2000), 248.
7 Pound, "The Renaissance" (*LE*, 221).
8 As D. Medina Lasansky has demonstrated, the use of such terms as "Renaissance" and "medieval" is complicated and loaded, particularly in discussions of the Fascist period. The periods that these terms demark were hardly solidified, and different groups chose to use different terms, often for political rather than any kind of purely historical or chronological reasons. For a rich discussion of the historiography of these terms, and especially of their deployment during the Fascist period, see Lasansky's *The Renaissance Perfected: Architecture, Spectacle, and Tourism in Fascist Italy* (University Park, Pennsylvania: The Pennsylvania State University Press, 2004), 19–25. Following her lead, I use "Renaissance" "to signify the artistic and political culture of the fourteenth, fifteenth, and sixteenth centuries and 'medieval'

to describe that of the eleventh, twelfth, and thirteenth centuries" (25). It is interesting to note, in the course of our discussion, how Pound uses these two terms.
9   On Anglo-American touristic investment in Renaissance Tuscany, particularly in the context of the Grand Tour, see Lasansky, *The Renaissance Perfected*, 25–55.
10 Carlo Carrà, *Giotto* (London: A. Zwemmer, 1925), 15.
11 Carrà, *Giotto*, 7.
12 Philip V. Cannistraro and Brian R. Sullivan, *Il Duce's Other Woman: The Untold Story of Margherita Sarfatti, Benito Mussolini's Jewish Mistress, and How She Helped Him Come to Power* (New York: William Morrow and Company, 1993), 139–286.
13 Sarfatti, "Lettera da Berlino," 903.
14 Bernhard Berenson, *The Florentine Painters of the Renaissance, with an index to their works* (New York and London: G. P. Putnam's Sons, 1896), 8–9. Further references to this text will use this edition and be cited parenthetically using the abbreviation *FP*.
15 Soffici's comment is quoted as an epigraph for Carlo Carrà's essay, "Paolo Uccello Costruttore," *La Voce* (30 September 1916): 377; my translation.
16 Carrà, "Paolo Uccello Costruttore," 378; my translation.
17 Carrà, "Paolo Uccello Costruttore," 379; my translation.
18 Carrà, "Paolo Uccello Costruttore," 384; my translation.
19 Berenson's analysis of Masaccio focuses primarily on that artist's works in the Brancacci Chapel of Santa Maria del Carmine. Because Masaccio's frescoes are interspersed with works by his compatriot Masolino and his follower Filippino, Berenson is able to compare the three artists' work to show why Masaccio's is superior (*FP*, 28–31). Berenson visited numerous works—by Andrea Buonaiuti, Domenico Ghirlandaio, Andrea Orcagna, Paolo Uccello—in Florence's largest and most important Gothic cathedral, Santa Maria Novella—a church still in use (*FP*, 21–22, 63–65, 22–23, 33–39). Similarly, part of his discussion of the work of Andrea del Sarto is rooted in the Chiostrino dei Voti of the church of the Santissima Annunziata (Florence) (*FP*, 79–80). Because this space is a sort of anteroom to the church itself, a visitor could look at these frescoes even during services. Considering a different sort of building, Benozzo Gozzoli's frescoes for the Chapel of the Magi in the Palazzo Medici-Riccardi serve as the foundation of Berenson's study of that artist's work (*FP*, 61–63). On the use of that palace by the federal government while Florence was briefly the capital of a united Italy, see Walter Adamson, *Avant-Garde Florence: From Modernism to Fascism* (Cambridge and London: Harvard University Press, 1993), 38–39.
20 F. T. Marinetti, "Fondazione e Manifesto del Futurismo" (1909), in Lawrence Rainey, Christine Poggi, Laura Wittman (eds), *Futurism: An Anthology*, trans. Lawrence Rainey (New Haven and London: Yale University Press, 2009), 51.

21 T. Nanni's *Benito Mussolini* is discussed in Anna Nozzoli, "Margherita Sarfatti, Organizzatrice di Cultura: 'Il Popolo d'Italia,'" *La Corporazione delle donne: ricerche e studi sui modelli femminili nel ventennio fascista* (Florence: Vallecchi, 1988), 242. The series also featured Ardengo Soffici's *Cubismo e oltre* (1913), Roberto Longhi's *Scultura futurista Boccioni* (1914), and Giuseppe Prezzolini's *Discorso su Giovanni Papini* (1915), among others. Longhi's translation was never published. See Cesare Garbo and Cristina Montagnani (eds), *Bernard Berenson – Roberto Longhi: Lettere e Scartafacci, 1912–1957* (Milan: Adelphi, 1993).

22 Bernhard Berenson, *I Pittori Italiani del Rinascimento*, trans. Emilio Cecchi (Milan: Ulrico Hoepli, 1936). For the same series, Cecchi translated the lists of paintings compiled in Bernhard Berenson, *Pitture Italiane del Rinascimento: Catalogo dei Principali Artisti e delle loro opere con un indice dei luoghi*, trans. Emilio Cecchi (Milan: Ulrico Hoepli, 1936).

23 Margherita G. Sarfatti reviewed an exhibition of *Valori Plastici* artists, organized by Broglio, in "Lettera da Berlino," 902–04.

24 Paolo Fossati, et al., *"Valori Plastici" 1918–22* (Torino: Giulio Einaudi, 1981).

25 Emily Braun, *Mario Sironi and Italian Modernism: Art and Politics under Fascism* (Cambridge: Cambridge University Press, 2000), 57.

26 Carrà, *Giotto*, 7.

27 Margherita Sarfatti, *Fiaccola accesa*, 155, quoted in Cannistraro and Sullivan, *Il Duce's Other Woman*, 192. On Sarfatti's cultural Nationalist objectives, see Paul and Zaczek, "Margherita Sarfatti and Italian Cultural Nationalism," 889–94.

28 Ardengo Soffici, "Fascism and Art," *Gerarchia* (1922), quoted by Soffici in his contribution to Jeffrey Schnapp and Barbara Spackman (eds), "Selections from the Great Debate on Fascism and Culture: *Critica Fascista* 1926–1927," *Stanford Italian Review* 8 (1990): 239.

29 Alessandro Pavolini's contribution to *Critica Fascista* 4:21 (1 November 1926): 393–95, trans. Elizabeth MacIntosh and Barbara Spackman, in Schnapp and Spackman (eds), "Selections from the Great Debate on Fascism and Culture: *Critica Fascista* 1926–1927," *Stanford Italian Review* 8 (1990): 242–48.

30 Cipriano Efisio Oppo's contribution to *Critica Fascista* 5:3 (1 February 1927): 44, trans. Jennifer Roberts and Barbara Spackman, in Schnapp and Spackman (eds), "Selections from the Great Debate on Fascism and Culture: *Critica Fascista* 1926–1927," *Stanford Italian Review* 8 (1990): 265.

31 On Giacomo Leopardi's appropriation of the Italian poets of the *trecento*, and on his interest to Pound, see Reed Way Dasenbrock, *Imitating the Italians: Wyatt, Spenser, Synge, Pound, Joyce* (Baltimore and London: Johns Hopkins University Press, 1991), 107–24. On Leopardi's goal of using his poetry to "arouse my poor fatherland," see Christopher Duggan, *The Force*

of Destiny: A History of Italy since 1796 (Boston and New York: Houghton Mifflin, 2008), 115.
32 Oppo, "Selections from the Great Debate," 265.
33 Carrà, *Giotto*, 7.
34 Carrà, *La mia vita* (Milan, 1942), trans. and quoted in Cannistraro and Sullivan, *Il Duce's Other Woman*, 192.
35 Although we are focused here more on Sarfatti's interest in the Renaissance, she devoted a significant amount of writing to celebrating ancient Rome as a model for Fascist Italy. For instance, she argued in 1926 that a new Italy should be built with an eye to ancient Rome, noting that "the idea of the empire—today less a material reality than a consolidated spiritual ideal-in-the-making—flashes in the consciousness of fascism like a profound intuition." See "Promesse e azioni: l'Accademia d'Italia," *Il Popolo d'Italia* (15 January 1926), trans. Paul and Zaczek, "Margherita Sarfatti and Italian Cultural Nationalism," *Modernism/modernity* 13:1 (2006): 903. Her contributions to Fascist *romanità* will be treated more extensively in Chapter 3.
36 Cannistraro and Sullivan, *Il Duce's Other Woman*, 192.
37 Margherita Sarfatti, "Achille Funi," from the catalogue of the exhibition at Galleria Arte, Milan, 1920, reprinted in Elena Pontiggia (ed.), *Da Boccioni a Sironi: Il mondo di Margherita Sarfatti* (Milan: Skira, 1997), 198; my translation. Sarfatti's remark also appeared in a review of that exhibition, "Cronache d'Arte: La Mostra Funi," published in *Il Popolo d'Italia* (27 October 1920).
38 Anselmo Bucci to Margherita Sarfatti, 3 June 1925, published in Rossana Bossaglia, *Il "Novecento italiano": Storia, documenti, iconografia* (Milan: Feltrinelli Editore, 1979), 93; my translation.
39 Sarfatti's remarks appeared in the catalogue of the Novecento Italiano, exhibited in Buenos Aires in 1930, and they are reprinted in Bossaglia, *Il "Novecento italiano,"* 118–20; my translation.
40 Braun, *Mario Sironi and Italian Modernism*, 101–02.
41 Braun, *Mario Sironi and Italian Modernism*, 58.
42 Francesco Monotti to Ezra Pound, 4 February 1932, Ezra Pound Papers, Yale Collection of American Literature, Beinecke Rare Book and Manuscript Library. Monotti offers to help arrange this meeting.
43 Ezra Pound, "Marches Civilization …," *Chicago Tribune* (Paris) 5:975 [?31 December 1933), Italian Supplement 1933, 21; *P&P*, 6:121.
44 Ezra Pound, "I Gather the Limbs of Osiris, III. Guido Cavalcanti," *New Age* 10:7 (14 December 1911), 155–56; *P&P*, 1:47–48.
45 Ezra Pound, "I Gather the Limbs of Osiris, [II]: A Rather Dull Introduction," *New Age* 10:6 (7 December 1911), 130–31; *P&P*, 1:44–45.
46 Pound, "Marches Civilization" (*P&P*, 6:121).
47 Pound could not have anticipated the failing of the Aquila Press in late 1929, but his conception of his book's physical look was so strong that he could not accept the earlier compromise position offered by Faber and

Gwyer in January 1929. For the complete details of the publication of this book—both the earlier unsuccessful attempts in England and the later published edition as it appeared in Italy in 1932—see Donald Gallup, *Ezra Pound: A Bibliography* (Charlottesville: The University Press of Virginia, 1983), 152–54. Peculiarities of this edition make bibliographic references difficult: not only do the cover and title page disagree as to the year of publication—Anno IX on the title page and Anno X on the cover—but the pages of the volume are not numbered in one long sequence. Cavalcanti's poems in Italian have one set of page numbers, the pages of photographic plates are not numbered but have only plate numbers, and the "Fragments of a Bilingual Edition" section has its own set of page numbers. My references to the "Fragments from a Bilingual Edition" section include first the page numbers as printed, and then a second set of bracketed page numbers, clarifying the position relative to the preceding sections. Page numbers from other sections of the book are given in brackets only.

48 On the history of this volume's compilation and its relationship to other editions of Cavalcanti produced by Pound, see David Anderson's introduction to *Pound's Cavalcanti: An Edition of the Translations, Notes, and Essays* (Princeton: Princeton University Press, 1983), ix–xxx.

49 Mario Praz, "Due Note su Ezra Pound" (1932), *Cronache Letterarie Anglo-sassoni*, vol. 1 (Roma: Edizioni di Storia e Letteratura, 1950), 180. Praz's phrase, which I have translated, reads "un divertente *bric-à-brac* squisitamente poundiano." Anderson briefly addresses the book's reception in England and Italy in *Pound's Cavalcanti*, xxii–xxiv. On the reception of *GCR*, see Anderson, *Pound's Cavalcanti*, xxii–xxiii.

50 Pound published work on Cavalcanti in three installments in the *Dial*: "Mediaevalism and Mediaevalism (Guido Cavalcanti)" [called just "Mediaevalism" in the 1932 edition], *Dial* 84:3 (March 1928), [231]–37 (*P&P*, 5:19–25); "Donna mi prega" with "Partial Explanation," "The Canzone," "The Other Dimension," and "Hendecasyllables," *Dial* 85:1 (July 1928), [1]–20 (*P&P*, 5:32–49); "Guido's Relations," *Dial* 86:7 (July 1929), [559]–568 (*P&P*, 5:164–73). "Sonnets and Ballate: Introduction" had appeared in his *Sonnets and Ballate of Guido Cavalcanti* (Boston: Small, Maynard, and Company, 1912; London: Stephen Swift and Co., 1912).

51 Ezra Pound, "Possibilities of Civilization: What the Small Town Can Do," *Delphian Quarterly* 19:3 (July 1936): 15–17, 44; *P&P*, 7:66–67. The dedication reads "A Manlio Dazzi che ha mangiato 'Ai Dodici Apostoli' e con me diviso le fatiche di quest' edizione (1928–31)."

52 Stefano Maria Casella, "Ezra Pound and Cunizza da Romano: Fragments of an Unfinished Epic Poem," in Helen M. Dennis (ed.), *Ezra Pound and Poetic Influence: Official Proceedings of the 17th International Ezra Pound Conference* (Amsterdam and Atlanta: Rodopi, 2000), 74–79.

53 Mussolini instituted the *Era Fascista* in December 1926, part of a larger program of iconography stressing Fascist Italy's connection to ancient

Rome. On this program and its relationship to the regime's cultural objectives, see Chapter 3 and Cannistraro and Sullivan, *Il Duce's Other Woman*, 304.

54 For a general treatment of Dante's prominence in Italian Nationalist thinking, see Charles T. Davis, "Dante and Italian Nationalism," in William de Sua and Gino Rizzo (eds), *A Dante Symposium* (Chapel Hill: University of North Carolina Press, 1965), 199–213. Luigi Scorrano's *Il Dante "fascista": saggi, letture, note dantesche* (Ravenna: Longo, 2001) examines Dante's appropriation and interpretation during the Fascist period. Risorgimento-era Nationalist Giuseppe Mazzini's "Dell'amor patrio di Dante" and "Dante" are reproduced in *Pensiero e Azione*, ed. Alessandro Levi, 2nd ed. (Florence: La Nuova Italia, 1914). For two important treatments of Dante during the Fascist period, see Giovanni Gentile, "La profezia di Dante" (1918), *Dante e Manzoni* (Florence, 1923), 9–61; Gentile, "Il canto di Sordello," *Nuova antologia* (16 May 1939), 130–39. On celebrations of the sexcentenary of Dante's death in Florence in 1921, and the subsequent mapping of history onto the urban fabric of Florence, as well as wider Fascist celebrations of Dante as a cultural icon, see Lasansky, *The Renaissance Perfected*, 57–63. For a compilation of materials published on this occasion, see *Dante e l'Italia: nel VI cenetenario della morte del poeta, mcmxxi* (Rome: Fondazione Marco Besso, 1921). Numerous articles about Dante and his writings appeared in 1924 in the Fascist journal *Gerarchia*. Domenico Venturini's *Dante Alighieri e Benito Mussolini* (Rome: Nuova Italia, 1927) draws specific parallels between the ideas espoused by Dante and those implemented by the Fascist dictator. Thomas L. Schumacher's *The Danteum: Architecture, Poetics, and Politics under Italian Fascism* (Rome: Officina Edizioni, 1980; Princeton: Princeton Architectural Press, 1985) offers a thorough and rich treatment of Rationalist architect Giuseppe Terragni's plans for a Danteum (1938), well received by Mussolini but never built. Schumacher also addresses Rino Valdameri's plans for a deluxe edition of the *Commedia*, to be illustrated by Amos Nattini and produced under Fascist auspices; only the *Inferno* (1932) and *Purgatorio* (1938) were completed (Schumacher, *The Danteum*, 58).
55 Ezra Pound, "Ad Lectorem E. P.," *GCR*, [5], my translation.
56 Ezra Pound, "Sonnets and Ballate," [39], [149]; "The Other Dimension," *GCR*, [22] [132]; "Mediaevalism," *GCR*, [1] [111]. The bulk of Cavalcanti's philosophical context is offered in "Partial Explanation," where Pound repeats in slightly different phrasing his comment about Cavalcanti's family's place in Inferno X and asserts again Cavalcanti's "familiarity … with dangerous thinking" ([11], [121]). Pound goes on to examine Cavalcanti's familiarity with the thinking of Aristotle, Albertus Magnus, Grosseteste, and suggests that Cavalcanti is not overly invested in the thinking of Thomas Aquinas and other specifically Christian thinkers ([11]–15, [121–25]).
57 Ezra Pound, "Mediaevalism," *GCR*, [1] [111].
58 Pound, "Sonnets and Ballate," *GCR*, [39] [149].

59 Pound, "Sonnets and Ballate," *GCR*, 41 [151].
60 Pound, "Mediaevalism," *GCR*, 4 [114].
61 Pound, "Mediaevalism," *GCR*, 4–5 [114–15]. The irony of Pound dismissing Petrarch so consistently and heartily given his own similarities to him, does not, as Dasenbrock has noted, stop him from making similar remarks as late as *Guide to Kulchur* (*Imitating the Italians*, 107–09).
62 Adamson, *Avant-Garde Florence*, 27. Adamson specifically addresses "the generation of 1880," contemporaries of Pound, and the literary generation that would form the Florentine avant-garde and continue to be very active in the cultural endeavors of the Fascist regime.
63 Pound, *The Spirit of Romance* (1910; New York: New Directions, 1968), 104.
64 Pound, *The Spirit of Romance*, 110. He added the following footnote to that phrase: "1929: I retract this expression."
65 Pound, "Mediaevalism" *GCR*, 2 [112]. "Mediaevalism" is an important part of the *Rime* edition, and was earlier published as "Mediaevalism and Mediaevalism (Guido Cavalcanti)" in the *Dial* in March 1928, when Pound was trying to publish the book in England.
66 As we have seen, Berenson's concept of "tactile values," crucial to the ideology and work of the Novecento and *Valori Plastici* schools, led to an emphasis on the plasticity of painted figures and the admiration of Giotto, Piero, Masaccio, and others known for their innovations in this realm: Italian tradition was identified with plasticity (Braun, *Mario Sironi and Italian Modernism*, 58). These same "Tuscan primitives" were the artists whom the Novecento painters saw as their models and predecessors.
67 Pound, "Mediaevalism," *GCR*, 3 [113].
68 Dasenbrock, *Imitating the Italians*, 158. In Chapter 3, I discuss *virtù* in the context of *Mussolinismo*.
69 Duggan, *The Force of Destiny*, 260.
70 Duggan, *The Force of Destiny*, 433, 495. Other Fascist leaders similarly drew inspiration from Machiavelli.
71 Pound, "Mediaevalism," *GCR*, 3 [113].
72 Sarfatti, *Segni, colori e luci* (Bologna, 1925), reproduced in Pontiggia, *Da Boccioni a Sironi*, 200; my translation.
73 Pound, "Mediaevalism," *GCR*, 3 [113].
74 Carrà, "Paolo Uccello Costruttore," 378–79; my translation.
75 Libero Andreotti, *Art and Politics in Fascist Italy: The Exhibition of the Fascist Revolution (1932)* (PhD thesis, Massachusetts Institute of Technology, 1989), 169.
76 Pound, "Mediaevalism," *GCR*, 4 [114].
77 Pound, "Mediaevalism," *GCR*, 4 [114].
78 Sarfatti, "Art and Fascism," 242.
79 Dasenbrock, *Imitating the Italians*, 148–49. Dasenbrock treats Pound's interest in Renaissance humanism on pages 144–79.

80 Pound, "Ad Lectorem E. P.," *GCR*, [6]; my translation.
81 On this reaction against the "absurd specialization" of universities and the separation of high culture from the masses, see Adamson, *Avant-Garde Florence*, 79–80.
82 Pound, "[Italy: The Second Decennio]," leaf [11], Pound Papers.
83 Giovanni Papini, "Firenze Centro di Studi sul Rinascimento," *Firenze* (May 1937), 198, trans. Lasansky, *The Renaissance Perfected*, 253.
84 Pound, "[Italy: The Second Decennio]," leaves [11]–[12], Pound Papers.

Notes to Chapter 3

1 Ezra Pound, "Ave Roma," *Il Mare* 26:1243 (7 January 1933): 3, 4 (*P&P*, 6:8–9); my translation.
2 Walter L. Adamson, "Modernism and Fascism: The Politics of Culture in Italy, 1903-1922," *The American Historical Review* 95:2 (April 1990): 381–84.
3 Margherita G. Sarfatti, "Art and Fascism" (originally published as "L'Arte e Fascismo" in Giuseppe Luigi Pomba [ed.], *La civiltà fascista* [Torino: Unione Tipografico Editrice Torinese, 1928]), trans. Olivia E. Sears and Jeffrey T Schnapp in Jeffrey T. Schnapp (ed.), *A Primer of Italian Fascism* (Lincoln and London: University of Nebraska Press, 2000), 249.
4 F. T. Marinetti, in *Critica Fascista* 5:1 (1 January 1927): 3, trans. Jennifer Roberts and Barbara Spackman in Jeffrey Schnapp and Barbara Spackman (eds), "Selections from the Great Debate on Fascism and Culture: *Critica Fascista* 1926–1927," *Stanford Italian Review* 8 (1990): 261.
5 Ardengo Soffici, in *Critica Fascista* 4:20 (15 October 1926): 383–85, trans. Elizabeth MacIntosh and Barbara Spackman in Schnapp and Spackman, "Selections from the Great Debate," 240.
6 For a greater representation of the issues at stake and the voices involved, see Schnapp and Spackman, "Selections from the Great Debate."
7 On the mobilization of the peasantry in Sicily during the 1890s, see Christopher Duggan, *The Force of Destiny: A History of Italy since 1796* (Boston and New York: Houghton Mifflin, 2008), 340.
8 These ambitions for *sindicati*, of course, would form the basis of the Fascist conception of corporations. See David D. Roberts, *The Syndicalist Tradition and Italian Fascism* (Chapel Hill: University of North Carolina Press, 1979).
9 Alexander J. De Grand, *The Italian Nationalist Association and the Rise of Fascism in Italy* (Lincoln and London: University of Nebraska Press, 1978).
10 On this heterogeneity of the early Fascist Party, see Duggan, *The Force of Destiny*, 416.
11 Simonetta Falasca-Zamponi, *Fascist Spectacle: The Aesthetics of Power in Mussolini's Italy* (Berkeley, Los Angeles, and London: University of

California Press, 1997), 95–96. On the Sicilian *Fasci* of the early 1890s, see Duggan, *The Force of Destiny*, 338–45. Shortly after the March on Rome, Margherita Sarfatti sent a public and prearranged letter to Mussolini, advocating the use of the *fascio* on all Italian coinage, which began a year later. See Philip V. Cannistraro and Brian R. Sullivan, *Il Duce's Other Woman: The Untold Story of Margherita Sarfatti, Benito Mussolini's Jewish Mistress, and How She Helped Him Come to Power* (New York: William Morrow and Company, 1993), 304.

12 The *fascio* also appears in radical imagery of the French Revolution, in American architecture and coinage, and on Italian buildings preceding the Fascist period. See Falasca-Zamponi, *Fascist Spectacle*, 95–96.
13 Ezra Pound, "Intellectual Money," *British Union Quarterly* 1:2 (April–June 1937): 24–34; *P&P*, 7:144–45.
14 Emilio Gentile, "Mussolini: i volti di un mito" (1983), in *Fascismo: storia e interpretazione* (Rome-Bari: Laterza, 2002), 113.
15 Schnapp and Spackman, "Selections from the Great Debate," n. 237.
16 Gentile, "Mussolini," 114–30.
17 Gentile, "Mussolini," 114–30.
18 Quoted in Falasca-Zamponi, *Fascist Spectacle*, 49–50.
19 For examples of such photos, see Falasca-Zamponi, *Fascist Spectacle*, 69, 74.
20 Falasca-Zamponi, *Fascist Spectacle*, 64–84.
21 Duggan, *The Force of Destiny*, 475–80.
22 See, for instance, Ezra Pound, "The Acid Test," *Biosophical Review* (New York) 4:2 (Winter 1934–35), 22–30 (*P&P*, 6:218) and "The Truth about Italy," *Saturday Review* (London) 161:4205 (9 May 1936), 598 (*P&P*, 7:56).
23 *J/M*, 88. Pound formulates the same point slightly differently when he says, "When a human being has an analogous completeness of knowledge, or intelligence carried into a third or fourth dimension, capable of dealing with NEW circumstances, we call it genius" (*J/M*, 18–19).
24 Pound makes a similar assertion a few pages earlier: "Nevertheless Mussolini has a more responsive instrument than any other I can think of, something does appear to get started with 'bewildering frequency,' grain, swamps, birds, yes, gentle reader, birds, there are more birds in the olive yards, 'birds friendly to agriculture.' W. H. Hudson wrote a lot about the subject, the aged Munthe wrote a book about Capri, but the BOSS does something about it" (*J/M*, 91).
25 Gentile, "Mussolini," 115.
26 Ezra Pound, *ABC of Economics* (London: Faber, 1933); *SP*, 261.
27 For a rich treatment of this concept in Pound's poetry and thought, see Peter Liebregts, *Ezra Pound and Neoplatonism* (Madison and Teaneck: Fairleigh Dickinson University Press, 2004).
28 Gentile, "Mussolini," 127.
29 Falasca-Zamponi, *Fascist Spectacle*, 85.

30 Falasca-Zamponi, *Fascist Spectacle*, 85.
31 Sarfatti, "Art and Fascism," 247–48. Similarly influential was the aggressive style employed by such Nationalist writers as Enrico Corradini—a style described later as "all nerves and muscles." See Richard Drake, "The Theory and Practice of Italian Nationalism, 1900–1906," *Journal of Modern History* 53:2 (June 1981), 217.
32 Sarfatti, "Art and Fascism," 248.
33 *J/M*, 59; emphasis original. Pound would still be exploring issues of snobbism in his essay "Snobismi e sindacati," *Meridiano di Roma* (2 June 1940); *P&P*, 8:40–42.
34 *J/M*, 66. Elsewhere Pound attributes this same ability to Thomas Jefferson, using language that connects him to the Duce: "in his range of knowledge and empirical curiosity, [Jefferson] was the heir of the encyclopedists, but he was Aquinian in his tendency to fit everything observable into an order system. He had the totalitarian view, seeing forces not in isolation but as interactive." See Ezra Pound, "The Jefferson-Adams Correspondence," *North American Review* (New York) 244:2 (Winter 1937–38): 314–24; *P&P*, 7:267.
35 In "Ave Roma," Pound explores the idea of the "authentic genius" through filmmaker Pietro Francisci. Pound was especially interested in his documentary film, made for the Istituto LUCE, about the Mostra della Rivoluzione Fascista (*P&P*, 6:8–9). For more on this film in Francisci's career, see Ezra Pound, *Carte italiane 1930–1944, letteratura e arte*, ed. Luca Cesari (Milan: Archinto, 2005), 259. That Pound applied the label of "authentic genius"—a title he had previously reserved for the likes of Gaudier-Brzeska and Brâncuși—to Francisci shows his shift in focus to Italian arts, and his willingness to take propaganda art seriously (*P&P*, 6:9). On the Istituto LUCE and its contributions to Fascist cultural Nationalism, see James Hay, *Popular Film Culture in Fascist Italy: The Passing of the Rex* (Bloomington and Indianapolis: Indiana University Press, 1987), 201–32.
36 On Sarfatti's ghostwriting for Mussolini, see Cannistraro and Sullivan, *Il Duce's Other Woman*, 360ff.
37 Duggan, *The Force of Destiny*, 478. Giuseppe Prezzolini came up with the idea for the biography in 1924, and arranged for Sarfatti to be the author: as a person intimate with Mussolini and a devoted Fascist, she could provide a more personal yet still ideologically rich portrait of the leader (Cannistraro and Sullivan, *Il Duce's Other Woman*, 299–303).
38 Cannistraro and Sullivan, *Il Duce's Other Woman*, 91–94.
39 Cannistraro and Sullivan, *Il Duce's Other Woman*, 100–05.
40 Ezra Pound, "Murder by Capital," *Criterion* 12:49 (July 1933), 585–92; *P&P*, 6:58.
41 Margherita G. Sarfatti, *Dux* (Milan: Mondadori, 1926), 42.

42 Ezra Pound to Margherita Sarfatti, 25 February [1934], Ezra Pound Papers, Yale Collection of American Literature, Beinecke Rare Book and Manuscript Library.
43 Pound to Sarfatti, [9 October] 1934, Pound Papers. This item has been misdated as "August?" in Beinecke.
44 The anecdote about the pre-Fascist working day and wage, set in the town of Orbe (*C*, 41:203, lines 46–53), and mention of the bombing of Mussolini's hospital (*C*, 41:204, lines 75–76), for instance, come from Sarfatti (*Dux*, 58–59 and 185 respectively).
45 Cannistraro and Sullivan, *Il Duce's Other Woman*, 303.
46 For some of Pound's critiques of the Venice Biennale, see his letter to P. M. Bardi, quoted in Bardi's column "Busta da Roma," *L'Ambrosiano* (Milan) (29 December 1931): 3 (*P&P*, 5:333); Pound, "Appunti," *Il Mare* 25:1235 (12 November 1932): 4 (*P&P*, 5:379-81); and Pound, "The Biennale," *New English Weekly* 7:7 (30 May 1935): 140 (*P&P*, 6:290).
47 David Barnes, "Fascist Aesthetics: Ezra Pound's Cultural Negotiations in 1930s Italy," *Journal of Modern Literature* 34:1 (Fall 2010): 27–32.
48 P. M. Bardi, *Rapporto sull'architettura (per Mussolini)* (Rome, 1931), 101, trans. Esther da Costa Meyer, *The Work of Antonio Sant'Elia: Retreat into the Future* (New Haven and London: Yale University Press, 1995), 194–95. Meyer also notes supportive comments made by other Rationalist and Futurist proponents of Sant'Elia. Although Italian Rationalism, aligned with the International Style, had a mixed reception in Italy—ranging from outright rejection to the acceptance of individual projects or works—Sant'Elia could be distinguished from its internationalizing tendencies, since his work was completed before the real rise of the Rationalist movement.
49 Pound might also have started paying attention to Sant'Elia's work as early as 1932, when he quoted comments by F. T. Marinetti that included reference to the "Futurist genius Antonio Sant'Elia." See Pound, "Appunti," *Il Mare* 25:1235 (12 November 1932): 4; *P&P*, 5:381. See also Barnes, "Fascist Aesthetics," 27–28.
50 Ezra Pound, "Un magnifico libro di P. M. Bardi," *Il Mare* (24 February 1934); *P&P*, 6:133.
51 Luigi Colombo Fillia and E. Prampolini, "Futurismo!" *Futurismo* (20 November 1932): 6, trans. in Meyer, *The Work of Antonio Sant'Elia*, 202.
52 Ezra Pound, "Rapallo centro di cultura," *Il Mare* (2 May 1936): [1]; *P&P*, 7:52–53.
53 Ezra Pound, "L'arte di Sant'Elia a Rapallo," *Il Mare* (28 March 1936); *P&P*, 7:40. Pound expressed a similar optimism about Sant'Elia's work in *J/M*, 106.
54 Pound, "Rapallo centro di cultura" (*P&P*, 7:52).
55 For discussion of noteworthy examples, see V. Fagone, G. Ginex, and T. Sparagni (eds), *Muri ai Pittori: Pittura murale e decorazione in Italia,*

1930–1950 (Milan: Mazzotta, 1999); R. Barbiellini Amidei et al., *La Casa Madre dei Mutilati di Guerra* (Rome, 1993).

56 Mario Sironi, "Manifesto della pittura murale," originally published in *La Colonna* (December 1933), trans. by Jeffrey T. Schnapp in Claudia Lazzaro and Roger J. Crum (eds), *Donatello among the Blackshirts: History and Modernity in the Visual Culture of Fascist Italy* (Ithaca and London: Cornell University Press, 2005), 238–40. The manifesto was also signed by Massimo Campigli, Carlo Carrà, and Achille Funi. Mural art did not become as popular as Sironi had predicted or hoped, in part because some prominent critics, including Roberto Farinacci and Ugo Ojetti, objected to the way that muralism displaced private patronage with public commissions. See Schnapp, "Flash Memories (Sironi on Exhibit)" in Lazzaro and Crum, *Donatello among the Blackshirts: History and Modernity in the Visual Culture of Fascist Italy* (Ithaca and London: Cornell University Press, 2005), 234–35.

57 In "Ubicumque Lingua Romana" (1938), Pound asserts that if he were asked to devise a syndicate for writers, "Among other things I should treat literature as communications service, not as the quantitative production of merchandise" (in Erminio Turcotti (ed.), *Fascist Europe/Europa Fascista: An Anglo-Italian Symposium* [Milan: National Institute of Fascist Culture of Pavia, 1938], 1:45).

58 Jeffrey T. Schnapp, "Fascism's Museum in Motion," *Journal of Architectural Education* 45:2 (February 1992): 88–89.

59 Attendance was stimulated in part, Libero Andreotti explains, "by the 70% discounts on train fares from Italy and abroad." See Andreotti, *Art and Politics in Fascist Italy: The Exhibition of the Fascist Revolution (1932)* (PhD thesis, Massachusetts Institute of Technology, 1989), 214. The notion of using the railways as a way to bring tourists to Italy's cities had also been important to Nationalist Count Camillo di Cavour. See Duggan, *The Force of Destiny*, 147–48.

60 Ezra Pound to Olga Rudge, 25 December 1932, Olga Rudge Papers, Yale Collection of American Literature, Beinecke Rare Book and Manuscript Library.

61 Pound, *J/M*, 51. He makes a similar comment in Italian in "Ave Roma" (*P&P*, 6:9).

62 Partito Nazionale Fascista, *Mostra della Rivoluzione Fascista: Guida Storica a cura di Dino Alfieri e Luigi Freddi* (Rome: Officine dell'Istituto Italiano d'Arti Grafiche di Bergamo, 1933), 9; my translation.

63 See, for instance, Marinetti's "Fondazione e Manifesto del Futurismo," trans. Rainey in *Modernism*, 5. On the importance of the Futurist influence on early Fascist thinking about culture, see Stone, *The Patron State*, 19.

64 Valuing its subjectivity, the MRF emphasized its solicitation of artifacts from those who had participated in the early days of Fascism.

65 Pound, "Ave Roma" (*P&P*, 6:9); my translation. Pound's comment follows the ideology of the process used to collect the artifacts for the exhibition. See Stone, *Patron State*, 137; PNF, *Mostra della Rivoluzione Fascista*, 7.
66 Ezra Pound, "Intellectual Money," *British Union Quarterly* 1:2 (April/June 1937): 24–34; *P&P*, 7:144–45.
67 Libero Andreotti, "The Aesthetics of War: The Exhibition of the Fascist Revolution," *Journal of Architectural Education* 45:2 (February 1992): 78.
68 *J/M*, 51. Pound makes a similar comment in Italian in "Ave Roma" (*P&P*, 6:9).
69 Although only twenty-eight years old when he was invited to participate in creating the *MRF*, Terragni already had several buildings to his credit. His *Danteum*, perhaps the greatest example of Terragni's ability to translate narrative elements (whether historical or literary) into an architectural composition, was still several years in the future, but its concerns are already visible here. Similarly, already present is his "insistent preoccupation with effects of (literal and phenomenal) transparency, and with related concepts of 'interpenetration,' overlapping, or layering" (Andreotti, *Art and Politics in Fascist Italy*, 130). On the *Danteum*, see Thomas L. Schumacher, *The Danteum: Architecture, Poetics, and Politics under Italian Fascism*, 2nd ed. (New York: Princeton Architectural Press, 1993).
70 Terragni's first task was to digest that information: his early sketches show this process (Andreotti, *Art and Politics in Fascist Italy*, 129–45).
71 Andreotti, *Art and Politics in Fascist Italy*, 138–40. Andreotti notes that "this layering effect was supposed to evoke the dense succession, even simultaneity, of events during 'insurrection.'"
72 Andreotti, *Art and Politics in Fascist Italy*, 123.
73 Andreotti, *Art and Politics in Fascist Italy*, 138.
74 For a more detailed description of the imagery at work, see Andreotti, *Art and Politics in Fascist Italy*, 141–42.
75 Andreotti's translation (*Art and Politics in Fascist Italy*, 54).
76 Pound, "Appunti," *Il Mare* (Genoa) 25:1235 (12 November 1932), 3 (*P&P*, 5:381); my translation.
77 For a more detailed description of the *Strapaese* faction, see Andreotti, *Art and Politics in Fascist Italy*, 115–18.
78 On Nizzoli's design work in the rooms documenting events from March–December 1918, see Andreotti, *Art and Politics in Fascist Italy*, 112–15.
79 All the information in this paragraph comes from Andreotti's dissertation, particularly its useful biographical notes.
80 Ezra Pound, "Canto XLVI," *New Democracy* 6:1 (March 1936): 14–16; *P&P*, 7:28; *C*, 46:231.
81 Braun, *Mario Sironi and Italian Modernism*, 149–51.
82 Andreotti's translation (*Art and Politics in Fascist Italy*, 169).
83 Andreotti, *Art and Politics in Fascist Italy*, 166.
84 PNF, *Mostra della Rivoluzione Fascista*, 211–15.

85 Andreotti, *Art and Politics in Fascist Italy*, 184.
86 Andreotti, *Art and Politics in Fascist Italy*, 185–86.
87 Andreotti, *Art and Politics in Fascist Italy*, 182.
88 As Claudio Fogu has noted, these two reconstructed offices—Mussolini's first and last at *Il Popolo d'Italia*—are unified by the same rhetorical thread, the rooms functioning as the site of the Fascist revolution, and "as a visualization of the fascist historic imaginary itself." See *The Historic Imaginary: Politics of History in Fascist Italy* (Toronto: University of Toronto Press, 2003), 151–52.
89 See Schnapp and Spackman, "Selections from the Great Debate."
90 Roberto Farinacci, "Fronte, cobezzoli!, unico," *Il Regime Fascista* (20 June 1933), qtd and trans. in Schnapp, "Flash Memories," 235.
91 Braun, *Mario Sironi and Italian Modernism*, 191.
92 This system of dating was adopted in 1927. See Duggan, *The Force of Destiny*, 480.
93 On the various images and tropes of Fascist *Romanità*, see Duggan, *The Force of Destiny*, 493–500; Falasca-Zamponi, *Fascist Spectacle*, 90–99; Fogu, *The Historic Imaginary*, 23–24; Roger Griffin, *Modernism and Fascism: The Sense of a Beginning under Mussolini and Hitler* (Basingstoke and New York: Palgrave Macmillan, 2007), 222–23; Claudia Lazzaro, "Forging a Visible Fascist Nation: Strategies for Fusing Past and Present," in Lazzaro and Crum, *Donatello among the Blackshirts: History and Modernity in the Visual Culture of Fascist Italy* (Ithaca and London: Cornell University Press, 2005), 13–31.
94 Joshua Arthurs, *Excavating Modernity: The Roman Past in Fascist Italy* (Ithaca and London: Cornell University Press, 2013), 5.
95 Cannistraro and Sullivan, *Il Duce's Other Woman*, 219.
96 Benito Mussolini, "L'Azione e la dottrina fascista dinnanzi alle necessità storiche della nazione," delivered 20 September 1922, published in *Il Popolo d'Italia* (21 September 1922), also in Mussolini, *Opera Omnia*, ed. Edoardo and Duilio Susmel (Florence: La Fenice, 1956), 18:412, trans. In Duggan, *The Force of Destiny*, 431.
97 Giuseppe Bottai, "Roma e Fascismo, *Roma: Rivista di studi e di vita romana* 15:10 (1937): 350.
98 Benito Mussolini, "La Nuova Roma," originally delivered 31 December 1925 and published in *Il Popolo d'Italia* (1 January 1926): 13; see Mussolini, *Opera Omnia*, ed. Edoardo and Duilio Susmel (Florence: La Fenice, 1957), 22:48.
99 Romke Visser, "Fascist Doctrine and the Cult of Romanità," *Journal of Contemporary History* 27:1 (January 1992): 17.
100 Peter Aicher, "Mussolini's Forum and the Myth of Augustan Rome," *The Classical Bulletin* 76.2 (2000): 119.

101 For discussions of this change, see Peter Bondanella, *Eternal City: Roman Images in the Modern World* (Chapel Hill: University of North Carolina Press, 1987) and Stone, *The Patron State*.
102 Visser, "Fascist Doctrine and the Cult of Romanità," 6–7. On the use of the journal *Roma* (first published in 1923) as an unofficial outlet of the Institute of Roman Studies and a means of encouraging classical education and the furthering of the cult of Rome, see Antonio La Penna, "Il culto della romanità nel period fascista: La rivista 'Roma' e l'Istituto di studi romani," *Italia contemporanea* 27 (December 1999), 605–30. On the deployment of *Romanità* in the iconography of the "E '42" (or the International Exhibition of the year 1942) and the Foro Mussolini, see Paolo Montorsi, "Il mito di Roma nella pittura di regime (1937–1943): i mosaici del Viale dell'Impero e le opera decorative per l'E 42," *Bollettino d'Arte* 78 (November–December 1993): 87–112. On the use of Augustan history in the conception of the Fascist revolution, see Mariella Cagnetta, "Il mito di Augusto e la 'rivoluzione fascist,'" *Quaderni di Storia* 3 (1976): 139–81. On the continuity in ideology and archaeology starting with the Exhibition of the Provinces of the Empire (organized in 1911 by Rodolfo Lanciani), continuing through the Exhibition of Augustus and Romanness (1937–38), and culminating in "E '42," see Eugénie Sellers Strong, "'Romanità' throughout the Ages," *Journal of Roman Studies* 29 (1939): 137–66.
103 Strong, "'Romanità' throughout the Ages."
104 Visser, "Fascist Doctrine and the Cult of Romanità," 8.
105 Antonio Cederna, *Mussolini urbanista: Lo sventramento di Roma negli anni del consenso* (Rome: Laterza, 1980), 11.
106 A. W. Van Buren, "Art Activities in Italy," *Parnassus* 1:1 (January 1929): 4. *Parnassus* was published by the College Art Association until 1941, when it became *College Art Journal* (1941–60) and later *Art Journal* (1960–present).
107 Stephen L. Dyson, *In Pursuit of Ancient Pasts: A History of Classical Archaeology in the Nineteenth and Twentieth Centuries* (New Haven and London: Yale University Press, 2006), 98.
108 *J/M*, 85. Similarly, in May 1931, Pound celebrated the Fascist regime's "service of the public interest" in the restoration of architectural treasures throughout Italy ("In difesa del paesaggio: non deturpare," *Giornale di Genova* (25 May 1931[?]); *P&P*, 5:293–94). He distinguishes the grace of the modern restorations of Romanesque architecture from earlier attempts, namely those undertaken by Viollet-le-Duc, whose so-called "restorations" transformed monuments of the past into fantasies of medievalism and revived Gothic.
109 On the alterations made to the Tempio under the direction of Leon Battista Alberti—much admired by Pound—see Lawrence S. Rainey, *Ezra Pound and the Monument of Culture: Text, History, and the Malatesta Cantos* (Chicago and London: University of Chicago Press, 1991), 8–14. Attempts to reveal traces of the ancient Roman past routinely demolished medieval

neighborhoods in Rome. As building materials were rarely wasted in the medieval period and beyond, later developments were commonly built on ancient foundations or reused ancient materials.

110 Pound, "In difesa" (*P&P*, 5:293). A. W. Van Buren of the American Academy in Rome in 1929 singled out Agrigento as one of three places (together with Ravenna and Pisa) in the provinces demonstrating "judicious restoration": "Agrigento in Sicily (no longer barbarously styled Girgenti), where many of the massive columns of that incomparable line of Greek temples have been put back in their original positions" ("Art Activities in Italy," [January 1929], 4). In April 1929, he brought readers' attention to "the continued discovery of structures and small objects of a cult nature on the slope near the 'temple of the Dioskouroi.'" Noting that "The existence of a sanctuary at this point, with a rectangular and a circular stone altar, had been revealed in March of the year 1927," Van Buren revealed that "There has now come to light another massive circular altar," which excavators dated to the first half of the sixth century BCE ("Art Activities in Italy," *Parnassus* 1:4 [April 1929]: 7).

111 Pound, "In difesa" (*P&P*, 5:293). Pound is quick to say that he is not trying "to start a battle in the name of aesthetics against the utility of commerce." At this time these two forces were frequently in conflict. Archaeologist and restorer Antonio Muñoz, appointed by Mussolini as director of antiquities and fine arts for the Governatorato, and responsible for many archaeological and restoration projects in the center of Rome (including overseeing the building of the via del Mare and the via dell'Impero, as well as restorations at Santi Quattro Coronati, Santa Sabina, and San Giorgio al Velabro, and work on such monuments as the Tempio della Fortuna Virile), wrote in *Roma di Mussolini* (1935) that the archaeological restorations going on in Rome (which often required the demolition of existing buildings) demonstrated the "triumph of Archeology against the strong forces of economic interest" (qtd. and trans. Borden W. Painter, Jr., *Mussolini's Rome: Rebuilding the Eternal City* [Basingstoke and New York: Palgrave Macmillan, 2005], 9).

112 Pound, "In difesa" (*P&P*, 5:294).

113 Pound, "In difesa" (*P&P*, 5:293).

114 Ruth Ben-Ghiat, *Fascist Modernities: Italy, 1922–1945* (Berkeley and Los Angeles: University of California Press, 2001), 4. See also Philip V. Cannistraro's entry "Bonifica Integrale" in Philip V. Cannistraro (ed.), *Historical Dictionary of Fascist Italy* (Westport and London: Greenwood Press, 1982), 80–81.

115 Benito Mussolini, "Per la cittadinanza di Roma" (21 April 1924), in *Opera Omnia* 20:235.

116 Pound, "In difesa" (*P&P*, 5:293).

117 Van Buren, "Art Activities in Italy" (January 1929): 4.

118 On Fascist-era efforts to increase touristic interest in Italy's cultural heritage, see D. Medina Lasansky, *The Renaissance Perfected: Architecture, Spectacle,*

and Tourism in Fascist Italy (University Park: The Pennsylvania State University Press, 2004). On similar efforts in colonized Libya, see Brian L. McLaren, *Architecture and Tourism in Italian Colonial Libya: An Ambivalent Modernism* (Seattle and London: University of Washington Press, 2006).

119 Giuseppe Bottai, "Il Rinnovamento di Roma," *Nuova Antologia* (1 January 1937), reprinted in *Politica Fascista delle Arti* (Rome: Angelo Signorelli, 1940), [5]; my translation. Bottai refers to Mussolini's speech, "La Nuova Roma," discussed above, and see n. 97.

120 Mussolini's plan made an explicit link between the via della Conciliazione and the Lateran Pacts, signed in 1929: these accords put to rest conflicts between the Vatican and the Italian nation, since the taking of Rome in 1870 involved a seizure of that land from the Pope. The Lateran Pacts recognized the Vatican as an independent state, regulated relationships between Church and state in Italy, and compensated the Holy See for its financial losses during the Risorgimento. As Painter has observed, this was one of many projects where Mussolini himself appeared at the beginning of the demolitions, with Giuseppe Bottai, at that time serving as governor of Rome (*Mussolini's Rome*, 68–71). The road became a symbol of the regime's new relationship with the Vatican, but it also rendered more visible the workings of the independent state within Rome's borders. Indeed the modern building facades that line the via della Conciliazione put a distinctly modern and Fascist architectural stamp on views of St. Peter's basilica.

121 On the mausoleum and piazza, see Spiro Kostof, "The Emperor and the Duce: The Planning of the Piazzale Augusto Imperatore in Rome," in Henry A. Millon and Linda Nochlin (eds), *Art and Architecture in the Service of Politics* (Cambridge and London: The MIT Press, 1978), 270–325. The original site of the Ara Pacis, about 30 feet below the roadway near the Palazzo Fiano in the via in Lucina, was on the Campus Martius, and because it is in a low-lying area, which receives drainage from the Quirinal, the subsoil is saturated with water, and issues of drainage presented frequent impediments to excavation. The first fragments of the monumental altar (consecrated in 13 BCE) were unearthed in 1568 on the site of the Palazzo Fiano (on the Piazza San Lorenzo along the via del Corso), and blocks found at that time and shortly thereafter made their way to the Uffizzi, Louvre, and Vatican Museums. In 1859, further excavations revealed other parts, which were taken to the Museo Nazionale Romano. After further incomplete excavations in 1903, the technique of freezing the subsoil was employed in 1937, regaining the rest of the monument which, together with copies of the pieces held in other museums, was reconstructed in 1938 on its present site between the Tiber and the Piazza Augusto Imperatore, where a formal opening occurred on 23 September 1938, marking the close of the bimillennium of Augustus. For details about the freezing techniques used and the reassembly of the monument, see C. A. Ralegh Radford, "Some Recent Discoveries in Rome and Italy," *The Journal of Roman Studies* 29:1

(1939): 48–49. The Fascist-era pavilion was later demolished, and the Ara Pacis is now housed in a controversial building by Richard Meier, opened 2006.
122 Not all of the restoration work in Rome was reserved for buildings of antiquity; one of the most visible projects involving a more modern building was that of the Palazzo di Venezia. Pound closes a discussion of the cultural evidence of the reawakening in Italy by saying that "The term 'gerarchia' is perhaps the beginning of a critical sense, vide the four tiles and the dozen or so bits of insuperable pottery, pale blue on pale brownish ground, in the ante-room of the Palazzo Venezia" (*J/M*, 85). A. W. Van Buren similarly praised the regime's use of the Palazzo Venezia—"the former seat of the Venetian ambassadors to the Holy See"—"to serve as the residence of the Head of the Government" as "one of the most ambitious attempts at restoring a historic monument to something resembling its original function that our time has seen" ("Art Activities in Italy" [January 1929]: 4). The palace was begun in 1455 and completed in the sixteenth century, and built partly of stone from the Colosseum. Having become the property of the Italian nation after the First World War, the building was to be used as a museum of the Middle Ages and the Renaissance and the seat of the Istituto Nazionale di Archeologia e Storia dell'Arte. While these plans went forward, the building also became the official residence of the government. Restorations in the late 1920s and early 1930s included the building of a monumental staircase designed by Luigi Marangoni as well as, in Van Buren's words, the removal of "two partition walls of the eighteenth century" and "various Barock accretions" to reveal "the original frescoes, which include great medallions containing portraits of the Roman emperors, and an intricate frieze with Centaurs and architectonic motives in the tradition of imperial Rome, attributable to Bramante." Removal of stucco and whitewash in the Hall of the *Mappamondo*, which Mussolini used as his office, allowed restoration of frescoes assigned to Mantegna ("Art Activities in Italy," *Parnassus* 1:4 [April 1929]: 8).
123 Roads like the via Cavour (opened in the 1870s, linking the Stazione Termini to the old center of the city) and the via Nazionale (also opened in the 1870s, connecting the Piazza Venezia to the Piazza della Repubblica) were part of that project, and the new via dell'Impero would serve as a means of linking the via Cavour to other parts of the city. On the building projects of the 1870s, see Duggan, *The Force of Destiny*, 302–05.
124 Peter Aicher summarizes some of the disputes surrounding the Fascists' role in determining the look of this project in "Mussolini's Forum," 119–21.
125 Spiro Kostoff, *The Third Rome, 1870–1950: Traffic and Glory* (Berkeley: The University Art Museum, 1973): 18.
126 A detailed chronology of Ricci's career and publications appears in *In memoria di Corrado Ricci: Un saggio ineditio nota delle pubblicazioni scritti di*

amici e collaborate (Rome: Istituto d'Archeologia e Storia dell' Arte, 1935), 7–11.
127 Rainey, *Ezra Pound and the Monument of Culture*, 191–97.
128 For an example of this kind of celebratory rhetoric in Ricci's work, see "Corrado Ricci e l'archeologia romana" by Giulio Q. Giglioli, archaeologist and Mussolini's chief archaeological spokesman in Rome, in *In memoria di Corrado Ricci: Un saggio ineditio nota delle pubblicazioni scritti di amici e collaboratori* (Rome: Istituto d'Archeologia e Storia dell' Arte, 1935), 247–50.
129 Bondanella, *Eternal City*, 182.
130 F. P. Mulè, "MCMXXII – Ottobre – MCMXXXII: Le grandi arterie monumentali di Roma, Il Duce sulla via dell'Impero," *Capitolium* 8:11 (November 1932): 559.
131 For treatment of the *fori imperiali* excavations, see James E. Packer, *The Forum of Trajan in Rome: A Study of the Monuments in Brief* (Berkeley, Los Angeles, and London: University of California Press, 2001), 32–47; Italo Insolera and Francesco Perego, *Storia moderna dei Fori di Roma*, expanded edition (Rome: Editori Laterza, 1999); James E. Packer, "Report from Rome: The Imperial Fora, a Retrospective," *American Journal of Archaeology* 101:2 (April 1997): 307–30; James E. Packer, "[Review]: Politics, Urbanism, and Archaeology in 'Roma Capitale': A Troubled Past and a Controversial Future," *American Journal of Archaeology* 93:1 (January 1989): 137–41. For reports from the time, see Corrado Ricci, "La liberazione dei resti del Foro d'Augusto," *Capitolium* 1:1 (April 1925); Ricci, "Il mercato di Traiano," *Capitolium* 5:8 (November 1929); Ricci, "Il Foro di Autusto e la Casa dei Cavalieri di Rodi," *Capitolium* 6:4 (July 1930); Ricci, "Il Foro di Cesare, I," *Capitolium* 8:4 (April 1932): 157–72; Ricci, "Il Foro di Cesare, II," *Capitolium* 8:8 (August 1932): 365–90; Ricci, *Via dell'Impero* (Rome: La Libreria dello Stato, [1933]); and Antonio Muñoz, "La Via dell'Impero e la via del Mare," *Capitolium* 8:11 (November 1932): 521–56.
132 As Packer notes, ornaments, columns, and other elements from the Forum of Trajan were reused in such still-extant Roman structures as the Arch of Constantine, Church of the Madonna of Loreto, the base of the equestrian statue of Marcus Aurelius (in the Piazza del Campidoglio), the Church of St. Peter in Chains, the Church of St. Mary Navicella, and St. Peter's Basilica; parts were also taken for reuse in Constantinople, though they were taken en route by Arab raiders (*The Forum of Trajan in Rome*, 5–17).
133 William L. MacDonald observes that the retaining wall along the Velian Hill contains architectural echoes of the surrounding classical structures, especially the great basilica across the street. See "Excavation, Restoration, and Italian Architecture of the 1930s," in Helen Searing (ed.), *In Search of Modern Architecture: A Tribute to Henry-Russell Hitchcock* (New York: The Architectural History Foundation; Cambridge and London: The MIT Press, 1982), 303.

134 Although the first four maps remain to this day, the fifth was removed in November 1945. See Heather Hyde Minor, "Mapping Mussolini: Ritual and Cartography in Public Art during the Second Roman Empire," *Imago Mundi* 51 (1999): 147–62.
135 Painter, *Mussolini's Rome*, 24–25.
136 For instance, Packer cautions that even as the excavations revealed unseen sections of these *fora*, poor cataloguing, rough handling of physical remains, reuse of fragments in new walls, and even disposal of remains has also insured that there is much that will never be learned about these important structures ("Report from Rome," 307). Because of the traffic and pollution of the via dei Fori Imperiali, as well as the awareness of important sites hidden under its pavement, there have been plans to do away with the road, but none has ever been followed through.
137 G. Marchetti Longhi, "La via dell'Impero, nel suo sviluppo storico-topografico e nel suo significato ideale," *Capitolium* 10:2 (February 1934): 53; my translation.
138 For numerous additional examples, see Italo Insolera, *Roma fascista, nelle fotografie dell'Istituto Luce* (Rome: Riuniti, 2001).
139 Lazzaro, "Forging a Visible Fascist Nation," 20. On the use of this language, see also Cederna, *Mussolini urbanista*, x.
140 Pound, "Ave Roma" (*P&P*, 6:9); my translation. Similar rhetoric appears in Roberto Paribeni, "Lo scopritore dei fori imperiali," in *In memoria di Corrado Ricci: Un saggio ineditio nota delle pubblicazioni scritti di amici e collaborate* (Rome: Istituto d'Archeologia e Storia dell' Arte, 1935), 121. Similarly, Corrado Ricci's own publication *Via dell'Impero*, co-authored with Antonio Maria Colini and Valerio Mariani (Rome: Libreria dello Stato, 1933), contains an "avvertenza" noting that the project began in 1924 "per volontà di S. E. Benito Mussolini, Capo del Governo" (3). F. P. Mulè emphasizes the verb *spazzare*, meaning "to sweep out or away," related to Pound's emphasized *spazzatura*: "Un ordine di Benito Mussolini, e tutto ciò che era indegno è stato spazzato via". See "MCMXXII – Ottobre – MCMXXXII: Le grandi arterie monumentali di Roma, Il Duce sulla via dell'Impero," *Capitolium* 8:11 (November 1932): 557.
141 Fogu, *The Historic Imaginary*, 13. For a more detailed treatment of actualism and its relationship to Fascism, see Fogu, *The Historic Imaginary*, 36 51; Roger Griffin, *Modernism and Fascism: The Sense of a Beginning under Mussolini and Hitler* (Basingstoke and New York: Palgrave Macmillan, 2007), 191–95.
142 Griffin, *Modernism and Fascism*, 193.
143 As Fogu notes, this motto derived from a more complex statement made by Mussolini in 1929: "No wonder, gentlemen, if side by side the shirkers of war we find the shirkers of history, who, having failed—for many reasons and maybe because of their creative impotence—to produce the event, that is, to make history before writing it, later on consume their revenge

diminishing it without objectivity or shame" (qtd. and trans. in Fogu, *The Historic Imaginary*, 21).
144 Pound makes the same point in nearly the same language in "A Social Creditor Serves Notice," *Fascist Quarterly* (London) 2:4 (October 1936), 492–99; *P&P*, 7:95.
145 MacDonald, "Excavation," 298–319.
146 MacDonald, "Excavation," 306. As MacDonald notes, Calza was responsible for the major excavations and publications of their findings in 1915–46.
147 MacDonald, "Excavation," 306. MacDonald has demonstrated strong resemblances between such buildings as the Casa di Diana at Ostia and the new apartment buildings built in the Piazza Roma in the new Agro Pontino town of Littorio (now Latina), and the rows of unadorned arches on the flanks of the Stazione Termini in Rome. Similarly, modern structures designed for the Università di Roma, for Fascist ministries, for the E'42 complex (now called EUR), showed further evidence of this new style, rooted very much in the ancient past but modern in its use of Roman building types not seen in earlier eras of classical imitation. A 1700-year-old column from Ostia was sent to Chicago for the "Century of Progress" exhibition, as an emblem of the triumph of modernity in Italy. See Griffin, *Modernism and Fascism*, 19.
148 Aicher has observed that the construction of the Forum began in 1927 with the building of the Academy for Physical Education, "which trained instructors for the Fascist youth organization Opera Nazionale Balilla" ("Mussolini's Forum," 124).
149 The obelisk is at one end of the forum, adjoining the Tiber and beside the bridge built to allow access to the forum. Inscribed in vertical block capitals on the shaft of the obelisk is "MUSSOLINI" and at its base "OPERA BALILLA / ANNO X."
150 A. W. Van Buren, "Art Activities in Italy," *Parnassus* 1:8 (December 1929): 12. Van Buren added more detail about this monument in 1933, after it was placed at the entrance to the Foro Mussolini: "The block is the largest worked mass of marble in existence, 17.10 meters high, 2.3 meters wide at its base and 2 meters at the top; it weighs 270 metric tons; in the whole monument there have been used 650 metric tons of Carrara marble. The erection of this monument represents no small technical achievement; for this purpose, hydraulic pressure was used up to four hundred atmospheres" ("Art Activities in Italy," *Parnassus* 5:2 [February 1933]: 7). Aicher demonstrates that the obelisk is not simply an element of *Romanità*, but an evocation of Augustus, who had first erected obelisks in Rome, not just as offerings to the sun god, but also as monuments of conquest over Egypt ("Mussolini's Forum," 129).
151 On this relationship, see Paolo Montorsi, "Il mito di Roma nella pittura di regime (1937–1943): I mosaici del Viale dell'Impero e le opera decorative per L'E 42," *Bollettino d'Arte* 78 (November–December 1993): 94–96.

152 Peter Aicher comments that one of the mosaics features Roman monuments exposed and isolated in the via del Mare project—including the Theater of Marcellus; the Temple of Fortuna Virilis (now known as that of Portunus); the "round temple" (now known as the Temple of Hercules Victor, but long thought to be a temple to Vesta); and the remains of the Janus, Spes, and Juno at San Nicola in Carcere ("Mussolini's Forum," 121, 134). Aicher provides a more extensive discussion of the iconography and ideological implications of the mosaics (132–38).

153 As Simonetta Falasca-Zamponi has demonstrated, Mussolini frequently used the image of himself as an artist to describe his crafting of the Italian masses into a Fascist people (*Fascist Spectacle*, 15–26).

154 Emil Ludwig, *Colloqui con Mussolini* (Milan: Mondadori, 1932), 125, trans. Falasca-Zamponi, *Fascist Spectacle*, 21.

155 For a summary of the urban planning problems that accompanied these demolitions, see Kostoff, *The Third Rome*, 18–20.

156 Dyson, *In Pursuit of Ancient Pasts*, 176–82.

157 See, for instance, A. W. Van Buren, "News Items from Rome," *American Journal of Archaeology* 44:3 (July–September 1940): 376–97. Van Buren had published similarly enthusiastic reviews in 42:3 (July–September 1938): 405–23; and 43:3 (July–September 1939): 508–21. In 1929, he had also celebrated discoveries around Rome, many dependent on the demolition of later additions—and his enthusiasm was hardly reserved exclusively for the monuments of ancient Rome. He commented, for instance, that such churches as Santa Sabina and Santa Pudenziana "are now recovering their true mediaeval form after the transformations of the Baroque age," and he highlighted "the precious architectural bits which the demolition of later structures has revealed, such as the mediaeval house that has been brought to light from amid the squalid dwellings that had clustered about the Theater of Marcellus (Van Buren, "Art Activities in Italy" [January 1929]: 6).

158 On the discoveries made in Rome as a result of pre-liberation bombings, see C. Bradford Welles, "Archaeological News," *American Journal of Archaeology* 52:4 (October–December 1948): 507.

Notes to Chapter 4

1 Ezra Pound, "Ubicumque Lingua Romana" (1938), in Erminio Turcotti (ed.), *Fascist Europe, Europa Fascista: An Anglo-Italian Symposium*, 2nd ed. (Milan: Salesian, 1939), 1:43.

2 Ezra Pound to Margherita Sarfatti, 25 February [1934], Ezra Pound Papers, Yale Collection of American Literature, Beinecke Rare Book and Manuscript Library, Yale University.

3 Philip V. Cannistraro and Brian R. Sullivan, *Il Duce's Other Woman: The Untold Story of Margherita Sarfatti, Benito Mussolini's Jewish Mistress, and How She Helped Him Come to Power* (New York: William Morrow and Company, 1993), 331. Although Cannistraro and Sullivan apply this responsibility to Sarfatti, I believe that it can be extended more widely to include such others as Bottai, Prezzolini, Ricci, and Sant'Elia.
4 This note also appears in the same place in the first American edition, published in January 1936 in New York by Liveright Publishing Corporation.
5 Ezra Pound to Galeazzo Ciano, [April? 1934], Pound Papers.
6 Qtd Margherita G. Sarfatti, *The Life of Benito Mussolini*, trans. Frederic Whyte (New York: Frederick A. Stokes, 1925), 289–90.
7 On the workings of Fascist corporations, or syndicates, see Alexander J. De Grand, "Corporativism and the Corporative State," in Philip V. Cannistraro (ed.), *Historical Dictionary of Fascist Italy* (Westport and London: Greenwood Press, 1982), 138–40. On corporativism's roots in French syndicalism, see David D. Roberts, "Syndicalism," in Philip V. Cannistraro (ed.), *Historical Dictionary of Fascist Italy* (Westport and London: Greenwood Press, 1982), 523–25.
8 Qtd Sarfatti, *The Life of Benito Mussolini*, 288.
9 When *Gerarchia* was founded, Sarfatti was its editor, but in January 1934 she was replaced by Vito Mussolini, nephew of the Duce. On Sarfatti's initiation and early administration of the journal, see Cannistraro and Sullivan, *The Duce's Other Woman*, 252–53.
10 *J/M*, 85. A. W. Van Buren of the American Academy in Rome similarly praised the regime's use of the Palazzo Venezia—"the former seat of the Venetian ambassadors to the Holy See"—"to serve as the residence of the Head of the Government" as "one of the most ambitious attempts at restoring a historic monument to something resembling its original function that our time has seen" ("Art Activities in Italy," *Parnassus* 1:1 [January 1929]: 4). Tim Redman treats this same comment in the context of Pound's visit to Mussolini in *Ezra Pound and Italian Fascism* (Cambridge and New York: Cambridge University Press, 1991), 94–97.
11 Ezra Pound, "The Truth About Italy," *Saturday Review* (London) 161:4205 (9 May 1936): 598; *P&P*, 7:56.
12 Pound, "Ubicumque Lingua Romana," 43. The title page of the volume notes in Italian and English that it is published "under the auspices of the National Institute of Fascist Culture of Pavia."
13 Ezra Pound to Ubaldo degli Uberti, 5 April XII [1934], Ezra Pound Miscellany, Yale Collection of American Literature, Beinecke Library.
14 Ezra Pound to Odon Por, 18 March 1935 (*EPEC*, 143).
15 Ezra Pound to Margherita Sarfatti, [May 1936], Pound Papers. Odon Por wrote to Pound on 13 May 1936, saying that both the Foreign Office and Ministero Stampa were afraid of him (Pound Papers).

16 By May 1936, in addition to their personal difficulties, Sarfatti and Mussolini had sparred over Italy's affiliation with Germany and over Italy's desire to conquer Ethiopia, and Sarfatti's writings had a harder time finding publication in Italy (Cannistraro and Sullivan, *Il Duce's Other Woman*, 480–92).
17 Ezra Pound to Camillo Pellizzi, 26 January [1937] (*EPEC*, 203). In the same letter, Pound catalogues a lengthy series of solicitations and rejections: "Ambrosiano asked for 12 articles/ got three, then pissed its pants. Civilta Ital/ asked me 'not to say it with gloves' that was I_ months ago/ and nothing printed Por told Riforma Letteraria to have me/ Izzo offered to EXPLAIN what I mean/ silence ensues. Bardi says he will print ANYTHING I send him/ and then the Meridiano ceases to arrive here."
18 Ezra Pound to Alexander Raven Thomson, 15 April 1934 (*EPEC*, 97).
19 Ezra Pound to Roberto Farninacci, 23 October [1939] and [November 1939], Pound Papers.
20 Pound, "Ubicumque Lingua Romana," 1:45.
21 Ezra Pound to Ubaldo degli Uberti, 1 July XII [1934], Pound Miscellany.
22 Ezra Pound to Margherita Sarfatti, 25 February [1934], Pound Papers.
23 Redman, *Ezra Pound and Italian Fascism*, 83–84.
24 Redman, *Ezra Pound and Italian Fascism*, 83–84.
25 Margherita G. Sarfatti, "Art and Fascism" (1928), trans. Olivia E. Sears and Jeffrey T. Schnapp, in Jeffrey T. Schnapp (ed.), *A Primer of Italian Fascism* (Lincoln and London: University of Nebraska Press, 2000), 247–48. Sarfatti's discussion of Mussolini's style is treated at greater length in chapters 1 and 3.
26 Pound also supported the regime's attempts to eliminate the use of *lei* as a polite form of address in favor of the more Francophone *voi*, seen by some as less effete. See "Il giudizio di uno straniero," *AntiEuropa* 10 (November–December 1939): 718; *P&P*, 7:469.
27 Sarfatti, "Art and Fascism," 248.
28 Ezra Pound to Margherita Sarfatti, 9 October [1934], Pound Papers.
29 *J/M*, vii. See also Pound's letters to Galeazzo Ciano (7 Oct 1934), to Carlo Camagna (22 Feb 1935), and to Ubaldo degli Uberti (9 Oct 1934) (all Pound Papers). He also mentions the speech in "Ubicumque Lingua Romana."
30 *J/M*, ix. For more on the economic significance of the speech—and its significance to Pound's economic thinking—see Redman, *Ezra Pound and Italian Fascism*, 173–75.
31 Ezra Pound to Benito Mussolini, 17 November [1933], Pound Papers.
32 Ezra Pound to Ubaldo degli Uberti, 12 May XIV [1936], Pound Miscellany.
33 Ezra Pound to Camillo Pellizzi, 9 May [1936], Pound Papers.
34 Ezra Pound to Ubaldo degli Uberti, 12 May XIV [1936], Pound Miscellany.
35 Ezra Pound to Ubaldo degli Uberti, 4 August XVIII [1940], Pound Miscellany.

36 Ezra Pound to Odon Por, 14 November 1936, Pound Miscellany. In January 1937, Pound asked Camillo Pellizzi's help in getting Giuseppe Bottai's attention, hoping to set up a meeting with Bottai in Rome or Genoa (Pound to Pellizzi, 26 January [1937], Pound Papers).

37 Ezra Pound to Carlo Camagna, 30 December [1935], Pound Papers.

38 Ezra Pound to Vito Mussolini, 11 March [1937], Pound Papers. Pound's Italian, which I have paraphrased, reads, "NOI dobbiamo andare avanti (senza sabottagio) per gli edizioni microfotografici del TESORO enorme della musica Italiana sepolta nelle bibliotece (per es/ 309 concerti di Vivaldi, a Torino)." In a letter to Benito Mussolini, dated 15 May 1937, Pound argues for the importance of "Lo sviluppo della microfotografia nella studia della musica antica. Importantissimo per l'Italia, e per i grandissimi tesori di mss/ inediti in questo paese." Pound similarly pitched this technology to Odon Por in early 1938, even sending him a copy of Rudge's *Broletto* article about microphotography and music (Pound to Por, 25 February XVI [1938], Pound Miscellany; on Rudge's article, see Chapter 4, pp. 000–00).

39 Ezra Pound to Giuseppe Bottai, [1939], Pound Papers.

40 Pound saw significant differences between modern published editions on the one hand—they were easy to use in performance—and unpublished manuscripts and early printed editions—which were locked up in libraries and impossible to use for performance. "What is shut up in a single printed copy in a bibbyteker is just as hard to git at as if it wuz in mss," Pound wrote to Rudge in March 1936 (Ezra Pound to Olga Rudge, [March 1936], Olga Rudge Papers, Beinecke Rare Book and Manuscript Library, Yale University). In 1928, Pound published a similarly Futurist concern about museums:

> A museum is a sarcophagus. A museum is alive only at one phase of civilization, i.e., during the first revolt against some utter wreck, the first stirring of sentient men amid a barbarism or among debris. Kept on after that phase the museum is a confession of failure, a confession of incapacity to make any new unit comparable to that from which the fragments have been collected. The British Museum, as distinct from its library, is the grave of English mentality; the South Kensington Museum with its old furniture is the last funeral dirge of British life. We may still need a few museums in America, but it is atrophic to regard them with more than tolerance; they are there as a property room, or as a dictionary. Only the half-dead can mistake them for the play, or the book, or the aim of a civilization. ("Where Is American Culture?" *Nation* 126:3276 (18 April 1928): [443]–44; *P&P*, 5:28–29).

I address the importance of microphotography and unpublished music for Pound in Chapter 5.

41 Ezra Pound to Odon Por, 23 July XVIII [1940], Pound Miscellany. In May 1931, Pound commented further about these restorations. See "In difesa del

paesaggio: non deturpare," *Giornale di Genova* (Genoa), 25 May 1931[?]; *P&P*, 5:293–94.
42 Ezra Pound to Carlo Camagna, 22 February [1935], Pound Papers.
43 Camillo Pellizzi to Ezra Pound, 24 January 1937 XV, Pound Papers.
44 Odon Por to Ezra Pound, 2 June 1940, Pound Papers.
45 Ezra Pound to Odon Por, 4 June XVIII [1940], Pound Miscellany.
46 Camillo Pellizzi to Ezra Pound, 5 May 1940, Pound Papers.
47 Ezra Pound to Camillo Pellizzi, 9 May [1940], Pound Papers.
48 See especially "In difesa del paesaggio: non deturpare"; "Appunti. XVIII. Sperimentale," *L'Indice* (Genoa) 2:12 (5 June [probably actually July] 1931): 2 (*P&P*, 5:297–98); "Terra Italica," *New Review* 1:4 (Winter 1931–32): [386]–89 (*P&P*, 5:329–32); "[Letter to P. M. Bardi, quoted in his column 'Busta da Roma']," *L'Ambrosiano* (Milan), 2 December 1931: 3 (*P&P*, 5:333); "[Interview]," *La Stampa* (Turin), between Jan. and Apr. 1932 (*P&P*, 5:334); "Appunti," *Il Mare* 25:1235 (12 November 1932): 3 (*P&P*, 5:379–81).

Notes to Chapter 5

1 Ezra Pound, "The Vivaldi Revival," *Il Mare* (25 November 1939), trans. in *EPM*, 450.
2 Stephen J. Adams, "Pound, Olga Rudge, and the 'Risveglio Vivaldiano,'" *Paideuma* 4:1 (Spring 1975): 111–18; Anne Conover, *Olga Rudge and Ezra Pound: "What Thou Lovest Well ..."* (New Haven and London: Yale University Press, 2001); Giulio de Angelis, "Letteratura e Musica: Pound e il Rinascimento Vivaldiano," *Chigiana* 41, n.s. 21 (1989): 41–52; Archie Henderson, "'Townsman' and Music: Ezra Pound's Letters to Ronald Duncan," *The Library Chronicle of the University of Texas* 25–26 (1984): 119–35; R. Murray Schafer, *Ezra Pound and Music: The Complete Criticism* (New York: New Directions, 1977).
3 For further detail about the transcriptions and their identification during the late nineteenth century, see Michael Talbot, *Vivaldi* (New York: Schirmer, 1992), 3–4.
4 R[eginald] L[ane] P[oole], "Antonio Vivaldi," *Grove's Dictionary of Music and Musicians*, ed. H. C. Colles, 3rd ed. (New York: Macmillan, 1928), V:556. This short entry is less than a page long, lists little information about Vivaldi's lifespan—"b. Venice, latter half of 17th cent."—and acknowledges only about seventy concerti, twenty-eight operas, and a few cantatas and motets. Even with the publication of Arnold Schering's history of the concerto, *Geschichte des Instrumentalkonzerts* (1905)—which took into consideration the vast manuscript holdings in Dresden, put Vivaldi's work in historical perspective, and revealed Vivaldi to be a more interesting composer than had before been known—and of Wilhelm Altmann's thematic catalogue of

318 Notes to pages 161–62

Vivaldi's works (1922), only a small fraction of Vivaldi's work was known (Talbot, *Vivaldi*, 4–5). Earlier catalogues of Vivaldi's works—including Aloys Fuchs's manuscript *Thematisches Verzeichnis über die Compositionen von Antonio Vivaldi* (1839) and Alberto Bachmann's "Table thématique des Oeuvres d'Antonio Vivaldi" in his *Les grands violonistes du passé* (1913)—demonstrate early interest in Vivaldi but must be seen as exceptions to a wider pattern of disinterest.

5   Alceo Toni, "Una nuova antica gloria musicale italiana: Antonio Vivaldi," *Il Primato artistico italiano* (October 1919): 31–34, discussed in Michael Talbot, *Antonio Vivaldi: A Guide to Research* (New York and London: Garland, 1988), xviii and 44.

6   Raoul Meloncelli, "Antonio Vivaldi e il rinnovamento musicale a Roma tra le due guerre," *Chigiana: Rassegna Annuale di Studi Musicologici* 41, n.s. 21 (1989): 65–68. Meloncelli notes that Vivaldi's compositions appeared in 120 of the 1,290 concerts presented by Accademia di Santa Cecilia between 1914 and 1945—not bad, considering how little of Vivaldi's work was known at this time. Bernardino Molinari, artistic director of the Orchestra dell'Augusteo from 1912 to 1943, prepared numerous transcriptions of Vivaldi's work (many later published by Ricordi), including *The Four Seasons* (in 1927), two compositions from the *Estro armonico* (number 2 in 1921 and number 8 in 1930), and the *Concerto in A major* (RV 552, in 1933) (Cesare Fertonani, "Edizioni e revisioni Vivaldiane in Italia nella prima metà del novecento [1919–1943]," *Chigiana: Rassegna annuale di studi musicologici* 41, n.s. 21 [1989]: 240–41). These were performed by his orchestra as well as by others, and the success of Molinari's renditions is reflected in the number of recordings produced: his recording with the Orchestra dell'Accademia di Santa Cecilia of *The Four Seasons* (1942) is the earliest of this now widely recorded piece (Fertonani, "Edizioni e revisioni," 250).

7   Fertonani, "Edizioni e revisioni," 240–50. Fertonani's treatment does not single out Molinari for criticism: instead, he shows that most Italian editors of Vivaldi during this period made similar moves to "modernize" the composer.

8   Talbot, *Vivaldi*, 5–7. On Gentili's role as reader and publisher of this material, see Fertonani, "Edizioni e revisioni," 250–56.

9   "Feste," "Ad Libitum," *The Musical Times* 79:1149 (November 1938): 819. "Feste's" claim for the number of extant works by Vivaldi did not go uncorrected: W. Gillies Whittaker wrote to *The Musical Times* (79:1150 [December 1938]: 930) offering a clarification of Pound's assertion and noting the limitations of the old entry in the *Grove's*.

10 Stephen J. Adams, "Pound, Olga Rudge, and the 'Risveglio Vivaldiano,'" *Paideuma* 4:1 (Spring 1975): 117.

11 *Antonio Vivaldi: Note e documenti sulla vita e sulle opera* (Siena: Accademia Musicale Chigiana, 1939), 47–59.

12 Philip V. Cannistraro and Brian R. Sullivan, *Il Duce's Other Woman: The Untold Story of Margherita Sarfatti, Benito Mussolini's Jewish Mistress, and How She Helped Him Come to Power* (New York: William Morrow and Company, 1993), 193.
13 Margherita G. Sarfatti, "Lettera da Berlino: Un'affermazione d'arte italiana," *Il Popolo d'Italia* (30 April 1921), trans. in Catherine E. Paul and Barbara M. Zaczek, "Margherita Sarfatti and Italian Cultural Nationalism," *Modernism/modernity* 13.1 (2006): 903. As earlier chapters of this volume show, Sarfatti was hardly unique in making such an assertion.
14 Gianfranco Vinay, "Prefazione: *21 + 26* ma anche *13+19+8+7*," in Alfredo Casella, *21 + 26* (Rome and Milan: Augustea, 1931, ed. Alessandra Carlotta Pellegrini; Florence: Leo S. Olschki, 2001), v. English translation cannot do justice to the connotations in Casella's phrase (quoted by Vinay), "melodrammismo conservatore, passatista e strapaesano": his use of the word "passatista" echoes similar usage of the term by the Futurists, who condemned all such aspects of Italian culture. Similarly, his use of the word "strapaesano," which literally means something "super-countryside-ish" may echo the name *Strapaese*, denoting the artistic movement championing the power of the traditional associations of the Italian countryside, as opposed to more urban-oriented movements as Futurism.
15 Ezra Pound, "Music in Ca' Rezzonico," *The Delphian Quarterly* (January 1937): 2–4, 11; *P&P*, 7:120–23.
16 Alfredo Casella, *Music in my Time: The Memoirs*, ed. and trans. Spencer Norton (Norman: University of Oklahoma Press, 1955), 82.
17 Casella, *Music in my Time*, 115.
18 Casella, *Music in my Time*, 115–17.
19 Casella, *Music in my Time*, 131.
20 Casella, *Music in my Time*, 133–34. Casella encountered resistance from the editor, Raffaello de Rensis, who would later write the booklet *Mussolini musicista* (*Mussolini the Musician*, 1927) as part of a campaign to deify the dictator. On *Mussolini musicista*, see Harvey Sachs, *Music in Fascist Italy* (New York and London: W. W. Norton, 1987), 11–16.
21 Casella, *Music in my Time*, 139–45.
22 Casella, *Music in my Time*, 145–48. On the significance of *La Voce* and *Lacerba* to Italian and Fascist cultural Nationalism, see Chapter 3.
23 Casella, *Music in my Time*, 159–63.
24 Casella, *Music in my Time*, 232.
25 Ezra Pound, typescript (carbon) "VIOLINIST STIRS ENTHUSIAMS [sic] ON ITALIAN RIVIERA," accompanying a letter to Ethel de Courcy Duncan, 20 November 1933, Ezra Pound Miscellany, Yale Collection of American Literature, Beinecke Rare Book and Manuscript Library.
26 On the critique of Casella in "A Manifesto of Italian Musicians for the Tradition of Nineteenth-Century Romantic Art," published simultaneously in December 1932 in three of the most important Italian newspapers, *Il*

popolo d'Italia (Rome), *Il Corriere della Sera* (Milan), and *La Stampa* (Turin), see Sachs, *Music in Fascist Italy*, 23–25.
27 Casella, *Music in my Time*, 172–73.
28 Jeffrey Schnapp and Barbara Spackman (eds.), "Selections from the Great Debate on Fascism and Culture: *Critica Fascista* 1926–1927," *Stanford Italian Review* 8 (1990): 234.
29 On *Pulcinella*'s negotiation of source material and new tendencies, see Joseph N. Straus, *Remaking the Past: Musical Modernism and the Influence of the Tonal Tradition* (Cambridge and London: Harvard University Press, 1990), 58–64.
30 Casella, *Music in my Time*, 172–73.
31 Fiamma Nicolodi, *Musica e musicisti nel ventennio fascista* (Fiesole: Discanto, 1984), 243.
32 Casella, *21+26*, 41.
33 Casella was hardly alone in so doing. See Chapter 3, and Spiro Kostof, "The Emperor and the Duce: The Planning of the Piazzale Augusto Imperatore in Rome," in Henry Millon and Linda Nochlin (eds), *Art and Architecture in the Service of Politics* (Cambridge: MIT Press, 1978); Claudia Lazzaro and Roger J. Crum (eds.), *Donatello among the Blackshirts: History and Modernity in the Visual Culture of Fascist Italy* (Ithaca and London: Cornell University Press, 2005); Marla Susan Stone, "A Flexible Rome: Fascism and the Cult of *Romanità*," in *Roman Presences: Receptions of Rome in European Culture, 1789–1945* (Cambridge: Cambridge University Press, 1999), 205–20.
34 Casella, *Music in my Time*, 202–03. Included in the first concert of the Sienese Vivaldi Week was Vivaldi's Concerto in G minor for violin, strings, and continuo (RV334), one of the works that Casella found at the Library of Congress. Following standard practice in discussions of Vivaldi's music, I include parenthetically after descriptions of individual pieces the catalogue numbers from Peter Ryom's catalogue.
35 The previous two comments are quoted in Sachs, *Music in Fascist Italy*, 139. Casella's "mystery" for the stage, *Il deserto tentato*, composed 1936–37 and first performed in Florence in May 1937, was conceived as a musical tribute to Italy's "great African adventure" (Casella, *Music in my Time*, 211).
36 Fertonani, "Edizioni e revisioni," 256–61.
37 The extent to which Casella's edition remains a respected staple of many collections of choral music, despite recognition of its many "errors," may be seen from the conversation in the *Choral Journal* initiated by Barrow and continuing in the letters to the editor, most notably that by Eric Nisula (21:7 [March 1981]: 41).
38 As R. Murray Schafer notes, the Amici del Tigullio performed publicly not *all* but only twelve (of thirty-four) of Mozart's violin sonatas, although Pound claims they listened to the rest privately (*EPM*, 331–33). Schafer gives an excellent sense of the chronology and aims of the Rapallo concerts

as well as presenting translations of Pound's essays about them (*EPM*, 321–463).
39 Ezra Pound, "Second Concert: Tuesday 14th November, 9 p.m. in the Town Hall," *Il Mare* (11 November 1933), trans. *EPM*, 347. Also performed were a sonata in A major for piano and two violins by Arcangelo Corelli; a number of other works by Jean Bésard, including one that Pound called "Chorea Angliacana Doolandi"; two arias by Francesco Severi; a dance suite compiled by Münch from various composers, including Giovanni Antonio Terzi, of about 1600; and a "Fantasia contrappuntistica" by an unknown seventeenth-century composer. For the programs of the Chilesotti concerts and some context for Münch's acquisition of these manuscripts, see Lina Urban, "Ezra Pound direttore artistico e critico musicale a Rapallo," *Rassegna Veneta di Studi Musicali* 4 (1988): 264–72.
40 Ezra Pound, "Warm Reception in Genoa for the Tigullian Musicians," *Il Mare* (25 November 1933), trans. *EPM*, 352.
41 Schnapp and Spackman, "Selections from the Great Debate on Fascism and Culture," 235.
42 B[asil] B[unting], "Musical Notes from Abroad: The Rapallo Manuscripts," *The Musical Times* 75:1098 (August 1934): 750.
43 Ezra Pound, "The Pianist Münch," *Il Mare* (23 September 1933), trans. *EPM*, 340. Fiamma Nicolodi notes a similar claim by Alfredo Casella: he justified the insertion of an adagio movement from a separate concerto into his transcription of the Concerto in C minor (RV198a) as "obedience to the principle that archaeology is one thing while living and performed music is another thing entirely" ("Vivaldi nell'attività di Alfredo Casella organizzatore e interprete," in Francesco DeGrada (ed.), *Vivaldi veneziano europeo* [Florence: Leo S. Olschiki, 1980], 307; my translation).
44 Pound's words were related in "Tigullian Studies," *Il Mare* (11 April 1936); *EPM*, 388–89.
45 Ezra Pound, "Tigullian Studies," *Il Mare* (14 March 1936), trans. *EPM*, 387.
46 Conover describes Rudge's work at Cambridge and Rudge's discovery of "Vivaldi's Concerto no. 7 in A Major for Violin (with the name Fitzwilliam and date 1706 inscribed on the title page), and a large-scale masterpiece, *Juditha Triumphans*, about the biblical heroine Judith who beheads the Assyrian general Holofornes" (*Olga Rudge and Ezra Pound*, 125).
47 Olga Rudge to Ezra Pound, [January 1936], Olga Rudge Papers, Yale Collection of American Literature, Beinecke Rare Book and Manuscript Library.
48 Conover notes that Rudge had spent only one day in this collection in 1935, so for this return trip she was more prepared to undertake extensive work, looking for music to perform, and creating her thematic catalogue of Vivaldi's work (*Olga Rudge and Ezra Pound*, 127).

49 Olga Rudge to Ezra Pound, [30? October 1936], Rudge Papers. In this initial group, Rudge identified sixty for violin; eighteen for cello; six for oboe; twenty-nine for bassoon; six for viola; five for two violins; two for two oboes; one for four violins; one for violin and cello; one for violin, oboe, and organ; one for violins and oboe; and one for oboe and bassoon.
50 Olga Rudge to Ezra Pound, [26 November 1936], Rudge Papers.
51 Ezra Pound to Olga Rudge, 26 [October 1936], Rudge Papers.
52 Ezra Pound to Olga Rudge, [28 October 1938], Rudge Papers.
53 Ezra Pound to Olga Rudge, 9 February [1936], Rudge Papers.
54 For instance, the Concerto in D major for violin, orchestra, and continuo known as "Grosso Mogul" (RV 208), is listed with the other concerti from Volume V, and numbered 21 within that volume and 137 overall. The publication includes articles about Vivaldi's life and work by Casella, Count Guido Chigi-Saracini, S. A. Luciani, and Virgilio Mortari, as well as catalogues of Vivaldi's known works (Olga Rudge's *Catalogo tematico delle opere strumentale di A. Vivaldi esistenti nella Biblioteca Nazionale di Torino*, U. Rolandi's *Opere ed oratorii di Antonio Vivaldi*, and Rudge's unsigned *Opere vocali attribuite ad A. V. nel Bibl. Naz. di Torino*). Rudge's thematic catalogue was later reprinted in M. Rinaldi's *Antonio Vivaldi* (Milan: Istituto d'Alta Cultura, 1943). Rudge published a similar thematic catalogue of unpublished vocal works from the Turin collection in the Accademia Musicale Chigiana's *La Scuola Veneziana (secoli XVI–XVIII): Note e documenti, raccolti in occasione della settimana celebrativa* (Siena: Libreria Editrice Ticci, 1941), 74–80. See also Michael Talbot, *Antonio Vivaldi: A Guide to Research* (New York and London: Garland, 1988), 42.
55 Rudge's letters document her difficulties with Gentili—his overprotectiveness of the manuscripts, reluctance to let her see them, preventing her from copying the music, and repeatedly cautioning her against publishing a catalogue. By this time the Milanese publishing house Ricordi had an exclusive contract for the publication of the works in this collection, and although Rudge and Pound believed that small performances of the music would not interfere with Ricordi's aims, Gentili was less convinced. Gentili wanted a copy of Rudge's catalogue made for the library, and although she was willing for them to have one, she feared giving hers over to their copyist, worrying that she might not get it back or that it would be greatly delayed. Rudge enumerates her tribulations in Turin in letters to Pound, 30 October–29 November 1936, Rudge Papers. Her letter of 9 November 1936 narrates events to date, at the advice of Pound, who worried that she might need documentation. By September 1938, when Alfredo Casella was going to Turin to find music for the performances of the Settimana Celebrativa, Rudge still had not sent a copy of her catalogue to Turin. She hesitated to give Casella her only copy, and considered instead sending a copy to Turin and urging him to find it there (Olga Rudge to Ezra Pound, [27 September 1938], Rudge Papers). In September 1939, Rudge reported to Pound that

Casella had accepted her "Ceni biografici" of Vivaldi for the *Note e documenti* publication, and that "He wanted some photos of Vivaldi mss for Illustrazione Italiane but I didn't give mine—correct?" (Olga Rudge to Ezra Pound, [11 September 1939], Rudge Papers).

56 Peter Ryom, *Répertoire des œuvres d'Antonio Vivaldi: les compositions instrumentales* (Copenhagen: Engstrøm & Sødring, 1986), liii.
57 Ezra Pound, "Tigullian Musical Life," *Il Mare* (4 December 1937), trans. in *EPM*, 426–27. Pound must not have known about the work in Rome, underway since the mid-1910s, to revive Vivaldi's music.
58 Ezra Pound to Olga Rudge, 17 [February 1936], Rudge Papers.
59 Ezra Pound to Olga Rudge, 5 May [1936], Rudge Papers.
60 See Ezra Pound to Olga Rudge, [14 March 1936] (folder 436); Ezra Pound to Olga Rudge, [March 1936] (folder 436); Ezra Pound to Olga Rudge, [March 1936?] (folder 455); Ezra Pound to Olga Rudge, undated [November or December 1936] (folder 455); Ezra Pound, typescript "The Instrumental Music of Vivaldi in Turin: An Impression" (probably November or December 1936) (folder 455), all from Rudge Papers.
61 Olga Rudge, "Vivaldi: La sua posizione nella storia della musica," *Il Mare* (9 May 1936); my translation.
62 Olga Rudge to Ezra Pound, 26 May [1939] and 2 June [1939], Rudge Papers.
63 Reginald Lane Poole, "Antonio Vivaldi," in H. C. Colles (ed.), *Grove's Dictionary of Music and Musicians*, 3rd ed. (New York: Macmillan, 1928), V:556.
64 O[lga] R[udg]e, "Antonio Vivaldi," in H. C. Colles (ed.), *Grove's Dictionary of Music and Musicians*, 4th ed., supplementary volume (New York: Macmillan, 1940), 653–57.
65 Olga Rudge, "Antonio Vivaldi," in Eric Blom (ed.), *Grove's Dictionary of Music and Musicians*, 5th ed. (New York: St. Martin's Press, 1954), IX:26–32.
66 Rudge's article was replaced by one by the musicologist Michael Talbot when the first edition of the *New Grove Dictionary of Music and Musicians* was published in 1980, edited by Stanley Sadie.
67 Ezra Pound, "Tigullian Studies," *Il Mare* (14 March 1936), trans. in *EPM*, 384.
68 In a move atypical of the usual tropes of newspaper writing, he provides a full listing of Vivaldi's published instrumental works from Altmann's catalogue (1922) and then reference to the Foà and Giordano collections at Turin.
69 Pound, "Tigullian Studies," trans. In *EPM*, 386–87. On two occasions, the Sonata in A major (Op. 2, No. 2, RV 31) was performed, and the Concerto in D major (Op. 3, No. 9, RV 230) similarly made two appearances. In one case, it was followed by J. S. Bach's Concerto in D major for harpsichord, adapted from that same concerto (BWV 972). Including the Bach piece

indicated the extent to which Vivaldi influenced Bach but also emphasized that for centuries Vivaldi was best known as source material for Bach. A similar pairing appeared in the Vivaldi Week in Siena in 1939, perhaps indicating a formal influence of the Tigullian Studies venture on that enterprise. Also performed were the Concerto in E major (Op. 3, No. 12, RV 265) and Concerto in A minor (Op. 3, No. 6, RV 356). All these pieces were taken from the starred works on Pound's first published list, perhaps indicating that the group followed through on its intentions.

70 See Pound's correspondence with Gerhart Münch, especially that from 1933–37 (Ezra Pound Papers, Yale Collection of American Literature, Beinecke Rare Book and Manuscript Library).

71 Olga Rudge, "Venice and Vivaldi," *Delphian Quarterly* 21 (January 1938): 7.

72 The concert for 5 February 1938 included a "free interpretation" by Gerhart Münch of a concerto in D, evidence of the use of Münch's contributions in the performances. Although a score for that transcription is not extant, we do have the score for Münch's transcription of the Concerto in G minor, originally for solo violin, orchestra, and continuo, but arranged for solo violin and keyboard (RV 324).

73 Münch mentions having the materials in Dresden photostated in a postcard to Pound ([25 October 1937], Pound Papers). Pound makes frequent reference to the copying of these scores in his correspondence with Olga Rudge during 1937 and 1938 and her papers contain numerous Vivaldi scores in Pound's hand (Rudge Papers).

74 Ezra Pound to Gerhart Münch, 1 August 1938, Pound Papers.

75 Pound wrote to Münch in August 1938 that he was disappointed to find how many had been transcribed already, either by Molinari or Casella (Pound Papers). Pound and Rudge had been frustrated by how slowly Ricordi was publishing the works of Vivaldi, and indeed, the Ricordi edition of the Concerto in A, edited by Gian Francesco Malipiero, was not published until 1960—twenty-two years after the Rapallo performance.

76 Ezra Pound to Olga Rudge, [March 1936?], Rudge Papers.

77 See, for instance, his preference for applicable over factual knowledge (28), his favoring of understanding over memorizing (51), emphasis on active learning (52), and concerns about putting the vast cultural heritage to use (54).

78 I discuss Pound's use of the material in the British Museum Library in *Poetry in the Museums of Modernism: Yeats, Pound, Moore, Stein* (Ann Arbor: University of Michigan Press, 2002), 65–94.

79 *GK*, 151. Pound makes a similar plea on page 148.

80 Olga Rudge, "La rivista *Broletto* di Como e la Microfotografia," *Il Mare* (26 February 1938): 1.

81 D[esmond] C[hute], "La 'Settimana Musicale' di Rapallo: i concerti del 2–3–4–5 febbraio," *Il Mare* (12 February 1938).

82 His catalogue includes twenty-one pieces, although one of his listings (#2) is actually the third movement of another item (#10). There are also two other pieces that, for one reason or another, never made it into his catalogue. These pieces are a sinfonia in G major for string orchestra (RV149) and a concerto in D minor for solo violin, orchestra, and continuo (RV241). There may well be others among the small unidentifiable fragments extant in Pound's and Rudge's papers.

83 "Stasera, Sabato, ore 21: ultimo concerto," *Il Mare* (5 February 1938); my translations. Pound was dismayed to find that the Concerto in A had already been published by Molinari: "NOT that his arrangement wd/ have been of any use to me here. BUT I didn't know he had done it" (Pound to Münch, 1 August 1938, Pound Papers). In the same letter he notes that another piece he had transcribed, the Concerto in C minor for solo violin, orchestra, and continuo (clavecin) (RV 198), had been partially mined by Casella.

84 "Stasera, Sabato, ore 21."

85 Ezra Pound to Olga Rudge, [7 July 1938], Rudge Papers.

86 Ezra Pound to Olga Rudge, [12? June 1938], Rudge Papers. Here he seems to refer to the concerto in C minor for solo violin, orchestra, and continuo, "Il sospetto" (RV 199), but he could as easily have had a piece written in E-flat major.

87 Ezra Pound to Olga Rudge, [4? June 1938], Rudge Papers. In August 1938, Pound makes a similar complaint about a score written with two sharps: "Did three pages, i;e; one quarter of a Viv/ wiff two sharps/ not much fun; as nothing much left to do after one has copied the notes/ in that one" (Pound to Rudge, 19 August [1938], Rudge Papers).

88 Fertonani, "Edizioni e revisioni," 239.

89 Archie Henderson has demonstrated that Pound defended the practice of reduction as a means of getting music performed, and often as a way of sifting through the extra silt that might accumulate in over-orchestrated arrangements ("'Townsman' and Music: Ezra Pound's Letters to Ronald Duncan," *The Library Chronicle of the University of Texas* 229:5–26 (1984): 124ff.).

90 Ezra Pound to Olga Rudge, 19 August [1938], Rudge Papers. Pound may be referring here to the Concerto in D major for solo violin, orchestra, and continuo (RV 226) or to the Concerto in B minor for solo violin, orchestra, and continuo (RV 384).

91 Ezra Pound to Olga Rudge, 24 September 1938, Rudge Papers.

92 Ryom, *Répertoire des œuvres d'Antonio Vivaldi*, 228–29. According to Ryom's catalogue, the title to which Pound refers reads "Con.to facto p M.r Pisende[l] / Del Vivaldi."

93 Ezra Pound to Olga Rudge, [15 July 1938], Rudge Papers.

94 Ezra Pound to Olga Rudge, 8 [September 1938], Rudge Papers.

95 Ezra Pound to Olga Rudge, [10 September 1938], Rudge Papers.

96 Both Noel Stock and Murray Schafer had concluded that Pound was primarily an organizer of events and a supporter of Rudge. See Stock, *The Life of Ezra Pound* (New York: Pantheon, 1970), 337–38; *EPM*, 329.
97 Ezra Pound to Olga Rudge, [7 August 1938], Rudge Papers. At the time, Pound was working on the Concerto in D major for solo violin, orchestra, and continuo (RV 226). The next day, he added, "Wall he has finished draft of Viv 2 sharps/ or Re/ maj (I suppose it iz maj, as it aint loaded wiff accidentals ALL over/ lin a MIN/ seems to be" (Pound to Rudge, [8 August 1938], Rudge Papers).
98 Ezra Pound to Gerhart Münch, 19 November [1937], Pound Papers. Pound was especially interested in having Münch find more unpublished material in Dresden beyond what they already had in microphotographic form, and offered to send a copy of Rudge's catalogue for Münch's use—or anything else he might need. Münch's responses were less enthusiastic: hardly a letter from 1938 to 1939 does not include an apology for his lack of progress on Vivaldi.
99 Gerhart Münch to Ezra Pound, 8 March 1939, Pound Papers.
100 Ezra Pound to Gerhart Münch, [March or April 1939], Pound Papers.
101 See *EPM*, 449–50; Ezra Pound to Tibor Serly, April 1940 (*SL*, 344).
102 Ezra Pound to Gerhart Münch, [March or April 1939], Pound Papers.
103 Ezra Pound, "The Vivaldi Revival," *Il Mare* (25 November 1939), trans. *EPM*, 450–51.
104 Pound, "The Vivaldi Revival," trans. *EPM*, 450.
105 See Philip V. Cannistraro's entry on "Autarchy" in Philip V. Cannistraro (ed.), *Historical Dictionary of Fascist Italy* (Westport and London: Greenwood Press, 1982), 43–44.
106 Pound, "The Vivaldi Revival," trans. in *EPM*, 451.
107 On the larger sequence of the Accademia's celebratory weeks, see Adams, "Pound, Olga Rudge, and the 'Risveglio Vivaldiano,'" 117.
108 One concert was dedicated exclusively to the music of Claudio Monteverdi. There were two multi-composer concerts, one showcasing orchestral and vocal music and the second instrumental and vocal chamber music. These concerts contained music by Giovan Battista Bassani, Francesco Antonio Bonporti, Antonio Caldara, Francesco Cavalli, Andrea Gabrieli, Giovanni Gabrieli, Baldassare Galuppi, Benedetto Marcello, Giovanni Platti, Agostino Steffani, and Giuseppe Torelli.
109 Anne Conover, *Olga Rudge and Ezra Pound: "What Thou Lovest Well ..."* (New Haven and London: Yale University Press, 2001), 141.
110 Ezra Pound, "Books and Music," delivered 26 October 1941; *EPS*, 9.
111 The entire program may be seen in Accademia Musicale Chigiana, *Settimana Celebrativa della Scuola Veneziana (secoli XVI–XVIII), sotto gli auspici del Ministero della Cultura Popolare e della Reale Accademia d'Italia: Programma delle Manifestazioni*, Siena 5–10 Settembre 1941—XIX (Siena: Stab. Arti Grafiche Lazzeri, 1941), in the Rudge Papers (YCAL MSS 54, box 143,

folder 3357). For a listing of the works by Vivaldi performed there, see Table 2.
112 Fertonani, "Edizioni e revisioni," 261–66.
113 Because it is not widely available outside of the Rudge Papers, I quote here at length a clipping from June 1948 titled "The Vivaldi Revival: Unpublished Scores," written by the Rome correspondent for an unidentified newspaper. It treats this very matter of the interpretation of Vivaldi's music according to the musical practice of his time or norms of modern listening. It explains the contrast between Casella's and Ephrikian's respective approaches to Vivaldi's music, deploying lengthy quotations from these two musicians:

> Casella in his notes on Vivaldi (*Quaderni dell'Accademia Chigiana*, xiii, 15) says:
>> There are many transcriptions of Vivaldi and first among them those of Bach. I myself have published two such works, in which I have frankly taken certain liberties with the Vivaldi text. But for this occasion (the 1939 Siena Festival) there was no question of presenting transcriptions but of reconstructing the original thought as far as possible. So I and my collaborators have followed principles of extreme stylistic purity, seeking (wherever the text was incomplete) patiently and diligently to reconstruct what was missing in the manuscript. It is well known that in those days orchestral scores were more than summary. Often one only finds the air and the bass. The organ and clavichord scores are always missing, for they were entrusted in those days to the interpretation and skill and imagination of the performer. Where intermediary scores were missing (second violins and violas) an attempt has been made to use all the knowledge there is of Venetian style. Thus it has been possible to reconstruct with much labour the original Vivaldi text, in all conscience reducing to a minimum eventual divergencies between this work and the author's idea.
>
> In an introductory note to the first volumes of the Vivaldi Institute written since the war, Angelo Ephrikian, then head of the Vivaldi Institute in Venice, writes:
>> On first perusal of the Vivaldi texts it looks as though there are vast lacunae in the intermediary parts. Thus in the past there were many interferences, integrations, and completions of the text which to-day seem, in the majority of cases, absolutely unjustified. The truth is that Vivaldi scores are almost always complete in every part. The lacunae are deliberate; graphic signs, quite clearly discernible, indicate the author's intention that certain instruments should remain silent or that the parts should be reduced and more instruments be made to sound in unison.
>
> This revolutionary approach to Vivaldi is shared by the Italian composer Malipiero, a Venetian and the head of the Conservatoire in Venice. At

> the end of January this year in Rome Ephrikian conducted a concert of unpublished works of Vivaldi, consisting of seven concertos, of which Malipiero had edited the Concerto in G minor for strings and clavichord and the conductor had edited all the others. It was an enchanting concert with two especially remarkable works: the Concerto in E major for violin, strings, and clavichord called "Rest," and the Concerto in B major for bassoons, violin, strings, and clavichord ended the concert. One heard Vivaldi for the first time in the way he would have wished to be performed. One felt his complete originality, instead of being reminded of Bach or some other transcriber. How much Bach owes to Vivaldi is a subject that has hardly been studied yet; the material has only now become available. The Vivaldi Institute in Venice is doing a great service to lovers of early eighteenth-century music by gradually publishing all his works.

The article continues by connecting this controversy to an upcoming third Settimana Celebrativa at the Accademia Musicale Chigiana:

> This year in Siena, on Tuesday, September 21, the third of the Chigiana's festival concerts will be devoted to Vivaldi's unpublished works, including the last concerto of Ephrikian's Rome concert, two other concertos, three arias for soprano, two arias for contralto, and a cantata for contralto, strings, and clavichord.
>
> It remains to be seen whose edition will be used. The editorial controversy is one for the "expert," but in time the public too will have to decide which Vivaldi it likes best: the revised or the "bare" score. ("The Vivaldi Revival: Unpublished Scores," author and place of publication unknown, June 1948, Rudge Papers.)

114 For the full listing of the works in this series, see *Opere strumentali di Antonio Vivaldi (1678–1741): Catalogo numerico-tematico secondo la catalogazione Fanna*, 2nd ed. (Milan: Ricordi, 1986). As this catalogue notes, there were 530 volumes in the first series (1947–72). A second edition of Vivaldi's works was initiated in 1978, when the Istituto Italiano Antonio Vivaldi became part of the Fondazione Giorgio Cini of Venice, and by 1985, when the series was completed, an additional nineteen volumes had been published. The Fondazione Cini also sponsors the Vivaldi yearbook, *Informazioni e studi vivaldiani* (1980–2000), later replaced by *Studi vivaldiani* (2001–present).

115 Talbot, *Antonio Vivaldi: A Guide to Research*, xx–xxi.

116 Antonio Vivaldi, *Due Concerti Manoscritti della Sächsische Landesbibliothek di Dresda*, ed. Olga Rudge (Siena: Accademia Musicale Chigiana, 1950).

117 A full list of the Dresden microfilm donated by Pound, along with other microfilm owned by the Accademia, appears in *Antonio Vivaldi: Note e documenti sulla vita e sulle opera* (Siena: Accademia Musicale Chigiana, 1939), 70–72.

118 On the postwar state of the Vivaldi holdings in Dresden see Walter Kolneder, "Zur Frage der Vivaldi-Kataloge," *Archiv für Musikwissenscaft* 11 (1954): 323–23, and Hans Rudolf Jung, "Die Dresdener Vivaldi-Manuskripte," *Archiv für Musikwissenschaft* 12 (1955): 314–18.

119 For analyses of the limitations of the early catalogues, see Jonathan Schiller's review of *Antonio Vivaldi; Catalogo numerico tematico delle composizioni di Antonio Vivaldi; Antonio Vivaldi et la musique instrumentale* in *Journal of the American Musicological Society* 2:2 (Summer 1949): 117–20; Lewis S. Salter, "An Index to Ricordi's Edition of Vivaldi," *Notes* (1953–1954): 366–74; Richard D. Seidler, "Vivaldi's 'Thirteen' Concertos for Trumpet(s)," *International Trumpet Guild Newsletter* 6:2 (February 1980): 15–17.

Notes to Chapter 6

1 Ezra Pound, "Ubicumque Lingua Romana" (1938), in Erminio Turcotti (ed.), *Fascist Europe, Europa Fascista: An Anglo-Italian Symposium*, 2nd ed. (Milan: Salesian, 1939), 1:45.

2 Ezra Pound, "How to Read, or Why. Part I: Introduction," *New York Herald Tribune Books* 17 (13 January 1929): [1], 6; *LE*, 16.

3 Ezra Pound to Frank Morley, [February 1937], Ezra Pound Papers, Yale Collection of American Literature, Beinecke Rare Book and Manuscript Library.

4 Frank Morley to Ezra Pound, 11 February 1937, Pound Papers.

5 These articles appear on page 1 ("IL DUCE ANNUNZIA ALL'ITALIA ED AL MONDO LA COSTITUZIONE DELL'IMPERO FASCISTA") and page 4 ("L'ITALIA HA FINALMENTE IL SUO IMPERO") of *Il Popolo d'Italia* (10 May 1936). Pound's copy is preserved in the Pound Papers. The title of Mussolini's speech became a widely used imperialist slogan, appearing, for instance in the mosaic work of the Foro Mussolini, now renamed Foro Italico (Rome).

6 On the images of Romanness that this exhibition presented for Italian citizens, see Marla Susan Stone, "A Flexible Rome: Fascism and the Cult of *Romanità*," in Catharine Edwards (ed.), *Roman Presences: Receptions of Rome in European Culture, 1789–1945* (Cambridge: Cambridge University Press, 1999), 205–20.

7 Ezra Pound, "Individual and Statal Views: Mr. Ezra Pound's Views," *Plain Dealer* (Brighton, England) 13, n.s. 1 (July 1934), supplement: [3]; *P&P*, 6:185.

8 Ezra Pound, "Trees Without Roots," *New York Herald* (Paris, 1 November 1934): 4; *P&P*, 6:207.

9 "Selections from the Great Debate on Fascism and Culture: *Critica Fascista* 1926–1927," Jeffrey Schnapp and Barbara Spackman (eds.), *Stanford Italian Review* 8 [1990]: 235).

10 On the Mostra Anti-*lei* planned by Achille Starace in 1939, and the cultural context for banning the use of *lei* for formal address, see Simonetta Falasca-Zamponi, *Fascist Spectacle: The Aesthetics of Power in Mussolini's Italy* (Berkeley, Los Angeles, and London: University of California Press, 1997), 106–09.
11 Ruth Ben-Ghiat, *Fascist Modernities: Italy, 1922–1945* (Berkeley and Los Angeles: University of California Press, 2001), 7.
12 Ezra Pound to Frank Morley, 2 July [1937], Pound Papers. Morley's request came in a letter of 30 June 1937.
13 Ezra Pound, "Affirmations" III, *New Age* (21 January 1915); *GB*, 102.
14 Benito Mussolini (Giovanni Gentile), *La Dottrina del Fascismo, con una storia del movimento fascista di Gioacchino Volpe*, Biblioteca della Enciclopedia Italiana 1 (Milan and Rome: Edizioni Fratelli Treves, 1932), 10; trans. Jeffrey T. Schnapp in Jeffrey T. Schnapp (ed.), *A Primer of Italian Fascism* (Lincoln and London: University of Nebraska Press, 2000), 48. On the original preparation of *The Doctrine of Fascism* for the 1932 edition of the *Enciclopedia Italiana*, and on its separate publication and foreign translation, see Mabel Berezin, *Making the Fascist Self: The Political Culture of Interwar Italy* (Ithaca and London: Cornell University Press, 1997), 58.
15 Mario Sironi, "Manifesto della pittura murale," originally published in *La Colonna* (December 1933), and trans. Jeffrey T. Schnapp in Claudia Lazzaro and Roger J. Crum (eds.), *Donatello among the Blackshirts: History and Modernity in the Visual Culture of Fascist Italy* (Ithaca and London: Cornell University Press, 2005), 238–40.
16 Ezra Pound, "Intellectual Money," *British Union Quarterly* 1:2 (April–June 1937): 24–34; *P&P*, 7:144–45.
17 Marla Susan Stone, *The Patron State: Culture and Politics in Fascist Italy* (Princeton: Princeton University Press, 1998), 227.
18 Diane Ghirardo, "Architects, Exhibitions, and the Politics of Culture in Fascist Italy," *Journal of Architectural Education* 45:2 (February 1992): 70–71.
19 Jobst Welge, "Fascism *Triumphans*: On the Architectural Translation of Rome," in Claudia Lazzaro and Roger J. Crum (eds.), *Donatello among the Blackshirts: History and Modernity in the Visual Culture of Fascist Italy* (Ithaca and London: Cornell University Press, 2005), 83.
20 *Mostra Augustea della Romanità: Catalogo*, 4th ed., definitive (Rome: C. Colombo, 1938), 3.
21 Claudia Lazzaro, "Forging a Visible Fascist Nation: Strategies for Fusing Past and Present," in Claudia Lazzaro and Roger J. Crum (eds.), *Donatello among the Blackshirts: History and Modernity in the Visual Culture of Fascist Italy* (Ithaca and London: Cornell University Press, 2005), 24.
22 Lazzaro, "Forging a Visible Fascist Nation," 23.
23 *Mostra Augustea della Romanità*, illustration LXXIV.
24 *Mostra Augustea della Romanità*, 434; my translation.

25 As Cipriano Efisio Oppo had argued in 1927, in the *Critica Fascista* debate about Fascist art, Rome was hardly an untapped source of iconography for rulers, its imagery was borrowed even by Napoleon, no hero to the Italians (Schnapp and Spackman, "Selections from the Great Debate," 265). On Napoleon's deployment of Augustan imagery to empower himself as a Roman emperor, and for a deconstruction of the myth of Napoleon, see Valérie Huet, "Napoleon I: A New Augustus?" in Catharine Edwards (ed.), *Roman Presences: Receptions of Rome in European Culture, 1789–1945* (Cambridge: Cambridge University Press, 1999), 53–69. Nineteenth-century Italian Nationalists, struggling toward independence, had used Rome's republican past to justify their image of the new Italy, in contrast to the Church-centered Rome that the Catholic Church had celebrated for centuries. Although a more imperial *Romanità* came to the fore during Italy's campaigns in Libya during 1911–12, the intensity of the propaganda is shadowed by that of Mussolini's Imperial Italy of the late 1930s. See Maria Wyke, "Screening Ancient Rome in the New Italy," in Catharine Edwards (ed.), *Roman Presences: Receptions of Rome in European Culture, 1789–1945* (Cambridge: Cambridge University Press, 1999), 189–92. See also Welge's notion that the "juxtaposition of ancient material with its modern reutilizations" was more far more important to this exhibition than "museological notions of authenticity and archaeological documentation" ("Fascism *Triumphans*," 86).

26 *Mostra Augustea della Romanità*, illustration LXXV; my translation.

27 On the history, form, and significance of the stele brought to Rome and erected in the Circus Maximus in October 1937, see "Stele di Axum," *Capitolium* 12 (1937): 604–07. Italy's claim to this stele was the subject of long dispute and it was finally repatriated in 2005.

28 Pound's earlier view of Rome might best be summarized by this comparison between the Roman empire and the late Italian renaissance:

> And in the midst of these awakenings Italy went to rot, destroyed by rhetoric, destroyed by the periodic sentence and by the flowing paragraph, as the Roman Empire had been destroyed before her. For when words cease to cling close to things, kingdoms fall, empires wane and diminish. Rome went because it was no longer the fashion to hit the nail on the head. They desired orators. And, curiously enough, in the mid Renaissance, rhetoric and floridity were drawn out of the very Greek and Latin revival that had freed the world from mediaevalism and Aquinas (Pound, "Affirmations: Analysis of this Decade," *New Age* [11 February 1915]; *GB*, 113–14).

29 Ezra Pound, "Paris Letter, December 1921," *Dial* (January 1922): 73–78; *P&P*, 4:212.

30 Ezra Pound, "Europe—MCMXXXVI: Reflections Written on the Eve of a New Era," *Globe* 1:2 (May 1937): [106]–10; *P&P*, 7:191.

31 Pound, "Europe—MCMXXXVI" (*P&P*, 7:191–92). Pound makes a similar assertion in "A Cultural Level (Or should we say Possibilities of Cultural Eminence?)," *British Union Quarterly* 2:2 (April–June 1938): 37–42; *P&P*, 7:308–13.

32 On the larger history of Italian stamps, see Federico Zeri, "I francobolli italiani: grafica e ideologia dalle origini al 1948," *Storia dell'arte italiana, 2: Grafica e immagine* (Turin: Einaudi, 1980), 287–319. Zeri also discusses the ideology of the Horace bimillenium stamps together with the mention of the stamps issued to honor Virgil (1930), Augustus (1937), and Titus Livy (1941) in the context of the regime's larger interest in Rome.

33 The only surviving Roman representations of this column can be seen on the reverse of Roman coins from the Augustan period, which show a statue of Augustus atop the column. Around the column were the prows and anchors of ships: the assembled parts became a trophy of victory, much like the assembled arms and armor represented on the stamp marking Augustus's victories on land. Paul Zanker demonstrates how the use of prows continued well into the imperial period in Rome, noting how monuments to Augustus's victory at Actium used this same imagery. See *The Power of Images in the Age of Augustus*, trans. Alan Shapiro (Ann Arbor: University of Michigan Press, 1998), 81–85.

34 Ezra Pound to Olga Rudge, 7 October 1938, Pound Papers. Olga and Mary Rudge were on their way to Rome, and Pound seems to have been wondering whether Olga could take Mary to see the Mostra Augustea. The exhibition closed on 5 November 1938.

35 Zanker, *The Power of Images*, 156–59.

36 Spiro Kostof, "The Emperor and the Duce: The Planning of Piazzale Augusto Imperatore in Rome," in Henry A. Millon and Linda Nochlin (eds), *Art and Architecture in the Service of Politics* (Cambridge and London: The MIT Press, 1978), 303–04. For a detailed history of the monument, its recovery, the Fascist-era building made to house it, and Richard Meier's new exhibition structure, see Orietta Rossini, *Ara Pacis* (Rome: Electa, 2006).

37 *Mostra Augustea della Romanità*, 105. For details about the reconstruction of these pieces—the museums where they were held and how long it took to bring them together—see Kostof, "The Emperor and the Duce," 304.

38 Stone, "Flexible Rome," 205–20.

39 Ezra Pound, "Marconi's Violins," *Il Mare* (18 July 1936); *P&P*, 7:76; trans. Maria Chiara Zanolli, Mary de Rachewiltz, and R. Murray Schafer (*EPM*, 393).

40 Ben-Ghiat, *Fascist Modernities*, 17–18.

41 Marinetti's comment trans. Olivia E. Sears and Jeffrey T. Schnapp in Schnapp, *Primer*, 277.

42 Margherita Sarfatti, "Art and Fascism" (1928), trans. Sears and Schnapp in Schnapp, *Primer*, 251.

43 Pound, "Marconi's Violins" (*P&P*, 7:76; *EPM*, 393).

44 Ben-Ghiat, *Fascist Modernities*, 126.
45 Fredric Jameson, "Modernism and Imperialism," *Nationalism, Colonialism, and Literature* (Minneapolis: University of Minnesota Press, 1990), 43–66.
46 For instance, see Benito Mussolini, "Declino," *Il Popolo d'Italia* (17 January 1937) reprinted in Mussolini, *Opera Omnia di Benito Mussolini*, ed. Edoardo e Duilio Susmel (Florence: La Fenice, 1957), *Opera Omnia* 28:106–07; "Il Canale di Suez," *Il Popolo d'Italia* (14 January 1937), *Opera Omnia* 28:102–03; "'Siamo Noi Decadenti?'" *Il Popolo d'Italia* (16 June 1937), *Opera Omnia* 28:198.
47 Jameson, "Modernism and Imperialism," 57–58.
48 Libero Andreotti, "The Aesthetics of War: The Exhibition of the Fascist Revolution," *Journal of Architectural Education* 45:2 (February 1992): 78.
49 Pound, "Intellectual Money" (*P&P*, 7:144–45).
50 Ezra Pound, "The Jefferson-Adams Correspondence," *North American Review* (New York) 244:2 (Winter 1937–38): 314–24; *P&P*, 7:266.
51 Pound makes similar observations in "No Tame Robots in Fascist Italy. The Intellectual Frontier," *British-Italian Bulletin* 2:4 (25 January 1936): 2 (*P&P*, 7: 20); "Italy's Frame-up," *British-Italian Bulletin* 2:5 (1 February 1936): 2 (*P&P*, 7:23).
52 In his "Government" chapter of *Guide to Kulchur*, Pound makes a similar assertion in slightly different language: "The best government is (naturally?) that which draws the best of the nation's intelligence into use" (*GK*, 242).
53 In *Italy: Inventing the Nation* (New York: Oxford University Press, 2001), Nicholas Doumanis suggests that Italian leaders invested in Italy's independence from Austria and France recognized that the cultural divisions within the Italian Peninsula made resistance to foreign domination difficult. As a result, a coherent sense of Italian culture, complete with linguistic uniformity, the history of a glorious Risorgimento, as well as the artistic and intellectual past of the Renaissance and Roman Empire, was crucial to Italy's remaining together in the uncertain years following the consolidation of the nation.
54 *GK*, 33. As is often the case with Pound's long works, he is not entirely successful in following the method he outlines for himself. Indeed, he does quote text, including all of Gaudier's Vortex (*GK*, 63–70), writings by Katue Kitasono concerning the relation between imagery and ideoplasty (*GK*, 137–39), and passages from ancient Roman texts concerning the abuses of usury (*GK*, 269–70).
55 Michael North, "Where Memory Faileth: Forgetfulness and a Poem Including History," in Marcel Smith and William A. Ulmer (eds), *Ezra Pound: The Legacy of Kulchur* (Tuscaloosa: University of Alabama Press, 1988), 147.
56 Ezra Pound, "[A review of] *The Quattro Cento*, by Adrian Stokes," *Symposium* (Concord) 3:4 (October 1932): 518–21; *P&P*, 5:375.

57 Pound expresses that notion explicitly earlier in the review when he celebrates the book's plates, saying, "I don't honestly know whether the 'reader' can learn more from Stokes's printed text than he can from that illustration" (P&P, 5:375).
58 This aspect of aesthetic criticism remains an issue for Pound in *Guide to Kulchur*, where he addresses Dante's "undiscussable Paradiso": "There is nothing in modern critical mechanism to deal with, and I doubt if there is anything handy in our poetic vocabulary even to translate, the matter of this and the following Cantos" (*GK*, 292). Reflecting on his entire undertaking, Pound later says: "I cannot state my beliefs about art more succinctly than I have done by naming particular works and makers" (*GK*, 347).
59 *Mostra Augustea della Romanità*, 726. The model is now displayed in Rome's Museo della Civiltà Romana.
60 Falasca-Zamponi, *Fascist Spectacle*, 93. For images of the architectural and archaeological projects undertaken in Rome by the Fascist regime—and of the demolition that came with these projects—see Chapter 3 of the present volume and Italo Insolera, *Roma fascista, nelle fotografie dell'Istituto Luce* (Rome: Riuniti, 2001).
61 Ben-Ghiat, *Fascist Modernities*, 4.
62 *GK*, 30. Pound does not reserve such thinking for history, and in fact such assertions appear throughout *Guide to Kulchur* in numerous contexts. For instance, he makes a similar observation about how a poor performance of a musical piece can make "the best qualities of concerti disappear; or at least so much of the fine carving is blunted that one's rage outweighs one's pleasure" (*GK*, 251).
63 Mussolini, "Per la nuova sede del Fascio di Milano," *Il Popolo d'Italia* (11 May 1922), qtd. Emily Braun, *Mario Sironi and Italian Modernism: Art and Politics under Fascism* (Cambridge: Cambridge University Press, 2000), 103. For examples of Fascist-era building projects that emulated those of ancient Rome, see Chapter 3; Peter Aicher, "Mussolini's Forum and the Myth of Augustan Rome," *The Classical Bulletin* 76:2 (2000): 117–39; William L. MacDonald, "Excavation, Restoration, and Italian Architecture of the 1930s," in Helen Searing (ed.), *In Search of Modern Architecture: A Tribute to Henry-Russell Hitchcock* (Cambridge and London: MIT Press, 1982), 298–320.
64 Braun, *Mario Sironi and Italian Modernism*, 103.
65 Ezra Pound, "Civilization," *Polite Essays* (London: Faber & Faber, 1937), 193–95; *EPM*, 399.
66 Pound had long believed that art should be integrated into architectural creation. For an early and clear statement of the importance of employing artists in the decoration of buildings, see his "Paris Letter, December 1922" *Dial* (January 1923): [85]–90; *P&P*, 4:274–79.
67 Stone, "Flexible Rome," 215.

68 See Catherine E. Paul, *Poetry in the Museums of Modernism: Yeats, Pound, Moore, Stein* (Ann Arbor: University of Michigan Press, 2002), 65–139.
69 Ezra Pound, "The Serious Artist" (1913; *LE*, 46).
70 Pound, "The Serious Artist" (1913; *LE*, 46).
71 Pound, "Ubicumque Lingua Romana," 45.
72 Mark Wollaeger, *Modernism, Media, and Propaganda* (Princeton and Oxford: Princeton University Press, 2006), 264–65.
73 Ezra Pound to Odon Por, 4 June [1940], Ezra Pound Miscellany, Yale Collection of American Literature, Beinecke Rare Book and Manuscript Library.

Notes to Chapter 7

1 H. D., *End to Torment: A Memoir of Ezra Pound, with the poems from "Hilda's Book" by Ezra Pound*, ed. Norman Holmes Pearson and Michael King (New York: New Directions, 1979), 44.
2 For a more expansive treatment of Ezra Pound's propagandistic writings, see Matthew Feldman, *Ezra Pound's Fascist Propaganda, 1935–45* (Basingstoke and New York: Palgrave Macmillan, 2013).
3 H. D., *End to Torment*, 48.
4 J. J. Wilhelm, *Ezra Pound: The Tragic Years, 1925–1972* (University Park: The Pennsylvania State University Press, 1994), 189–93.
5 The complete text of the second indictment appears in C. David Heymann, *Ezra Pound: The Last Rower, A Political Profile* (New York: Viking, 1976), 180–85. Heymann treats the original indictment of 25 July 1943 on 135–36.
6 Mark Wollaeger, *Modernism, Media, and Propaganda: British Narrative from 1900 to 1945* (Princeton and Oxford: Princeton University Press, 2006), 3.
7 Ezra Pound to Francis Biddle, 4 August 1943, reproduced in Heymann, *The Last Rower*, 137.
8 *EPS*, 340. In a letter of 5 October 1945 to Shakespear and Parkyn, his late father-in-law's law firm, Pound makes a similar claim, saying "I was not sending axis propaganda but my own" (Heymann, *The Last Rower*, 168–69).
9 Richard Sieburth, annotation in Ezra Pound, *The Pisan Cantos* (1948), ed. Richard Sieburth (New York: New Directions, 2003), 143.
10 W. B. Yeats, *Later Essays*, ed. William H. O'Donnell with Elizabeth Bergmann Loizeaux, Collected Works 5 (New York and London: Charles Scribner's Sons, 1994), 193.
11 Lina Caico to Ezra Pound, 14 March 1937, Ezra Pound Papers, Yale Collection of American Literature, Beinecke Rare Book and Manuscript Library.
12 Ezra Pound to Lina Caico, [March 1937], Pound Papers.
13 H. D., *End to Torment*, 44.

14 H. D., *End to Torment*, 32.
15 Ezra Pound, "Ubicumque Lingua Romana" (1938), in Erminio Turcotti (ed.), *Fascist Europe, Europa Fascista: An Anglo-Italian Symposium*, 2nd ed. (Milan: Salesian, 1939), 1:45. Pound similarly treated the importance and benefits for the *sindacati* in his radio broadcast of 20 April 1942, noting that even if a worker "don't join us, his interests are nevertheless looked after," and adding:

> I, for example, would come under the confederation of artists and professional men, painters, doctors, writers, dentists, etc. WHAT Congressional representation or parliamentary representation have the professional classes had in the United States or England since the beginning of their government system? (*EPS*, 102).

16 *EPS*, 337. Pound makes a similar claim in his broadcast of 19 March 1943 (*EPS*, 254).
17 Cleanth Brooks, *Modern Poetry and the Tradition* (Chapel Hill: The University of North Carolina Press, 1939), 49–51; square brackets Brooks's own.
18 Toby Clark, *Art and Propaganda in the Twentieth Century: The Political Image in the Age of Mass Culture* (New York: Harry N. Abrams, 1997), 8.
19 Clark, *Art and Propaganda in the Twentieth Century*, 8–9.
20 Richard Wolin, "Introduction: 'Over the Line': Reflections on Heidegger and National Socialism," in Richard Wolin (ed.), *The Heidegger Controversy: A Critical Reader* (Cambridge and London: The MIT Press, 1993), 8.
21 Libero Andreotti, *Art and Politics in Fascist Italy: The Exhibition of the Fascist Revolution (1932)* (PhD thesis, Massachusetts Institute of Technology, 1989), 238–40.
22 Ezra Pound, "The Serious Artist" (1913; *LE*, 46).
23 Roger Griffin, *Modernism and Fascism: The Sense of a Beginning under Mussolini and Hitler* (Basingstoke and New York: Palgrave Macmillan, 2007), 31.
24 Griffin, *Modernism and Fascism*, 8.
25 Ezra Pound, *Personae: Collected Shorter Poems* (New York: New Directions, 1926), 187–88.
26 Touring Club Italiano, *Roma*, 9th ed. (Milan: Touring Editore, 1999), 238–39. The Egyptianizing lions and circular vases were added by Valadier in 1823.
27 H. D., *End to Torment*, 44.
28 H. D., *End to Torment*, 7.
29 H. D., *End to Torment*, 34.
30 Philippe Lacoue-Labarthe, "Neither an Accident nor a Mistake," trans. Paula Wissing, *Critical Inquiry* 15:2 (Winter 1989): 482.
31 Maurice Blanchot, "Thinking the Apocalypse: A Letter from Maurice Blanchot to Catherine David," trans. Paula Wissing, *Critical Inquiry* 15:2 (Winter 1989): 479–80.
32 In "Aesthetics at the Limits of the Nation: Kant, Pound, and the *Saturday Review*," Wai Chee Dimock makes a similar claim, although the larger

argument of his essay disagrees with mine (*American Literature* 76:3 [September 2004]: 534).
33 Ezra Pound to Francis Biddle, 4 August 1943, reproduced in Heymann, *The Last Rower*, 137.
34 Homi K. Bhabha, *The Location of Culture* (London and New York: Routledge, 1994), 25.
35 Terry Eagleton, *The Ideology of the Aesthetic* (Oxford and Cambridge: Blackwell, 1990), 3.

Index

Accademia Musicale Chigiana (Siena) 162–63, 170, 192–96, 318n6, 323–24n69, 327–28n113
Adams, John 243, 257
Aeneas 98
Alberti, Leon Battista 60, 64, 306–07n109
Altmann, Wilhelm 176, 317–18n4, 323n68
Ambrogio de Predis, Giovanni 62, 78
Andrea del Sarto 78, 293n19
Antonini, A. 25
Antoninus Pius 218
Ara Pacis Augustae (Rome) 126, 154, 216–17, 308–09n121
Arditi 88
Aristotle 233
Arnold, Matthew 201
Ars Nova (Rome) 166
Arrigotti, Enrico 105
Augustine of Hippo 206
Augustus Caesar, Gaius Octavius 16, 115, 117, 118, 124–25, 127–28, 130, 135, 201, 205–17, 261, 306n102, 312n150, 331n25, 332n32
autarchy 193, 252
Avanti! (Milan) 51
Axum, Stele of 118–19, 135, 210–11, 261

Bach, Johann Sebastian 160, 162, 163, 168, 175, 179–80, 182, 188–90, 194–95, 323–24n69
Bachmann, Alberto 317–18n4
Balla, Giacomo 26–27
Bardi, Pietro Maria 100–01, 142, 302n46, 315n17
Bartók, Béla 100, 164, 166, 182, 257
Bartoli, Amerigo 109
Bauta, La (Venice) 20–21, 28
Beach, Sylvia 264, 266
Beardsley, Aubrey 243
Beethoven, Ludwig van 194, 204
Berenson, Bernard 14, 52–58
Bernart de Ventadorn 73, 78
Bésard, Jean 172
Bey, Osman 147
Bibliografia Fascista (Rome) 65, 145
Biennale (Venice) 26, 44, 100, 302n46
Blast (London) 38
Bloch, Ernest 166
Boccherini, Luigi 169, 193
Boccioni, Umberto 26–27
Bollingen Prize 264
Bonaparte, Napoleon 60, 92, 93, 155, 331n25
Boni, Giacomo 127
bonifica (reclaiming) 122–23, 139, 229, 243, 251
Bontempelli, Massimo 114

Borgia, Cesare 98
Bottai, Giuseppe 15, 58, 86, 114, 115, 118, 124, 142, 145–46, 153, 154, 167, 182, 193, 308n120, 314n3
Botticelli, Sandro 78
Brâncuși, Constantin 152, 257, 301n35
Braque, Georges 57
Breton, André 57
British Museum and Library (London) 200, 232, 252
Broglio, Mario 57, 166
Brooks, Cleanth 253
Brown, Horatio F. 21
Browning, Robert 20, 27–28
Brunelleschi, Filippo 59
Bucci, Anselmo 62–63
Bunting, Basil 172–73
Buonaiuti, Andrea 293n19
Burckhardt, Jacob 92
Byron, George Gordon Lord 20

Ca' Pesaro (Gallery of Modern Art, Venice) 26, 285n21
Caico, Lina 245–26
Calza, Guido 134
Camagna, Carlo 146, 153, 155
Campigli, Massimo 203–04, 303n56
Capitolium (Rome) 44, 128
Caravaggio, Michelangelo Merisi da 60
Carducci, Giosuè 33, 43, 95, 165
Carlyle, Thomas 91
Carrà, Carlo 14, 26–27, 39–40, 51, 55, 57–58, 61, 77, 92, 166, 203–04, 303n56
Casa Madre dei Mutilati (Rome) 262–63
Casella, Alfredo 15, 158, 160, 163–70, 176, 182, 185, 192–95, 256, 322–23n55, 324n75, 327–28n113
Cato the Younger (Marcus Porcius Cato Uticensis) 97

Catullus, Gaius Valerius 90
Cavalcanti, Guido 14, 48, 65–82, 153–54, 243, 286n34, 287n40
Cavour, Camillo di 303n59
Cecchi, Emilio 52, 56–57
Cellini, Benvenuto 59
Cézanne, Paul 54, 61, 290n74
Chilesotti, Oscar 171–72
Churchill, Winston 194
Chute, Desmond 184, 189
Ciano, Galeazzo 15, 142
Cicero, Marcus Tullius 157, 206
Cino da Pistoija 73
Civiltà Fascista (Rome) 153, 157–58
Clementi, Muzio 169
Colles, Henry Cope 180
Cocteau, Jean 57
Columbus, Christopher 157
Confucius 200, 223, 230, 231, 233, 243, 257
Constantine I 212–14, 218
Corelli, Arcangelo 321n39
Corporazione delle Nuove Musiche (CDNM, New Music Corporation) 166, 167
Corradini, Enrico 289n62, 301n31
Cosimo Tura 78
Cremonesi, Filippo 117
Croce, Benedetto 86
Critica Fascista (Rome) 35, 58–61, 86, 114, 145, 202, 331n25
Cuoco, Vincenzo 33

Daniel, Arnaut 73, 78
Dante Alighieri 8, 14, 24, 38, 44, 58, 60, 66, 69, 71–74, 80–81, 111–13, 153, 209, 286n34, 304n69, 334n58
D'Annunzio, Gabriele 25, 36, 43, 73, 290n74
d'Azeglio, Massimo Taparelli 287n39
Dazzi, Manlio 71
de Chirico, Giorgio 57, 166, 287n41

De Renzi, Mario 104, 110
De Sanctis, Francesco 74
Debussy, Claude 164, 165, 185,
degli Uberti, Ubaldo 146, 148, 152
Diaghilev, Sergei 167
Disciplinary Training Center (Pisa) 16–17, 237, 239, 264
Doolittle, Hilda (H.D.) 4, 16–17, 237–68
Dottori, Gerardo 109
Douglas, C. H. 3, 34, 89, 201, 233
du Bellay, Joachim 83, 101, 129
Duccio di Buoninsegna 174
Dudreville, Leonardo 61

Edizioni Marsano (Genoa) 69
Eliot, Thomas Stearns 38, 115
empire, Italian pursuit of 16, 81, 199–235, 243
Ephrikian, Angelo 195–96, 327–28n133
Epstein, Jacob 29, 100

Fanna, Antonio 196–97
Farinacci, Roberto 15, 114, 142, 146, 147, 303n56
Fasano, Renato 196
Fasci Italiani di Combattimento 88
fascio littorio 84–91, 104, 105, 113, 172, 249–50, 262, 299–300n11, 300n12
Fascist Party, Italian 88
Fascist revolution, *see* March on Rome
Fattori, Giovanni 54, 57, 61
Fauré, Gabriel 164
Foà, Roberto 161, 175, 269 70
Ford, Ford Madox (Hueffer) 71
Fontana, Domenico 261
Foscolo, Ugo 32
Frobenius, Leo 89
Foro Mussolini (Foro Italico) 133–35, 137–38, 262–63, 306n102
Francesco da Milano 172, 174, 244–45

Francisci, Pietro 301n35
Franco, Francisco 17
Frescobaldi, Girolamo 169
Fuchs, Aloys 317–18n4
Funi, Achille 61–62, 109, 203–04, 303n56
Futurism 18, 26–27, 37–40, 56, 85–88, 101, 103–04, 108–09, 164–65, 166, 174, 231, 316n40

Galileo Galilei 74
Gaudier-Brzeska, Henri 29, 100, 219, 221, 243, 249–50, 257, 301n35, 333n54
Gentile, Giovanni 32–33, 131, 146, 203, 297n54
Gentili, Alberto 161, 176
Gerarchia (Milan) 52, 144–46, 154, 297n54
Ghiberti, Lorenzo 59
Ghirlandaio, Domenico 121, 293n19
Giardini, Felice 169
Giordano, Filippo 161, 175, 269
Giotto di Bondone 47–64, 69, 77, 163, 172, 174, 290n74, 298n66
Gozzoli, Benozzo 293n19
Greenberg, Clement 254
Gris, Juan 57
Guarnieri, Antonio 194
Guinicelli, Guido 73

Handel, George Frideric 179
Hardy, Thomas 234
Hare, Augustus 21, 23–24
Heidegger, Martin 265–66
Hindemith, Paul 100, 166, 182
Hitler, Adolf 17, 237, 242, 265
Horace (Quintus Horatius Flaccus) 90
Howells, William Dean 21
Hunt, Violet 71

Istituto de Studi Romani 118, 306n102

342 Fascist Directive

Istituto LUCE 301n35
Italianità (Italianness) 39–40, 44, 76, 79–82, 168, 192

Jacob, Max 57
Jacopo da Sellaio 78
Jacopo della Quercia 60
James, Henry 20–22, 24
Janequin, Clément 174, 182, 244–45
Jefferson, Thomas 155, 157, 243, 257, 301n34
Joyce, James 38, 115, 257
Julius Caesar, Gaius 92, 93, 98, 115, 218
Justinian I 212–14, 218

Kitasono, Katue 333n54
Kodály, Zoltán 166
Kolneder, Walter 196
Křenek, Ernst 166

Lacerba (Florence) 85, 166
Lanciani, Rodolfo 229, 306n102
Lateran Pacts 308n120
League of Nations sanctions 266
Le Bon, Gustav 92
Léger, Fernand 57
Leibniz, Gottfried Wilhelm 98
Lenin, Vladimir Ilyich Ulyanov 93
Leonardo da Vinci 69
Leonardo (Florence) 34
Leopardi, Giacomo 60, 286n34
Lewis, Percy Wyndham 29, 100, 223, 257
Libera, Adalberto 104, 110
Lincoln, Abraham 93
Lipchitz, Jacques 57
Lippi, Fra Filippo 78
Livy (Titus Livius) 206, 332n32
Londonio, Marco 20–21, 28
Longanesi, Leo 109–14
Longhi, G. Marhetti 128
Longhi, Roberto 56–57
Lope de Vega 8

Maccari, Mino 109
Machiavelli, Niccolò 52, 74
Mahler, Gustav 164
Malaparte, Curzio 99
Malatesta, Sigismondo 98, 204, 243
Malipiero, Gian Francesco 165, 166, 196, 324n75, 327–28n113
Manin, Daniele 42, 284n2
Manzoni, Alessandro 32
March on Rome (28 October 1922) 14, 19, 40, 41, 65, 92, 105, 114–15, 117, 126, 300n11
Mare, Il (Rapallo) 174–75, 177–85, 192
Marinetti, Filippo Tommaso 14, 25–26, 37–38, 56, 86, 100, 103, 108–09, 142, 164–65, 218, 302n49
Marussig, Pietro 61
Masaccio (Tommaso di Ser Giovanni di Simone) 47–64, 69, 77, 163, 293n19, 298n66
Mascagni, Pietro 25
Matteotti, Giacomo 43
Mauri, Guido 105
Mazzini, Giuseppe 32–34, 90, 286–87n35, 297n54
Medici, Cosimo de' 98
Meier, Richard 309n121
Melchior, Alessandro 108
Mencius 243, 257
Meridiano di Roma (Rome) 157–58
Michelangelo di Lodovico Buonarroti Simoni 59, 60, 74
Miró, Joan 182
Mocenigo, Count Nani 26
Molinari, Bernardino 161, 318n6, 324n75
Monotti, Francesco 65, 145, 152
Montanelli, Indro 220
Monteverdi, Claudio 166, 167, 169
Morandi, Giorgio 39–40, 57
Morley, Frank 200, 203
Mostra anti-*lei* 202, 291n90, 315n26

Mostra Augustea della Romanità (Exhibition of Augustus and Romanness) 16, 40, 60, 118, 201, 205–17, 226–28, 231, 234–35
Mostra della Rivoluzione Fascista (Exhibition of the Fascist Revolution) 60, 80, 89, 101, 102–14, 204–05, 211, 221, 227, 255–56, 301n35
Mozart, Wolfgang Amadeus 172, 194–95
Münch, Gerhart 158, 159, 170–98, 244–45, 321n39, 324n72, 326n98
Muñoz, Antonio 307n111
Museum of Modern Art (New York) 254
Mussato, Albertino 71
Mussolini, Benito 1–6, 9, 11–17, 27, 29, 32–33, 35, 41–43, 47, 50–52, 57, 65, 69, 74, 81, 83–84, 88, 90–99, 110–14, 115–18, 120–24, 129–40, 141–59, 169–70, 182, 192–93, 199–203, 206–07, 209, 218, 220, 223, 227, 229–30, 233, 237–40, 243, 251–52, 255–56, 260–61, 265, 300n24, 307n111, 308n120, 316n38
Mussolini, Vito 146, 154
Mussolinismo 91–99, 110–14, 136

Nationalist Party, Italian 18, 36–37, 39–40, 86, 89, 331n25
Nattini, Amos 292n92
Nietzsche, Friedrich 91, 98
Nizzoli, Marcello 109
Norton, Charles Elliot 24
Novecento Italiano 14, 39–40, 61–64, 80–81,109–14, 163, 169, 172

Ojetti, Ugo 114, 303n56
Oppo, Cipriano Efisio 14, 60–61, 70, 108–09, 331n25
Orage, A. R. 10
Orcagna, Andrea 293n19

Ostia Antica 94, 123, 133–35, 172

Palagi, Pelagio 33
Palazzo Venezia 126, 144, 309n122, 309n123, 314n10
Papini, Giovanni 38–40, 81, 166, 290n74
Pascoli, Giovanni 43
Pavolini, Alessandro 59
Pellizzi, Camillo 15, 145, 147, 152, 155–58
Pergolesi, Giovanni Battista 167, 185
Petrarch, (Francesco Petrarca) 72–74, 286n34
Piazza Augusto Imperatore (Rome) 124–26, 130, 262, 308n121
Picasso, Pablo 57
Piero della Francesca 58–64, 69, 172, 298n66
Pietro Lombardo 102, 204, 225–27
Pincherle, Marc 196–97
Pizzetti, Ildebrando 165
Pliny (Gaius Plinius Secundus) 206
Poe, Edgar Allan 21
Poole, Reginald Lane 180
Popolo d'Italia, Il (Milan) 27, 42, 47, 50, 51–52, 110–113, 117, 127, 143, 145, 161, 201, 283n23, 294n21, 295n35, 295n37, 305n88
Por, Odon 35, 146, 153, 316n38
Poulenc, Francis 166
Pound, Ezra
  A Lume Spento (1908) 25
  ABC of Economics (1933) 6, 95, 151, 248
  ABC of Reading (1934) 6, 7, 84, 96, 102, 148–51, 200, 248, 258
  "The Acid Test" (1936) 94, 300n22
  "Affirmations" (1915) 203, 211, 331n28
  L'America, Roosevelt e le cause della Guerra presente (1944) 6

"A Pact" (1913) 165
"Appunti" (*Il Mare*, 1932) 100, 109, 157, 302n46, 302n49
"L'arte di Sant'Elia a Rapallo" (1936) 102
"Ave Roma" (1933) 83, 104, 105, 117–18, 129–31, 301n35, 303n61, 304n68
"The Biennale" (1935) 302n46
Cantos 4, 9, 16–17, 23, 98–99, 110–14, 172, 204–05, 234–35, 237–68
Carta da Visita (1942) 6
"Civilization" (1937) 231
"Concerts of March 29 and April 1" (1937) 178
"A Cultural Level" (1938) 331n31
"Europe MCMXXXVI" (1937) 117–18, 211–14
Exultations (1909) 78–79
Gaudier Brzeska (1916) 203, 211, 331n28
"Il giudizio di uno straniero" (1939) 315n26
Guide to Kulchur (1938) 1–3, 6, 16, 91, 162, 183–84, 198–235, 248, 250–52, 258, 333n52
Guido Cavalcanti Rime (1932) 14, 48, 64, 65–82, 153–54, 224
How to Read (1931) 6, 7, 149, 200
Hugh Selwyn Mauberley (1920) 258
"I Gather the Limbs of Osiris" (1911–12) 7–8, 28–29, 65–66, 229–30
"In difesa del paesaggio: non deturpare" (1931) 120–22, 157, 306n108, 316–17n41
Indiscretions: or, Une Revue de Deux Mondes (1923) 42–43
"Individual and Statal Views: Mr. Ezra Pound's Views" (1934) 34, 201

"Intellectual Money" (1937) 89, 104, 205–06, 221
Introduzione alla natura economica degli S.U.A. (1944) 6
"Italy's Frame-up" (1936) 333n51
"Italy: The Second Decennio" (1935 or 1936) 47, 81
"The Jefferson-Adams Correspondence" (1937/1938) 221–22, 301n34
Jefferson and/or Mussolini (1935) 6, 9, 14–15, 41–43, 84, 89–90, 93–98, 103, 105, 119–23, 131–32, 136–39, 142–45, 147–48, 151–52, 155, 157–58, 195, 205, 223, 229, 300n23, 302n53, 309n122
"Marches Civilization" (1933) 65–66
"Marconi's Violins" (1936) 217–18
"Murder by Capital" (1933) 98
"Music in Ca' Rezzonico" (1937) 164
"No Tame Robots in Fascist Italy. The Intellectual Frontier" (1936) 333n51
Orientamenti (1944) 6
Oro e lavoro (1944) 6
"Paris Letter, December 1921" (1922) 211
"Paris Letter, December 1922" (1923) 231, 334n66
Patria Mia (1950) 49
"The Pianist Münch" (1933) 174
Pisan Cantos (1948) 4, 12, 16–17, 235, 237–68
"Possibilities of Civilization: What a Small Town Can Do" (1936) 71
radio broadcasts 4, 10, 16–17, 158, 194–95, 237–68, 336n15
"Rapallo Centro di Cultura" (1936) 101–02, 285n20
"The Renaissance" (1915) 49–50

"[A Review of] *The Quattro Cento* by Adrian Stokes" (1932) 226–27
"A Retrospect" (1918) 29
"Second Concert: Tuesday 14th November" (1933) 172
"The Serious Artist" (1918) 3, 29, 233–34, 255
"Snobismi e sindicati" (1940) 301n33
Social Credit (1935) 6
"A Social Creditor Serves Notice" (1936) 312n144
The Spirit of Romance (1910) 8, 28–29, 73–74, 78–79, 200, 224
"Stasera, Sabato, ore 21: ultimo concerto" (1938) 185
"Terra Italica" (1931/1932) 157
"Three Cantos" (1917) 21–23
"Tigullian Musical Life"(1937) 178
"Tigullian Studies" (1936) 174–75, 178, 181–82
"Trees Without Roots" (1934) 35, 202
"The Truth About Italy" (1936) 94, 144, 300n22
"Ubicumque Lingua Romana" (1938) 3, 103, 117–18, 141, 144–45, 148, 199, 233–35, 249–50, 303n57, 315n29
"Un magnifico libro di P. M. Bardi" (1934) 100–01
"The Vivaldi Revival" (1939) 159, 178, 192
"Warm Reception in Genoa for the Tigullian Musicians" (1933) 172
What Is Money For (1939) 6
"Where Is American Culture?" (1928) 316n40
Prampolini, Enrico 109
Pratelli, Esodo 105
Praz, Mario 70
Prezzolini, Giuseppe 25, 39–40, 92, 290n74, 301n37, 314n3

Quadriennale (Rome), 44, 109

Radio Rome 4, 10, 16–17, 158, 194–95, 237–68, 336n15
Rationalism 18, 103–04, 110, 302n48
Ravel, Maurice 164, 166
Regime Fascista, Il (Cremona) 114, 146
Respighi, Ottorino 165, 166,
Ricci, Corrado 118, 126–28, 142, 314n3
Richards, Ivor Armstrong 253
Rinaldi, Mario 196–97
Risorgimento 1–2, 25, 30–34, 141, 207, 224, 297n54, 333n53
Roma (Rome, periodical) 306n102
Romanità (Romanness)14–15, 16, 18, 44, 52, 60–61, 84, 98, 114–19, 201, 205–17, 230, 251, 295n35, 312n150
Rossini, Gioacchino 169
Rudge, Olga 12, 15–16, 103, 135, 153, 158, 159–60, 164, 170–98, 214–16, 269–75, 316n38, 316n40
Ruskin, John 20, 23
Russolo, Luigi 26–27
Ryom, Peter 176–77, 182, 190, 197, 269–75

Salò Republic (Italian Socialist Republic) 238
Salvemini, Gaetano 92
Sammartini, Giovanni Battista 169
San Zeno (Verona) 120
Sansoni, Luigi 184
Sant'Elia, Antonio 100–02, 302n48, 314n3
Santa Maria dei Miracoli (Venice) 102, 204, 225–27
Sarfatti, Margherita 14, 15, 47–52, 55, 58, 61–64, 74–76, 78, 79, 95, 97, 115, 118, 141–42, 145–47, 149–51, 163, 182, 193, 218, 256, 299–300n11

Savinio, Alberto 57
Scarlatti, Domenico 169, 185
Schering, Arnold 317n4
Schoenberg, Arnold 164, 166
Scriabin, Alexander 182
Severi, Francesco 321n39
Severini, Gino 26–27, 57
Sgambati, Giovanni 161
Shakespeare, William 234
Sironi, Mario 54, 61, 63–64, 77, 102, 109–14, 142, 163, 203–04, 256
Sixtus V, Pope 260–61
Socialist Party, Italian 18, 86, 92
Società Italiana di Musica Moderna (SIMM, Italian Society of Modern Music) 165
Socrates 93
Soffici, Ardengo 39–40, 55, 57–58, 86, 114, 290n74
Spenser, Edmund 83, 129
St. Elizabeths Hospital 237, 239, 267–68
Starace, Achille 291n90, 330n10
Stokes, Adrian 226–27
Stracittà (Super-city) 39–40, 88
Strapaese (Super-country) 18, 39–40, 88, 109–14
Stravinsky, Igor 100, 164–69, 182, 185, 257
Strong, Eugénie Sellers 117, 306n102
Summerville, Robert 34
Syndicalists, Italian 86, 299n8, 314n7

Tacitus, Publius Cornelius 98
Tempio Malatestiano (Rimini) 120, 127, 204, 306n109
Terragni, Giuseppe 105, 110, 113, 163, 256, 297n54
Terzi, Giovanni Antonio 321n39
Tigullian Studies 15–16, 102, 153–54, 157–58, 159–62, 166, 170–98, 244–46, 323–24n69
Toni, Alceo 161, 189
Torrefranca, Fausto 195

Toscanini, Arturo 194
Toscanità (Tuscanness) 39–40, 66, 69–81, 290n74
Twain, Mark 21

Uccello, Paolo 47–64, 77, 163, 293n19

Valdameri, Rino 292n92, 297n54
Valori Plastici (Rome) 14, 56–57, 166, 287n41, 298n66
Van Buren, Albert W. 119, 123, 135, 139, 307n110, 309n122, 314n10
Van Buren, Martin 243
Verdi, Giuseppe 60, 164–65
via della Conciliazione 124–26, 308n120
via dell'Impero (via dei Fori Imperiali) 101, 115, 116, 125–29, 131, 307n111, 309n123
via del Mare 307n111, 313n152
Villon, François 191
Viollet-le-Duc, Eugène 306n108
Virgil (Publius Vergilius Maro) 332n32
Vittorio Emanuele III 201
Vittorio Emanuele monument (Rome) 33, 58
Vivaldi, Antonio 15–16, 154, 158, 159–98, 255–56, 269–75
Vivaldi Week (Settimana Celebrativa di Antonio Vivaldi) 162–63, 170, 192–95, 322n55, 323–24n69, 327–28n113
Voce, La (Florence) 18, 25, 38–40, 56–57, 66, 85–88, 92, 166, 290n72, 290n74
Volpi, Albino 291n85

Washington, George 93
Weber, Max 92

Yeats, William Butler 243, 245, 253

www.ingramcontent.com/pod-product-compliance
Lightning Source LLC
Chambersburg PA
CBHW061423300426
44114CB00014B/1512